Martha Jefferson Randolph, Daughter of Monticello

Her Life and Times

CYNTHIA A. KIERNER

The University of North Carolina Press

CHAPEL HILL

This book was published with the assistance of the Thornton H. Brooks Fund of the University of North Carolina Press.

Set in Utopia and Celestia types
by Tseng Information Systems, Inc.

Manufactured in the United States of America

The paper in this book meets the guidelines for permanence and durability of the Committee on Production Guidelines for Book Longevity of the Council on Library Resources.

The University of North Carolina Press has been a member of the Green Press Initiative since 2003.

Library of Congress Cataloging-in-Publication Data
Kierner, Cynthia A., 1958–
Martha Jefferson Randolph, daughter of Monticello : her life and times / by Cynthia A. Kierner.
p. ; cm.
Includes bibliographical references and index.
ISBN 978-0-8078-3552-4 (cloth)
1. Randolph, Martha Jefferson, 1772–1836. 2. Children of presidents—United States—Biography. 3. Jefferson, Thomas, 1743–1826—Family. I. Title.
E332.25.R18K54 2012
973.4′6092—dc23
[B]

2011042856

16 15 14 13 12   5 4 3 2 1

Martha Jefferson Randolph, Daughter of Monticello

For Zack and Anders

contents

illustrations

Note on Names and Sources

Observant readers will note my frequent use of first names to refer to Martha Jefferson Randolph—known in girlhood as Patsy and later as Martha—and to others. Modern scholars typically refrain from referring to women by their first names because the archaic practice of using surnames for men (e.g., Jefferson) and first names for women (e.g., Martha), like the custom of referring to men as men and grown women as "girls," suggests that women were neither full-fledged adults nor serious historical actors. Yet the presence of so many Randolphs in this biography makes the consistent use of surnames impossible. In the Jefferson-Randolph family circle, however, referring to people by their first names also causes problems. Martha Jefferson Randolph shared her mother's name; her father, husband, father-in-law, and son were all named Thomas.

For the most part, I use first names to refer to women and men alike. The main exceptions to this rule are cases in which the use of a surname would not confuse the reader, which include most references to Thomas Jefferson. Because his wife died in 1782 and because he had only daughters, whose names changed when they married, Martha's father was the only Jefferson with whom she interacted on a regular basis—and thus the only bearer of that surname to appear frequently in these pages (at least after the first chapter). Moreover, however appealing on ethical grounds, referring to Jefferson by his first name would be confusing, given the preponderance of Thomases in the immediate family of Martha Jefferson Randolph.

Historians are exceptionally fortunate in having access to the Jefferson and Jefferson-Randolph family papers in a variety of formats—manuscripts, edited volumes, newly available digitized collections—all of which are cited in my notes. Particular documents, however, are accessible to researchers in multiple formats. A letter written by Jefferson to Martha's husband, Thomas Mann Randolph, for instance, might be available in the manuscript collections of the Library of Congress, on the Library's website, and also in published paper volumes such as *The Family Letters of Thomas Jefferson*, edited by Edwin Morris Betts and James Adam Bear Jr., and the multi-volume *Papers of Thomas Jefferson*, the definitive (but still unfinished) edition of Jefferson's correspondence and other documents, which is also now available in a digital format. A letter exchanged by two Randolph daughters would likely be in the manuscript collections of the University of Virginia, but it might also be included in the excellent and growing selection of documents that are obtainable digitally via the *Family Letters Digital Archive*, based at the International Center for Jefferson Studies at Monticello.

My notes generally cite documents in the format I used when conducting the research for this biography. For letters to and from Jefferson, I cite the published volumes of *Papers of Thomas Jefferson* when possible. For family letters, I cite mostly manuscripts, using the *Family Letters Digital Archive* mainly to augment my research in manuscript sources, most of which I conducted before this authoritative digital source became a viable alternative.

Martha Jefferson Randolph, Daughter of Monticello

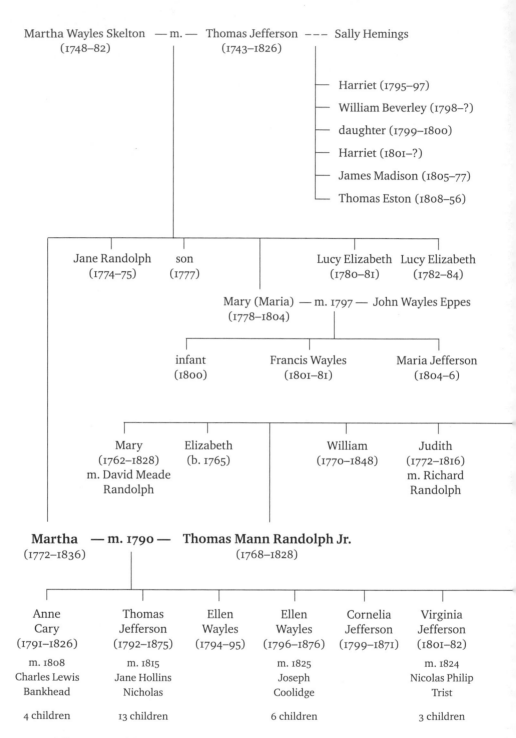

Martha Wayles Skelton — m. — Thomas Jefferson --- Sally Hemings
(1748–82)   (1743–1826)

— Harriet (1795–97)
— William Beverley (1798–?)
— daughter (1799–1800)
— Harriet (1801–?)
— James Madison (1805–77)
— Thomas Eston (1808–56)

Jane Randolph   son   Lucy Elizabeth Lucy Elizabeth
(1774–75)   (1777)   (1780–81)   (1782–84)

Mary (Maria) — m. 1797 — John Wayles Eppes
(1778–1804)

infant   Francis Wayles   Maria Jefferson
(1800)   (1801–81)   (1804–6)

Mary   Elizabeth   William   Judith
(1762–1828)   (b. 1765)   (1770–1848)   (1772–1816)
m. David Meade   m. Richard
Randolph   Randolph

Martha — m. 1790 — **Thomas Mann Randolph Jr.**
(1772–1836)   (1768–1828)

Anne   Thomas   Ellen   Ellen   Cornelia   Virginia
Cary   Jefferson   Wayles   Wayles   Jefferson   Jefferson
(1791–1826)   (1792–1875)   (1794–95)   (1796–1876)   (1799–1871)   (1801–82)

m. 1808   m. 1815   m. 1825   m. 1824
Charles Lewis   Jane Hollins   Joseph   Nicolas Philip
Bankhead   Nicholas   Coolidge   Trist

4 children   13 children   6 children   3 children

Jefferson-Randolph Family Tree

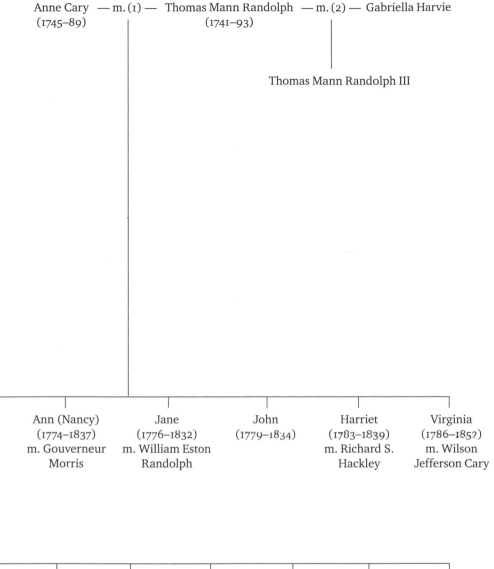

Anne Cary — m. (1) — Thomas Mann Randolph — m. (2) — Gabriella Harvie
(1745–89)   (1741–93)

Thomas Mann Randolph III

Ann (Nancy)	Jane	John	Harriet	Virginia
(1774–1837)	(1776–1832)	(1779–1834)	(1783–1839)	(1786–1852)
m. Gouverneur Morris	m. William Eston Randolph		m. Richard S. Hackley	m. Wilson Jefferson Cary

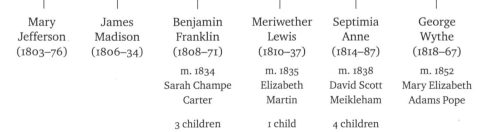

Mary Jefferson	James Madison	Benjamin Franklin	Meriwether Lewis	Septimia Anne	George Wythe
(1803–76)	(1806–34)	(1808–71)	(1810–37)	(1814–87)	(1818–67)
		m. 1834 Sarah Champe Carter	m. 1835 Elizabeth Martin	m. 1838 David Scott Meikleham	m. 1852 Mary Elizabeth Adams Pope
		3 children	1 child	4 children	

introduction

One sunny November afternoon in 1824, fifty-two-year-old Martha Jefferson Randolph stood beside her father, Thomas Jefferson, and welcomed the Marquis de Lafayette to Monticello. The aging French hero, who was touring the United States to commemorate the fiftieth anniversary of American independence, kissed her hands and offered kind words, while his hostess, according to one report, "received him with a grace peculiarly her own." Widely regarded as an exemplary woman and an accomplished plantation mistress, Martha Randolph presided over a celebration that showcased the Virginia gentry's gracious style of living and traditional rites of southern hospitality. After receiving Lafayette on Monticello's columned portico, twenty "ladies & gentlemen," including several of her own "white robed" daughters and nieces, enjoyed a pleasant dinner indoors. By all accounts, the food was good and the company was congenial. As the sun set behind the distant Blue Ridge mountains, Martha Jefferson Randolph and her guests basked in the nostalgic glow of the reunion of the old revolutionaries.[1]

Years later, Jane Blair Cary Smith, Martha's niece and a frequent visitor to Monticello, described Lafayette's visit in terms that cast her aunt as an exemplar of genteel white womanhood and rural domesticity. When Martha received her famous guest at Monticello, Smith recalled, she exuded "the charm of a perfect temper—the grace of a nature which . . . possessed the truest dignity." Her unselfish cheerfulness, she opined, was "the result of an unambitious spirit, and a contentment that lived in a sunshine all its own." Martha Jefferson Randolph, she wrote admiringly, was "highly cultivated and accomplished . . . [but] nevertheless happy in the domestic life of Monticello." This Paris-educated daughter of a president and wife of a governor was "universally popular" in large part because she downplayed her own notable experiences and accomplishments and projected to everyone she encountered an "utmost simplicity of character and the most unaffected humility."[2]

Martha's relaxed and welcoming demeanor on this and other occa-sions is all the more striking in light of the deepening crisis that engulfed the Jefferson-Randolph household. By 1824, Martha's husband, Thomas Mann Randolph, was penniless and increasingly estranged from his wife and children. Thomas Jefferson's finances were equally imperiled, despite the efforts of his oldest grandson, Thomas Jefferson Randolph, to manage his extensive but devalued properties and pay down his mounting debts. Martha's oldest daughter, Anne, who suffered a failed pregnancy nearly every year, lived unhappily with her insolvent and drunken husband, while her younger sisters faced the looming prospect of permanent spinsterhood. Still, Martha, her father, and their supporting cast staged quite a show when Lafayette came to visit, providing their guests with a pleasing meal as they flawlessly performed their respective domestic roles. Martha's "perfect temper" was part of a persona that, while neither fake nor insincere, some-times masked the realities of a troubled and complicated life.

❖ To a surprising extent, historical treatments of the life of Martha Jeffer-son Randolph mirror contemporary images of women as either beneficia-ries or victims of men's patriarchal power. Most traditional Jefferson biog-raphers present Martha as the devoted daughter who existed mainly as a beloved accessory to her famous father and, if they consider the question at all, presume that she benefited prodigiously from her close connection to the Sage of Monticello. Other, mostly more recent, accounts emphasize the negative consequences of Jefferson's vast influence within his family circle and on his daughters in particular. This Jefferson is often portrayed as an ex-pert manipulator whose emotional demands on Martha especially doomed her marriage to Thomas Mann Randolph—intentionally or not—and whose disparaging assessment of the female sex consigned his daughters and all women to a largely ornamental education and exclusion from the dynamic and potentially satisfying civic life of the postrevolutionary era. At Monti-cello, this Jefferson subjected Martha to daily encounters with her mixed-race half-siblings, his children by the enslaved woman Sally Hemings, and to the public opprobrium and ridicule that his relationship with Hemings engendered. To varying degrees, authors of these revisionist interpretations conclude that though Jefferson loved Martha—and she, in turn, adored her father—she paid a high price for her dependence and devotion, as did the other women he loved.[3]

Both traditional and revisionist approaches share a Jefferson-centered perspective that, though admittedly important, cannot tell the entire story of his daughter's life. For example, while Jefferson-centered treatments of Martha Jefferson Randolph generally portray her marriage to Thomas Mann Randolph as doomed from the start, in large part due to the unusually close bond between daughter and father, a more wide-ranging perspective—with Martha herself at its center—suggests that the Randolphs' marriage was surprisingly resilient for many years, despite its ultimate collapse in the 1820s. Martha and Tom's marital problems, moreover, owed at least as much to the personal feuds and financial problems that plagued Tom's family, the Randolphs of Tuckahoe, as to Jefferson's preference that Martha and her family reside with him at Monticello. Martha also outlived her father by eleven years; though Jefferson's famously ruined finances and resurgent popularity (at least in some circles) shaped her life during these later years, so, too, did her experiences as a penurious mother of a large family in an unfamiliar and changing world, away from Monticello. Throughout her life, Martha Jefferson Randolph made choices—some good, some bad. Her relationship to her father was one of many factors that informed her personal agency.

Randolph's story is that of an intelligent, patriotic, but in most respects conventional woman who never attained the iconic status of Abigail Adams (who is sometimes lionized as a protofeminist today) or Dolley Madison (the prototypical "first lady" of the American republic and namesake of ice cream and cupcakes in our own era).[4] Born at Monticello in 1772, Martha Jefferson married Thomas Mann Randolph in 1790, bore twelve children, and died in 1836 at Edgehill, the Randolph family plantation in Albemarle County, within sight of the house her father built. As a girl, she accompanied Jefferson to Paris, where she attended a French convent school. As a young matron, her status as the president's daughter exposed her to the best and brightest society of the American republic. When Jefferson retired from public life, his (and her) home at Monticello became a magnet for visitors, a cosmopolitan salon in the rural Virginia Piedmont. Throughout her life, however, such demonstrable privilege coexisted with great sorrow. When she was ten years old, Martha lost her mother; four of her five siblings died in childhood or infancy, and her sole surviving sister died, in 1804, at the age of twenty-six. Conflict and scandal embroiled her Randolph in-laws, while her beloved father suffered repeated public attacks on both his policies and his character. Over time, Martha's marriage deteriorated, as did her family's finances. Widowed and homeless, she spent her last years residing with her adult children in Virginia, Boston, and Washington.

Any biographer must make the case that her subject's story is worth telling—and worth reading—and my case for Martha Jefferson Randolph rests on two seemingly contradictory facts. On the one hand, at its best, her life was extraordinary. She knew interesting people, including eight of the first nine American presidents—she apparently never met George Washington—and many of the most influential women of her era, including among her closest friends the remarkable Dolley Madison. At a time when most white southern women were illiterate, Randolph spoke and read four languages, won near-universal praise for her conversational skills, and (in the opinion of the Spanish ambassador) was "fitted to grace any court in Europe."[5] On the other hand, much of her life and work in Virginia as a wife, mother, and plantation mistress was ordinary, tedious, and dull. As a wife, she was loyal to—and legally dependent on—a volatile and ultimately impoverished spouse. As a mother, she labored to prepare her children for adult lives that would be significantly less privileged than her own. The domestic life of Martha Jefferson Randolph reveals to modern readers the challenges, complexities, and frustrations that dominated the lives of many women of her era, even those who were members of a privileged social elite.

Women's stories matter not only for their contributions to American history but also because the historical narrative often looks somewhat different from the perspective of female protagonists—an observation that rings especially true when Martha Randolph is the central character in the Jefferson family narrative. For better or worse, Jefferson-centered accounts of Martha's life at Monticello assume that its master, like other southern planters, was a patriarch who had near-absolute authority over (and responsibility for) his wife, children, servants, and slaves. Martha Jefferson Randolph's story, however, can be read as a narrative of lived experience that counters the rhetoric of southern patriarchy to the extent that she herself had significant authority and influence—along with myriad responsibilities and obligations—throughout her adult life.[6]

Martha's story can also be read as a case study of what could happen when patriarchy malfunctioned because men were unable or unwilling to fulfill their prescribed domestic roles. When her husband and her father lost their property, and with it their capacity to maintain the family, Martha, like other women, filled the void, using her skills and connections to generate opportunities and income and to marshal her household's scant resources. When marriages went awry but divorce was unacceptable (or unavailable), some women suffered egregiously, but others instead found creative ways to live independently from their estranged spouses. Fending for herself and for her family in the absence of male providers, Martha, like many women who had some autonomy, often exercised hers unhappily. Significantly, the pervasive economic problems of Virginia's old plantation gentry may have inspired the adoption of an aggressively patriarchal worldview in some quarters by the 1820s—a decade or so before white southerners deployed patriarchal rhetoric in their vigorous defense of chattel slavery. Not coincidentally, Martha's sister-in-law, Virginia Randolph Cary, was an impoverished and opium-addled widow when she wrote her *Letters on Female Character*, a prescient treatise in which she sought to convince her readers that women should be dependent on and subordinate to benevolent men who would protect and govern them both at home and in society.[7]

So, too, does Thomas Jefferson's renowned hospitality look different from the perspective of the daughter who not only oversaw the production of meals and other domestic amenities but also personified civility and sociability as she mediated guests' access to her famous father. "A good Virginia housekeeper," as one of Martha's nieces observed, "was a very busy woman," especially compared with her eminent father, who in retirement presented himself to a near-constant parade of visitors as a sort of genial and leisured philosopher king. Jefferson scholars have long recognized the role of Martha and her children in protecting the great man's legacy after his death in 1826. But a careful analysis of the domestic tableaux that she constructed with her father in Washington and, later, at Monticello reveals Martha's recurrent efforts to mold and to burnish her father's public image as a family man long before she and her children published a purposefully edited version of his papers in 1829.[8]

Like most women of her era, Martha spent much of her life at home, and her political engagement was typically subtle, intermittent, and sometimes mainly symbolic. Early accounts of women's place in postrevolutionary America portrayed even elite women as largely excluded from public life and relegated to the domestic sphere, where, as republican wives and mothers, their ability to deploy feminine virtue to promote good citizenship was their most significant permissible political role. More recent historians have found women playing self-consciously political roles in a variety of public venues. Women populated the refined salons and drawing rooms of Philadelphia and, later, Washington, as well as the era's raucously partisan rallies and civic festivals, where their visibility elicited a powerful backlash by the 1820s.[9] Neither an invisible "republican mother" nor a "female politician," Martha Jefferson Randolph stood between these two extremes. In an era that valued polite manners, domestic virtues, and women's influence (at least within their households), her performance as her father's hostess or representative in carefully staged domestic contexts brought her and her family access to political influence, patronage, and pleasant society.

Martha's unusually well-documented life also offers a window onto the complicated personal relationships and seemingly endless work of a Virginia plantation mistress, whose real-life experiences belie the caricatures of strong men and frail ladies who still inexplicably people the present-day mythology of the Old South. Despite Martha's uniquely privileged status as the daughter of Thomas Jefferson, the challenges she faced as a daughter, wife, and mother—and her virtually lifelong struggle to balance the competing needs of those to or for whom she deemed herself responsible—characterized the lives of countless women of her era. Neither ornament nor cipher, Martha was often the most clearheaded and practical person in her domestic circle, though her "perfect temper" often masked her exasperation, enabling her to disagree with the men and sometimes even to get what she wanted.

As a historian of early America and of women and gender, I have written a biography that places my protagonist's life in its appropriate historical context. While some readers will prefer to focus exclusively on the story, others will doubtless wonder about its larger significance. Aside from my most basic argument—that American women's stories are important and that we know too few of them, especially for the period before 1830—my historiographical insights are mostly implicit or in the endnotes. Nevertheless, by way of introducing my narrative, I should explain what I hope readers will learn from it, more generally speaking, and clarify where I stand on issues ranging from Thomas Jefferson's alleged misogyny to the paternity of the light-skinned slaves who worked, mostly as house servants, at Monticello.

For starters, Martha Jefferson Randolph's life story is added evidence that early American women, even those who resided in the southern plantation regions, could and did venture beyond their prescribed domestic roles without jeopardizing their reputations or undermining their respectability. Born into a society in which law, custom, and religion upheld the near-absolute authority of white men over their wives, children, slaves, and other dependents, Martha did not see much change in the formal rules that governed relations between women and men during her sixty-four-year lifetime. Yet moments of self-assertion punctuated her life, from her adolescent chiding of her father for not writing her more and better letters to her carefully orchestrated efforts to secure government jobs for members of her family. Martha's connections were extraordinary—few other women could call on President James Madison at his central Virginia plantation to seek political patronage—but her sometimes successful attempts to dilute the authority of her husband or her father were not. Even in the slaveholding states, where patriarchal values were most deeply entrenched, tactfully assertive females could sometimes challenge those values and social conventions without sacrificing either domestic peace or their status in society.

Even in Martha's time, Americans organized their families and households in many ways, only one of which was the idealized nuclear family composed of two parents and their offspring. Neither Martha nor her children spent much of their lives in such supposedly normative households. The early death of her mother unavoidably disrupted the nuclear family of her childhood, while Martha's own decision to move herself and her children—and to a lesser extent her husband, too—to Monticello in 1809 departed from convention, though it did not necessarily mark an ominous turning point in the Randolphs' marriage, as some historians have argued.[10] As mistress of Monticello, Martha shared the house at various times with her father, her husband, her children, her sisters-in-law, her nieces and nephews, an aunt, at least one family friend, an unrelated young man or two (who were students of Jefferson's), assorted short- and long-term guests, and, of course, the family's slaves. Later, her domestic life was even more unsettled, as she moved among the homes of her adult children, accompanied by varying entourages of dependent children, grandchildren, and enslaved domestics.

Martha's interactions with enslaved people support the findings of historians who contend that slaveholding women generally experienced slavery as more of a personal relationship than a political issue and that mistresses strove to be benevolent, particularly toward familiar slaves who worked as domestic servants in their households. Like many Virginia women of her era, Martha claimed that she detested slavery, both for making white people cruel and immoral and for being unjust to blacks. At the same time, when forced to choose, like her father and countless other self-consciously benevolent slaveholders, she consistently put the economic interests of her white family ahead of any genuine desire she may have had to prevent the breakup of enslaved families or to emancipate her bondpeople. Like other slaveholders, for her entire life she profited, either directly or indirectly, from unfree labor.[11]

On at least one occasion, Martha lamented what she called the "discomforts of slavery," which included not only the problem of slave discipline and the horror of slave auctions as indebted Virginians sold their human chattel in staggering numbers, but also persistent rumors about her father's long-term sexual relationship with Sally Hemings, an enslaved woman at Monticello. Beautiful and light-skinned, Hemings was the mixed-race daughter of Martha's maternal grandfather, John Wayles, making her also the half-sister of Jefferson's wife (and Martha's mother). Until recently, Jefferson's white descendants and most historians did not believe that he was the father of Sally Hemings's children, but now the preponderance of evidence—from documents, oral tradition, and DNA testing—strongly supports the contention of Hemings's son, Madison, that his mother was "Mr. Jefferson's concubine" for many years, during which she gave birth to four children who survived to adulthood and became free.[12]

From Martha's perspective, however, whether Jefferson was truly the father of Hemings's children probably mattered less than the fact that so many people believed that he was. Whatever their paternity, the Hemingses posed no financial threat to Martha and her sister. The law guaranteed that Sally's children would inherit their mother's enslaved status, and as the offspring of an unsanctioned interracial union, they could press no legal claim against their white father's estate. Nor did revelations about Jefferson's relationship with Hemings, first published in a Richmond newspaper in 1802, impede his reelection to the presidency or diminish his subsequent popularity. But salacious gossip about Thomas Jefferson's relationship with Sally Hemings seemed to circulate everywhere, and especially in the hands of his political enemies, those stories portrayed him in an extremely unflattering light. The gossip saddened Martha and eventually led her children to concede that Hemings gave birth to a white man's children at Monticello, though they claimed that their cousin Peter Carr—and perhaps also his brother Samuel—had fathered the Hemings offspring. Martha, who knew the Hemingses better than any other family save possibly her Randolph in-laws, "took the Dusky Sally stories much to heart," according to her oldest son.[13]

Indeed, Martha's active involvement in deflecting and discounting hurtful gossip about her father and Sally Hemings shaped the performance of her duties as her father's hostess in Washington and later at Monticello. Historians have seen Jefferson's administration as a low point in the history of women's involvement in the civic life of the early republic. The third president abolished his predecessors' opulent salons and receptions, which included both gentlemen and ladies, thereby depriving women of access to political news and networks until the advent of Dolley Madison's drawing rooms and "crushes" when her husband succeeded Jefferson as president in 1809. But a careful examination of Martha Randolph's occasional trips to

Washington, as well as her style of entertaining at Monticello, reveals her ongoing involvement in efforts to display what she paradoxically referred to as her father's "private character" or "private virtue"—by which she meant his wholesome and benevolent relations with his white family. Jefferson wholly supported and, indeed, encouraged these efforts. Although historians typically portray Jefferson as critical of women who had political agendas, he apparently approved when his daughter shared his own.[14]

Even if Jefferson disliked and distrusted women, as some recent historians have argued, his problems were mostly with those who—by virtue of their age, intelligence, independence, or wealth—could challenge him intellectually, reject him romantically, or in any way claim to be his equals. Relations between daughters and fathers were inherently unequal, at least until old age debilitated and in some sense unmanned the latter. At any rate, Jefferson was devoted to his daughters and to Martha especially. She, in turn, loved him unconditionally, though it would be wrong to see her devotion as either unquestioning or mindless.[15]

Although this biography places Martha Jefferson Randolph at the center of her own story, her relationship with her father shaped most aspects of her life, in greater or lesser degrees. Martha was so extremely sensitive to any criticism of her father's character or conduct in part because they shared such an extraordinarily close relationship but also because she grew to regard her father's fame and reputation as her own and her children's chief inheritance. In addition, from her love of reading and her determination to see her own children appropriately educated, to her struggles as a penurious plantation mistress and her hostility toward banks and evangelical Christianity, Martha Randolph's life reflected important facets of her father's ideals and habits. Generally well-meaning but nonetheless meddlesome, Jefferson also complicated Martha's marriage to Thomas Mann Randolph, who both benefited and suffered as a result of his close connection to the great man who, even after his death, remained a continual and influential presence in his daughter's life.

Martha's status as the beloved daughter of Thomas Jefferson was a source of both undeniable privilege and largely unspoken problems. Jefferson's wealth in land and slaves staked her to a Parisian education, marriage into a prominent gentry family, and the land and slaves to begin life as a young matron, just as his financial ruin (and that of her husband, erstwhile heir to a grand estate) eventually impoverished her. Jefferson's fame and political success afforded the Randolphs access to illustrious and interesting people and occasional political patronage, while exposing them to painfully vicious allegations about Jefferson's supposedly debauched character. Even Jefferson's legacy as a hero of the republic's founding era was a double-edged sword for his daughter, who valued her family above all else. Justifiably proud of her father's achievements as a public man, she nonetheless believed that her own "honorable poverty," which occasioned the loss of Monticello and the dispersal of her children, was the "price we have paid, for a long and useful life devoted to the service of his country."[16]

There is no evidence that Martha ever sought to escape her father—quite the opposite—nor do I avoid him in this biography. Indeed, through his copious letters and other writings, his house, and even his physical resemblance to his eldest daughter, Jefferson is omnipresent here, just as he was in Martha's life. That said, this is Martha's story, and I have chosen to situate it in a broad historical context because the fact that she was a female member of the Virginia gentry and the mother of many children shaped her life at least as much as her relationship to her famous father. Martha Jefferson Randolph's status sometimes made her situation unique, but in some important respects her experiences were emblematic of those of many elite women of her place and time.

chapter 1

Love and Death at Monticello

Sunday, 27 September 1772, was a happy day for those who gathered at the bedside of Martha Wayles Skelton Jefferson in the small brick building that for the time being served as her husband's mountaintop home. With the assistance of their friend and neighbor physician George Gilmer, and perhaps a sister or a skilled domestic servant, Martha safely delivered a baby girl, the first offspring of her union with Thomas Jefferson, whom she had married nine months earlier. The twenty-four-year-old mother, whose first husband died in 1768 at the age of twenty-four and whose four-year-old son, John, followed his father to the grave in 1771, again survived the treacherous ordeal of childbirth to begin a second family. Thomas, who had craved the domestic life his wedded friends enjoyed before he himself married at the relatively advanced age of twenty-nine, was now a father, too. The new parents, following the common practice in the colony, named their firstborn daughter Martha, after her maternal grandmother. The child, who became known as "Patsy," did poorly during her first six months, in part because of her mother's lack of milk. Happily, "a good breast of milk" from Ursula, the family's enslaved housekeeper, restored the baby's health.[1]

❖ If she remained healthy, Patsy Jefferson could expect to enjoy a privileged life as a member of Virginia's gentry elite. Though her father's house, Monticello, was still a rudimentary work-in-progress, like most gentry homes, it was destined to be a two-story brick mansion that would appear both massive and stylish compared with the plain, two-room wooden "Virginia houses" of their less affluent neighbors.[2] Like most children of the gentry, Patsy would grow up surrounded by slaves, a few of whom would become familiar to her as servants in her family's house. At a time when fewer than half of the white men in Virginia were literate, the Jeffersons' daughter would be reared in a world of books. She would be educated, though her father (like most men) did not consider females his intellectual equals.

Thomas Jefferson's father, Peter, asserted his family's claim to gentry status by marrying well, amassing property, and providing his children with the accoutrements of gentility. A successful but by no means aristocratic surveyor, Peter Jefferson married Jane Randolph, a member of one of Virginia's oldest and most influential families. Between 1740 and 1755, Jane bore five daughters and four sons, though two of the boys died in infancy. The third child and oldest son, Thomas spent his youth at Tuckahoe, a Randolph plantation in Goochland County, where Peter managed the estate and oversaw the education of his own son and his orphaned cousin, Thomas Mann Randolph. In 1752, the Jeffersons moved to Shadwell, Peter's house in Albemarle County. When Peter Jefferson died in 1757, he had accumulated substantial landholdings in central Virginia and claimed ownership of more than sixty slaves. His house was stocked with furniture, silver, china, and books denoting his family's membership in Virginia's gentry elite.[3]

Along with property and prestigious personal contacts, education and public service were key gentlemanly attributes in eighteenth-century Virginia.[4] Accordingly, young Thomas Jefferson enrolled in the College of William and Mary in 1760, enjoying both the intellectual and social life of Williamsburg, Virginia's colonial capital. He also studied law there and, in 1766, was admitted to the bar, which enabled him to practice law in the colony. In 1769, Jefferson took his seat in the colonial legislature, the House of Burgesses, as a representative of his home county of Albemarle. Although not yet famous, he had begun the process of distinguishing himself in Virginia politics and society.

By the standards of his time, moreover, Thomas Jefferson married well. While financial considerations trumped emotion in the marriage choices of earlier generations of Virginia gentry, those of Jefferson's era, though still eager to acquire property, increasingly idealized unions based on companionship and romantic love. By all accounts, Thomas Jefferson and Martha Wayles Skelton were affectionate and compatible. Contemporaries described the young widow as a beautiful and amiable companion who shared certain common tastes and interests with her future husband. Like Thomas, Martha enjoyed reading, and both admired Laurence Sterne's novel *Tristram Shandy*, which they sometimes read together. Both were also avid and accomplished musicians: Thomas played the violin, while Martha played harpsichord and pianoforte—the most highly regarded instruments for females—and perhaps also the guitar. Music played an important role in the couple's courtship. The first substantial gift that Jefferson purchased for his future wife was an expensive harpsichord "of fine mahogany . . . worthy [of] the acceptance of a lady for whom I intend it."[5]

As her refined tastes and accomplishments suggest, Martha Wayles Skelton also hailed from an affluent Virginia family. She was the eldest of four daughters—there were no sons—of John Wayles, a lawyer, merchant, and slave trader who acted as an agent for English tobacco merchants in Virginia. Her mother, the first of Wayles's three wives, was Martha Eppes, who died a month after her daughter's birth. A propertied widow when she married Jefferson in 1772, Martha Wayles Skelton received some 11,000 acres and 135 slaves when her father died the following year. Among these slaves were a mulatto woman named Elizabeth (or Betty) Hemings and her children, some of whom were the offspring of Jefferson's late father-in-law and, therefore, half-siblings to Martha Wayles Skelton Jefferson (and half-aunts and -uncles to the infant Patsy). The presence of the Hemingses eventually would vastly complicate the lives of Thomas Jefferson and his family. In 1772, however, what was most apparent was the fact that, though Thomas Jefferson had married for love, his union with Martha Wayles Skelton also made him one of the wealthiest planters in the colony, at least in terms of ownership of land and slaves. Only thirty-four Virginians owned more acreage; only thirty-six had more bondpeople.[6]

A literate person who visited Virginia in 1772 might gauge the cultural aspirations and concerns of the Jeffersons and their peers by perusing the colony's newspapers. Established in 1736 and published in Williamsburg, the provincial capital, the *Virginia Gazette* aspired to provide its readers with the "freshest Advices, Foreign & Domestick." It featured news from Europe (especially England), polite essays, and commercial notices that both signified and enhanced the gentry's privileged access to information, which, in turn, strengthened their collective claim to political and social authority. In 1766, another Williamsburg weekly that published similar fare (and was also named the *Virginia Gazette*) became the second newspaper in the colony. Newspaper issues that bracketed the birth of Patsy Jefferson at Monticello on 27 September 1772 revealed the vitality of Virginia's gentry culture while signaling the imminent disruption of the routines of provincial life.

Even the most casual reader of the *Virginia Gazette* in 1772 would notice its cosmopolitan, outward-looking perspective. British and European news typically occupied the paper's front page, where this week's readers learned about the introduction of a new order of knighthood by King George III "for the Encouragement of Literature, the fine Arts, and learned Professions" and savored an essay titled "On the Power of England," which celebrated the mother country's commercial prowess and "the peculiar Felicity of our Constitution."[7] On subsequent pages—there were only four in all—local merchants and storekeepers proudly advertised apparel, patent medicines, stationery, and books recently imported from Britain, attesting to readers' membership in a transatlantic cultural and commercial community. Histories, novels, and conduct manuals were especially popular among provincial readers who turned to books to acquire the etiquette and information they needed to shine in conversation and polite society.

Yet a cursory reading of the *Virginia Gazette* in September 1772 also would have revealed colonists' incipient discomfort with their ties to Great Britain, despite their resumption of civil, if tense, relations with imperial officials in the wake of colonial resistance to parliamentary taxation, which resulted in the Stamp Act and Townshend Duties crises of the 1760s. A Latin motto added to the masthead of the original *Virginia Gazette* on 19 November 1767 asserted the necessity of free speech and free thought to the preservation of liberty—perhaps alluding to recent imperial political controversies—as did ongoing coverage of the saga of John Wilkes, an English radical who supported colonial rights and (seemingly partly for that reason) was repeatedly denied a seat in Parliament and persecuted by British authorities. Other front-page stories noted the extensive and dangerous power of allegedly corrupt Scots in the London-based imperial regime and reported that Scots emigrants fled to America to escape "the Oppression of their Superiours." Readers also learned of the British crisis of credit, both public and private, which had dire implications for Virginia planters who were heavily indebted to English and Scottish merchants, who sold them imported consumer goods on credit and marketed their tobacco.[8]

Signs of planter indebtedness, which had worried Jefferson's merchant father-in-law as early as 1764, were by 1772 ubiquitous in the province, as well as in the pages of the Williamsburg press. Perhaps responding to pressure from their own creditors in Britain, local agents for one London partnership demanded payment of outstanding debts by 20 October 1772, tersely adding that "no indulgence can be given" to delinquent debtors. Meanwhile, countless newspaper notices informed readers of local storekeepers seeking to settle their accounts, while others advertised the sale or auction of lands, slaves, livestock, and other property seized for debt. By 1772, when he advertised the sale of more than 2,000 acres, a tobacco warehouse, livestock, and "upwards of ONE HUNDRED FINE SLAVES, many valuable Tradesmen among them," William Byrd III was only the most prominent of many casualties of insolvency born of unstable tobacco prices and planters' unremittingly extravagant consumption of imported goods. Dissipated and penniless, Byrd committed suicide in 1777.[9]

Despite the political, economic, and cultural dominance of the gentry, cautionary vignettes suggesting the limits of their authority punctuated the pages of the *Gazette*. The issue published for 24 September 1772, for instance, contained ample evidence of dissatisfaction among the gentry's imagined inferiors. One way for bonded workers to express their discontent was by running away from their masters. In this issue of the *Gazette*, eight masters placed newspaper notices seeking the return of a total of eight runaway slaves (six men and two women), a skilled white servant, and an English convict laborer. Another advertisement noted the capture of "a runaway woman named MOLLY" and requested that her "Owner" retrieve her from the James City County jail. Evidence from the *Gazette* suggests that free laborers, too, sometimes chafed under the bridle of gentry rule. On 24 September, the editors published an advertisement condescendingly encouraging "Any discreet Tradesman (especially a CARPENTER), content if he can make a genteel provision for himself and Family, by an honest Industry, and not ambitious to rank as a Gentleman," to settle in the growing town of Richmond. In the paper's next issue, "Mechanicks in the lower Parts of Virginia" responded angrily to these advertisers, who, they asserted, were "not *simply* [equipped with] the Qualifications of *Extortion, Insolence,* and *Laziness,* but rather *Adepts* therein; and, perhaps, may have the Addition of . . . *Pride, Envy,* and *Malice.*"[10]

But public outbursts of this sort were uncommon, and Virginia's gentlemen expected to govern not only laboring men but also women of all social ranks. The law prescribed the subordination of women to men, and especially the authority of husbands over wives. The common-law doctrine of coverture erased a wife's legal identity, making her husband her sole representative at law and thereby preventing her from controlling property, filing lawsuits, or executing contracts. The virtual nonexistence of legal divorce further institutionalized women's formal subordination to men in both Britain and its colonies. At the same time, however, popular writers increasingly lauded feminine virtue as a potentially civilizing influence in families and—to a lesser extent—in society. This new appreciation of the possible benefits of women's moral influence, in turn, generated concerns about the education of young females, at least within the colony's elite.[11]

During the week of Patsy Jefferson's birth, evidence from the *Virginia Gazette* pointed to both the opportunities and limits of female education in the province. On the one hand, the long list of books for sale in Williamsburg in September 1772 contained titles specifically aimed at female readers. These included prescriptive literature, such as *Instructions for a young Lady in every Sphere and Period of Life*, *Moore's Fables for the Female Sex*, *Letters to the Ladies on the Preservation of Health and Beauty*, and *The School, being a Series of Letters between a young Lady and her Mother*. Also advertised were many novels whose titles bore the names of their heroines, which appealed to female readers. Such circumstantial evidence indicates that the wives and daughters of the gentry were reading at least certain types of literature by the 1770s.[12]

On the other hand, schools for girls were uncommon in Virginia, and on 24 September 1772, the editors of the *Gazette* reprinted an English essay that provided a rationale for parents' preference for keeping their daughters (unlike their sons) at home to be educated. "*The first Seeds of Vice* are imbibed at a Boarding School," this critic observed, where "vicious Girls" and other unsavory characters "will find sufficient Opportunities to taint the tender Minds of unsuspecting Innocence." Loss of virtue meant utter ruin for young women, as the author of a poem that appeared in the *Gazette* a week later advised:

Virtue is Grace and Dignity,
'Tis more than Royal Blood,
A Gem the World's too poor to buy;
Would you be fair, be good.[13]

The infant Patsy Jefferson was born into a seemingly genteel and orderly world that prized feminine virtue, masculine independence, and a social hierarchy in which gentlemen with polite manners and cosmopolitan tastes governed peaceably on behalf of their presumed inferiors. In fact, Virginia was on the threshold of dramatic change in 1772. The imperial crisis that began with the Stamp Act in 1765 and occasioned the establishment of a second (and more outspokenly critical) *Virginia Gazette* in Williamsburg in 1766 would lead to the Royal Navy's bombardment of the Virginia coast a decade later, when Patsy's own father would pen a manifesto that the Continental Congress in distant Philadelphia used to declare and justify the independence of Virginia and twelve other insurgent provinces. The ensuing years of war and revolution would aggravate the economic problems that already afflicted many Virginia planters in 1772 and—more troubling still, from the perspective of white Virginians—sow the seeds of slave rebellion.

The war also disrupted the normal routines of family life. Only four years old in 1776, Patsy Jefferson was too young to remember the earliest stages of the Revolution, but the military and political conflicts of the era profoundly shaped her childhood. Her father's increasing prominence in the revolutionary movement affected where she lived and whom she met and—in the longer run—adversely affected her family's finances. The Revolution was a formative experience for Patsy Jefferson, whose family in some respects sacrificed mightily for the patriot cause.

❖ Children's experiences in revolutionary America ranged from the prosaic to the profoundly unsettling. Those who lived far from the battlefields and army encampments and whose parents avoided military or political service could enjoy a secure and stable family life, perhaps blissfully unaware of the war and its attendant hardships. Others, by contrast, experienced wartime violence in communities under siege or as camp followers or underage soldiers; many more lost a father or another close relation in the unexpectedly long war that eventually claimed more than 25,000 American lives.[14]

Patsy Jefferson's first decade—which coincided with the rise, progress, and ultimate triumph of the American Revolution—fell between these two extremes. Although the war brought military prisoners and eventually armed conflict to their Albemarle County neighborhood, the adult Jeffersons were surprisingly successful in isolating their home and family from the ill effects of war. Years later, when Patsy wrote a brief account of her childhood, her memories of the personal tragedies and political controversies of the era overshadowed those of the war itself.[15]

Patsy spent most of her first decade at Monticello, her father's house in Albemarle, located just a few miles from Peter Jefferson's Shadwell, which had been destroyed by fire in 1770. Begun in 1772, the first version of Monticello was nearly completed by the war's end. Jefferson clearly planned his home as a bucolic refuge. It was far removed from the bustle of town life, perched atop an 867-foot mountain that took half an hour to climb, despite the road that his enslaved workers had laboriously cut through the heavily forested slopes. The nearest town was Charlottesville, Albemarle's county seat, which consisted of "only of a Court-house, one tavern, and about a dozen houses" in the 1770s.[16]

In the serene isolation of Monticello, Patsy's family cultivated the affectionate domestic ideal that they and their contemporaries increasingly valued. Jefferson regarded parental love as "the strongest affection known ... greater than even that of self-preservation," and by all accounts his was a loving and harmonious household. Visitors routinely noted the amiable company and comforts they enjoyed as guests at Monticello, conveying the impression that Jefferson's family circle was loving, sociable, and virtuous— an atmosphere that Jefferson and, later, his daughter fostered for their entire adult lives. To outsiders at least, it seemed that the sentimental ideal of affectionate domesticity had been attained at Patsy Jefferson's childhood home.[17]

In reality, love and death together marked the years of Patsy's infancy and early childhood. On the one hand, the adult Jeffersons expressed affection openly to their child and to each other. Patsy later recalled that her father's "manners in his family were familiar and affectionate" and that "we always kissed him good night . . . unless strangers were present." On the other hand, the pervasiveness of mortality made family ties both precarious and precious. In 1773, Patsy's grandfather, John Wayles, and Dabney Carr, Thomas Jefferson's brother-in-law and intimate friend, died suddenly. The next year brought the death of Jefferson's sister Elizabeth. In April 1774, Martha Jefferson gave birth to a second daughter, Jane, who died in October 1775. The death of Jane Randolph Jefferson, Patsy's paternal grandmother, followed five months later.[18]

By then, Thomas Jefferson had begun his career as a peripatetic revolutionary, leaving his family for long intervals to serve in the Continental Congress. While Jefferson had represented Albemarle in the House of Burgesses since 1769, the sessions of that colonial assembly, which convened in Williamsburg, were typically brief; by contrast, Congress met in Philadelphia, which was roughly twice as far from home, and its sessions lengthened as its members moved cautiously toward declaring independence. Although some members of Congress brought their families with them, concerns about his wife's health, his daughter's youth, and his own decided aversion to city life probably led Jefferson to conclude that his family would be better off in Virginia. During the Revolution, when he journeyed to Williamsburg or Philadelphia on public business, Jefferson corresponded with his wife and with friends and family near home, as he had done since his marriage in 1772. When he came home, he arrived bearing gifts—chocolate, lace, shoes, a doll for Patsy—which must have conveyed a sense of well-being to his family, despite the troubled times.[19]

Soon, however, the crisis between the colonies and Great Britain escalated, bringing war to Virginia. In late 1775, when the colony's royal governor, Lord Dunmore, bombarded the coastal towns of Hampton and Norfolk and promised freedom to slaves who joined the king's forces, civilians experienced violence firsthand, sometimes in their own houses. Mary Webley of Norfolk was "suckling her child" in her home when her leg was broken by an exploding British cannonball. Webley and her "little Children" survived, but their house was destroyed by fire during the bombing, and like many other women and children, the Webleys became refugees after the destruction of the coastal town by soldiers on both sides. When young Jenny Steuart visited Norfolk in 1779, she found that only about fifteen houses had been rebuilt, though she noted that there were "a great many small huts" to shelter townspeople who "cannot be happy anywhere else."[20]

The fact that Patsy's memories of her childhood at Monticello focused overwhelmingly on her relations with her parents suggests that they largely succeeded in protecting her from the ill effects of war. Thomas Jefferson believed that his family would be safe in Albemarle, which was far removed from the early fighting, and he probably imparted that confidence to his wife and daughter. As he put it in a letter to his uncle in the summer of 1776, "Our interior situation is to me the most agreeable as withdrawing me in a great measure from the noise and bustle of the world. . . . Our idea is that every place is secure [from enemy attack] except those which lie immediately on the water edge."[21]

When public business took Thomas Jefferson away from home, he and Martha relied on family or friends for protection and companionship and to maintain a semblance of normal domestic life. In particular, they turned to Francis Eppes and his wife Elizabeth Wayles Eppes (Martha's half-sister), who lived at The Forest in Charles City County, just west of Williamsburg. During Dunmore's raids, Jefferson unsuccessfully pressed Francis Eppes and his family "to keep yourselves at a distance from the alarms" by moving farther inland to Albemarle, where they would be welcome additions to the Monticello household while he attended to political business in Philadelphia. Instead, Patsy and her mother spent July and August at The Forest, where Elizabeth saw Martha through a seemingly dangerous illness and four-year-old Patsy enjoyed the company of her three-year-old cousin, John Wayles Eppes.[22]

These domestic arrangements would not have seemed extraordinary to Patsy, who was only three in 1775 when her father made his first trip north to Philadelphia to attend Congress, nor would they have seemed entirely strange to her mother, who was the product of a gentry culture in which long-term visits to close kin were common. Many white Virginians lived far from their relatives and friends on widely dispersed plantations, and Martha Jefferson had spent much of the time immediately after her marriage visiting her sister Elizabeth Eppes and other members of her family. Especially for the gentry, who had some time for leisure, visiting provided opportunities for socialization and sociability. Women, who often were lonely and isolated at home, particularly valued time spent with distant mothers, sisters, and other female relatives.[23]

At the same time, like other revolutionary wives, Martha Jefferson regretted and possibly even resented her husband's frequent absences. Perhaps for that reason, in October 1776, Thomas turned down a judicial appointment that would have required his continual attendance at court. Citing domestic concerns, he also declined Congress's offer of a diplomatic post in Europe. Alluding to his wife's recent illness and yet another pregnancy in its early stages, and perhaps also thinking of his four-year-old daughter's need to begin her education, he explained that "circumstances very peculiar in the situation of my family, such as neither permit me to leave nor to carry it, compel me to ask leave to decline a service so honorable & at the same time so important to the American cause."[24]

Jefferson's decision to turn his attention to state politics after 1776 allowed Patsy, for the first time, to live in a conventionally patriarchal two-parent household for an extended period. Between 1777 and 1779, Jefferson's membership in Virginia's state legislature required his presence in Williamsburg for weeks or even months at a time, but he still spent less time away from home than he had in previous years. On at least one occasion, Martha (and possibly Patsy, too) accompanied him to the capital. During these years, Jefferson devoted his time primarily to revising Virginia's colonial legal code to make it more compatible with the republican political values of a now-independent commonwealth. This project enabled his family to enjoy a relatively stable domestic life as he worked in his personal library at Monticello.[25]

Safe from the violence of war, the Monticello family nevertheless experienced personal anguish and loss as a result of Martha Jefferson's continued bad health and another ill-fated pregnancy. Despite her husband's frequent absences, Martha became pregnant roughly every two years, an interval that was typical for elite Virginia women in the eighteenth century, though the mortality rate of her offspring far exceeded contemporary averages. The family mourned another infant, an unnamed boy, who was born in late May 1777 and died three weeks later. In August 1778, however, they rejoiced in the birth of a daughter—Mary, known as "Polly"—the only Jefferson child besides Patsy who lived to adulthood.[26]

Between 1777 and 1779, with the armies fighting in the Middle States and then in Georgia and the Carolinas, Jefferson stepped up construction at Monticello, planted fruit trees in his orchards, and resumed the scientific activities and research that were among his lifelong avocations. At Monticello, the main discernable impact of the war during these years probably came in the form of shortages as the disruption or stoppage of trade in wartime meant that goods that Virginians normally imported became either extremely expensive or completely unavailable. One woman in central Virginia lamented a shortage of ink that prevented her from writing longer letters to her husband. In Albemarle, the army's demand for food, especially meat, diminished supplies for the civilian population. Meanwhile, plantation mistresses and their enslaved workers began sewing and spinning to make or mend clothing and other necessary items. Martha Wayles Skelton Jefferson, perhaps assisted by her young daughter, oversaw the production of cloth at Monticello.[27]

In this precariously safe environment, the Jeffersons began childrearing in earnest, and Patsy embarked on an educational regimen designed to make her—in her father's words—"good and accomplished." Jefferson's library holdings and sentiments he later expressed in letters to both his daughters and granddaughters show that his attitudes toward childrearing were conventional for the times. His ideas about the education and training of young females in particular were far from revolutionary. The essays of Joseph Addison and Richard Steele—*The Tatler* and *The Spectator*—along with *A Father's Legacy to His Daughters*, by the Scotsman John Gregory, were the most influential texts on genteel femininity among eighteenth-century Americans. Jefferson owned copies of these works, and he featured *The Spectator* (a series of essays first published in London six decades before Patsy's birth) on his recommended "List of Books for a Lady's Library."[28]

These popular writers believed that girls should be educated, but they also assumed that female education should serve the interests of husbands and children—and thus, by extension, those of the larger society. Contemporary moralists and social critics generally valued the influence of literate and sensitive females, which they believed improved men by promoting virtue and civility at home and in society. But Addison and Steele, in particular, ridiculed politically minded women and praised those who wholeheartedly embraced their prescribed domestic roles. The primary concerns of good women, in other words, were the comforts and virtues of men. As one contributor to the *Virginia Gazette* put it in 1773, "if Men did not converse with Women, [men] would be less perfect and less happy than they are."[29]

Like most Virginia fathers of his generation, Thomas Jefferson directed his child's education and intellectual development. Patsy later recalled that her father "bestowed much time & attention" on her education during the war years. Although little is known about the precise nature of this first phase of her education at Monticello, Patsy probably learned to read and write by age five, as did her younger sister Polly; her father also began to teach her French and the basic arithmetic skills needed to run a plantation household. Jefferson urged his daughter to read, though the reading lists he compiled for young men, such as his kinsmen Robert Skipwith and Peter Carr, were far more specific and varied than what he prescribed for his daughters, for whom he believed reading would be chiefly a weapon "against ennui" born of rural isolation and ultimately "useful only for filling up the chinks of more useful and healthy [domestic] occupations." Like most gentry parents, Jefferson also stressed the importance of what contemporaries called "accomplishments," especially music (at which Patsy, like her parents, excelled) and drawing (at which she did not). Although Jefferson could be a demanding taskmaster, his daughter remembered her early years under his tutelage as cherished quality time spent with a man she loved.[30]

Patsy's relations with Martha Wayles Skelton Jefferson appear to have been more distant. Years later, she remembered her mother as "having a vivacity of temper that sometimes bordered on tartness" toward her children, though not toward her husband, whom she deeply loved. As an adult, Patsy told a story that cast her mother in a comparatively negative light. On one occasion, she later recalled, her mother had punished her "for some fault, not harshly nor unjustly, but in a way to make an impression." Some time later, when Martha was displeased with her daughter "for some trifle," she "reminded her in a slightly taunting way of this painful past." Some forty years after this incident, Patsy still recalled feeling "deeply mortified" and tearful, until her father rose to her defense. "My dear, a fault in so young a child once punished should be forgotten," he gently suggested to his wife. Patsy "could never forget the warm gush of gratitude that filled her childish heart at these words, probably not intended for her ear."[31]

As a young child, Patsy almost certainly did not appreciate the toll that illness, repeated pregnancies, and grief exacted from a woman already burdened by the onerous domestic responsibilities of a plantation mistress, which Martha Jefferson by all accounts performed well. Although Patsy recalled that her mother's virtues included "neatness, order, good housewifery and womanly accomplishment," Martha Jefferson apparently did not impart her domestic skills to young Patsy, who years later claimed to be "well grounded in all the solid branches of a woman's education, save only the arts of housewifery," which she "attained with pain & difficulty, by untiring perseverance" only after she married.[32]

An exemplary hostess, Martha Jefferson probably played a more active role in introducing Patsy to the forms and rituals of genteel sociability. The Jeffersons had welcomed European guests to their home as early as 1773, when Thomas persuaded the Florentine Philip Mazzei to settle at nearby Colle plantation. Impressed by the taste and hospitality of his hosts, Mazzei reported to a friend in Italy in 1775, "If you knew Mr. Jefferson and his worthy spouse I am certain you would not seek any benefit other than that of living with them." Patsy herself remembered her mother as "a very attractive person . . . with considerable powers of conversation, some skill in music, all the habits of good society, and the art of welcoming her husband's friends to perfection"—all womanly attributes that Thomas Jefferson clearly valued and that would later characterize his daughter's conduct as hostess at Monticello. Guests described Martha Wayles Skelton Jefferson as "gentle and amiable," "very agreeable, sensible, and accomplished," an adept performer on both the harpsichord and pianoforte. Patsy, who also became an expert harpsichordist, probably had her first music lessons from her mother at Monticello.[33]

The arrival of thousands of military prisoners in Patsy's Albemarle neighborhood in 1778 unexpectedly made her father's house a center of polite sociability. In October 1777, American troops defeated a combined force of British regulars, Germans, and loyalists in a pivotal battle at Saratoga in upstate New York. Congress later interred prisoners from Saratoga in and around Charlottesville. Although some Albemarle residents resented the prisoners' presence, Jefferson extended his hospitality to captured officers, who, in eighteenth-century European armies, invariably held elite social status. "It is for the benefit of mankind to mitigate the horrors of war as much as possible," he wrote to Governor Patrick Henry in 1779. "The practice . . . of treating captive enemies with politeness and generosity," he asserted, "is not only delight in contemplation, but really interesting to the world—friends, foes, and neutrals."[34]

Although the Jeffersons did not socialize with the common soldiers who were imprisoned in Albemarle, the presence of officers, who were educated members of Europe's upper social strata, afforded Patsy her first exposure to genteel cosmopolitan society. A family dinner at nearby Blenheim plantation, hosted by a captive British major general, included an invitation for

seven-year-old "Miss Jefferson" and her parents, along with Baron von Riedesel and his wife and three daughters, who had accompanied the Hessian
officer on his tour of duty in America. The Monticello family especially enjoyed the agreeable society of the accomplished, English-speaking Riedesels, whose eldest daughter, Augusta, was a year older than Patsy. The Jeffersons hosted many musical evenings for the Riedesels and other paroled
officers and their families. Patsy's mother played the harpsichord or pianoforte, and the Baroness von Riedesel often sang.[35]

The fact that Patsy did not recall any discussion of the war during these
mostly happy years suggests that, from her perspective as a young child,
Monticello was a safe haven from the mixture of good and bad news about
a revolution whose failure would result in the ruin (and perhaps the execution) of its leaders, including, of course, her own beloved father. Jefferson
corresponded regularly with prominent officials and military command-
ers, so he (and possibly his wife) knew that the war, having been fought
to a stalemate in the Middle States, moved decisively southward with the
British capture of Savannah and then all of Georgia beginning in December 1778. Patsy's youth and her residence on a mountaintop, where she was
isolated from local militia musters and other troop movements and far from
the seat of government, made it somewhat easier for her parents to shield
her from war-related issues and anxieties. By contrast, Betsey Ambler, who
lived in York, a coastal town near Williamsburg, and who was seven years
older than Patsy, had strong recollections of the war from its beginning and
acute awareness of the movement of troops in its later stages.[36]

Nevertheless, Patsy must have become increasingly conscious of the war
and its consequences after June 1779, when the Virginia legislature chose
her father to be the state's new governor. Thomas Jefferson's assumption
of the governorship changed his family's circumstances in at least two respects.

First, because Thomas Jefferson's new office necessitated his presence
in the capital, Martha Jefferson and her daughters, like many political and
military families, left home, joining Thomas in Williamsburg, where they
took up residence in the Governor's Palace in the old colonial capital. A
massive three-story structure that had been completed in 1722 and enlarged to include a ballroom in the 1750s, the Governor's Palace served as a
military hospital in 1776 before becoming the residence of Governor Patrick
Henry and members of three generations of his unusually large family, who
moved with him to Williamsburg. In 1779, when Jefferson became governor,

Governor's Palace in Williamsburg. Completed in 1722, this English-style mansion was large and fashionable by American standards, though much smaller and less opulent than the palaces of Europe. The Jeffersons were the last family to reside in the house, which was destroyed by fire in 1781 and rebuilt with the help of Jefferson's drawings in the 1930s. The Library of Virginia.

he drew a floor plan of the building and apparently considered remodeling to make it more suitable for his own, much smaller family.[37]

Second, because Jefferson was now responsible for overseeing the state's war effort, his residence became a central clearinghouse for military and political information. Under these circumstances, it was unlikely that Patsy—who was now seven years old and quite intelligent—could remain unaware of the war, especially as the contending armies moved inexorably toward Virginia. Indeed, not long after Patsy arrived in Williamsburg, her father issued a proclamation, pursuant to a recommendation from the Continental Congress, that set aside a day of "public and solemn thanksgiving and prayer" to commemorate recent military successes and seek "the continuance of [God's] favour and protection to these United States." The governor encouraged "all the good people of this commonwealth," including presumably his own family (who were not ordinarily regular churchgoers), to pray and attend church services to support the war effort. Such activities must have given young Patsy at least a vague understanding of current events.[38]

Notwithstanding her growing awareness of the war raging in Georgia and then in the Carolinas, Patsy may have enjoyed her first year as the governor's daughter. During Jefferson's initial one-year term as governor, no major military engagements occurred in Virginia. In Williamsburg, Patsy had her first taste of town life, which included regular lessons at Sarah Hallam's dancing school for young ladies, where she learned the basics of the social skill that more than any other was essential for young Virginians. The installation of some Monticello slaves as a domestic workforce in the Governor's Palace also must have fostered an atmosphere reminiscent of the Jeffersons' normal family life at Monticello. The family's domestic servants accompanied them to Richmond when the state capital moved there in 1780. Unlike Williamsburg, however, Richmond was a rustic village that offered few opportunities for sociability. Fifteen-year-old Betsey Ambler, daughter of another state official who moved his family, sullenly predicted that "this famous Metropolis . . . will scarcely afford one comfort in life."[39]

By spring 1780, the Jefferson family—which now included Patsy's widowed aunt, Martha Jefferson Carr, and her six children—had moved with their slaves to a rented house in Richmond. In June, Thomas reluctantly accepted a second one-year term as governor. His wife, in response to an appeal from Martha Washington, wrote letters urging other Virginia ladies to support the efforts of the Philadelphia-based Ladies Association to raise money to benefit poorly supplied Continental soldiers, perhaps imparting some civic values to her daughter in the process. "I under take with chearfulness the duty of furnishing to my country women an opportunity of proving that they also participate of those virtuous feelings" of patriotism, Martha wrote in August 1780, during the second trimester of yet another difficult pregnancy. In November, she gave birth to another daughter, Lucy Elizabeth. Meanwhile, her husband devoted himself to official paperwork and teaching his elder daughter and her Carr cousins, despite the discouraging war news from the southern states, where British forces had reclaimed Georgia and most of South Carolina by the end of 1780.[40]

For both his family and his state, Jefferson's second term as governor was significantly more turbulent than the first. Enemy forces converged on Virginia from both north and south, and, beginning with a British attack on

Richmond and the surrounding area in January 1781, war-related violence affected large numbers of Virginia civilians for the first time since 1776. Some families fled their homes in anticipation of enemy raids, while others braved the onslaught in hope of preserving their property. Widow Mary Willing Byrd, who lived with her eight children on her James River plantation, was poorly treated by soldiers on both sides. In February, Americans who suspected Byrd of aiding the British imprisoned her entire family in their home and, she later claimed, inflicted "*savage* treatment" on them. A few months later, the British commandeered Byrd's house as temporary quarters. When they left, forty-nine slaves and several of Byrd's horses departed with them.[41]

In January, rumors that the enemy planned to attack Richmond led Jefferson to send his wife and children to Tuckahoe, the nearby home of his childhood friend Thomas Mann Randolph, who was now himself the father of five daughters and three sons. The next day, the family moved to Fine Creek, a Goochland County property that Thomas had inherited from his father. Although the governor considered the situation to be sufficiently serious to ensure the safety of his family, he delayed calling out the militia until it was too late to mount an effective defense of the capital. With the Continental Army occupied elsewhere, Richmond was therefore undefended when the enemy arrived on 5 January. "In ten minutes, not a white man was to be seen in Richmond," recalled the slave Isaac Jefferson, son of Ursula, both of whom had remained behind at the governor's house. The British searched the house, plundered its wine cellar, and took the family's meat and grain, aggravating any food shortages the Jeffersons experienced during their stay in Richmond. The soldiers also burned public buildings and warehouses, destroyed records, and looted ships docked at the James River wharves as they made their way back toward the coast.[42]

When the British withdrew from Richmond, ten of the Jeffersons' slaves left with them: Jupiter (Jefferson's personal attendant since his college days), Sukey (the cook), Ursula (the family's housekeeper and Patsy's erstwhile wet nurse), George (Ursula's husband), Mary (a seamstress), and five children, including Isaac. Slaveowners liked to believe that their bondpeople were "carried off" forcibly by the British, but thousands left of their own accord in hopes of obtaining freedom. Though no member of the Jefferson family commented on the loss of these enslaved workers, with whom they were on familiar or even intimate terms, they must have keenly missed both their company and their labor. Like most white Virginians, the adult Jeffersons also must have harbored a profound fear of wartime slave insurrections, which had led to more rigorous policing of slave activities as early as 1775. Governor Jefferson himself pondered the possibility of race war. In 1781, all ten of his escaped slaves went to Yorktown, where, according to Isaac Jefferson, the British "treated them mighty well," though American forces recaptured them after the battle and returned them to slavery at Monticello.[43]

By spring 1781, Virginia was the war's main theater, as British forces commanded by the traitor Benedict Arnold and General William Phillips again moved toward Richmond, and General Charles Cornwallis marched northward from North Carolina to join them. Awaiting the arrival of Continental forces in Richmond, the Jeffersons mourned the death of the infant Lucy, the family's youngest member. Two weeks later, on 29 April, the Marquis de Lafayette, the idealistic young aristocrat who came from France to fight for liberty, arrived with a force of some 1,200 men to save Richmond and its military stores from falling into enemy hands. On 1 May, however, the state's legislators decided to flee westward and reconvene in Charlottesville.[44]

The ensuing months must have been exciting (and frightening) for Patsy and her family. In roughly five weeks, the family lived in at least six different places—Richmond, Tuckahoe, Monticello, Blenheim and Enniscorthy (both plantations in Albemarle), and Poplar Forest (roughly ninety miles southwest of Monticello in Bedford County)—sometimes with and sometimes without its esteemed patriarch. The family of Betsey Ambler, whose father chaired Virginia's Board of Trade, undertook a similar wartime odyssey from Richmond to Louisa County to Charlottesville and then back to Louisa. Betsey found the situation both horrifying and inspiring. "What an alarming crisis this is," she wrote to her friend Mildred Smith from Louisa in 1781. "War in itself, however distant is indeed terrible, but when it is brought to our very doors—when those we love are personally engaged in it, when our friends and neighbors are exposed to its ravages, when we know how assuredly that without sacrificing many dear to us as our own lives, our country must remain subject to British tyranny, the reflection is overwhelming."[45]

When the state legislature convened in Charlottesville on 28 May, the entire Jefferson family was at Monticello, as were the speakers of both legislative houses. Thomas's term as governor was due to expire on Saturday, 2 June, but the legislators postponed selecting his successor until Monday. By that time, a messenger had interrupted breakfast at Monticello to inform the Jeffersons and their guests that Lieutenant Colonel Banastre Tarleton was moving toward Albemarle in hopes of capturing Virginia's chief gov-

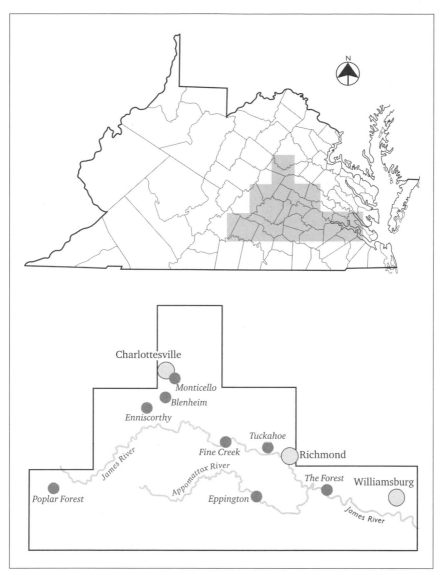

Patsy Jefferson's Virginia. This map shows the various plantations where Patsy and her family stayed during the war. When Thomas Jefferson was governor, his family lived with him in Williamsburg and then in Richmond, until the spring of 1781, when they fled westward to escape advancing enemy forces. In all, the Jeffersons covered approximately 100 miles, going as far west as Poplar Forest, in Bedford County. The state map shows Virginia counties in 1781.

ernment officials. The legislature resolved to reconvene in Staunton, thirty-three miles to the west, while Jefferson—whose official status was at that point ambiguous—prepared to leave Monticello. The family moved several times before settling at Poplar Forest, Jefferson's Bedford County property, where they remained for six weeks while he recovered from a fall from his horse that resulted in a broken arm. The fact that no one in the family wrote letters describing their flight or informing friends or relatives of their changing circumstances suggests that their priorities were, first, to ensure their personal safety and, then, to set up housekeeping in the two-room cottage at Poplar Forest plantation.[46]

The 1781 campaigns hurt Jefferson and his family, both personally and politically. Besides the losses he had already sustained at his Richmond residence, Jefferson later reported that, though Tarleton and his men "behaved very genteelly," doing no real damage at Monticello, Cornwallis's troops destroyed crops, barns, and livestock at Elk Hill, his wife's James River plantation, from which they "carried off also about 30 slaves," of whom three may have attained permanent freedom. Even more painful, however, was the damage Jefferson's reputation suffered as a result of his alleged failings as Virginia's war governor. After reconvening and choosing a successor on 7 June 1781, the legislature resolved that "an inquiry be made into the conduct of the Executive of this State for the last twelve months." Jefferson's political enemies spearheaded this effort to—in his words—"stab a reputation by general suggestion under a bare expectation that facts might be afterwards hunted up to bolster it." In particular, they hoped to censure him officially for his failure to summon the militia to defend Richmond. Although these efforts ultimately failed, the accusations, a disheartened Jefferson confided, "inflicted a wound on my spirit which will only be cured by the all-healing grave."[47]

The pain of public dishonor coupled with the fact that Martha was again pregnant and in poor health led Thomas Jefferson to retire from public life. Again he refused a diplomatic post in Europe, explaining to Lafayette, "The independence of private life under the protection of republican laws will I hope yeild me that happiness from whi[ch] no slave is so remote as the minister of a Commonwealth." After the American victory at Yorktown in October virtually ensured an ultimate American triumph, Jefferson clearly hoped to make Monticello once again a center of civil discourse and polite sociability. In December, he invited General Horatio Gates—the hero of the Battle of Saratoga—and his old law teacher, George Wythe, to visit him and his family. He also planned to rekindle his scientific interests, asking a friend to send him "some teeth of the great animal whose remains are found on the Ohio" because "the retirement into which I am withdrawing has increased my eagerness in pursuit of objects of this kind." But more than anything, retirement meant family time and the resumption of lessons for nine-year-old Patsy, three-year-old Polly, and their cousins at Monticello.[48]

By the spring of 1782, the construction of Patsy's girlhood home was more or less complete, though the house was not fully decorated and the kitchen and other so-called dependencies—work and storage facilities that were to flank the main house—had not yet been built. When Jefferson's friend the Marquis de Chastelleux visited in April, he found the family residing in a house "constructed in an Italian style . . . quite tasteful, although not however without some faults." The house consisted of, he wrote, "a large square pavilion, into which one enters through two porticoes ornamented with columns." Visitors proceeded into a spacious, high-ceilinged drawing room, or salon, which was the house's main public room. Small wings on either side of the salon contained a dining room and a parlor. On the second floor were the family's sleeping quarters and, in the larger center room, Jefferson's library. Though still unfinished and a mere fraction of its eventual size, Patsy's house was nonetheless the biggest and the most unusual in the county.[49]

The birth of a baby girl in May 1782 may have signaled a return to the normal rhythms of domestic life as the war drew to a close, but that brief period of contentment ended abruptly with the death of Martha Jefferson in September due to complications arising from the birth of Lucy Elizabeth (who was named for her deceased sister, a common practice at this time). Patsy and her sister Polly apparently were not at her mother's bedside at the very end, but members of the Hemings family, who were there, recalled that concerns about her daughters' future preoccupied the dying woman. Perhaps because she had been raised by two successive stepmothers before her father settled into a long-term relationship with Betty Hemings—who was now among those attending her on her deathbed—Martha Jefferson declared that she "could not die happy if she thought her . . . children were ever to have a stepmother brought in over them." Acceding to this dying request, a tearful Jefferson promised that he would never take a second wife, despite the fact that Virginia widowers, especially those with young children who needed tending, typically remarried.[50]

Of all the events and episodes that transpired during the revolutionary years, the death of her mother and especially her father's reaction to it inspired Patsy, as an adult, to write the most evocatively. "As a nurse no female ever had more tenderness or anxiety," she recalled years later, than what her father gave his ailing wife. He "nursed my poor Mother in turn with Aunt Carr and her own sister [Elizabeth Wayles Eppes] setting up with her and adminstring her medicines and drink to the last," she explained. "For the four months that she lingered . . . when not at her bedside he was writing in a small room which opened immediately at the head of her bed" so that he could come quickly if she called. Other sources corroborate Jefferson's deep devotion to his wife and his profound grief on her demise. One friend worried that Jefferson was "inconsolable" after Martha's death and that he was reportedly "swooning away whenever he sees his children" because the girls reminded him of his lost "domestic happiness."[51]

The death of Martha Jefferson marked a turning point in the life of ten-year-old Patsy, who purposefully became her father's sole companion, while her aunts cared for Polly and the infant Lucy Elizabeth and attended to domestic matters at Monticello. Although Jefferson tried to distance his daughters from both their mother's suffering and his own intense grief after the "closing scene"—when he "fainted and remained so long insensible that they feared he never would revive"—Patsy later recalled that she "almost by stealth . . . entered his room," where she found him emotionally prostrate. The distraught widower remained in his room for three weeks, during which his ten-year-old daughter was always by his side, though he "walked almost incessantly night and day only lying down occasionally." By early October, the grieving widower had left his room, but he was constantly on horseback. Patsy was "in those melancholy rambles . . . his constant companion, a solitary witness to many a violent burst of grief," which she remembered vividly decades later. Riding "5 or 6 miles a day," Patsy and her father forged bonds of mutual devotion that would last their entire lives.[52]

In his grief, Jefferson acted to protect what was left of his family by having his daughters inoculated against smallpox. He himself had traveled to Philadelphia to receive this treatment sixteen years earlier, in 1766, when inoculation was still controversial and not readily available in Virginia. But the dreaded disease had spread throughout the United States with the movement of troops during the War of Independence, reaching epidemic proportions at Yorktown, where thousands of escaped slaves succumbed to the highly infectious variola virus. Though soldiers were inoculated, Jefferson knew the dangers smallpox posed for the largely unprotected civilian population. The fact that some Monticello slaves had escaped to the British only to be recaptured and returned to their master by the victorious Americans probably heightened Jefferson's concerns for his daughters' safety and explains the timing of his decision to have them undergo inoculation in November 1782. He then nursed the girls through the aftermath of their treatment—which often included fever, nausea, vomiting, and some pustules—at Ampthill, his friend Colonel Archibald Cary's Chesterfield County plantation.[53]

By mid-November, while the girls were still recovering, Jefferson had formally accepted a diplomatic appointment as one of three ministers representing the United States at the peace negotiations in Paris. As he informed a friend, "the catastrophe" of his wife's death had "wiped away all my plans" to retire to Monticello and devote himself to "domestic & literary objects." Now he planned to leave Virginia as quickly as possible. "I shall lose no time . . . preparing for my departure," he assured his friend James Madison in late November 1782. Jefferson hoped to be in Philadelphia, which he expected to be his first stop en route to Paris, by 20 December. Immediately before his departure, he penned a notice to be published in the *Virginia Gazette*, announcing his intention to be "absent from the State for some time" and directing "all persons having business with him" to contact either Nicholas Lewis of Albemarle or Francis Eppes of Chesterfield, to whom "he had confided the care of his affairs."[54]

Jefferson entrusted Francis and Elizabeth Eppes with the care of his younger daughters, though there was never any doubt that Patsy would accompany her father to Europe. The bond between them was strong, and Jefferson believed that his oldest daughter was ready to embark on the next phase of her education, which he wished to oversee and which he hoped would be superior to anything she would get with her cousins in rural Virginia. In January 1783, he consulted John Jay, an American diplomat in Paris, about lodgings in the French capital. He inquired specifically about accommodations near the Hôtel de Vendôme, where Mrs. Izard of South Carolina was staying with her daughters, "with whom a little motherless daughter accompanying me might sometimes be able to associate." A few months later, when it became apparent that his departure would be delayed, he asked Madison about suitable lodgings for Patsy in Philadelphia.[55]

❖ Patsy Jefferson's childhood, which effectively ended in the months following her mother's death, taught her three great lessons that would profoundly shape her life. She learned that her parents—and her father especially—valued learning and good manners, both for the private pleasure they brought and for their usefulness in fostering polite sociability. She learned that the domestic sphere, and especially her family circle at Monticello, could be both a nurturing environment for parents and children and the public face that the family presented to outsiders, such as the European guests who marveled at the civility and refinement they found at Jefferson's American home. Finally, Patsy also learned that her father, whatever his importance in the wider world, was emotionally vulnerable, both to personal losses and to assaults on his public reputation and honor.

Leaving behind her sisters, aunts, and other relatives in Virginia, Patsy went off with her father to begin what would be the most unusual phase of her life. At a time when families were large and children grew up surrounded by siblings and legions of nearby cousins, Patsy left familiar people and places to accompany Jefferson when his public business took him away from the Old Dominion. She would experience life in the wider world, first in Philadelphia and then in Paris, though most of her contemporaries, even among the gentry, never ventured beyond Virginia. Years later, Patsy fondly recalled the time she spent in Philadelphia and Paris. But aside from her self-evident trust in and devotion to her father, she left no clues about how she felt, as a girl, embarking on this great adventure.

chapter 2

The Education of Patsy Jefferson

Unlike their brothers, daughters of Virginia gentlemen rarely left home to be educated and almost never had adventures. In a society that considered white females the "weaker sex," respectable girls and young women could not travel, either near or far, without the supervision and protection of a trusted escort. When they reached their midteens, they entered society, began attracting suitors, and perhaps went with their families to attend balls in the capital. But even then, young women found their social networks and experiences continually monitored and circumscribed, as they circulated mainly among the offspring of familiar gentry families.

By contrast, Patsy Jefferson left Virginia as a ten-year-old girl and came home as a young woman seven years later. During those years, she lived in Philadelphia and Paris, mostly among strangers, and she visited other places in Europe and America. Just as Patsy's parents had shielded her from the most disruptive effects of the American war, her father would try to insulate her from the foreign social customs and political excesses that characterized Paris on the threshold of revolution. In Philadelphia and Paris, Patsy Jefferson completed her education, acquiring accomplishments and knowledge—both academic and social—that would distinguish her from her peers at home, even as she came to think of herself as a Virginian and an American.

❖ "Set out from Monticello for Philadelphia, France, &c.," Thomas Jefferson wrote blandly in his memorandum book for 19 December 1782. He and Patsy bade farewell to four-year-old Polly and little Lucy Elizabeth, who remained with their aunt, uncle, and cousins at Eppington, the plantation on the banks of the Appomattox River where the Eppes family now lived. Accompanied by Robert Hemings, Jefferson's valet and the eldest son of Elizabeth Hemings and John Wayles, father and daughter journeyed northward in a four-wheeled carriage he borrowed from a kinsman, Richard Randolph of Curles. The roads were rocky and often hilly and sometimes difficult to follow. On the third day of the trip, Jefferson employed a guide to help him find his way through part of northern Virginia. The road between Baltimore and Philadelphia was wider and more heavily traveled, but it was full of ruts and holes. Carriages easily overturned, so passengers sometimes got out and walked instead. Waterways posed other obstacles for eighteenth-century travelers. En route to Philadelphia, Jefferson's party relied on local ferrymen to carry them, their horses, carriage, and baggage across the Potomac, Patapsco, Susquehanna, and Schuylkill rivers.[1]

In all, the trip took eight days, which was roughly average for the times. On 27 December, the trio arrived in Philadelphia, where they lodged at the city's largest public house, the Indian Queen, a three-story brick building on Fourth Street, near the Pennsylvania State House (later known as Independence Hall). While Patsy and her father occupied one of the sixteen rooms that the tavern's proprietors rented to overnight lodgers, Robert Hemings spent the night in a fourth-floor garret with other servants and slaves. The next day, the travelers moved to more congenial accommodations at a private boardinghouse, owned by Mary House, on the corner of Fifth and Market streets, where Jefferson's friend and fellow Virginian James Madison stayed while he served in Congress. Jefferson probably expected to remain with Mary House and her daughter, Elizabeth House Trist, only a short time before sailing for France. He soon learned, however, that his departure would be delayed, leaving him and Patsy with a month to spend in the city that some contemporaries called the "Athens of America."[2]

With some 40,000 inhabitants from a diverse array of ethnic backgrounds, Philadelphia was the largest city in the United States and unlike any place Patsy Jefferson had ever visited. Laid out on a rectangular grid a century earlier by William Penn, its Quaker founder, Philadelphia boasted spacious streets lined with impressive private dwellings and public buildings. Although the British had destroyed and burned some houses when they occupied the city in 1777–78, both trade and social life had rebounded by the early 1780s. When the Marquis de Chastellux visited Philadelphia in 1780—even before the war was over—there were frequent balls and formal dinners, and some 300 ships jammed the city's "magnificent" harbor. A year later, Martha Bland of Virginia, who enjoyed a ball, a concert, and a theatrical performance there within a single week, wrote home extolling the "Gay Scenes of Philadelphia" as the country's preeminent social venue. The presence of the American Philosophical Society, whose members included Patsy's own father, also attested to the city's status as the leading center of science and learning in eighteenth-century America.[3]

While none of the letters Patsy wrote during her initial stint in Philadelphia survive, and her father's letters shed little light on what they did
during their stay there, Jefferson's memorandum books indicate that they
took advantage of the unique shopping opportunities that such a large and
prosperous city offered. Patsy's aunt, Lucy Jefferson Lewis, had given her
brother money to purchase some fashionable items that were easier to obtain in Philadelphia than in Albemarle, and Jefferson bought chessmen
and a chessboard, boots, shoes, shoe buckles, gloves, and books for himself. He also visited William McIlhenny, a tailor on Arch Street, where he
spent nearly £15 on clothing. Although Jefferson did not employ a milliner
or dressmaker to outfit his daughter, on eight occasions he bought unspecified "sundries for Patsy."[4]

During her first weeks in Philadelphia, Patsy became acquainted with
Elizabeth House Trist, an intelligent, strong, and sociable woman who be-
came a maternal figure and lifelong friend to the youngster from Virginia.
Elizabeth House was born in Philadelphia in 1751. She married Nicholas
Trist, a British army officer, in 1774 and gave birth to their only child, Hore
Browse Trist, the following year. In 1775, with revolution approaching,
Nicholas resigned his commission and bought land in British West Florida,
where he planned to resettle his family. When Patsy and her father arrived
in Philadelphia in late 1782, Elizabeth Trist was living with her mother, but
she planned to leave soon to join her husband in the western territory.[5]

Jefferson's interest in the West, as well as the fact that he and Elizabeth
Trist shared a common friend in James Madison, provided the basis for
mutual respect and lasting friendship. As it became clear that his departure
for Europe would be delayed even longer than expected, Jefferson relied on
Trist's assistance to arrange lodging and lessons for Patsy. He advised his
daughter that "as long as Mrs. Trist remains in Philadelphia cultivate her
affections," adding, "She has been a valuable friend to you and her good
sense and good heart make her valued by all who know her and by nobody
on earth more than me." When she finally left Philadelphia in late 1783,
Trist, who kept a detailed diary of her voyage to Natchez, furnished Jefferson with firsthand information about the geography, plant life, mineralogy,
and other features of the West. She and Jefferson continued their correspondence after he left for Paris. In her letters, Trist always asked to be remembered affectionately to Patsy, who, in turn, addressed a long and lively
account of her transatlantic journey to this "dear friend" in America.[6]

Throughout 1783, however, the Jeffersons' travel plans were in a state of
flux. In late January, Patsy and her father left Philadelphia for Baltimore,

where they expected to board a French ship that would carry them to Paris. But because the war between the United States and Great Britain had not formally ended, British naval vessels still loomed along the American coast, making sailing potentially dangerous. Patsy and her father waited nearly a month in Baltimore without boarding the ship, and by 26 February they had given up and gone back to Philadelphia. A few days later Jefferson wrote to Francis Eppes that Patsy was well and that he expected Congress to cancel his appointment, thereby freeing them both to rejoin their family in Virginia. While they waited to hear from Congress, Patsy got new shoes and visited the milliner's shop. Perhaps her father also began to teach her how to manage money. When they first arrived in Philadelphia, Jefferson had made all their purchases himself, but on several occasions he now "gave Patsy" sums to "purchase sundries."[7]

In early April, Congress notified Jefferson that his services were not needed in Paris, at least for the time being, so he settled his account with Mary House and returned to Virginia. Traveling southward by way of Baltimore to Richmond, father and daughter stopped at Tuckahoe, the home of Jefferson's friend and kinsman Thomas Mann Randolph, where for the first time in months Patsy enjoyed the company of familiar people her own age. By 1783, the Randolphs had nine children, including eleven-year-old Judith, with whom Patsy became friendly. From Tuckahoe, father and daughter proceeded west to Monticello and then eventually on to Eppington, where Patsy reunited with her younger sisters. By August, however, Jefferson learned that the state legislature had chosen him as one of Virginia's delegates to Congress. Accepting the appointment, he returned to Philadelphia with Patsy—this time accompanied by James Hemings, Robert's younger brother—though the recent mutiny of some Pennsylvania soldiers demanding back wages meant that a wary Congress would probably reconvene elsewhere.[8]

Although the meeting place of the next Congress was still undecided, Jefferson wanted to establish Patsy in a stable and secure environment where she could begin her formal education. Because Congress would likely convene nearby and because Jefferson had many trusted friends in the city, Philadelphia was the logical place for his daughter to stay. Although the city had many schools for girls by the 1780s, Jefferson preferred to find Patsy living quarters in a private home where she could experience some semblance of parental supervision and family life—in other words, where she would be in an environment as similar as possible to that which she experienced before her mother's death at Monticello. Aware that Elizabeth

Trist's departure was imminent, Jefferson asked James Madison to solicit "the favor of Mrs. Trist to think for me on that subject, and to advise me as to the person with whom [Patsy] may be trusted." On 19 November 1783, about three weeks after the Jeffersons arrived in Philadelphia, Patsy left Mary House's boardinghouse and, as Jefferson reported in his memorandum book, "removed to Mrs. Hopkinson's." He left to attend Congress in Annapolis three days later.[9]

Mary Johnson Hopkinson was an educated, patriotic, and pious widow with strong ties to the local intelligentsia whose erudite company Jefferson so highly valued. Her husband, Thomas Hopkinson, a merchant and civic leader, had been the first president of the American Philosophical Society and Benjamin Franklin's collaborator in his famous electrical experiments. After Thomas Hopkinson died in 1751, Mary raised their seven children, including several daughters, whom (in Franklin's words) she managed to "carefully educate, genteelly, but frugally, out of the income of a small estate." Hopkinson's oldest son, Francis, had been Jefferson's colleague in Congress in 1776 when he signed the Declaration of Independence, as well as a fellow member of the American Philosophical Society. Though trained as a lawyer, Francis Hopkinson also wrote poetry, essays, and music and was an acknowledged authority on harpsichords. His mother, who was known for her piety and intellect, was a patriot whose house was burned by British soldiers in 1778.[10]

For nearly six months, Patsy did not see her father, who relied on the Hopkinsons and other friends in Philadelphia to care for his daughter and oversee her studies. Before he left for Annapolis, Jefferson hired Gaspard Cenas, a dancing master from Paris, to teach his daughter to dance, supplementing the lessons she had briefly in Williamsburg. Possibly on Francis Hopkinson's recommendation, he also employed the English organist and harpsichordist John Bentley, one of the best musicians in Philadelphia, as her music tutor. Hopkinson himself secured the services of Pierre Eugène du Simitière, the Swiss-born artist, engraver, and proprietor of the recently opened American Museum, to teach Patsy drawing. Jefferson relied on his friend the French diplomat François du Marbois to find a French tutor and to recommend some books for his daughter to read in his absence. Patsy's tutors—two Frenchmen, one Englishman, and one Swiss—were emblematic of Philadelphia's ethnic diversity and its status as a cosmopolitan cultural center. The fact that two of her teachers, Bentley and Simitière, were accomplished artists who took on pupils to make ends meet attests to the difficulty of making a living by art alone in postrevolutionary America.[11]

While Jefferson relied on his male friends to engage tutors and recommend books, he looked to Elizabeth Trist and, after Trist's departure, to Mary Hopkinson to monitor his daughter's daily life and conduct. When Trist informed Jefferson that Patsy was somewhat careless about her clothing, he wrote a letter cautioning his daughter to "let your clothes be clean, whole, and properly put on" because a woman's dress reflected her moral character and, indeed, her sexual probity (or lack of it); "nothing is so disgusting to our sex," Jefferson warned, "as a want of cleanliness and delicacy in yours." When Trist informed her friend in Annapolis that the pious Mary Hopkinson believed that "the Earthquake we had the other night is only a prelude to something dreadfull that will happen," he encouraged Patsy to "have good sense enough to disregard those foolish predictions that the world is to be at an end soon." Jefferson used the occasion to teach Patsy a lesson in morality inspired as much by the Enlightenment as by orthodox Christianity. "Our maker has given us all, this faithful internal Monitor, and if you always obey it," he advised, "you will always be prepared for the end of the world: or for a much more certain event which is death."[12]

Despite his tacit disagreement with Mary Hopkinson about the causes and meanings of earthquakes, Jefferson instructed his daughter to be "obedient and respectful to her in every circumstance" and to "consider her . . . as your mother." Thus Jefferson sent Patsy a detailed daily schedule for her studies, which he told her to share with Hopkinson and "if she approves it pursue it." When Patsy asked for permission to have her drawing lessons at the home of David Rittenhouse, whose daughter also studied with Simitière, Jefferson deferred to Hopkinson's judgment. Patsy may have shared her father's high opinion of her caretaker, but she and Hopkinson do not appear to have developed a close personal relationship. After she left Philadelphia, Patsy stayed in contact with Elizabeth Trist, and she once dutifully closed a letter to Trist by sending her regards both to Mary Hopkinson and Mrs. Rittenhouse. But Patsy and Hopkinson never exchanged either letters or visits, though the older woman lived until 1804.[13]

The first letter Patsy received from her father after he left for Annapolis established the tone of their relationship and delineated his expectations for her during his absence. Revealing both the authority of a patriarch and the anxiety of a distant parent who had suffered grievous personal losses, Jefferson attempted to protect his daughter and train her for her future life as a Virginia matron by rigorously circumscribing her activities. Cautioning her to avoid offending Mary Hopkinson by "any unguarded act," Jefferson prescribed for Patsy the following daily schedule:

from 8. to 10 o'clock practice music.

from 10. to 1. dance one day and draw another.

from 1. to 2. draw on the day you dance, and write a letter the next day.

from 3. to 4. read French.

from 4. to 5. exercise yourself in music.

from 5. till bedtime read English, write &c.

In impressing upon his eleven-year-old daughter the seriousness of her studies, Jefferson emphasized not the pleasure such "acquirements" could afford Patsy herself but, rather, the pride and affection that he as her father would feel as a result of her achievements. Excellence in music, drawing, and the rest would, he declared, "render you more worthy of my love." Finally, in this initial letter, as in most of his others, Jefferson instructed Patsy to write him weekly to inform him of her progress. He also asked that she correspond with her aunts in Virginia and "take care that you never spell a word wrong" because "it produces great praise to a lady to spell well."[14]

Even by contemporary standards, there were notable omissions in the schedule Jefferson prescribed. Presumably, meals would be before 8:00, at 2:00, and after 5:00, but Jefferson left no time in Patsy's schedule for visiting or social life of any sort (though she attended at least one party on New Year's Eve, at which she "danced out the old Year" with the Hopkinsons and Rittenhouses, according to Francis Hopkinson). Jefferson did not counsel his daughter to allot a portion of her day to prayer and devotional reading, though Scriptures and pious books were long-standing staples for female readers especially. Nor did he advise her to practice needlework or other domestic skills that he nonetheless believed would be essential in her future life. Perhaps he expected Mary Hopkinson to attend to these parts of his daughter's education.[15]

Jefferson compiled a "plan of reading" for Patsy in his absence, and he repeatedly asked her to let him know what books she read. Although Patsy rarely supplied her father with the detailed information he requested, Jefferson insisted that reading "the best poets and prosewriters" would prepare his daughter for life as an American wife and mother. "The plan of reading I have prepared for her is considerably different from what I think would be most proper for her sex in any other country than America," he explained to the Frenchman Marbois. The dearth of quality education in the United States meant that "the chance that in marriage she will draw a blockhead I calculate at about fourteen to one," leaving the education of her children to "rest on her own ideas and direction without assistance." To that end, Jefferson also intended to have Patsy read scientific works, though he believed that portion of her education could wait "till she returns to me."[16]

Jefferson was one of several luminaries who seriously pondered the distinctive educational needs of the new American nation and advocated the expansion of schooling to foster republican citizenship. American men generally did not share the protofeminist views of Judith Sargent Murray, who saw equal education as a potential route to female independence, but some nonetheless publicly championed substantive improvements in women's education. Benjamin Rush, a prominent Philadelphia physician who was Jefferson's friend and a fellow signer of the Declaration of Independence, prescribed an ambitious curriculum that included reading, writing, rhetoric, geography, mathematics, the classics, and moral philosophy to enable women to assume a "principal share of the instruction of children" and, when necessary, to act as "stewards and guardians of their husbands' property." Noah Webster, author of both the popular *American Spelling Book* and the famous dictionary, also supported formal schooling for females because, in his view, the republic needed wives and mothers who were "possessed, not only of amiable manners, but of just sentiments and enlarged understandings." Both Rush and Webster downplayed the significance of ornamental accomplishments for American females, whose main task, they believed, was to instill civic values in the rising generation. Though Jefferson shared their belief that education prepared girls to be better mothers and wives, he never discerned a political significance in women's domestic role, and consequently, unlike them, he never saw the education of females as a public responsibility or objective.[17]

Jefferson clearly was interested in Patsy's intellectual development, but he candidly admitted that during these months in Philadelphia she would be "chiefly occupied in acquiring a little taste and execution in such of the fine arts as she could not prosecute to equal advantage in a more retired situation," such as rural Albemarle. In terms of its short-term value, dancing, which contemporaries regarded as both a form of exercise for young people and an integral part of sociability and genteel courtship, was the most important of these arts, though Jefferson valued music almost equally as "delightful recreation for the hours of respite from the cares of the day [which] lasts us through life." Jefferson also hoped that Patsy would excel in drawing, which he considered a "pretty and pleasing accomplishment." He repeatedly asked her to send him her recent drawings and—despite Patsy's lack of both enthusiasm and aptitude—was deeply disappointed when the temperamental Simitière ceased her lessons because, according to Francis Hopkinson, he resented "the Drudgery of teaching those who have no Capacity." Otherwise, Hopkinson reported in January, two months after Jefferson's departure, that Patsy "comes on finely in her Education."[18]

Jefferson also closely monitored his daughter's progress in French, which many of his contemporaries considered a desirable, if largely ornamental, accomplishment. Jefferson shared the belief of many of his well-heeled contemporaries that learning French was an appropriate accomplishment for children of both sexes. Because Patsy still expected to go to Paris, however, her acquiring some proficiency in French would have added practical benefits. Jefferson urged his daughter to study the language every day, and he expressed "great satisfaction" when she wrote him a letter in French just two months after commencing her lessons with the tutor in Philadelphia.[19]

How did Patsy react to her father's detailed instructions and schedules, his combined criticism and encouragement, and his unceasing demands for letters? Jefferson, who told his daughter that his business in Congress precluded his writing often, sent her a total of eight letters of varying lengths during a separation that lasted nearly six months, but he expected his daughter to write to him weekly. He depended on letters to monitor Patsy's behavior and to solidify their relationship with each other, despite their separation, while recognizing letter-writing itself as an increasingly valued feminine accomplishment. Nevertheless, Jefferson's records indicate that Patsy sent him only eight letters during these months, none of which apparently have survived. Small wonder that he complained that she was "inattentive." That Patsy wrote to her father only exactly as often as he wrote to her may have been the coincidental result of childish laziness, but more likely it signaled her resentment at having been left alone among strangers. Ignoring her father's requests that she resume her drawing lessons and send him copies of her artwork also may have been ways for Patsy to express her discontent in a manner that stopped short of blatant disrespect or outright rebellion.[20]

That Jefferson apparently preserved none of the letters he received from Patsy during this period is striking, given his generally careful record-keeping and the survival of much of his other personal correspondence, including a letter from young Polly (in her aunt's writing) asking him to visit Eppington. Jefferson may have mislaid or destroyed Patsy's letters because their contents did not reflect his idealized view of family life. He loved his daughters and sought to do what in his view was best for them. He left the younger girls at Eppington because he believed they needed maternal care, and he brought Patsy to Philadelphia because—as he put it in the first letter he wrote to her after his departure—she "would be more improved" there. Roughly two weeks after Jefferson went to Annapolis, Elizabeth Trist optimistically reported that Patsy "seems happy much more so than I expected," but the congenial Trist soon left Philadelphia (and Patsy) for the West. In early January, Francis Hopkinson informed Jefferson that his daughter was well and progressing in her studies—except for drawing—and that she had enjoyed New Year's Eve with the Rittenhouses. Otherwise, there is no evidence of how Patsy spent her time in Philadelphia, no indication of whether she was happy. Perhaps in her letters she complained of loneliness or sadness, which would have hurt her father deeply.[21]

By mid-May, however, Jefferson was back in Philadelphia, having received his long-awaited appointment as Congress's minister to France. While in Philadelphia, he bought two tickets to see an exhibition of hot air balloons—perhaps taking Patsy with him—and prepared for their departure. By 26 May, nineteen-year-old James Hemings had come from Virginia to accompany them to Paris. Two days later, the trio ferried across the Delaware River to New Jersey, thus beginning the journey that ultimately took them to the French capital. On the last day of May, the travelers arrived in New York City, where they spent six days before proceeding north through Westchester County and then east through Connecticut to Rhode Island. After leaving Providence on 17 June, Jefferson's party arrived in Boston one day later. In all, it took twenty-one days to travel some 270 miles from Philadelphia to Boston. The trip included passage on eleven ferries and multiple stops en route to repair their carriage, shoe the horses, and mend their harnesses.[22]

Then, after spending a hectic month with her father, Patsy again found herself unexpectedly adrift in an unfamiliar city. From Boston, Jefferson had planned to travel to Europe with Abigail Adams, who was joining her husband, John, in the Netherlands, where he was the American minister. When he and Patsy arrived in Boston, however, they discovered that Adams had already left and that there would be no other suitable ships departing for Europe until early July. So, after spending three days with his daughter in Boston, Jefferson—who, among other things, was to represent American trading interests abroad—left to tour the ports of Massachusetts and New Hampshire to better his understanding of New England's commerce.[23]

Again among strangers, Patsy lodged with the family of John Lowell, a Boston judge. There is no evidence that Jefferson knew Lowell before they arrived in Boston, though Lowell was acquainted with Jefferson's friends James Madison and John Adams. When Adams left home to represent Massachusetts in Congress, he recommended Lowell as one of the "2 or 3 gentlemen" to whom his wife might "apply for advice and assistance" during his absence. These personal connections, along with the fact that Lowell had a big house and lots of children who could be companions for Patsy, probably led Jefferson to believe that leaving her in Boston was preferable to taking her with him to tour New England's ports. Patsy left no account of her time with the Lowells, but she may have encountered antislavery sentiments for the first time in their household. In 1780, John Lowell had been a member of the constitutional convention that effectively ended slavery in Massachusetts. After the convention, he offered his legal services to anyone held in bondage who went to court to sue for freedom.[24]

In Boston, as in Philadelphia, Patsy often found herself among people she barely knew, with neither family nor friends to mitigate the impact of alien ideas or customs or to help her to navigate unfamiliar social networks. Although Jefferson made sure that his daughter associated with only respectable people in both locales, her socialization was in many ways the antithesis of what it would have been had she remained in Virginia. There is no way to know whether these social challenges enthralled or unnerved Patsy, but her experiences in Philadelphia and Boston prepared her for Europe. In the long run, they also helped her to become an adult who, as many observers noted, was at ease and gracious with all sorts of people in virtually any social situation.[25]

By 26 June, Jefferson was back in Boston, and he and Patsy anticipated their departure, which was scheduled for 3 July. They were to sail to England on the ship *Ceres*, which was owned by Nathaniel Tracy of Newburyport, Massachusetts. In fact, their departure was again delayed, but this time only for little more than a day. "Sailed from Boston at 4 o'clock A.M. in the Ceres," Jefferson reported in his memorandum book. "We had a lovely passage in a beautiful new ship that had only made one voyage before," Patsy later informed Elizabeth Trist. "There were only six passengers, all of whom papa knew, and a fine sun shine all the way, with the sea which was as calm as a river," she added. Unlike Abigail Adams, who experienced constant seasickness and was revolted by the "horrid dirtiness of the Ship," Patsy enjoyed her nineteen-day trip across the ocean. "I should have no objection at making another voyage," she wrote gaily, "if I could be sure it would be as agreeable as the first."[26]

❖ While elite Americans often had journeyed to Europe, especially Britain, during the colonial period, the Revolution disrupted transatlantic travel and transformed the meaning of Americans' travel experiences. Before 1776, well-heeled colonists self-consciously strove to acquire the polish of Europe's cosmopolitan culture to enhance their stature both at home and abroad. But during and after the Revolution, Americans sought to distinguish themselves and their country from Europe, even as they indulged in Old World pleasures. Benjamin Franklin, who as a diplomat immersed himself in the social whirl of Paris, famously sported the fur hat of a frontiersman, which marked him as an exotic American visitor. Jefferson, who was both less flamboyant and more ambivalent toward French society and toward city life in general, was also self-consciously American. As a father, he shielded Patsy from what he saw as corrupting French customs and manners, encouraging her to cultivate instead her own distinctly American identity and values.[27]

Patsy's first European experiences were at best mixed. After she, her father, and James Hemings landed in England, at West Cowes on the Isle of Wight, they spent four days at nearby Portsmouth, where Patsy saw a physician who treated her for a fever. From there they crossed the English Channel to France, but that short trip took thirteen hours because of bad weather. Patsy was seasick and confined to a small, windowless cabin the entire time. Moreover, her first impressions of the French were not good. Patsy believed that people aboard the ship and on land alike cheated them because "papa spoke very little french and me not a word," and she was alarmed by the beggars who accosted their carriage as they traveled the 125 miles from the coastal town of Le Havre to Paris. But the young Virginian also appreciated the beauty of the French countryside and the grandeur of the cathedral at Rouen and the gothic church at Mantes, both of which were bigger, more ancient, and more ornate than anything she had seen in America. The church of Notre Dame in Mantes, she explained breathlessly to Elizabeth Trist, "had as many steps to go to the top as there are days in the year. There are many pretty statues in it. The architectures is beautiful. All the winders are died glass of the most beautiful colours that form all kinds of figures."[28]

Arriving in Paris on 6 August 1784, father and daughter passed the next few weeks getting accustomed to their new surroundings and acquiring the things they needed to commence housekeeping and socializing in Europe's largest and most fashionable metropolis, which, with some 600,000 denizens, was roughly fifteen times the size of Philadelphia. They spent their

first few days at an inn near the Palais Royale, the newly renovated pleasure gardens and shopping arcade, which one recent English visitor had
described glowingly as "a Scene of Gaiety and Business, and Chearfullness!"
Soon they moved to larger quarters in the Hôtel d'Orléans on the Left Bank.
Jefferson hired two house servants and purchased wine, household goods,
a map of the city, and clothes for his daughter and himself. "I wish you could
have been here when we arrived," Patsy wrote to Elizabeth Trist. "I am sure
you would have laughfed, for we were obliged to send imediately for the
stay maker, the mantuamaker, the milliner and even a shoe maker, before I
could go out." She resisted, however, the *friseur*'s attempts to dress her hair
in the tall, elaborate style that Parisian women favored. On 15 August, father
and daughter dined with Abigail and John Adams, whose nineteen-year-old
daughter, Nabby, pronounced Patsy a "sweet girl" with "amiable and lovely
manners."[29]

The next item on Jefferson's agenda was to make suitable arrangements
for his daughter to continue her education in the French capital. Patsy
could study with private tutors, as she had done in Philadelphia, or she
might attend one of the city's many day schools. In either case, she would
have needed a female companion or governess to watch over her when her
lessons were over. Jefferson knew no one in Paris who could recommend
such a person, and he could not entrust his daughter's well-being to anyone
who lacked reassuringly stellar personal references. Abigail Adams, who
sharply criticized the manners and morals of French women, may have
made Jefferson even more cautious about exposing Patsy to their influence.
Boarding schools were another option: Paris had more than forty convent
schools, as well as some newer secular establishments, that took in boarders. On 24 August, the Marquis de Chastellux recommended to Jefferson the
prestigious convent school at the Abbaye Royale de Panthemont, where the
Comtesse de Brionne agreed to sponsor Patsy's admission. Two days later,
Jefferson paid the first installment of his daughter's tuition at the Panthemont.[30]

Patsy would spend much of the next four and a half years at this convent
school acquiring what in many respects was the antithesis of an American
education. For one thing, the fifty or sixty students at the Panthemont were
mainly daughters of French and English aristocrats; at least two French
princesses attended the school, and the future empress Josephine de Beau-
harnais lodged there during the 1780s. With the exception of Kitty Church,
whose father was English but whose mother was a New Yorker, Patsy was
the only American student. In keeping with the Panthemont's aristocratic

Jeune Dame se faisant coëffer à neuf; elle est en peignoir et sa juppe de gaze d'un jaune très tendre, Le Coëffeur en veste rouge un peu poudrée, culotte noire et bas de soie gris.

Dessiné par LeClerc

Gravé par Dupin

French Fashion. This plate from the Galerie des Modes, *an elegant precursor to the modern fashion magazine, shows a woman having her hair dressed in the large, upswept style many Parisian women favored in the early 1780s. When she arrived in Paris in 1784, twelve-year-old Patsy Jefferson acquired a wardrobe of fashionable clothes, but she apparently resisted the* friseur. *Author's collection.*

orientation, its curriculum emphasized manners and ornamental accomplishments, such as music and drawing, but students also learned arithmetic, geography, history, Latin, and modern languages. Although the few Protestant students were exempt from catechism and the sacraments, they often attended the convent's Catholic religious services.[31]

Wariness of foreign education for Americans, regardless of gender, paradoxically led Jefferson to place his daughter in this most un-American environment. In 1785, Jefferson cautioned a fellow Virginian against sending his son abroad to be educated, lest he acquire "a fondness for European luxury and dissipation and a contempt for the simplicity of his own country." Jefferson, who believed that foreign travel was especially dangerous for young Americans, also advised Patsy's cousin Peter Carr to complete his education in Williamsburg, though the seventeen-year-old Carr professed "an invincible inclination to see the world . . . [and] get the polish of Europe."[32]

Given his belief that exposure to European society would ruin even hardy young Virginia males, Jefferson chose the Panthemont as his best option for protecting his young daughter from what he saw as the potentially dangerous excesses of Parisian life. In Philadelphia, Jefferson had relied on Elizabeth Trist and Mary Hopkinson to be surrogate mothers to Patsy. Now he deemed the nuns of the Panthemont the most viable source of quasi-maternal care he could hope to find for his daughter in the French capital.

Still, Jefferson must have been aware of the growing criticism in France of convent education. Enlightenment rationalism led some French intellectuals to condemn convent schools and their curricula on pedagogical grounds. Others, who, like Jefferson, believed that young females should be trained for domesticity, assailed convent schools as impediments to the attainment of girls' true callings as wives and mothers both because the nuns taught their pupils no domestic skills and because some of their charges decided to become nuns themselves. Some critics argued that life secluded within the convent's walls left young women ill-equipped to meet life's moral challenges, while others conversely portrayed the convent as a place where vice flourished, hidden from public view. The most prestigious convent schools, such as the Panthemont, were suspect on political grounds, too, because of their close ties to the aristocracy and its interests. In sum, many liberal-minded people—just the sorts toward whom Jefferson himself gravitated—questioned the desirability of convent education for girls and young women by the 1780s.[33]

So, too, did American family and friends challenge Jefferson's decision to send Patsy to the Panthemont. Their objections, however, were based on religious considerations, deriving specifically from the profound anti-Catholicism that still pervaded the popular culture of what was once British colonial America. The Panthemont, Jefferson explained defensively to his sister in Virginia, "is a house of education altogether the best in France, and at which the best masters attend." He insisted that the school had "as many protestants as Catholics, and not a word is ever spoken to them on the subject of religion." Even after spending three years in Europe, Abigail Adams confessed that she still had "many, perhaps false prejudices" against sending Protestant girls to Catholic convents for their education.[34]

Patsy's first months in the convent were difficult. She missed her father so much that he visited her there every evening "for the first month or two," she recalled years later, until she felt more comfortable. Part of the problem was that Patsy suddenly found herself in a large and imposing building full of peculiarly dressed women—nuns in habits and students in uniform crimson frocks—who did not (or would not) speak her language. Although there were several English students roughly her own age enrolled at the Panthemont, Patsy told Elizabeth Trist that "no one here knew english but a little girl of 2 years old." Maybe the other students refused to speak English as part of a hazing ritual directed at the American newcomer, or perhaps the nuns hoped to hasten Patsy's progress in French by preventing her from using her native tongue. Patsy's French, indeed, improved quickly, and by November she was sending entertaining accounts of convent life to her envious friend Judith Randolph at Tuckahoe.[35]

At the Panthemont, for the first time since her mother's death, Patsy was part of a stable domestic community. She and her classmates slept in four "exceedingly large" rooms, used another room for their lessons, and had a sixth as a parlor for socializing and other daytime activities. They strolled and played in the vast courtyard inside the convent walls. Some came to see favorite nuns as surrogate mothers, though there is no evidence that Patsy, like some students, adopted one of the sisters as her special mentor or confidante. She did, however, develop a crush on a kindly abbot a few months after her arrival. She must have blushed deeply when a classmate teased her about her feelings, playfully reminding her that Catholic clergy could not marry.[36]

Patsy soon developed a circle of school friends, some of whom she kept up with after she left Paris. Her closest friends were the daughters of the Earl of Thanet, Elizabeth and Caroline Tufton, whom Patsy remembered

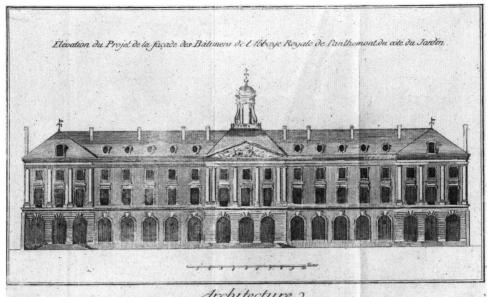

Abbaye de Pentemont. This imposing building housed the Abbaye de Panthemont, a convent whose school was one of the most prestigious in France. Patsy spent more than four years as a student at the Panthemont. Though she was initially uncomfortable in such an alien environment, her school days in Paris were among the happiest of her life. Author's collection.

so fondly that she persuaded her father to name a farm near Monticello in their honor. She corresponded with the sisters for at least twenty years after she returned to Virginia. Julia Annesley, another English student, who later married an earl, confessed a deep love for her "Dear Jeffy," while Bettie Hawkins cherished a lock of reddish hair from her "Dear Jeff." Patsy's closest French friend at the Panthemont was Marie de Botidoux, who enjoyed the company of the young American and idolized her father. Botidoux, who stayed at the Panthemont until the revolutionaries closed it in 1790, kissed a ring that Patsy gave her "20 times a day" after they parted and wrote to her American friend from time to time for more than two decades. Throughout her life, Patsy spoke affectionately of the convent school and the friends she made there, which made her years in Paris the "brightest part" of her life.[37]

Although Patsy's letters to her classmates have not survived, those they wrote to her provide a glimpse of this lively and youthful community. Despite their seclusion from the outside world—or perhaps because of it—Panthemont students shared information and opinions about balls, fashion, theater, and even politics. They also gossiped about one another and their families, foibles, and eventual marriage prospects. Through gossip, they articulated, pondered, and ultimately embraced the moral standards that they, as young ladies, were expected to uphold. Thus, Julia Annesley explained to Patsy that one of their fellow students, Mademoiselle Broadhead, had done something for which she "lost her Character," but Julia suggested that because her transgression occurred at such a young age, possibly "the world will forget it." Another student, Rachel Dashwood, the illegitimate daughter of an English libertine, acquired a reputation for "boldness" around young men. "I hope she will get better principles & get a little more virtue," her friend Bettie Hawkins observed. Scandal followed the beautiful but apparently incorrigible Dashwood, who later became notorious as an outspoken critic of Christianity and the victim of an alleged abduction (which was probably her botched attempt, in 1803, to elope with a married man).[38]

Patsy was popular among her convent classmates, whose letters portray her as an intelligent and gregarious adolescent who liked jokes, mixed readily with others, and relished her limited independence. In the convent, as in Philadelphia, she enjoyed music, struggled with her drawing lessons, and was occasionally careless with her clothing and her manners. The most vivid picture of Patsy during her student days in Paris comes from the pen of Marie Botidoux, who, in 1798, was incredulous to learn that her old schoolmate was now the mother of three children. Botidoux wondered if her friend had become calmer and more mature. She remembered Patsy as a wild and playful girl who never walked when she could run, her petticoats dragging often and her clothing stained and disheveled. Not surprisingly, her father worried that she did not "employ yourself as closely as I could wish" while she was with her classmates in Paris.[39]

Once she was comfortably established at the convent, Patsy enjoyed unprecedented independence, in part because her father had so many new duties and distractions. In 1784–85, learning the ropes of French politics and diplomacy and finding suitable living arrangements preoccupied Jefferson, who, two months after settling at the Hôtel d'Orléans, signed a lease on a house in a newer residential district farther from the convent. A year later, in October 1785, after learning of his appointment to succeed Benjamin Franklin as U.S. minister to France, he moved to the Hôtel de Langeac, a new two-story house with a neoclassical facade, which had been built for the then-exiled mistress of a French count. Located on the Champs-Élysées, this larger house required more servants and more fur-

*Hôtel de Langeac. Jefferson's largest and most elegant residence in Paris appears
to the left, behind the gate known as the "Grille de Chaillot." The Champs-Élysées,
a fashionable venue for carriage rides and strolls, is in the foreground. Courtesy of
Bibliothèque Nationale de France.*

niture than his previous residence. Jefferson spent much time and money
acquiring horses, carriages, furniture, and other household items, making
the Hôtel de Langeac the site of one of the city's most hospitable diplomatic legations. Years later, Patsy remembered the house as "elegant even
for Paris with an extensive garden court and out-buildings in the handsom-
est style."[40]

Jefferson may have decided he needed a larger house in part because he
was determined to have his second daughter, Polly, join them in Paris after
his youngest child, Lucy, died of whooping cough at Eppington in October 1785. Nabby Adams reported in her journal that news of Lucy's death
"greatly affected" father and daughter alike. Jefferson did not dine out for
at least four months after he learned of the tragedy, and he wrote frequent
letters to the Eppeses to orchestrate Polly's removal to Europe. "I must
have Polly," he explained impatiently to Francis Eppes in May 1785. "Poll . . .

hangs on my mind night and day," he declared mournfully in another letter three months later. Patsy was much more reticent—her few surviving letters from the two years following Lucy's death mention neither of her sisters— and seven-year-old Polly's unwillingness to leave Eppington and her relatives' reluctance to send her delayed her departure. Nevertheless, by spring 1787, when Polly's arrival seemed imminent, Patsy dutifully affirmed that reuniting with her younger sister would make her "the happiest of mortals."[41]

During these years, travel and female companionship interrupted— and perhaps assuaged—Jefferson's grief over Lucy's death and his near-obsessive determination to bring Polly to Paris. In March 1786, he embarked on a two-month trip to England on official business, leaving Patsy behind at the Panthemont. Not long after he returned to Paris, Jefferson enjoyed his famous flirtation with Maria Cosway, the beautiful and talented Italian-born wife of the English artist Richard Cosway and an accomplished artist in her own right. Jefferson and Maria Cosway enjoyed opera, theater, art, and each other's company during the early autumn of 1786, when she returned to London. In late February 1787, Jefferson left Paris for a tour of France and northern Italy that lasted three and a half months.[42]

While Jefferson traveled, he had his secretary, the young Virginian William Short, look in on Patsy at the Panthemont from time to time, though he also sought to monitor her conduct via fatherly letters of instruction, as he had done during her stay with Mary Hopkinson. "The more you learn the more I love you," he wrote before leaving for London in 1786, "and I rest the happiness of my life on seeing you beloved by all the world, which you will be sure to be if to a good heart you join those accomplishments so peculiarly pleasing in your sex." On this occasion, the final advice Patsy received from her father was to "lose no moment in improving your head, nor any opportunity of exercising your heart in benevolence." Perhaps she lived up to his expectations, or maybe he felt a tinge of guilt for leaving her behind, especially when Short informed him that Patsy was well but "wanting to hear more frequently from you to make her still more happy." In any event, Jefferson consulted Francis Hopkinson about choosing a harpsichord as a special gift for his daughter shortly after he returned to Paris that May.[43]

Patsy's visits with her father were sometimes frequent, but at other times much less so, even when he was not traveling. Jefferson's account books indicate that in some months he saw Patsy (and gave her money) as many as four times, or roughly once a week, but that at other times they may have gone for weeks without seeing each other. For instance, in 1785, Patsy was with her father at his house when the Adamses came to dine there twice in late January and early February, but from mid-March through early May she got her allowance from Jefferson's maître d'hôtel—the male employee who oversaw the household and its accounts—rather than directly from her father. Patsy was with Jefferson again when the Adamses came to dinner on 9 May 1785, and she saw him at least three times in June and at least twice a month for the rest of the year, except possibly in August and November, when he reported giving her money only once. Although Patsy typically left the convent to visit with her father, he sometimes went to Panthemont to see her. In the years that Patsy was enrolled in the convent school, he generally went there periodically to pay her tuition personally.[44]

Jefferson took his daughter on occasional outings to cautiously introduce her to life outside the convent. On 24 May 1785, father and daughter watched the ceremonial procession of Queen Marie-Antoinette to Notre Dame, where she gave thanks for the recent birth of a son. Losing sight of the queen amid the crowds, Jefferson reported to John Adams, "I carried my daughter to the Abbaye and came home to bed myself." Jefferson, like many of his French friends, disliked the extravagant Austrian queen and was somewhat more sympathetic toward King Louis XVI, who he believed "*loves his queen* and is too much *governed by her*." Neither half of the royal couple impressed Patsy, who nonchalantly informed Elizabeth Trist that she had "seen the king and queen but at too great a distance to judge if they are like their pictures in Philadelphia." Jefferson's account books indicate that Patsy was in Paris for more than a year before she went to her first concerts in December 1785. They also appear to have attended the theater to see a French comedy together a few months later.[45]

Jefferson was adamant that Patsy's Parisian adolescence would not undermine her American roots and impede her from returning happily to Virginia. To that end, he made sure that she socialized with admirable American women whenever possible, having her leave the convent to dine with him at home when her "country-women" were among his guests. He also emphasized his own "perfect knowledge of the situation" in which she would "be placed" as an adult and sought to prepare her for what he saw as her destiny as a wife, mother, and mistress of an American household. As early as 1785, Jefferson bemoaned the fact that "domestic bonds . . . are absolutely done away with" among Parisians, mostly because of the assertiveness and promiscuity of French women. As a result, he believed, the French were an unhappy and "wretched" people. In his letters to Patsy— and presumably in their conversations, too—Jefferson lauded domesticity, thrift, and industry as specifically American virtues. He also urged her to delight in music, sewing, reading, and other solitary pastimes that could be "resources . . . against ennui" once she returned to the "country life of America." Although Patsy grew intellectually and became adept at genteel accomplishments at the Panthemont, Jefferson confided pointedly to Elizabeth Eppes, "She will have to learn from you things which she cannot learn here, and which after all are among the most valuable parts of education *for an American*."[46]

Following her father's lead and at least partly for his benefit, Patsy self-consciously identified with certain aspects of these American ideals and values. In one letter to Jefferson, she implicitly contrasted unhappy Parisian marriages—and unruly French wives—with their superior American counterparts. "There was a gentleman, a few days ago, that killed himself because he thought that his wife did not love him," Patsy wrote in 1787. "I believe that if every husband in Paris was to do as much," she observed mischievously, "there would be nothing but widows left." Likewise, she reported with tacit disapproval that the only kind of needlework she could learn at the Panthemont was fancy embroidery, which would not be terribly useful to her in America.[47]

At the same time, however, Patsy appears to have had some misgivings about the prospect of her eventual return to Virginia. She was happy among her friends at the Panthemont and in Paris generally, and on at least one occasion she strongly criticized one of the fundamental institutions of Virginia society: chattel slavery. "I wish with all my soul that the poor negroes were all freed," she wrote to her father in May 1787. "It grieves my heart when I think," she opined, "that these our fellow creatures should be treated so terribly as they are by many of our country men." Jefferson, who a few years earlier had contended that the "unfortunate difference of colour, and perhaps of faculty, is a powerful obstacle to the emancipation of these people," did not respond to his daughter's protest.[48]

Overall, the letters Patsy wrote to her father during his 1787 tour of France and Italy reflected a new confidence and assertiveness in the fifteen-year-old Virginian. Although she dutifully updated her father on her progress in drawing, dancing, and Latin—with which she struggled—she also conveyed to him political news from Paris, where the king's government was in the throes of the financial crisis that eventually led to its downfall. In contrast to their separation in 1783, when Jefferson relentlessly demanded letters from Patsy, she now chided him for not writing to her during his extended absence. "Being disapointed in my expectation of receiving a letter from you my dear papa, I have resolved to break so painful a silence by giving you an example that I hope you will follow," she wrote cheekily about a week after he left Paris in 1787. She reiterated this complaint two weeks later, noting that he had "not kept your word in the least . . . but I hope you will make up for your silence by writing me a fine, long letter by the first opportunity." Her third letter acknowledged receipt of his first, but she playfully ended hers with a postscript requesting "a long letter, without a margin."[49]

Patsy wrote her father five letters during his three-and-a-half-month trip, and he wrote five letters to her. This rough parity of letter-writing—and perhaps of the affection and obligation the letters signified—is reminiscent of that of the months, years earlier, when Patsy stayed in Philadelphia while her father attended Congress, but the tenor of their relationship had changed as Patsy matured and grew comfortable in her environment and confident in her abilities. Jefferson saved these letters and responded to them affectionately, though he could not prevent himself from peppering his missives with fatherly advice to exercise moderately, study hard, and eschew idleness. Jefferson still set high standards for Patsy, and he still appealed to her in emotion-laden rhetoric. "My expectations for you are high: yet not higher than you may attain," he wrote from Provence in March. "No body in this world can make me so happy, or so miserable as you."[50]

Patsy's progress to womanhood pleased her father both because he anticipated her future life in Virginia and because, before that, he would depend on her to care for "our dear Polly." Jefferson envisioned fifteen-year-old Patsy as a maternal figure for her younger sister, who was not yet nine in the summer of 1787 when she was due to arrive in Paris. Jefferson's advice to Patsy on assuming responsibility for this "precious charge" amounted to a summary of his own prescriptions for domestic tranquility, which he valued above all else. "Teach her above all things to be good. . . . Teach her always to be true. . . . Teach her never to be angry. . . . And teach her industry and application to useful pursuits. I will venture to assure you that if you inculcate this in her mind you will make her a happy being in herself, a most inestimable friend to you, and precious to all the world." Eagerly awaiting the arrival of his "dear Polly," he reminded his elder daughter that she, too, should practice these virtues "for the additional incitement of increasing the happiness of him who loves you infinitely."[51]

❖ In July 1787, Patsy saw her sister for the first time in nearly four years. At fifteen, Patsy was attractive but not beautiful, tall and red-haired like her father. By all accounts, Polly was pretty, dark-haired, and exquisitely delicate like her mother. Patsy was cheerful, gregarious, and accustomed to life in Paris. At least initially, Polly was shy and spoke no French, but Abigail Adams, with whom she stayed briefly in London en route to Paris, reported that "her temper, her disposition, her sensibility are all formed to delight." Jefferson's younger daughter was, in Adams's view, a "child of the quickest sensibility, and the maturest understanding, that I have ever met with for her years." John Adams agreed that he "never saw a more Charming Child."[52]

Another signal difference between Patsy and Polly was the latter's reluctance to travel to France. On learning that her father wanted her to come to Paris in 1785, Polly wrote him a one-sentence note: "I want to see you and sister Patsy, but you must come to Uncle Eppes's house." Polly was happy at Eppington. She was especially close to her aunt Elizabeth Eppes, and she knew her cousins much better than she knew Patsy, whom she had not seen since 1783. Jefferson promised Polly "as many dolls and playthings as you want" if she came to France without protest, but the youngster responded to this offer by asserting that she "had rather stay with Aunt Eppes." To no avail, both Elizabeth Eppes and Martha Jefferson Carr, Jefferson's sister, tried to dissuade him from forcing his daughter to make the trip to Europe. In January 1787, Carr informed her brother bluntly that "Pollys aversion to going to France Increases dayly, and . . . she fears she must at last be draged like a calf to the Slaughter." Jefferson nonetheless insisted that joining him and Patsy in Paris was "necessary for her happiness."[53]

Not only did Polly explicitly oppose her father's wishes; she also criticized him, most likely during her time with the Eppeses and most certainly while she stayed in London with the Adamses. When Polly arrived in London on 26 June 1787, she was demonstrably "unhappy being wholly left to strangers," according to Abigail Adams. In an effort to calm the tearful girl, Adams told her that she had never seen Patsy cry, but Polly replied that her sister "was older and ought to do better, besides she had her pappa with her." By 6 July, Jefferson's French maître d'hôtel, Adrien Petit, had arrived to accompany Polly on the final leg of her journey to Paris. Polly, who had tearfully resisted leaving first the Eppeses and then the ship captain who befriended her during the transatlantic crossing, now clung to Abigail Adams, claiming that she neither remembered her father nor desired to go to him. Polly resisted leaving with Petit in part because she was angry with her father. According to Adams, "She did think [Jefferson] would have taken the pains to have come here for her, and not have sent a man whom she cannot understand" because she did not yet know French.[54]

Polly soon renewed her ties with her father and her sister, but her arrival irrevocably changed life at the Hôtel de Langeac, in part because Jefferson's younger daughter did not come alone. Although Jefferson initially hoped that either "some good lady" or "a careful gentleman" or even "a careful negro women . . . under the patronage of a gentleman" would accompany Polly on her journey to Europe, none of those options materialized. Instead, the child traveled with a female slave who was, at fourteen, a year younger than Patsy and just five years older than Polly herself. "The Girl," as Abigail Adams called her, was, in fact, a blood relation to Jefferson's daughters. Known as Sally, Sarah Hemings was the youngest daughter of John Wayles and Betty Hemings and therefore the half-sister of Patsy and Polly's deceased mother.[55]

Patsy probably remembered Sally from Monticello, where the Hemingses had been favored house servants since their arrival in 1774 after the death of John Wayles and the dispersal of his estate. Sally was almost two years old when she came to Monticello with her mother, so Patsy and Sally were probably playmates. Enslaved children often played with their masters' offspring until they were old enough to be put to work, and the light-skinned Sally was no ordinary slave. Even if the Jeffersons shielded Patsy and her sister from the truth—that Sally was their half-aunt—the Hemingses were well-aware of their connection to the mistress of Monticello. In 1782, nine-year-old Sally had been among a circle of Hemings females who attended the deathbed of Patsy's mother. According to family tradition, on her deathbed, Martha Wayles Jefferson gave Sally Hemings a handbell as a memento, a gift that ambiguously signified both their close personal connection and the fact that "one sister was the slave of the other."[56]

When Patsy left Virginia with her father, Sally stayed with Polly at Eppington. Together they weathered the threat of whooping cough, which carried off young Lucy Jefferson and one of her Eppes cousins. Elizabeth and Francis Eppes must have deemed Sally sufficiently capable and mature to send their beloved niece to Europe under her care, and Polly must have been comforted by the presence of the enslaved teen, whom she had known her whole life. In 1787, Sally looked two or three years older than her fourteen years, according to Abigail Adams. Isaac Jefferson, a Monticello slave who knew Sally Hemings well, described her as "very handsome, [with] long hair down her back." Her skin, he remembered, was "mighty near white."[57]

Once Patsy and Polly left for school in late July, Sally had no specific responsibilities. She probably did sewing and mending and ran errands for her brother James, who was completing the apprenticeship that would enable him to be Jefferson's French chef at the Hôtel de Langeac. As the only female servant in Jefferson's household, she also served as a chambermaid for him and for his daughters when they visited. Jefferson paid both Sally and James wages while they were with him in Paris, and both became proficient in French. Paradoxically, Sally had more freedom to explore Paris than the Jefferson girls did.[58]

At the convent, the formerly gregarious and carefree Patsy now found herself responsible for a skittishly homesick sister she barely knew. Although Polly had written her father occasional brief letters during their separation, the sisters apparently did not correspond directly with each other. While Patsy remembered Polly, Abigail Adams thought that the younger sister had "totally forgotten" the elder. Even Jefferson admitted that Polly "neither knew us, nor should we have known her had we met with her unexpectedly" when she first arrived in Paris. Patsy's first task, then, was to become reacquainted with her sister; her second was to ease her into the routine of school and convent life.[59]

From July 1787 until April 1789, Patsy and Polly studied and boarded together at the Panthemont. The sisters visited their father at the Hôtel de Langeac most weeks, though there was at least one two-month stretch, while Jefferson was in Amsterdam and the German states, when they remained at school. Patsy and Polly sometimes enjoyed special outings with their father, such as when he took them and their American schoolmate Kitty Church to Bagatelle, a fashionable pleasure garden and pavilion in the Bois de Boulogne, outside Paris. When the sisters were away from Jefferson, Patsy, who was six years older than Polly and by now fluent in French, was clearly in charge. Jefferson's account books show that he regularly gave small sums to his elder daughter, who presumably used part of the money for Polly, who received no money directly from her father until January 1789.[60]

In the throes of adolescence, even as she monitored the progress of her younger sister, Patsy experienced a religious awakening of sorts at the convent. Patsy may have been exposed to Protestant doctrines and devotional practices by her mother or by the pious Mary Hopkinson, but there is no evidence that Jefferson taught either her or Polly any religious precepts beyond belief in a Supreme Being and adherence to Christian morality, despite the fact that in old age Martha Jefferson Randolph claimed that she had been "most religiously brought up." At the Panthemont, however, Patsy appreciated the beauty and pageantry of Catholic ritual and admired the devout and kindly nuns. By 1788, she found Catholicism appealing and confided to at least one friend, Bettie Hawkins, her desire to become both a

Catholic and a nun. The incredulous Hawkins understandably wondered how this news would "be made known to your Father," who, as she correctly expected, would disapprove of Patsy's plan.[61]

Although family tradition holds that Patsy's interest in joining the convent so alarmed Jefferson that he abruptly withdrew both her and Polly from the Panthemont, what really happened was less dramatic. Jefferson asked his daughter to delay making such a momentous decision until she had more time to reflect and until her judgment "matured." At least partly to distract sixteen-year-old Patsy from her new religious interests, he also cautiously increased her exposure to social life outside the convent. As an antidote to her religious fervor and as preparation for her eventual reception of suitors in Virginia, Jefferson began spending large sums of money on clothes for Patsy, who began to attend balls and parties. He also bought clothes for Sally Hemings, who acted as Patsy's attendant when she appeared in society.[62]

Jefferson had begun Patsy's social education in a modest way even before Polly and Sally arrived in Paris. In March 1787, he asked his daughter to take her meals at the Panthemont with the abbess, Madame Béthisy de Mézières, who was herself a member of a noble family and who dined with the convent's most prestigious residents, who often included prominent women lodging there temporarily. Dining with the abbess and other ladies prepared Patsy for dinners—such as one she attended at the chateau of the Marquis de Lafayette that June—that would be more formal than those she enjoyed with her schoolmates at the convent or at her father's house. Jefferson also pressed his daughter to dress neatly and appropriately for social engagements. In June 1787, he instructed her to "make it a rule hereafter to come [to his house] dressed otherwise than in your uniform," so that she could present herself as a young lady, not as a schoolgirl, and so that he could monitor her sometimes slovenly tendencies. Patsy initially chafed at the new demands of fashion and sociability, but after some months her classmate Bettie Hawkins congratulated her on "getting rid of your bashfulness and diffidence," adding, "I find assurance very necessary in the world where every man judges you from the opinion you seem yourself to have of your own abilities."[63]

Patsy's illness during the winter of 1788–89, the coldest on record in half a century, also eased her transition from the Panthemont to the Hôtel de Langeac. Both Patsy and Polly contracted typhus while at school, and they came to their father's house to be treated. Patsy was ill for five or six weeks. Polly, whose case was more severe, suffered for more than two months and was, according to her sister, "for many weeks Deaf and stupid" as a result of her illness. Indeed, Patsy believed that her sister never entirely recovered the mental faculties she lost to typhus, "having always retained a *torpor* which I thought was not natural to her." The sisters spent most of the winter in their father's house, where he nursed them back to health, administering the rations of gruel and Madeira wine prescribed by an English doctor whom Jefferson praised as "the ablest I ever met with." Although the sisters returned to school when they recovered, Jefferson's fear of losing his two remaining children to some contagion may have contributed to his decision to withdraw them from the Panthemont that spring.[64]

Patsy spent her last six months in Paris in her father's house, where she shared living quarters with him, her sister, Sally and James Hemings, Adrien Petit, and five other Frenchmen whom Jefferson employed in various capacities at the Hôtel de Langeac. Jefferson's secretary, William Short, also lodged with the family when he was in Paris. The spacious and beautifully furnished house included some impressive modern conveniences, including indoor plumbing, and enough bedrooms to ensure the privacy of their occupants, including Jefferson's frequent guests.[65]

Since the death of her mother in 1782, Patsy had lived in a succession of unconventional domestic environments, a pattern that continued in her father's Parisian household. As the daughters of Virginia gentry, both she and Polly were accustomed to having servants in their home. But the domestic staff in Paris was unusual insofar as it was all male, except for Sally Hemings, and aside from the Hemingses, all free men who worked for wages and could leave at any time. The status of the Hemingses, moreover, was less straightforward than it had been in Virginia, where despite their white ancestry, they were both slaves. France, unlike Virginia, adhered to the "Freedom Principle," which held that once an enslaved person set foot in the country, he or she was free. In practice, a visiting slaveholder could register his bondpeople with the authorities to preserve their status, but Jefferson never did so, perhaps because he did not want to draw attention to the fact that he owned slaves. Though Jefferson still thought of James and Sally Hemings as his slaves, he paid them wages. There is also strong evidence that he began what would become a long-term sexual relationship with Sally, who, according to their son Madison Hemings, "became Mr. Jefferson's concubine, and . . . was *enciente* [pregnant] by him" when they returned to America in 1789.[66]

There is no way to know what Patsy thought of the odd composition of her father's household, whether she pondered the difference between French servants and African American slaves, and how much she thought about the status of Sally Hemings, with whom she interacted on a daily basis. Although she left Virginia at too young an age to know that masters often had sex with enslaved women, perhaps Sally's light skin and noted family resemblance to her own mother led her to conclude that such relationships were common. Perhaps Patsy's belief—which her father shared—that even married Parisians were promiscuous by American standards helped her to accept the extramarital exertions of her widowed father, who believed that sexual activity was essential to preserving men's (but not women's) physical and emotional health. Or maybe Patsy simply was unaware of what Jefferson and Hemings did together in some corner of his big Parisian house. In any event, if she wrote any letters during her last months in Paris when she and Polly resided with their father, they have not survived. Nor do her later letters mention Sally Hemings in any substantive way, though they often included news of other members of the Hemings family and of other Monticello slaves.[67]

Visitors found that an aura of domesticity prevailed at Jefferson's house, at least when his daughters returned from the Panthemont. As the American minister in Paris, Jefferson hosted official entertainments that, unlike the city's salons and fancy balls, followed a more domestic and patriarchal model. Gouverneur Morris, a wealthy New Yorker who visited Jefferson at least nine times in 1789, reported that Patsy and Polly dined with their father's guests, though the girls left the table after the meal was over.[68]

These sociable performances of domesticity served at least two purposes for Jefferson and his daughters. First, Patsy and Polly learned how to interact with genteel adults and no doubt acquired social skills that would be useful to them first as belles and later as wives and hostesses in Virginia. Second, Jefferson used his daughters to create a stable and amiable domestic tableau at the Hôtel de Langeac not long after he enjoyed a flirtation (and perhaps more) with a married woman, Maria Cosway, and at the very moment when many historians believe he began what became a long-term sexual liaison with Sally Hemings. Although Parisians took extramarital affairs in stride, many Americans did not. Family dinners and outings enabled Jefferson to present himself to guests and to the wider public as a family man who embraced wholesome American domestic values.[69]

During her busy final months in Paris, Patsy's social activities may have distracted her from the more quotidian aspects of life in her father's house. An avid shopper who filled the Hôtel de Langeac with art and furnishings that he would soon transport home to Monticello, Jefferson now set out to acquire for his elder daughter some material trappings of her new status as a young woman formally entering genteel society. Nearly every page of the account book Jefferson kept during these months includes an entry noting his expenditures on clothes, stays, shoes, or some other item "for Patsy." He paid tailors, seamstresses, and a "flower mistress" to outfit his daughter for social occasions. He bought her a ring—her first known piece of jewelry—and a "pocketbook," or wallet, which signified an adult's ability to carry and use money, a distinction also reflected in her greatly increased monthly allowance that was six times the sum Polly received. Patsy resumed riding and became a good horsewoman. Jefferson also hired a dancing master and made monthly payments to both a harpsichord teacher and a guitar master.[70]

In the spring and summer of 1789, Patsy Jefferson, who would turn seventeen that September, enjoyed an active social life, though she did not frequent the famous salons where enlightened women and men mingled amiably, discussed art and politics, and (from the perspective of American critics, including Jefferson) flirted shamelessly. Jefferson continued to shield his daughter from sophisticated French women, in part because he believed that a virtuous American woman should be content with "the society of [her] husband, the fond cares for the children, the arrangements of the house, the improvements of the grounds, [which] fill every moment with a healthy and an useful activity." Genteel dinners and carefully choreographed balls, unlike salons, enabled Patsy to practice conversation, dancing, and other social graces that were essential in Virginia, as in Paris, without compromising her manners and morals. According to family tradition, she loved to dance and danced well, but her father limited her to three balls a week.[71]

Patsy spent some evenings attending concerts with her father. The most notable of these was in May 1789, when a nine-year-old mixed-race violinist named George Bridgetower played at the Panthemont. Bridgetower, whose mother was Polish and whose father was a black Barbadian, was beginning what would be a long and distinguished career as a classical musician based in London. One Paris newspaper gave rave reviews to Bridgetower's debut performance that April, observing that "his talent is one of the best replies one can give to philosophers who wish to deprive people of his nation and his colour of the opportunity to distinguish themselves in the arts." Neither Patsy nor her father commented on the youngster's virtuosity, though a few years earlier, in *Notes on the State of Virginia*, Jefferson had suggested that people of African descent, though adept at certain simpler types of music, were not "equal to the composition of a more extensive run of melody, or of complicated harmony."[72]

At balls, concerts, and formal dinners, Patsy met famous and interesting people. During her last winter in Paris, she accompanied her friends the Tuftons to a dinner given by Georgiana, Duchess of Devonshire, at which the hostess, who was renowned as both a liberal political force and a fashionable trendsetter in Britain, remarked that Patsy was "the only lady present whose height was equal to her own." Patsy often saw Lafayette and his family and other prominent Frenchmen, such as the philosophes Condorcet and Rochefoucauld, who visited her father's house. She also met most of the important Americans who came to Paris. Patsy had tea with the wife of Nathaniel Barrett, who represented some Boston merchants in Paris, and she visited the young American widow Dorcas Montgomery. Ever mindful of the need to limit Patsy's independence, however, Jefferson politely denied Montgomery's "friendly offer" to take her on a grand tour of Europe because, as he explained awkwardly, he felt obliged to expose his daughters to "the fewest objectionable circumstances."[73]

Perhaps not surprisingly, during these months, Patsy had her first romance, though it probably did not proceed beyond the flirtation stage. Family tradition held that "more than one young man . . . paid his addresses" to Patsy in Paris, but her relationship to her father's Virginia-born secretary, William Short, seems to have been closer than most. The two had known each other slightly in America, though they became better acquainted in 1787, when father and daughter communicated with each other by sending their letters through his secretary. At the time, Short was Jefferson's most trusted subordinate in Paris; he was related to Jefferson's Wayles in-laws and, like Jefferson, had graduated from the College of William and Mary and studied law with George Wythe. Jefferson regarded Short, who was thirteen years older than Patsy, as a protégé and virtual adopted son. Nabby Adams, the daughter of John and Abigail, praised Short as "social and pleasant," adding, "He appears a well-bred man, without the least formality, of affectation of any kind. He converses with ease and says many good things."[74]

Other women also found William Short attractive. During most of his tenure as Jefferson's secretary, Short divided his time between the Hôtel de Langeac and the home of the Royer family in Saint-Germain-en-Laye, some fifteen miles from Paris, where he went initially in 1785 to immerse himself in French to become proficient in the language. While living with the Royers, he fell in love with their fifteen-year-old daughter. The two had an amorous relationship that lasted until roughly 1790, though the young woman, known as Lilite, had married Henri Denis and given birth to a son sometime in 1787; a second son followed. William Short's relationship with Lilite may or may not have included sexual relations, either before or after her marriage, though he later became a benefactor to her two adult sons. By 1790, however, Short had ended his visits to Saint-Germain, having begun an affair with Rosalie, the young wife of Jefferson's friend and contemporary the Duc de la Rochefoucauld.[75]

Although Short was away during much of the time Jefferson's daughters resided with him in Paris, he was there enough to make a deep impression on Patsy and her friends. Short was touring Europe when Patsy and Polly moved from the Panthemont to the Hôtel de Langeac in April 1789. He returned to Paris for a week in May before leaving again for Saint-Germain, but he returned to Paris after a few days and spent much of the next few months helping Jefferson plan for his impending departure. From May to September, Short was often in Paris, living with the Jeffersons, and he and Patsy saw each other daily. At the time, Lilite was a married woman with two children, and Short had not yet begun his affair with the duchess.[76]

Jefferson, who eagerly anticipated his return to America and claimed that Patsy shared his enthusiasm for leaving Paris, tried mightily to persuade Short that his future also lay in America rather than in Europe. Assuring Short that finding prosperity in Europe would be difficult, he concluded, "The only resource then for a durable happiness is to return to America," where he might earn enough to support a wife with whom he could enjoy "the amusement and comfort of children." Jefferson admitted that personal interest, along with a concern for Short's welfare, led him to advocate his return home. "For affection and the long habit of your society have rendered it necessary to me," he wrote in March 1789. "And how much more so will it be," he added, "when I shall have parted with my daughters?"[77]

Although there is no evidence that Jefferson considered Short a desirable suitor for his older daughter, letters written by Patsy's friend Marie de Botidoux soon after the Jeffersons left Paris suggest that her relationship with her father's secretary was affectionate and flirtatious—and possibly more. Botidoux believed that Patsy loved Short and that he attempted to persuade her to stay in Paris after her father left—an arrangement that, even if it included marriage, would have been unacceptable to Jefferson, who clearly expected both Patsy and Polly to return with him to Virginia. Botidoux indicated that Patsy was reluctant to leave France, and she implied that her flirtation with Short was at least one factor that influenced her friend's feelings on that subject. Conversely, when Patsy left Paris, Short profusely lamented her departure. In January 1790, Botidoux described him as angrily renouncing his affection for Patsy, though she believed he was still in love, a view she reiterated four months later. William Short, who never married, did not return to the United States until 1810.[78]

Meanwhile, during her last months in Paris, Patsy witnessed the first dramatic stages of the French Revolution in the summer of 1789. In June, the Third Estate—the non-noble, non-clergy majority of the Estates General, the French legislature—with some support from liberal clergy and aristocrats, such as Lafayette, declared itself a National Assembly and swore an oath that it would not disband until a new constitution was drafted. By mid-July, according to Gouverneur Morris, Paris was in a "Tumult," and the Jeffersons could hear gunshots in the distance from the Hôtel de Langeac. Then, on 14 July, hundreds of Parisians stormed a medieval fortress known as the Bastille in hopes of freeing prisoners and obtaining gunpowder and weaponry. Finding no weapons, the enraged crowd captured the Bastille's governor and some of his subordinates, several of whom they beheaded. An appalled Morris recorded in his diary that people "were carrying the Heads in Triumph thro the City." The next day, the streets remained dangerous even as the crowd rejoiced in its victory and Lafayette assumed command of the National Guard. On 17 July, Jefferson informed Thomas Paine, an important English supporter of both the American and French revolutions, "A more dangerous scene of war I never saw in America, than what Paris has presented for 5. days past."[79]

When Louis XVI came to Paris from Versailles in an attempt to restore order at Lafayette's behest, Patsy witnessed the king's dramatic entry from a window above the street, where some 60,000 angry citizens brandishing "pistols, swords, pikes, pruning hooks, [and] scythes" greeted their sovereign. The royal procession also included fifty members of the National Assembly, led by the popular Lafayette, who saw Patsy standing in the window and saluted her with a bow. Like her father, Patsy expressed support for the French Revolution, at least in its early stages, donning a revolutionary's tricolored cockade that she cherished as a memento for the rest of her life.[80]

When Patsy left Paris in late September 1789, she could not have known that the popular revolt whose inception she had witnessed would lead to pain and suffering for so many of her French friends. The revolutionary regime closed the convents, including the Panthemont, in 1790, but not before one Sister Catherine tarnished its reputation by fleeing its confines and telling Jean-Paul Marat, the radical newspaperman, that the nuns had per-

French Revolutionary Cockade. Women and men wore cockades—usually in their hair or on their hats—to show their political loyalties. In France, steadfast supporters of the Bourbon monarchy and its king, Louis XVI, wore the white cockade; the revolutionaries' cockade was red, white, and blue. Patsy Jefferson wore the revolutionary tricolor. Her cockade became a cherished memento of her time in Paris. Courtesy of the James Monroe Museum & Memorial Library, Fredericksburg, VA.

secuted her as a result of her prorevolutionary sympathies. Most of the nuns returned to their families or went into domestic service, according to Marie de Botidoux, though at least one married after the convent's dissolution. Botidoux still considered herself a *patriote* (a supporter of the revolution) in 1798, though she lost much of her small fortune during the upheaval. Lafayette, who had been influential during the revolution's early moderate phase, suffered as the revolutionary movement became more radical and more violent. This esteemed friend endured five years in an Austrian prison and lived quietly and in reduced circumstances after his release in 1799. Another close friend, the Duc de la Rochefoucauld, suffered a crueler fate.

In 1792, a crowd in the Norman town of Gisors stoned him to death as his wife and mother looked on.[81]

On 26 September 1789, a month to the day after the publication of the Declaration of the Rights of Man and the Citizen, which the National Assembly modeled in some respects on Jefferson's own revolutionary manifesto, the Declaration of Independence, Patsy left Paris. She traveled with her sister, her father, and James and Sally Hemings, both of whom were returning to their families in their native Virginia, even though doing so meant that they would remain enslaved. According to Madison Hemings, Sally, who was in the early stages of her first pregnancy, initially refused to leave Paris, but Jefferson changed her mind by promising her "extraordinary privileges" and making "a solemn pledge that her children should be freed at the age of twenty-one years." Jefferson, who dearly wanted James Hemings to be his French chef at Monticello, probably induced him to leave France by promising to emancipate him after he trained his substitute.[82]

The first leg of the trip homeward took Patsy and her companions to the coastal town of Le Havre, where she and her father had first set foot on French soil more than five years earlier. Bad weather delayed their departure for England for ten days. While they waited, Jefferson bought a dog, a Normandy shepherd, known as Bergère, or Buzzy. Finally, on 8 October, the Americans, their dog, and thirty-eight boxes of baggage left France and endured a turbulent, twenty-six-hour passage across the English Channel to Cowes, where they waited for nearly two weeks to board the ship that would take them home. The Jeffersons filled their time by touring the Isle of Wight, including Carisbrook Castle, and by visiting with Nathaniel Cutting, a Massachusetts sea captain who was then living in Le Havre. Cutting enjoyed the company of Jefferson and his daughters. He described Patsy as "an amiable Girl . . . tall and genteel . . . [who] though she has been so long resident in a Country remarkable for its Levity and the forward indelicacy of its manners . . . retains all that winning simplicity, and good humour'd reserve that are evident proofs of innate Virtue and an happy disposition." Like Jefferson, Cutting believed, with some satisfaction, that these "Characteristicks . . . eminently distinguish the Women of America from those of any other Country."[83]

Finally, at noon on 22 October 1789, the Jeffersons and the Hemingses boarded the *Clermont* as its only passengers. The ship, which sailed directly to Virginia, had two large staterooms, one for Jefferson and another for his daughters, and lesser accommodations for the Hemingses. The vessel was relatively new, and it had a spacious deck for strolling. Bergère gave birth to two puppies during the trip, which Patsy remembered as "quick and not unpleasant," though fog off the Virginia capes delayed their entry into Norfolk's harbor. When the ship docked in Norfolk on 23 November, the travelers went to a local inn. Patsy noticed that the town, which suffered heavy shelling during the Revolution, still bore the scars of war. A fire broke out aboard the *Clermont* not long after it docked, but the passengers' baggage—which included Patsy's French wardrobe, her revolutionary cockade, and other mementos of the past five years—were saved.[84]

❖ Patsy's education and social experiences in Philadelphia and especially in Paris were unique, and those around her knew it. Her friend Judith Randolph of Tuckahoe, who hungered for Patsy's news from "the Beau Monde," confided that her own "prospect for a tolerable education is but a bad one, which . . . is one of the greatest disadvantages which the Virginia Girls are attended with." So, too, did Jefferson's friend, the beautiful and brilliant Anne Willing Bingham, who found Paris so stimulating that she started her own salon in Philadelphia, describe Patsy Jefferson as "the envy of all the young Ladies in America."[85]

The last leg of the trip to Monticello, by horseback and ferry, which included stops in Williamsburg and Richmond as well as at Eppington and other family seats, took almost a month.[86] That journey reintroduced Patsy to once-familiar people and places, perhaps easing her reentry into a society and culture that was far different from what she left behind. She had left Virginia as a shy and unsophisticated ten-year-old in 1782. Now, seven years later, she returned as an accomplished young lady on the threshold of what were the most critical decisions of an eighteenth-century woman's life.

wife, мother, plantation мistress

Years after her return from Paris, Thomas Jefferson's older daughter romanticized the family's homecoming and her own first year as the de facto mistress of Monticello. She waxed nostalgic about the joyous reception they received from Monticello's African American residents, who, she recalled, "collected in crowds . . . and almost drew [the carriage] up the mountain by hand. When the door of the carriage was opened," she remembered, "they received [their master] in their arms and bore him to the house crowding round and kissing his hands and feet—some blubbering and crying, others laughing, it seemed impossible to satisfy their anxiety to touch and kiss the very earth that bore him." Years later, as an aging matron, she also reminisced about happily passing her first year back in her native Virginia sliding playfully on the ice with her cousin Peter Carr, developing her skills as a horsewoman, and socializing with her "country neighbors" in Albemarle.[1]

Notwithstanding these cheerful memories of a youth long since past, Patsy's early experience in Virginia as a grown woman was far more complicated. Although the enslaved people of Monticello surely rejoiced when the Jeffersons—and the Hemingses—returned from Europe, they did so at least partly because their own families were more likely to avoid dismemberment so long as their master lived and so long as Monticello prospered as a working plantation. By the same token, though Patsy clearly had some fun times on her return to Albemarle, she also took on new and sometimes daunting responsibilities. Exactly two months after that carriage ascended her father's mountain, she married, and just months later she became pregnant. Little more than a year after her return from Europe, her life was truly transformed. From the shops and balls of Paris, she was transported to the rustic world of wife, mother, and plantation mistress in rural Virginia. Between 1790 and 1800, as Thomas Jefferson served the republic first as secretary of state and then vice president, his daughter immersed herself in her domestic work and in a complex web of family relations, navigating the myriad challenges of her new adult life.

❖ Perhaps one reason for Patsy's reluctance to leave Europe was her expectation that her father would return to Paris to resume his diplomatic duties while she and Polly—whose formal name had evolved from Mary to Maria—lived sedately on some family plantation in Virginia. Not long after his arrival in Albemarle, however, Jefferson received an invitation from President George Washington to join his cabinet as secretary of state, which required his removal to New York, the first capital of the United States under its recently enacted constitution. Jefferson expected Polly to continue to attend school, but he concluded that seventeen-year-old Patsy could profit no more from "mere city education." Because a young woman could not live alone and unprotected, for Patsy there were only two options. She could stay at Eppington, where she could learn various domestic skills from her aunt and circulate socially under the supervision of the Eppeses and other relatives, or she could marry and reside with her new husband. Although there is no evidence that Jefferson led his daughter in one direction or the other, Patsy was engaged to be married within a month or so of their return to Virginia.[2]

Patsy's future husband was Thomas Mann Randolph Jr., the oldest son and presumptive heir of Thomas Mann Randolph of Tuckahoe. For two generations, kinship and friendship had united the Jefferson and Randolph families. Thomas Jefferson's father, Peter, married Jane Randolph and served as guardian for the children of his friend William Randolph, his wife's cousin, who died in 1745. One of William's orphaned children was the elder Thomas Mann Randolph, who spent his boyhood at Tuckahoe with Peter Jefferson and his family. Thomas Mann Randolph and Thomas Jefferson were best friends as boys, and as adults their relationship remained cordial. In 1790, Thomas Mann Randolph of Tuckahoe was the father of ten—three sons and seven daughters. Like Jefferson, he was a widower, since his wife, Ann Cary Randolph, had died in March 1789 at age forty-four.[3]

Patsy and Tom, who were third cousins, had met at least twice as youngsters. In 1781, when Patsy was nine and Tom was thirteen, the British invaded Virginia, and Tuckahoe was one of the Jefferson family's stops as they fled Richmond for Albemarle. Two years later, Patsy and her father went to Tuckahoe as they made their way south from Philadelphia while Jefferson waited to receive his assignment in Paris. During that visit, eleven-year-old Patsy struck up a friendship with Judith Randolph, who was also eleven years old. Patsy must have also made an impression on Judith's older brother Tom, who sent his "compliments to Miss Jefferson" when he wrote to ask her father's advice about his education in 1786. Although family tradition held that Patsy and Tom met again and fell in love in Paris, no evidence supports that story. Instead, Patsy renewed her acquaintance with Tom and his siblings when she, Polly, their father, and the Hemingses visited Tuckahoe on their way from Norfolk to Monticello in November 1790. Tom went to see Patsy and her father at Monticello not long thereafter. By December, Tom had fallen in love with Patsy, and she apparently returned the favor.[4]

Some historians have seen this match as doomed from the start, citing either the improbably close relationship between father and daughter or Tom Randolph's ill-tempered and highly emotional personality. Those who describe Tom as "an unstable and physically abusive man" who "moved in and out of psychosis" presume that the anxiety and rage that afflicted him in middle age—sometimes with dire consequences for those around him—also characterized him as a young man, a position supported only by the young man's admittedly strained relationship with his imperious father. In part because of this troubled relationship, young Tom probably saw in Jefferson a surrogate parent who, unlike his own father, shared his love of learning and revolutionary politics. If Tom's eventual marriage to Patsy "triangulated intimate family relations . . . in a way that routinely intruded on domestic tranquility," as one historian has argued, all parties optimistically embraced that arrangement, at least at the outset.[5]

One reason for their optimism was the fact that Patsy and Tom had much in common. They both had deep roots in Virginia and shared many mutual kin and acquaintances, though each had also experienced life in the wider cosmopolitan world. Both were comparatively well educated and valued learning and those who had it. Tom, for instance, believed that "an accomplished woman cannot be entirely ignorant" of science, though he also thought that his sisters and other members of the "delicate sex" were overall better suited to the "*elegant* and agreeable occupations of *Poetry* and the fine arts," especially music, at which Patsy, of course, excelled. Patsy and Tom were both tall, though she was red-haired and fair-skinned, while he had black hair and an olive complexion that the Randolphs attributed at least in part to their descent from the Powhatan princess Pocahontas. Both were skilled on horseback. And both felt deep affection for Thomas Jefferson, which he, in turn, professed toward them.[6]

Neither Patsy nor Tom left an account of their brief courtship, but Jefferson confided to a French friend that "according to the usage of my country,

Patsy Jefferson. This enamel miniature is the earliest known portrait of Patsy Jefferson—if, in fact, it is really her. One theory, once widely accepted, was that Patsy or her father had the miniature made as a gift for some French friends. Recent research suggests that Patsy may not have sat for this portrait, attributed to the French painter Joseph Boze, though its fair-skinned, red-haired subject resembled the young Virginian. Courtesy of the Diplomatic Reception Rooms, U.S. Department of State; photo by Will Brown.

I scrupulously suppressed my wishes, that my daughter might indulge her own sentiments freely." He also left no doubt that he thoroughly approved of Patsy's choice. Twenty-one-year-old Thomas Mann Randolph was educated and studious, having spent two years at the prestigious university in Edinburgh during which he exchanged letters with his future father-in-law, who offered advice about his education and prospects. Tom shared his mentor's passion for science and natural history, and he, too, aspired to public office, which he believed would "lead to the highest honours in a free state, and . . . would be of the greatest utility to the community in an infant one." All in all, Jefferson had good reason to rejoice in the prospects of Tom Randolph, who was not only the presumptive heir to Tuckahoe but also a young man whose "talents, dispositions, connections and fortune were such," he confessed, "as would have made him my own first choice."[7]

But even if Patsy's choice elated Jefferson, why did he encourage his daughter to wed so quickly? The fact that Tom was twenty-one and Patsy only seventeen—a young age for marrying even by the standards of the time—makes their extremely brief one-month engagement all the more striking. Virginia weddings usually took place in the bride's father's house, and participants in the ceremony did not require special clothing. The bride, for instance, usually wore her best dress, but she did not invariably dress in white or any other specific color. Aside from engaging the services of a clergyman, planning for a wedding and reception was no more time consuming than for any other genteel social gathering. But most young couples still wisely spent months courting and getting to know each other before taking their vows, and wary parents could delay their children's nuptials by withholding their financial support in the form of a marriage settlement. Jefferson, by contrast, did everything possible to expedite the negotiations, though, in a time and place where divorce was not an option, Patsy and Tom's decision to wed was effectively irrevocable.[8]

Tom's mother, Ann Cary Randolph, addressed this issue in September 1788 when her sixteen-year-old daughter, Judith, became romantically entangled with her kinsman Richard Randolph, who was himself only eighteen years old. Ann Cary Randolph attempted to prolong their courtship because, as she explained to Richard's stepfather, St. George Tucker, she hoped to prevent her daughters from marrying "'till they were old enough to form a proper judgment of Mankind, well knowing that a Woman's happiness depends intirely on the Husband she is united to" because both law and custom rendered wives dependent on and subservient to their spouses. Although any decision to wed was fraught with peril, she noted, "the risk

. . . is doubled when they marry very young" because "young people cannot have a sufficient knowledge of the World to teach them the necessity of making a proper allowance for the foibles . . . of Humanity," and "when the delirium of love is over, and Reason is allowed to reascend her Throne . . . if they are not so happy, as to find in each other a similarity of Temper, and good qualities enough to excite esteem and Friendship, they must be wretched without a remedy."[9]

The death of Ann Cary Randolph the following March removed the main impediment to her young daughter's marriage, and on the last day of 1789, Judith and Richard celebrated their nuptials at Tuckahoe. Tom Randolph certainly attended his sister's wedding, and maybe Patsy was also there. Indeed, the event probably inspired either Tom or Patsy—or maybe both—to consider marrying themselves, because they were soon engaged. If Martha Wayles Skelton Jefferson had lived, she might have echoed Ann Cary Randolph's concerns about her daughter marrying so young. By contrast, on learning his son's intentions, the elder Thomas Mann Randolph, who was the widowed father of seven unmarried children, expressed his "singular pleasure" and his preference for a brief engagement. Patsy's father's concurred, enthusiastically accepting a February wedding date, though he recognized that marriage was serious business and that his daughter's happiness would thenceforth depend—as he put it—"on the continuing to please a single person," namely her new husband.[10]

Well aware of the gravity of the marital commitment, Jefferson nonetheless did not encourage Patsy to delay her nuptials as he had pressed her to put off her decision to join the convent a few years earlier. Jefferson's response to this new, life-changing proposal was dramatically different because, while he did not want his daughter to become a nun, he most certainly did want her to marry, and considering his belief that the odds were good that she would marry a "blockhead," he must have concluded that Tom was a far better mate for Patsy than anyone she would meet at Eppington. Approving Patsy's choice and perhaps fearing that either moving her to Eppington would jeopardize her relationship with Tom or, conversely, that youthful passion would lead them to premarital indiscretions, Jefferson determined to see his daughter happily and safely settled before he left Virginia. He may have also viewed Tom as someone who could help manage his property, as well as his family, while he was away on government business. Finally, some scholars have interpreted Patsy's desire to wed quickly—and her father's acquiescence—as an attempt to distance her from his relationship with Sally Hemings, who by then was visibly pregnant. In sum, though Jefferson's willingness to allow Patsy to marry in haste might seem foolhardy or even negligent in retrospect, there were many reasons for him to consent to the couple's plan to wed in early 1790.[11]

Jefferson took the lead in orchestrating the negotiations that typically preceded weddings among the eighteenth-century Virginia gentry. In early February, informing the elder Thomas Mann Randolph that his departure for New York was imminent, he urged his old friend to come to Monticello soon so they could formalize the necessary transfer of land and slaves to Patsy and Tom. Despite his complaints of gout and other ailments, by 21 February, Randolph had arrived at Monticello.[12]

That day, the fathers formally gave their children title to the land and slaves that they hoped would afford them the financial wherewithal they needed to embark on married life. Randolph, who owned some 14,000 acres in four Virginia counties, along with 366 slaves—but who also had debts to pay and many other unmarried children to provide for—gave his son a 950-acre plantation called Varina in Henrico County "with 40 negroes . . . belonging to the same tract and the stocks and utensils thereto also belonging." Jefferson had fewer children than Randolph, but he, too, had debts and possessed less acreage and fewer slaves than the master of Tuckahoe. He gave Patsy 1,000 acres in Bedford County, which was part of the estate he called Poplar Forest, along with five families of enslaved people who currently resided there and one additional family of seven who would have to move to Poplar Forest from Monticello. Patsy also received "all the stock of work horses, cattle, hogs and sheep and the plantation utensils" on the Bedford County tract. By virtue of her father's contract, Patsy owned this property, but once she married, the common-law rule of coverture vested control of it in her husband.[13]

On Tuesday, 23 February 1790, Patsy Jefferson and Tom Randolph were married at Monticello. The only surviving evidence of their wedding is a brief entry in an account book kept by the bride's father: "My daughter Martha is this day married to Thos. Mann Randolph junr." Jefferson also recorded having paid the local Episcopal minister, the Reverend Matthew Maury, a fee of £4.16 for officiating at his daughter's nuptials. The wedding ritual, a passage to adulthood, initiated the transformation of "Patsy" into "Martha." Now Jefferson referred to his daughter either as "my daughter Randolph" or by her formal given name in his letters to those outside the family, and though he still sometimes addressed her by her childhood nickname, he gradually came to call her "Martha." At least initially, Tom Randolph spoke of his wife as "Patsy," while she, following the conventions of the time, referred to him as "Mr. Randolph." Outside the family, Patsy was now known as either "Martha" or "Mrs. Randolph."[14]

Like most newly married gentry, the Randolphs undertook a round of visits to various family members to cement new bonds of kinship and to ease their entry into the demands of life as independent adults in their own household. Jefferson accompanied his daughter and her new husband as far as Richmond before heading northward to New York. The first letter he addressed to her as a married woman indicates that Martha enjoyed her first months of married life. Jefferson, as usual, missed his daughter, but he admitted that it was "a circumstance of consolation to know that you are happier; and to see a prospect of it's continuance in the prudence and even temper of both Mr. Randolph and yourself." After Jefferson's departure, the newlyweds continued their trip, visiting aunts and uncles on both sides of the family, before depositing Polly at Eppington. Martha, too, stayed at Eppington until Tom prepared the small house at Varina for her eventual arrival.[15]

During their first year of marriage, Martha and Tom dealt with issues of property and family that would profoundly shape their future lives. As an aspiring planter couple, their most basic concerns involved where they would live, what crops they would grow, and the extent to which they would depend on enslaved labor. These discussions almost inevitably forced the newlyweds to make tough choices about their family loyalties. Nominal Randolphs, they nonetheless gravitated toward Jefferson, in part due to Martha's utter devotion to her father but also as a result of tensions and changes within the Tuckahoe family.

At least initially, both Tom and his father expected the young Randolphs to live at Varina, which was near Tuckahoe, and Jefferson probably shared that assumption because daughters ordinarily left home when they married and joined their husbands' families. Patriarchal traditions—such as the custom of a woman taking her husband's surname—and the entrenchment of a legal system that essentially deemed a wife her husband's chattel encouraged this phenomenon, as did the general preference for passing land from father to son while giving daughters moveable assets such as slaves and livestock. Yet Martha was devoted to her father, and Tom's rapport with Jefferson was warmer than his relationship with his own father. These factors complicated the related issues of Tom's career and the couple's future place of residence.[16]

Jefferson approved of his son-in-law's plan to study law even as he gave "a good degree of attention to the farm," because he believed these pursuits

Thomas Mann Randolph Jr. This unsigned and undated portrait is the only known image of the man who married Martha Jefferson at Monticello in 1790. Tom Randolph came from a large family with deep roots in Virginia and long-standing ties to Thomas Jefferson, who enthusiastically approved his daughter's choice. Virginia Historical Society (2007.5.31).

were complementary. As early as 1787, Tom had decided to study law, and Jefferson recommended that he take at least one year of formal instruction in Williamsburg with his own former mentor, George Wythe, one of the leading jurists in Virginia. When Tom came home from Edinburgh in 1788, however, he did not pursue that plan. Although in the months after he married Martha he reiterated his commitment to "the study of the law, and the attempt to acquire Political knowledge," both he and Jefferson recognized that his changed circumstances meant that his studies would have to be informal and combined with managing a plantation. Jefferson encouraged Tom, averring that legal knowledge "qualifies a man to be useful to himself, his neighbors, and to the public." In his opinion, the law also constituted "the most certain stepping stone to preferment in the political line."[17]

More difficult was the question of where the young couple would reside. This subject gave rise to complex negotiations between Martha, Tom, and their fathers. These exchanges in some ways set a precedent for Jefferson's well-intended but nonetheless invasive involvement in the couple's married life, which Martha sometimes encouraged and Tom accepted to varying degrees.

Months after their nuptials, as Tom commenced farming at Varina, Martha cautiously expressed a desire to live nearer to Monticello. In this first major disagreement with her husband, she did not openly dispute his authority or question his judgment. Instead, in April 1790, she carefully explained her dilemma to her father in terms that seemed to pit her devotion to him—without whose company her happiness, she declared, "can never be compleat"—against her commitment to please Tom "in every *thing* and . . . consider all objects as secondary to that *except* my love for you."[18]

Although she did not explicitly seek her father's intervention, Martha surmised that he, too, wanted her to settle somewhere in Albemarle, and she shrewdly initiated the discussion whereby she hoped that he would try to make that happen. In fact, on 26 April 1790, the day after Martha wrote the letter in which she expressed her reluctance to move to Henrico, Jefferson penned a letter to her in which he anticipated her distress and gently lobbied against her removal to Varina. "I hope Mr. Randolph's idea of settling near Monticello will gain strength," he wrote. That "idea" really originated not with Tom but, rather, with Jefferson, who now told his daughter that he hoped that she and Tom would delay settling anywhere until they found someplace suitable near Monticello. Specifically, Jefferson suggested that Tom ask his father to sell him a section of Edgehill, a desirable Randolph property located on the Rivanna River a few miles east of Monticello.[19]

Knowledge that Martha's wishes coincided with his own gave Jefferson all the incentive he needed to spearhead an effort to secure Edgehill for his son-in-law. He not only missed his daughter, but he also believed that Monticello and its vicinity were much healthier than most other places. At least one European visitor agreed with him on that point. Isaac Weld, an Irish traveler who toured North America in the 1790s, believed that Albemarle's climate was "equal . . . to that of any part of the United States" and especially notable, even in the hottest months, for a "freshness and elasticity in the air unknown in the low country" of Virginia. Weld praised the "healthy ruddy appearance" of the area's inhabitants, particularly the "females," whom he contrasted with the "pale, sickly, debilitated beings" he found elsewhere in the state.[20]

Jefferson was meddling, but he did so with Martha's encouragement and without serious opposition from Tom. The Randolphs spent much of the late spring and summer at Varina, but the fact that Tom suffered "excessive torture" from the heat there, even in May, probably made him more receptive to his father-in-law's suggestions that he abandon Henrico for a more healthful climate. By the end of May, uncomfortable weather, Martha's prodding, or Jefferson's letter—or possibly all three—led Tom to conclude that it was time to move. "We find that it will be necessary for us to fix on some other part of the country in which to pursue our plan of retirement and domestic Industry," he wrote to his father-in-law, adding, "No situation in America has so many allurements for us as Albemarle." At this point, Tom was still intent on continuing his studies. He hoped to purchase "a small farm . . . of 100 acres," which would be less likely than a large plantation to monopolize his time while he read law and perhaps ran for office in Albemarle, where his connection to Jefferson would help him attain his goal of entering public life. In July, however, Jefferson sought a much larger tract of land for his son-in-law when he asked Thomas Mann Randolph of Tuckahoe to sell part of Edgehill, which Tom would pay for with the profits from the plantation at Varina.[21]

In the protracted negotiations that followed, Jefferson frequently advised his son-in-law and sometimes spoke for him. He broached the subject of Edgehill not only with the elder Randolph but also with his friend Colonel John Harvie, another prospective buyer whose teenage daughter was destined to become the forty-nine-year-old Randolph's second wife in September 1790. That fall, Jefferson went to Tuckahoe to negotiate the purchase of 1,600 acres at Edgehill on his son-in-law's behalf. Though the elder Randolph initially accepted an offer of $1,700 to be paid in three installments, he then changed his mind and raised the price to $2,000. By late October, father and son had exchanged angry letters. Tom soon apologized to his father, however, and explained that his awkward attempt to buy Edgehill had been fueled by both Jefferson's encouragement and his own "desire to gratify Patsy."[22]

The impending marriage of the widowed Randolph to a much younger woman, however, further alienated his son and helped solidify his allegiance to Jefferson and to Albemarle. Both Tom and Martha worried about the consequences of Randolph's union with Gabriella Harvie, who would certainly bear children who would compete with Tom and his nine siblings for shares of an already debt-ridden estate. Jefferson, who knew the pain of losing a spouse but who, of course, had not remarried, defended his old friend, who, he maintained, "cannot live alone." Jefferson counseled his daughter and son-in-law to maintain cordial relations with that "excellent good man" and his "lady," even as he worked to move the young couple from Varina to Albemarle.[23]

The Randolphs' inability to come to terms on the issue of Edgehill, combined with Martha and Tom's growing desire to live in Albemarle, delayed the establishment of the couple's own separate household. They resided at Varina for several months before accepting Jefferson's invitation for them and Polly to "pass three or four weeks" with him at Monticello when he returned from New York that September. Perhaps because Martha was by then about four months pregnant, however, she and Tom stayed at Monticello, where the neighbors were familiar and the climate was healthful, when Jefferson resumed his official duties that November in Philadelphia, the nation's new temporary capital. Jefferson asked his friend and neighbor Nicholas Lewis, who oversaw his Albemarle farms during his absence, to provide "Mr. Randolph and my daughters" with "whatever the plantation will furnish, to wit, corn, fodder, wheat, what beeves there may be, shoats, milch cows, fire-wood to be cut by the plantation negroes, and brought in by the mule-cart or ox-cart." The Randolphs were to have nine "house-servants," including Ursula, who had nursed the infant Patsy Jefferson, and Sally Hemings and her sister Critta. As a prelude to a much larger renovation and expansion of the original house, Jefferson also ordered the construction of a washhouse, two "meat-houses," and a stable, as well as the repair of "fences which inclose the house, garden and orchard . . . and a partition fence run between the yard and the garden as formerly."[24]

By March 1791, the elder Thomas Mann Randolph was willing to sell Edgehill, but now Tom hesitated, due to his economic (and perhaps moral) qualms about increasing his reliance on slave labor. Reiterating his desire to obtain only a "small tract, just sufficient to supply me with provisions," Tom expressed concerns he shared with other Virginia planters as tobacco markets declined in the postrevolutionary era. "If my circumstances admitted of [buying the property] with the greatest of ease, still my aversion to increase the number of my negroes would be an insurmountable objection," he observed in a letter to his father-in-law. "My desire to gratify my Father would induce me to attempt it," he explained, "if there was a prospect of my making myself whole, without employing slaves in the cultivation of the lands." Perhaps Martha, who had declared her desire to see "the poor negroes . . . all freed" just a few years earlier, influenced her husband's thinking. In any event, Tom informed his father-in-law that she approved of his plan to engage in agriculture on a smaller scale so that he could reduce his use of enslaved labor.[25]

Tom's misgivings were emblematic of a trend among liberal-minded Virginians who questioned slavery, for the most part tentatively, in the postrevolutionary era. The libertarian ideals of the Revolution helped lead to the enactment of a statute in 1782 that allowed slaveholders to emancipate their bondpeople. Some did, but many more, like Jefferson, were more ambivalent about the future of slavery. In the end, on 1 January 1792, Tom overcame his reservations and agreed to pay his father $2,000 for 1,523 acres and the enslaved families that resided on them. Jefferson congratulated him on acquiring "a fine tract of land [that] will make you happier by furnishing a pleasing occupation."[26]

As it turned out, Tom's plan to diminish his reliance on enslaved workers never caught on in Albemarle. Although the tax lists indicate that he operated Edgehill with relatively few slaves for the first three years after he acquired the property, by 1795, he had 21 enslaved people over age twelve listed as his property on the Albemarle County tax rolls. Four years later, that number had risen to 38, making Tom Randolph one of the county's largest slaveholders. Overall, Albemarle's enslaved population grew, both in absolute terms and as a proportion of the total, in the coming decades. In 1790, 5,579 slaves accounted for 44 percent of Albemarle's inhabitants; the county's 9,226 enslaved people constituted a majority of the county's population in 1810.[27]

Because Tom's new Albemarle plantation had no habitable house, the Randolphs continued to reside at Monticello. Tom planted crops at Edgehill and occasionally went to Varina and to Richmond, where he marketed his produce and Jefferson's, too. He also became an asset to his father-in-law at

Monticello. Along with George Washington, who had made the switch years earlier at Mount Vernon, Tom persuaded Jefferson to abandon tobacco for wheat because the latter was more dependably profitable (though years later Martha claimed that her father changed crops because tobacco cultivation "was such hard work for the negroes"). At Jefferson's behest, Tom also kept daily meteorological data, a practice the older man had begun years earlier. He planted peach trees as part of an experiment to support Jefferson's notion that "5 acres of peach trees at 21 feet apart will furnish dead wood enough to supply a fire place through the winter, and may be kept up at the trouble of only planting about 70 peach stones a year." Jefferson also encouraged Tom's less practical "researches into the Opossum."[28]

Both Tom and Martha were busy but seemingly content. Tom never complained about the many tasks he performed for Jefferson, all of which took time away from his own plantation work and compromised any serious effort to continue his legal studies. Meanwhile, Martha plunged into the work of housewifery at Monticello, despite her lack of preparation for such a massive undertaking. Besides performing domestic work themselves, plantation mistresses supervised corps of domestic servants who scrubbed, laundered, sewed, and cooked. They also ran dairies, raised poultry, and grew vegetables, fruits, and herbs in household gardens. Perhaps most important, they were responsible for—as one of her Randolph sisters-in-law would later put it—"the grand arcanum of management."[29]

Martha had only dim memories of her mother as mistress of Monticello, and because she had lived mainly in cities since she was ten years old, she had no rural domestic role models. Jefferson initially expected both of his daughters to live at Eppington, where their aunt Elizabeth Eppes could teach them the useful domestic skills they would require to be successful plantation mistresses, but Patsy's decision to marry so soon after her return to Virginia scuttled that plan. Not long after the wedding, Patsy received a popular French cookbook, *La Cuisinière Bourgeoisie*, as a gift from her father, along with a parcel of cloth and patterns to make clothing for her three housemaids. Years later, Martha remembered that she learned by doing, attaining the "arts of housewifery with pain & difficulty, by untiring perseverance, so soon as she was placed in a situation which rendered a knowledge of them essential for the comfort of others."[30]

By mid-January 1791, Martha was sorting china, counting spoons, and otherwise preparing Monticello to become once again a fully functioning household. Though often barely visible, a woman's domestic work and stewardship was vital to the economic well-being of her family, and Martha knew it. "I have wrought an entire reformation," she wrote proudly to her father. "Nothing comes in or goes out without my knowledge and I believe there is as little waste as possible." The new mistress of Monticello visited the kitchen, smokehouse, and chicken coops "when weather permits." She also oversaw the butchering of livestock. She planted some seeds and wrote to her father to request others. In addition, she attended to the education of her sister, Polly, who stayed with her at Monticello. Martha was so busy that she had no time to read or to play her harpsichord when it eventually arrived from France. At the time, she was eight months pregnant and planning for the arrival of her first child. Her daughter was born a month prematurely on 23 January 1791.[31]

❖ Motherhood was the defining feature of Martha Jefferson Randolph's adult life, and family relationships dominated her comparatively insular world, as they did for most rural women of her time. Her children, husband, father, sister, aunts, and cousins, along with the Hemingses and other longtime house servants who constituted—in Tom's words—the "colored part of the family" (some of whom were actually blood relations), were familiar faces whose continuing presence remained important throughout her adult life. At the same time, marriage vastly expanded Martha's circle of kin to include the Randolphs. Tom had two brothers and seven sisters. His oldest sister, Mary, was ten years older than her new sister-in-law, while the youngest, Virginia, was fourteen years younger. These Randolph women became Martha's companions, with whom she exchanged visits and letters. Two of the sisters, Virginia and Nancy, lived for a time with her and Tom, and others visited frequently.[32]

The centrality of family and especially of female kin and friends was evident during the transformative months surrounding the birth of the Randolphs' first child. Because Martha's own mother was deceased and her only sister was young and inexperienced, other older women stepped in to assist the expectant mother in the final stage of pregnancy. By early January, Elizabeth Eppes had invited both of her nieces to stay with her for the month of February, but the sisters remained at Monticello, where the anticipated arrival of Tom's aunt, Mary Randolph Fleming, seemed to make the journey to Eppington unnecessary. As it turned out, Martha went into labor about five weeks early while Tom was away in Goochland County fetching his aunt. In her absence, Martha turned to Mary Walker Lewis, a neighbor who was a mother of twelve children and also an experienced nurse who had tended wounded soldiers on both sides during the Revolutionary War.

A somewhat chagrined Tom Randolph reported to his father-in-law that Lewis's "attention and tender concern supplied the place of Mrs. Fleming and made some amends for the want of my Sympathy" during his wife's ordeal.[33]

Martha continued to rely primarily on female assistance and support even after Tom returned to Monticello. Mary Fleming stayed while she recuperated and began to nurse her infant. Mary Lewis, who visited often, became friendly with Martha and offered her advice. Although Tom optimistically reported that "during the whole of her confinement, she has scarcely felt the smallest indisposition," Martha suffered occasionally from fever and other symptoms that were worrisome, especially in view of her own mother's tragic experiences with childbirth and its aftermath. Fleming and Lewis, along with other women, oversaw the new mother's recovery and helped her care for her infant until she could do so on her own. Child care was women's work. By mid-March, however, Tom was praising "Patsy's plan of nurture" and informing his anxious father-in-law that the baby was thriving and that the new mother was in good health.[34]

The infant remained nameless for more than two months because her parents wanted Jefferson to choose her name, and Tom's letter containing that request and Jefferson's response traveled slowly between Albemarle and Philadelphia. Jefferson gracefully accepted this honor, proposing the name Anne, which he surmised was "very dear" to his son-in-law (because it had been his mother's) and belonged "also to Patsy's family on both sides." The parents added the middle name Cary to make the commemoration of Tom's late mother more explicit. Anne Cary Randolph got her name from her father's family and blue eyes and fair skin from her mother's.[35]

Both before and after her confinement, Martha depended on female kin and some close friends for companionship and for help as she worked to establish a viable plantation household. Jefferson himself recognized how important Polly's continued presence would be for Martha when he delayed his younger daughter's departure, though she eventually resumed her schooling in Philadelphia in late 1791. In the meantime, tutoring Polly was work for Martha, but Polly also helped with the housekeeping, assisted by Tom's youngest sister, Virginia (known as Jenny), who lived more or less full time at Monticello after her father's new wife took over Tuckahoe in September 1790. Polly and Jenny were also company for Martha when Tom went to Varina or Richmond to attend to business or to Tuckahoe to see his family.[36]

Other short- and long-term guests, most of whom were female, completed the social circle during Martha's first years as mistress of Monticello. In the months between the birth of Anne in January and Jefferson's return from Philadelphia in mid-September, Martha's guests included another Randolph sister, Nancy, her aunt Mary Jefferson Bolling, and James Monroe's "charming wife" Elizabeth Kortright Monroe, who stayed at Monticello while her husband was in Williamsburg. Nancy Randolph came to Monticello again in the spring of 1792, as did Jefferson's widowed sister Martha Jefferson Carr and her daughter Jane, who shared Patsy's enthusiasm for gardening. These women helped their hostess care for her toddler daughter and six-year-old Jenny Randolph while Martha progressed through her second pregnancy and suffered through an unusually hot Virginia summer. The Carrs were still there when the Randolphs' second child, Thomas Jefferson Randolph, was born in September, and they stayed for some time thereafter.[37]

In the early years of her marriage, Martha forged close ties to most of her Randolph sisters-in-law and with them became enmeshed in their family's growing personal and financial problems. Neither she nor Tom was pleased when his father wed Gabriella Harvie, in part because they worried that the marriage would produce offspring whose claims would diminish the property inherited by the ten existing Randolph siblings. As the eldest son, Tom himself had expected to inherit Tuckahoe, the family seat, and when she married Tom, Martha probably had envisioned herself as the eventual mistress of that fine and venerable estate. As it turned out, the elder Randolph's second marriage, indeed, had far-reaching consequences for Martha and her husband. The entrenchment of Gabriella Harvie Randolph as the new mistress of Tuckahoe led to an exodus of unmarried Randolph daughters from their childhood home. Martha and Tom became, in effect, surrogate parents for Jenny, who was only four years old when her father remarried. More serious still, in 1792 Gabriella gave birth to a son, yet another Thomas Mann Randolph (later known as Mann), who supplanted his older half-brother as heir to Tuckahoe.[38]

As the economic and emotional consequences of Thomas Mann Randolph's second marriage unfolded, scandal and discord engulfed his offspring. The ensuing drama centered primarily on Nancy Randolph, who resided mainly with her sister Judith and her husband Richard Randolph on a Cumberland County plantation named Bizarre. In October 1792, Judith, Richard, and Nancy traversed the county to visit their cousins Mary and Randolph Harrison, a young couple with whom they socialized frequently. After everyone retired for the evening, loud screams awakened the Harri-

Tuckahoe. Tom Randolph believed that he would inherit this riverfront mansion that had been his childhood home, and perhaps Patsy imagined herself the future mistress of the elegant house, which had been built by Tom's grandfather in the 1730s. Not long after they married, however, Tom lost Tuckahoe to an infant half-brother, and his father's death made Patsy's husband, as the eldest son, in large part responsible for his family's financial problems. Photograph by the author.

sons, who found Nancy ill in her room, with Richard at her bedside. A day or two later, an unnamed slave woman told the Harrisons that Nancy had miscarried or delivered a child whose discarded body some slaves found hidden in a remote spot on their plantation. Although both the Harrisons and the Randolphs stoically ignored the slaves' gossip, many people came to believe that Nancy had, indeed, been pregnant, that Richard was the father of her unborn infant, and that he helped her either to abort the fetus or to murder a newborn child.[39]

Tom Randolph and his brothers certainly blamed Richard for the scandal that impugned their family honor, jeopardized their sister's reputation and future happiness, and threatened to make the disgraced and unmarried Nancy perpetually dependent on her already financially troubled family. Of Nancy's brothers, William was among Richard's most vocal critics, and when the Randolphs of Bizarre visited Tuckahoe in mid-March, he confronted Richard, who, in turn, challenged him to a duel. William did not accept the challenge, which would have been tantamount to acknowledging his brother-in-law as his equal and as a man of honor. For his part, Tom sent Richard an angry letter in which he threatened to "wash out with your blood the stain on my family" if he did not admit his culpability. The brothers did not publicly concede that Nancy was pregnant, seeking to protect their sister by holding Richard alone accountable for the rumors about her alleged misconduct while she resided at Bizarre.[40]

Martha was close to both Nancy and Judith. Nancy had visited her and Tom at Monticello. Judith had exchanged letters with her when she was a student in Paris. Judith and Martha had married within two months of each other; both soon experienced pregnancy and motherhood, as well as the problems of overseeing complex but poorly financed plantation households. These common experiences provided a basis for friendship. Although Martha rarely left Monticello, she made three extended visits to Bizarre in the early 1790s, including a three-month stay there with Tom in the snowy winter of 1791–92 when Judith was pregnant with her first child, and when both Nancy and Richard's sickly brother Theo (who, years later, Nancy claimed was the father of her stillborn infant) were also living at Bizarre.[41]

Martha made another social visit to Bizarre with Tom and his sister Jane in October 1792, not long after Judith, Richard, and Nancy returned from their fateful stay at the Harrisons' home. As a result, Martha was at Bizarre in late October when Randolph Harrison informed the family there that his slaves were still gossiping about Nancy and the tiny corpse they had found hidden among a pile of shingles on his plantation. Although no one else, including Harrison, had seen the body, the atmosphere at Bizarre was tense as it became increasingly clear that the slaves' story was spreading among the county's white inhabitants. Martha stayed with her friends at least until mid-November. In the coming months, relations among the Randolphs became strained, and popular outcry forced the authorities to take a stand in Cumberland.[42]

Although Martha for the most part watched in silent horror as her in-laws fought among themselves, she was forced to play an active role in the formal judicial resolution of the scandal at Bizarre. Martha was at Monticello when the crisis came to a head in April 1793. On Thursday, 18 April, at least partly in response to public pressure, two Cumberland County magistrates ordered the sheriff to arrest both Richard and Nancy. Although the authorities could not find Nancy, who was in Chesterfield County with Judith,

Richard surrendered himself and was taken into custody. The next day, the magistrates summoned eight "material witnesses" to "give such evidence as they know" about Richard's alleged misconduct. Martha was one of these witnesses, though the fact that the magistrates charged Richard just three days after issuing their summons (which had to travel some forty miles to reach Martha in Albemarle) suggests that they did so before hearing her testimony.[43]

On 22 April, three justices convened at the Cumberland County courthouse and charged Richard with "feloniously murdering a child delivered of the body of Nancy Randolph or [being] accessory to the same." A week later, he was to appear before the examining court, which was a tribunal of justices charged with deciding whether there was sufficient evidence to indict him for murder, a capital offense. The witnesses' testimony and the outcome of Richard's case would determine whether the authorities would attempt to prosecute Nancy for infanticide, which was also punishable by death.[44]

Eighteenth-century Virginia court records generally included neither transcripts of court proceedings nor summaries of witnesses' testimony, but one of Richard's attorneys, the future Supreme Court justice John Marshall, took extensive notes on the statements made by seventeen witnesses interviewed by the defense. Four of the men the defense called claimed they "knew nothing of the matter." Of the remaining thirteen deponents, seven women gave evidence that was overall more substantive because all were married women who had personal experience with pregnancy, childbirth, and related concerns, and most knew something about the use of medicinal herbs for matters related to pregnancy, abortion, and menstruation. While Tom and Martha's extended visits to Bizarre had given them both ample opportunity to observe the relationship between Richard and Nancy, the authorities sought only Martha's testimony because they believed that her insights might help them to determine whether Nancy was pregnant and, if so, what medicines she had ingested. Accordingly, the focus of Martha's testimony was not the alleged sexual liaison between Richard and Nancy but, rather, the more specific matter of Nancy's physical condition and whether she had attempted to terminate an illicit pregnancy.[45]

At issue was the medicine Nancy took to ease her pain when she was visiting the Harrisons. Randolph Harrison believed that she had used "essence of peppermint, which she had been accustomed to take for cholic." His wife, Mary, however, claimed that Nancy took gum guaiacum, and Martha buttressed Mary's testimony by stating that she herself had supplied Nancy, at her request, with gum guaiacum a few weeks earlier. In her deposition, Martha admitted that she suspected that Nancy was pregnant, and she described gum guaiacum as "an excellent medicine for the cholic, but . . . at the same time . . . a dangerous medicine, as it would produce an abortion." In fact, this medicinal herb was used primarily to treat rheumatism, and some experts explicitly warned that it could either cause or aggravate stomach and intestinal ailments, such as colic.[46]

Was Martha simply ill-informed, or did she purposefully seek to give Nancy a plausible excuse for claiming to have used gum guaiacum to relieve the pains in her stomach? This herbal medicine probably was not an especially effective abortifacient, but gum guaiacum was nevertheless one of the plants women sometimes used to stimulate menstruation and thus potentially to terminate a pregnancy. Although male physicians tended to be vague or evasive on the topics of abortion and birth control—neither of which were illegal—one observed that "several physicians have apprehended mischief from the use of the guaiacum in a spirituous tincture."[47]

Martha left no written record of her impressions of John Marshall, his more famous cocounsel Patrick Henry, the magistrates, or the crowded courtroom, where she herself—as the daughter of a former governor and the current secretary of state—must have been among the star attractions. Nor did she comment on others' testimony about a flirtation—or maybe more—between Nancy and Richard, or about what some perceived as the changing dimensions of Nancy's body and the blood that stained her bedclothes as she writhed in pain that night at the Harrisons' home. Martha did, however, remark on the court's finding "that the said Richard Randolph is not guilty of the felony wherewith he stands charged." Though her cousin John Wayles Eppes believed that the court's verdict vindicated Richard and Nancy and put the matter to rest, Martha disagreed. As she observed perceptively in a letter to her father, Richard (and, by extension, Nancy) was "*tried* and acquitted tho I am sorry to say his Lawers gained more honour by it than they did, as but a small part of the world and those more inconsiderable people in it were influenced in there opinion by the dicision of the court."[48]

Martha's observation proved prescient. Shortly after the court's ruling, she reported that the "divisions of the family encrease daily," despite Tom's attempts to rally his siblings around Nancy and restore peace. Martha herself followed her father's advice, showing affection toward Nancy, whom he deemed "the pitiable victim . . . of error or of slander," in keeping with the prevailing gender stereotypes of the era that cast genteel white women as weak and vulnerable. But Nancy persisted in her loyalty toward Richard, a man her closest kin maligned as a "vile seducer." Nancy returned to Bizarre, where she lived in comparative isolation with Judith and Richard, whose relationship predictably deteriorated, in part because of the persistent aura of scandal that surrounded their household. All three of the scandal's principals suffered long-term consequences. Nancy's reputation was forever tainted, as was that of Richard, who died at Bizarre in 1796 at age twenty-six. Judith spent an embittered and comparatively impoverished widowhood fulfilling the terms of her husband's will, which mandated that his debts be paid and then his slaves emancipated and given lands in neighboring Prince Edward County, an objective she finally attained in 1807.[49]

Despite their earlier intimacy with Judith and Richard, Martha and Tom did not visit Bizarre after 1793. Martha worried—unnecessarily, as it turned out—that the scandal at Bizarre would reflect badly on her own branch of the Randolph family. "I am too sensible of the illiberality of extending to one person the infamy of an other, to fear one moment that it can reflect any real disgrace on me in the eyes of people of sense," she declared, "yet the generality of mankind are weak enough to think otherwise and it is painful to an excess to be obliged to blush for so near a connection." Tom and his brothers remained estranged from their unrepentant brother-in-law. After Richard died, the continued taint of scandal, Judith's hostility and unceasing pathos, and the demands of Martha's own growing family deterred her from making the trip to Cumberland.[50]

But as the scandal and its consequences distanced Martha and Tom from certain members of his family, the unexpected death of the elder Thomas Mann Randolph in November 1793 embroiled Martha's husband, as the eldest brother, in a protracted effort to protect the material interests of his younger siblings. Appointed coexecutor of his father's estate with his brother William, Tom immersed himself in settling the complicated and precarious finances of the deceased, who, despite his prestigious lineage and his vast holdings in land and slaves, was, like many postrevolutionary Virginia planters, deeply in debt. While Tom had received his portion of his father's property in land and slaves at the time of his marriage, like each of his brothers, who also received a share of his father's property, he inherited a portion of roughly $64,000 in unpaid debts. The Randolph sisters were each to receive $6,000 from their father's estate. Their half-brother, the infant Thomas Mann Randolph III, inherited the family seat at Tuckahoe. Although Tom considered the executorship "an invidious, dangerous, and difficult" job, he accepted it to protect the interests of his younger siblings for whom he now felt keenly responsible.[51]

By then, Martha was pregnant with her third child and anticipating her father's full-time return to what he liked to call the "blessings of domestic society." Jefferson resigned his position as secretary of state when it became clear to him that President Washington consistently favored both the fiscal and foreign policies of his archrival, Secretary of the Treasury Alexander Hamilton. Jefferson had been at Monticello in September, seeking relief from politics and also from the yellow fever that ravaged Philadelphia. When he returned to the capital in November, he left Polly with the Randolphs, thereby ending her formal education. Jefferson resigned his post effective 31 December 1793. Five days later, he began his eleven-day journey southward to Monticello.[52]

Between 1794 and 1797, the Randolphs divided their time between Monticello and Varina. Although Jefferson wanted them to stay at Monticello, Tom had the Varina plantation to oversee in Henrico, and in 1796 Jefferson began to demolish his house, which was the first step in its much-anticipated renovation and redesigning on a much grander scale. Martha spent most of 1794 at Varina, but she was at Monticello when she gave birth to a daughter, Ellen Wayles Randolph, that September. Most years, the Randolphs spent the summer months with Jefferson, trading Henrico's uncomfortable climate for the more wholesome air of Albemarle. In June 1796, they were at Monticello to see the Duc de La Rochefoucauld Liancourt, who had known Jefferson and his daughters in Paris. The Frenchman, who fled his country as its revolution became increasingly violent, described the now-grown-up Martha and her sister as "handsome, modest, and amiable women" and noted the cordial relationship between Jefferson and Tom Randolph, who seemed "to be more his son than his son-in-law."[53]

The Randolphs' long-term plan was to build a house at Edgehill, and Tom sought to become active in the public life of his adopted county, as befitted his status as the son-in-law of its most prominent citizen and one of its largest landowners in his own right. In April 1794, Tom obtained an appointment as justice of the peace, an office that had signified gentry status in Virginia's county communities since the colonial era. He also applied for and received a captain's commission in the county militia, despite his self-professed ignorance of "the military art." After Jefferson became vice president in March 1797, his reliance on Tom to oversee his plantations led the Randolphs to spend even more time in Albemarle. That spring, with Jefferson's encouragement, Tom ran for the state legislature, but he lost the election, in part, because he stayed at Varina, where he and Martha nursed their children through the aftermath of smallpox inoculation, rather than return to Albemarle to canvass the voters.[54]

Though the Randolphs spent the first few months of 1797 at Varina, some time that year they decided to live permanently in Albemarle. They spent the spring, summer, and early autumn amid construction debris at Monticello, where Polly married her cousin and childhood playmate John Wayles Eppes in October. Tom retained his property at Varina, but he moved some of its enslaved workforce from Henrico to Albemarle. In November, Martha and Tom moved to Belmont, a farm that belonged to John Harvie, a friend of Jefferson's and the father of Tom's now-widowed stepmother. The family stayed at Belmont until the summer of 1799, when they returned to Monticello. Only in January 1800, after ten years of marriage, did Martha and Tom move into their own modest frame house at Edgehill, a two-story dwelling that measured eighteen feet deep and forty-four feet wide, located a few miles from Jefferson's still-unfinished house.[55]

Thus far, Martha's marriage seems to have been happy, though by no means typical for the times. In the 1790s, many Virginians moved to the southern and western frontiers, but the Randolphs' peripatetic style of living was uncommon. Debt and declining tobacco prices were partly responsible for their frequent movements, as they were for the displacement of so many Virginia planters, but Martha's continuing attachment to her father also profoundly shaped this first formative decade of her married life.

Because surviving family letters from these years include none that Martha and Tom exchanged, it is difficult to gauge how wife and husband interacted or even how they felt about each other. In her letters to her father, Martha expressed admiration for Tom as a loving father and also as a peacemaker among the Randolphs during the crisis at Bizarre. Although she may have disagreed with him occasionally—as in the case of his initial decision to settle at Varina—Martha never criticized her husband, at least in writing. At the same time, however, she openly professed a "Love and Reverence" for her father which was unusual by any standard. As she herself put it in 1798, the "*new* ties" of marriage and motherhood could never "weaken the first & best of nature . . . affection and respect for you and none others . . . have weakened or surpassed them." Jefferson, in turn, claimed that his love for his daughters "knows no bounds."[56]

❖ Despite the drama of the Jefferson-Randolph family saga, in other respects Martha's first decade as a wife, mother, and plantation mistress was fairly representative of the experiences of elite southern women of her era, though probably not at all what she expected when she returned from Paris. Between 1790 and 1800, she bore five children, added another five in the next decade, and then two more in 1814 and 1818. Large families were common in the southern states, where women married young and typically became pregnant every second year thereafter, though infant mortality rates remained high throughout the region. Martha and Tom were unusually fortunate in that only one of their children did not live to adulthood. Martha made the health and well-being of her children her chief preoccupation. As the mistress of a slaveholding family, she had time to devote to her children's nurturing and education in part because enslaved people performed the more routine and menial domestic chores in the Jefferson and Randolph households.[57]

Ever precarious, health pervaded the consciousness and correspondence of Martha's family circle. Virtually every letter she wrote, and most she received, included up-to-date reports on the health of near and sometimes more distant connections. Some letters were written for the sole purpose of conveying information about health or illness. For example, in June 1793, Jefferson wrote and mailed a letter from Philadelphia to his family in Albemarle that contained only eight words of text: "All well, but not a moment to write." Martha's health was generally good; but children were prone to sickness, and Tom's physical condition was a source of frequent anxiety.[58]

Even as a young man, Tom Randolph had suffered from various ailments. Although his sister Judith characterized the Tuckahoe Randolphs, herself included, as "a fanciful and hypochondriac family," as early as 1785 Tom's Scottish tutor had worried that his pupil lacked "the Stamina . . . for those exertions necessary for making the most distinguished figure in life." Aside from the severe skin disorder he suffered from the excessive heat at Varina in the spring of 1790 and a bout of "dysentery" in July 1793, Tom was reasonably healthy during his first years of married life. But in 1794 he was struck by an illness that no physician could identify, though Jefferson thought it might be gout.[59]

Beginning in July 1794, Tom spent nearly two years traveling—sometimes with Martha, sometimes alone—trying to regain his health. Martha and the children stayed at Monticello when he journeyed initially to Boston and New York seeking medical advice and a change of climate. Well aware that the proceeds from Tom's plantations might not fully fund these expensive excursions, Jefferson generously offered his son-in-law the use of his name to obtain additional credit as needed. It is unclear whether Tom was with

Martha when their daughter Ellen was born that September, but in January they were together with their infant at Varina, though their two older children remained at Monticello. The happy grandfather reported to Martha that three-year-old Anne and two-year-old Jefferson were "both well, and have never had even a finger-ache since you left us." He described Anne as a pleasingly "placid" little girl and Jeff as "robust" and prone to "tempests." Jeff resisted wearing shoes and gloves, despite the cold, and he developed a profound fear of dogs, which Jefferson tried to cure by allowing a puppy to live in the house.[60]

By mid-July, Tom was in a "nearly hopeless state" both physically and emotionally, so he, Martha, and nine-month-old Ellen set out for the springs of western Virginia in hopes of improving both his spirits and his health. Known for their healing waters and lively society, these mountain resorts were gathering places for elite southerners who sought to escape the summer heat, enjoy beautiful scenery, drink the springs' medicinal mineral waters, and experience the healthful and sensual effects of therapeutic bathing. Although accommodations were often primitive, men and women flocked to the springs for relief from grief, depression, and physical pain. Jefferson, who took the waters in 1787, believed Virginia's medicinal springs could "relieve rheumatisms" and that "other complaints . . . of very different natures have been removed or lessened by them."[61]

The Randolphs left Albemarle on 15 July 1795, planning to make the town of Staunton in Augusta County their first major stop. Little Ellen died suddenly in Staunton, and her body was sent back to Albemarle to be buried at Monticello. Her distraught parents proceeded, first to Warm Springs in Bath County, where Tom Randolph found no relief, and then northward to Sweet Springs, where he claimed to experience "an almost perfect recovery of his health." By October, after losing one child and being away from the others for more than two months, Martha and Tom returned to Monticello.[62]

During Martha's absence, Tom and his father-in-law exchanged occasional letters full of family and agricultural news, but she apparently wrote no letters at all to Jefferson, who ordinarily expected her to be a faithful and frequent correspondent. Jefferson's memory of his devastation on the deaths of so many of his own children may have deterred him from pressing her to write him. Martha and Tom deeply mourned the loss of their child, though the closest she came to committing her emotions to paper came a few years later when she sent her surviving children off with their father to be inoculated for smallpox. "I never look at them but my eyes fill with tears," she wrote poignantly, "to think how soon we shall part and *perhaps forever.*"[63]

Continuing concerns about Tom's susceptibility to illness and the well-being of her children increased Martha's desire to live near family and in the comparatively healthful climate of Albemarle. In early 1796, only a few months after they returned from the springs, Jefferson observed that his son-in-law's condition was "certainly bad" again. In the summer of 1796, Tom returned to the springs, but this time he went alone, leaving Martha and the children at Monticello. By the end of the summer he appeared to be better, and his condition did not worsen after he left the springs, though his health remained precarious and he continued to suffer intermittently from other relatively minor ailments from time to time.[64]

Although Martha surely worried about her husband's physical condition, she was more directly responsible for her children's health. Jefferson himself considered child care her domain, and Tom seemed to agree, though as a young father he also took a vital interest in his children's health. When Martha gave birth to her first child, Anne, in 1791, Jefferson sent his daughter a childrearing treatise by one of his most trusted authors, the Scottish physician John Gregory, who had also written *A Father's Legacy to His Daughters*, the popular advice manual for young women, which Jefferson also owned. Jefferson believed that Gregory's *Comparative View of the State and Faculties of Man with those of the Animal World* would be "very useful to her in her new character" as a mother, and Martha liked the advice the Scotsman offered. As Tom informed his father-in-law, "Patsy's plan of nurture, when not opposed by [aunt Mary Randolph] Flemings prejudices, has corresponded nearly with Dr. Gregories from the first."[65]

Above all, Gregory, whose book was first published in 1765, was an early advocate of breastfeeding, which he deemed beneficial to mother and child alike. Gregory informed readers that "one half of Mankind die under eight years of age" and that infant mortality was especially high among "the most luxurious part of Mankind" whose diet was rich and "unnatural." Gregory believed—correctly, as it turned out—that breastfeeding was nutritionally best for infants. He also maintained that nursing eased women's recovery from childbirth because a "sudden check given to the great natural evacuation of Milk, at a time when her weakly state renders her unable to sustain so violent a shock, is often of the worst consequence" to a woman who does not breastfeed. In keeping with the Enlightenment notion that social interaction bred human improvement and happiness, Gregory touted the social and emotional benefits of mothers nursing their infants themselves, rather than hiring wet nurses, because doing so fostered the ties of affection between mother and child that were fundamental to human society, though he was less prone to sentimentalizing the mother-child relationship than some other breastfeeding advocates.[66]

By the 1790s, the idea that mother's milk was best was current in Britain and America, promoted not only by conventional Enlightenment figures such as Gregory but also by Mary Wollstonecraft, the feminist author of *A Vindication of the Rights of Woman*. There is evidence that maternal breastfeeding was widespread among elite Virginia women and that some gentry couples recognized that prolonging lactation could curb fertility and enable women to extend the intervals between their pregnancies. In his *Comparative View*, the treatise that Martha owned and read, Gregory advised mothers to nurse their babies for nine to twelve months to limit their pregnancies and thereby preserve their own health. This advice perhaps retrospectively struck a chord in Jefferson, given his wife's debilitation and early death in childbirth. "A Woman who does not nurse, has naturally a Child every year," Gregory advised, but one "who nurses her Child, has an interval of a year and a half or two years betwixt her Children, in which the constitution has time to recover its vigour."[67]

The spacing of Martha's pregnancies suggests that she heeded this advice, but in at least one instance prolonged lactation did not delay her next pregnancy. In October 1796, Martha gave birth to her fourth child, Ellen Wayles Randolph, who was named for her dead sister, and then a fifth, Cornelia Jefferson Randolph, after a comparatively long hiatus in July 1799. In January 1801, Martha, who was still breastfeeding little Cornelia, correctly believed that she was again pregnant, and she gave birth to another daughter, Virginia Jefferson Randolph, in August. After less than eleven years of marriage, at age twenty-nine, Martha had five children to tend, though she enjoyed the assistance of the capable Critta Hemings Colbert, who joined the Randolph household in the mid-1790s.[68]

Martha's repeated and largely successful experiences with childbirth and infant care made her a natural choice to assist her younger sister, Maria, as she experienced motherhood for the first time at Eppington in January 1800. Petite and beautiful like her ill-fated mother, she, too, suffered dreadfully in childbirth and had the added sadness of having her firstborn die within a month. Although a snowstorm delayed Martha's departure from Albemarle, her brother-in-law was genuinely grateful when, in mid-February, "a visit from Patsy and Mr. Randolph . . . revived the drooping little spirits of my poor Mary," who still suffered from fever and a painful inflammation in her breasts, though she was under a physician's constant care. Influenced by Gregory, who believed that postpartum mothers needed exercise and cool air, the Randolphs urged Maria to get out of bed and stop taking the medicines prescribed by her doctor. Although Jack Eppes initially resisted their advice, Tom reported proudly that "it was attempted thro' Patsy entirely and so gently that there was no violence done to the feelings of the good [doctor] whom [Eppes] so much esteemed." Martha stayed with her sister for at least a month, and Maria recovered completely.[69]

For her own children, Martha approved Gregory's general scheme, which emphasized cleanliness, freedom of movement, a simple diet, and plenty of outdoor activities. "The mismanagement of Children is principally owing," Gregory declared, "to over-feeding, over-clothing, want of exercise, and fresh air." Jefferson generally shared these opinions, which he deemed equally applicable to adults. He continued to take long walks and rides on horseback well into his seventies and prescribed outdoor exercise as a remedy for his son-in-law's physical maladies during the 1790s. The fact that Jefferson informed Martha and Tom about their children's "sports" and outdoor play at Monticello suggests that they, too, as parents, valued outdoor activities. As an adult, their daughter Ellen, who happily remembered her childhood days at her grandfather's house, commissioned an artist to paint a watercolor showing her youngest brother playing on its vast lawn while two older sisters looked on.[70]

While Martha and Tom seem to have shared the responsibility for promoting and maintaining their children's physical well-being, their early education was her domain entirely. Martha was extremely well educated for a Virginia woman of her time. Her father had intended her education to prepare her to teach her own children, and in that sense, Patsy's expensive tuition at the Panthemont was an investment in cultural and intellectual capital that would yield dividends in future generations. Moreover, experts agreed that women's innate qualities made mothers ideal teachers for young children of both sexes during their formative years. Although men had the "power and authority, to direct the affairs of public societies and private families," John Gregory wrote, women were "designed to soften our hearts and polish our manners." Accordingly, mothers were best suited for teaching their children not only basic reading and writing but also morality and manners. Many postrevolutionary Americans also regarded instilling civic values in the next generation of citizens as mothers' special service to the young republic.[71]

Monticello. This 1825 watercolor, attributed to Jane Pitford Braddick Peticolas, a friend of Ellen Randolph's, portrays Jefferson's house as the backdrop for an idyllic rural life. Martha and her children enjoyed the civility and intellectual life that Monticello offered, as well as pleasant outdoor activities in a comparatively healthful mountain climate. Monticello/Thomas Jefferson Foundation, Inc.

Martha embraced her role as her children's first teacher more enthusiastically than she did any other aspect of motherhood. As early as 1793, she proudly informed her father that three-year-old Anne was "busily employed *yiting*," self-consciously adding that "a fond Mother never knows where to stop [boasting] when her children is the subject." Perhaps sharing Gregory's concern that "a too early application to different branches of education" might inhibit a child's ability to develop "a healthy and vigorous constitution, a cheerful temper, and a good heart," Martha did not teach Anne to read until she was eight years old. Jeff, however, attended what he later recalled as "Old Field Schools, located in the woods, in log cabins, or Meeting houses" from the time he was four years old, walking between one and four miles to attend classes with other neighborhood boys and carrying his "simple breakfast and dinner in baskets." But most schools in Albemarle were irregular and short lived, and Jeff eventually regretted what he called the "early deficiency" of his education, which may have impeded his progress when he later continued his studies in Philadelphia and then in Richmond.[72]

By January 1801, while she suffered the morning sickness of her sixth pregnancy in eleven years, Martha weaned her youngest child, Cornelia, and deloused Jeff, while devoting as much time as possible to the education of her three older children, Anne, Jeff, and Ellen. She worried that Anne and Jeff were not good students and "are uncommonly backward in every thing much more so than were many others who have not had half the pains taken with them." Four-year-old Ellen, by contrast, was "wonderfully apt." While Martha had great expectations for this scholarly younger daughter, she confided to her father that "the two others excite serious anxiety with regard to their intellect." Overall, however, Martha felt that teaching her children was a rewarding occupation. "I have lost my relish for what is usually deemed pleasure," she declared, "and duties incompatible with it have surplanted all other enjoyments in my breast—the education of my Children to which I have long devoted every moment that I could command."[73]

Because enslaved workers performed many of the routine domestic tasks at Varina, Belmont, and Edgehill—as they did at Monticello—Martha could devote hours each day to teaching her children's lessons and tending to their health. Great planters in Virginia devoted between one-fourth and one-third of their enslaved workforce to occupations other than fieldwork by the 1790s. At Monticello, for instance, female slaves who did not do fieldwork were likely to do spinning, sewing, or routine domestic chores; some male slaves who did not do fieldwork were house servants, though many more worked making nails or bricks or at some other artisanal or manufacturing occupation. Most domestic servants were either very young or very old. Regardless of age, however, the light-skinned Hemingses held special places atop the occupational hierarchy as privileged house servants and skilled craftsmen who sometimes earned wages by hiring themselves out for pay.[74]

Martha grew up in a household where persons of African descent outnumbered whites, and where she was on familiar, even intimate, terms with those who labored in her father's house. Ursula, the family housekeeper, had nursed Patsy Jefferson as an infant. Betty Hemings and her children cleaned, sewed, and were housemaids and valets in her childhood home, and James and Sally Hemings were later with her in Paris. Not surprisingly, the newly married Martha Jefferson Randolph yearned for some familiar faces among her workforce at Varina. A few months after she wed, she therefore asked her father to send her a maid from Monticello. Later that year, Jefferson gave Martha eight slaves, including Molly Hemings, who was the daughter of Mary Hemings, Sally's sister and a longtime Monticello house servant whom Martha knew well. Fourteen-year-old Molly became Martha's maid, a familiar presence who followed her from Varina to Belmont to Edgehill—and who presumably savored long visits to her own extended family when her mistress stayed at Monticello.[75]

In the Randolph household, Molly was one of perhaps six or eight slaves who worked directly under Martha's supervision in and around the house. Although Martha left little evidence of her interaction with her own house servants during this period, one surviving comment from Isaac Jefferson, Ursula's son and a Monticello blacksmith, suggests that she was a kind mistress, at least to those whom she knew well. Isaac Jefferson remembered Martha as "a mighty peaceable woman; never holler for a servant; make no fuss or racket." Her husband, Tom, also had "treated him mighty well" and was, in his opinion, "one of the finest masters in Virginia."[76]

Like most plantation mistresses, Martha rarely commented on slavery as an issue, though her letters contained occasional references to enslaved people as individuals. Because letters she wrote to her father constitute the main surviving documentation for this period of her life, the bonded laborers she mentioned were usually those who worked in and around the house at Monticello, including the Hemingses. In 1795, for instance, she informed her father that she had seen Robert Hemings—the first of the Hemingses Jefferson manumitted—in Richmond, where he resided with his enslaved wife and child. A sympathetic Martha interceded with her father at the behest of Hemings, whose departure had angered Jefferson, asserting that "he never would have left *you* to live with any person but his wife." In January 1798, reporting that her own servants at Belmont suffered "more sickness than I ever saw in a family in my life" during the damp winter, she added that the Monticello slaves were generally healthy "except Tom and Goliah . . . and poor little Harriot who died a few days after you left us" in December 1797. Tom also made a point of mentioning the death of this infant, whom he identified as "Sallies child."[77]

As his daughter and son-in-law must have known, Jefferson would have been especially interested in the death of "poor little Harriot" because "Sallies child" was also his own. Harriet, who was born in October 1795, was conceived during the hiatus between Jefferson's tenure as secretary of state and his term as vice president, when Martha and Tom were at Varina in early 1795. Jefferson surely took a special interest in the naming of this child, who took her name not from the Hemingses—as was customary in this large and tightly knit family—but from Jefferson's extended white family. Harriet Randolph was one of Tom's younger sisters, a favorite of Jefferson's, and a frequent guest at Monticello. Hemings's next child, a son born on 1 April 1798, was conceived during Jefferson's six-month stay at home in 1797. His name, William Beverley Hemings, had both familial and historical significance for Jefferson and his white family. William Beverley had surveyed western lands with Jefferson's father and later negotiated a pivotal treaty that gave white Virginians control of vast acreage in what was previously Indian territory. Moreover, several men in the Randolph family already bore this name or one similar to it. Tom had a young nephew named William Beverley Randolph; another Beverley Randolph had been governor of Virginia.[78]

That Martha mentioned none of these circumstances in her surviving letters should come as no surprise. In a time and place when respectable women were supposed to be genteel and pliant, what daughter would inquire about or meddle in the sex life of her father? Besides, white Virginians generally ignored sexual liaisons between slaveowning men and black women, especially if the men involved conducted their affairs discreetly and made no attempt to legitimate their relationships with their enslaved partners. What truly outraged white Virginians were illicit sexual relationships between men of any social status and white women, especially the wives and daughters of the propertied elite—hence the outcry against Richard Randolph of Bizarre for his alleged seduction of his unmarried sister-in-law. The relationship between Jefferson and Hemings, then, was not all that unusual, and equally important, it did nothing to undermine the status or prospects of Martha and Maria, unlike the marriage of Gabriella Harvie to Thomas Mann Randolph Sr., which severely diminished Tom's inheritance and caused his younger siblings to leave Tuckahoe. Whatever the nature and extent of Jefferson's relationship with Hemings, Martha was still effectively the mistress of Monticello. Although Jefferson's children by Hemings might expect to receive their freedom, they could not be legal claimants to rival his white daughters' rights to his estate.[79]

Amid the constant clamor of children, guests, and construction noise, it would have been easy enough for Martha to ignore or purposefully overlook the special relationship between Sally Hemings and her father. Jefferson and his adult daughter were not constant companions. Though the family took their meals as a group, Martha and her children spent the day together, apart from her father. Jefferson's sleeping quarters, even while Monticello was still under construction, were separate from those of his daughter's family and from those of other guests. Indeed, Jefferson scrupulously guarded the privacy of both his bedchamber and his library. Martha sometimes bemoaned how little she saw her father, even when they resided together in the same house. For instance, when she and her children lived with Jefferson at Monticello between May and November 1800, she complained that she "never had the pleasure of passing one sociable moment" with him, in part because he was "always in a croud" of guests. Yet sometime during these months Sally Hemings became pregnant again. She gave birth to a daughter, named Harriet for her dead sister, in May 1801.[80]

❖ Martha and her father were often "in a croud" at Monticello, in part because what her father called the "eternal presence of strangers" was the inevitable result of the "manner and usages of our country," which included, among gentlemen at least, the unstinting offer of hospitality. In the spring and summer of 1800, Jefferson's guests included the Eppeses, Elizabeth Kortright Monroe, and Dr. William Bache, a grandson of Benjamin Franklin who had purchased a 600-acre farm near Charlottesville. These and other less familiar visitors competed for Jefferson's attention with the voluminous influx of letters and newspapers containing political news—including erroneous reports of Jefferson's death—from every region of the country. The year 1800 was a presidential election year, and Vice President Jefferson was the leading candidate. As Martha and her children summered at Monticello, state elections decided the composition of legislatures that would choose delegates to the Electoral College, which, in turn, was supposed to decide the outcome of the bitterly partisan election of 1800.[81]

chapter 4 ┃ The President's Daughter

On 19 February 1801, Thomas Jefferson calmly informed his family that the House of Representatives had finally, after thirty-five inconclusive votes, elected him president. As they well knew, the vote in the Electoral College had been deadlocked, giving Jefferson and his putative running mate, the New Yorker Aaron Burr, each seventy-three votes. As mandated by the Constitution, the contest then moved to the House of Representatives, where, Jefferson reported, "After exactly a week's balloting there at length appeared 10 States for me, 4. for Burr, & 2 voted blanks. This was done without a single [Federalist] vote coming over." Jefferson hoped that the Federalist minority who had abstained from the final vote would be amenable to his new Democratic-Republican (or simply Republican) administration and that the virulent partisanship of the recent election would discredit the worst offenders. The "conduct of the [Federalist] minority," he wrote optimistically, "has done in one week what very probably could hardly have been effected by years of mild and impartial administration."[1]

What exactly did it mean to Martha Jefferson Randolph that her father was now president of the United States? Martha clearly hoped that Jefferson would win the election of 1800. She called the Republicans, the political party led by her father and James Madison, the "friends of Liberty," in contrast to the Federalists, whom many in their circle regarded as tyrants and even closet monarchists.[2] At the same time, Jefferson's ascent to the presidency did not necessarily confer special status on his daughters. Americans, especially Jefferson's partisans, spurned the notion of an unelected "first family," which seemed to smack of royalty.

"Women," as one historian has noted, "were everywhere in Washington City," the fledgling capital on the Potomac, especially during the annual social season.[3] As the president's daughter, Martha sometimes participated in the political business of the capital's social life. Her involvement was subtle and only intermittent, though, because like many female members of political families, she spent most of her time at home. Between 1801 and 1809,

Martha familiarized herself with her family's finances, educated her children, and performed domestic and agricultural tasks she had mastered as a young wife. Indeed, her oversight of the family's practical affairs and interests, especially after her husband's election to Congress, made the men's absence less costly. In two carefully timed visits, however, in her forays into public life, she helped Jefferson to manage his public image and to reshape Washington's official social life.

❖ Martha Jefferson Randolph was part of a generation of women who, inspired by their foremothers' support for the Revolution and building on that example of patriotism and public spirit, sustained their political consciousness in the postrevolutionary era. Some were "female politicians" who actively championed either the Federalists or the Republicans. "I am becoming an outrageous politician, perfectly *federal*[ist]," reported Eleanor Parke Custis, the adopted daughter of George Washington, in 1798. After the Federalists lost the election of 1800, Custis and her friends wore white plumes to balls and other public functions to signify opposition to Jefferson's administration and continuing loyalty to the defeated Federalist party. At the opposite end of the political spectrum, Martha's sisters-in-law, Judith and Nancy Randolph, wrote letters in which they addressed their correspondents as "Citizen" to show their support for Jefferson and the Republicans, and for the French revolutionaries, who adopted that title to signal their antiaristocratic political values.[4]

Martha had many politically conscious female friends and role models. She may have recalled her mother's quiet patriotism during the Revolution, when Martha Wayles Jefferson made homespun, raised money to help the troops, and endured life as the wife of an embattled wartime governor. In Paris, Patsy and Polly had known Abigail Adams, an intelligent and outspoken woman with whom their father had serious conversations about shopping and domestic matters as well as politics and women's rights. In the 1790s, Martha was on intimate terms with the Randolph sisters, who so admired the French revolutionaries, and she may have known Nelly Custis, who was Polly's friend in Philadelphia during Jefferson's tenure in Washington's cabinet. Jefferson's daughters, then, had been exposed to political people and information since childhood. They were well aware that respectable women could express political opinions and even, within certain parameters, participate in public life.[5]

But Martha and her sister also knew that their father often disapproved of politically minded women. In Paris, he balanced his admiration and respect for Abigail Adams with disdain for French women who talked politics with men in their salons or, worse still, sought to influence the government and its functionaries. Jefferson condemned elite and educated French *salonnières* as well as plebeian women who led bread riots in the streets of Paris, and he eventually blamed Queen Marie-Antoinette's influence over the king for "plung[ing] the world into crimes and calamities which will forever stain the pages of modern history." During his years in Paris, Jefferson took comfort in the notion that American women were altogether domestic and "too wise to wrinkle their foreheads with politics." Arguing that women's involvement in politics was detrimental both to the polity and to their own happiness, he smugly declared that female influence "does not endeavour to extend itself *in our country* beyond the domestic line." Committed to preserving his daughters' American identity and attributes, Jefferson must have shared these opinions with them from time to time.[6]

As it turned out, Jefferson was wrong about American women's supposed aversion to politics. In New York and, later, in Philadelphia, city ladies mingled with the wives and daughters of political dignitaries and diplomats, as Americans created an official society to complement their new political order. In Philadelphia especially, women orchestrated salons with a Federalist partisan flavor. Jefferson recoiled from the salons and from other politicized social gatherings because of the predominance of both Federalists and women in these venues. In 1798, in a letter to Martha, he deplored "the rancorous passions which tear every breast here, even of the sex which should be stranger to them," adding that "politics & party hatreds destroy the happiness of every being" in the capital. By early 1800, Vice President Jefferson, increasingly vilified by his opponents and estranged from the Federalist Adams administration, informed his daughter that he had given up political "dinners & parties" completely, instead "associating entirely" with men of science.[7]

Jefferson's correspondence with his daughters indicates that he wanted them to be knowledgeable about contemporary politics and especially to be wary of what he considered to be the corrosive effects of partisan intrigue, which he consistently contrasted with the wholesome tranquility of domestic life. For instance, in early February 1801, as he waited in Washington for the official outcome of the presidential election, Jefferson confided to Martha that he was "worn down with pursuits in which I take no delight, surrounded by enemies & spies catching & perverting every word which falls from my lips or flows from my pen, and inventing where facts fail them." He yearned "for that society where all is peace and harmony" among his family at Monticello. Federalists, who accused Jefferson of being an atheist, a spendthrift, a reckless admirer of French radicalism, and an enemy of the Constitution, made Jefferson's life unpleasant. But his frequent comparisons between home and politics aimed less to discourage his daughters from learning about the latter than to alert them to its nastiness and most especially to emphasize the crucial restorative function of family life and the signal importance of women's domestic role.[8]

Although some historians have characterized Jefferson as unequivocally hostile to politically minded women, his enduring friendship with Elizabeth Trist suggests that he respected knowledgeable and outspoken women who shared his own political views. In 1801, Trist unabashedly celebrated her friend's elevation to the presidency, which she believed would result in "a fair experiment of What a Republican Administration can effect as to the happiness of the people." She then boldly lectured Jefferson about the continuing "machinations" of his Federalist enemies, even as she rhetorically conceded the limits of women's political influence. "The only privilege our sex injoy is that of freely communicating our sentiments," she wrote. Although the bluntly opinionated Trist showed little restraint in sharing her political views with Jefferson, she also slyly—and, one suspects, only half-seriously—distanced herself from her own strident and seemingly unfeminine political rhetoric. "We [women] are generally thought of little consiquence in the Political World," she observed, "but if we are incompetent to decide properly on these subjects, we certainly can revibrate the opinion of others," especially, she might have added, if those opinions coincided with Jefferson's own.[9]

Similarly, while historians generally view Jefferson's administration as a low point in women's political influence, the new president actually sought to incorporate his daughters into what he envisioned as a new Republican approach to official social life in the nation's capital. Jefferson was determined to make his administration's official social rituals distinct from those of his Federalist predecessors. He especially disliked the Federalists' stiffly formal receptions (which only gentlemen attended) and the formal gatherings for ladies and gentlemen, known as levees, which Martha Washington had hosted, both of which he considered unacceptably elitist and quasi-monarchical. Jefferson also condemned the levees because, much like the salons he so reviled in Paris and Philadelphia, they afforded elite women such prominence and influence in official society.[10]

As he had done in Paris, Jefferson fashioned his official entertainments in Washington to conform to a more domestic model. In the process, he jettisoned customary diplomatic protocol in favor of *pêle mêle* etiquette, in which guests interacted on more or less equal terms when they visited the president's house. Jefferson replaced Federalist levees, salons, and receptions with intimate dinner parties, which he saw as politically effective and ideologically appropriate venues for conversing with congressmen, diplomats, and other dignitaries. Although his dinners often were for men only, Jefferson also brought women and men together to dine at his official gatherings. Only months into his first term as president, he declared that "it would be the greatest comfort imaginable" for Martha or Maria to join his household as its hostess, but in their absence he often relied on Dolley Madison, the wife of his newly appointed secretary of state, or another cabinet wife to fill that role.[11]

Jefferson repeatedly asked Martha and Maria to join him in Washington, where their presence would provide him with a domestic refuge from party politics while simultaneously marking him as a man of the people, the archetypical republican family man who governed, protected, and publicly represented his dependents in his household. Such performances of domesticity were doubly appealing to Jefferson because the use of casual domestic manners, which preserved inequalities between husbands and wives, and fathers and children, offered an alternative to the exclusive and carefully choreographed Federalist gatherings and ceremonies that accentuated sharp inequalities among white male citizens, while sometimes blurring distinctions between ladies and gentlemen. Because most Americans identified manhood with citizenship and because manhood itself depended to some extent on the ability to preside over an independent household of women, children, and servants (or slaves), when Jefferson appeared in a domestic setting he both embraced and embodied those popular political values.[12]

In sum, the president wanted his daughters to come to Washington to help him domesticate the capital's official society. When women attended his presidential dinners, their roles, which replicated gender distinctions prevalent at Monticello and other elite American domiciles, reflected his priorities. Jefferson used his dinners to solidify support for his policies among Republicans, woo Federalists critics, and cultivate good relations with foreign diplomats and local grandees. He seated a dozen or fewer guests at a round table to facilitate conversation and signify a rough equality among diners. Because he, like many of his contemporaries, believed that the society of virtuous women made men more agreeable and temperate, he sometimes relied on a feminine presence to encourage civility. Having

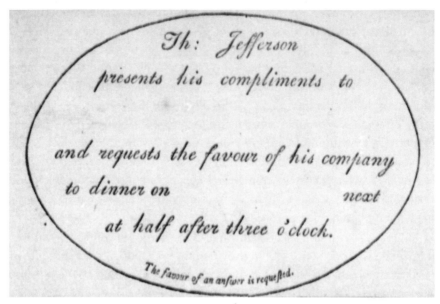

Dinner Invitation. Jefferson used these formal invitations to summon guests to dinner during his presidency. Although these dinners were plainly political, he modeled his entertainments on the casual family meals he enjoyed at Monticello. When she visited Washington, Martha attended her father's dinners and played an important role in the domestic tableaux visitors saw at the president's house. Courtesy of the Library of Congress.

served their function, the ladies then withdrew with their hostess, leaving the men to their political business. Women's ideal role at these events, then, was essentially domestic, therapeutic, and ornamental.[13]

Although Martha eventually played this role effectively and without complaint, she resisted her father's early entreaties to join him in Washington. The main deterrent to her visiting the capital was her situation as the wife, mother, and mistress in a household with increasingly evident financial problems. In March 1801, when Jefferson became president, Martha was responsible for the care and education of four children between the ages of ten and two, and pregnant with another child, who was born in August, the first of five she bore during her father's eight-year presidency. Although Martha Washington, Abigail Adams, and later Dolley Madison and her immediate successors resided full time or nearly full time with their spouses in the capital, these women were all mothers of grown children, and each was the wife of a president, not his daughter. Nelly Custis, who set a precedent for daughters of presidents being prominent in capital society during the

Washington administration, was young, unmarried, and childless during her time as a belle in Philadelphia. Martha's circumstances were entirely different, and whatever her desire to visit Washington, family considerations prevented her from doing so for nearly two years into her father's presidency.

In early 1802, Jefferson again asked his daughters to come to Washington, and by May he and Martha had begun planning the long-awaited visit. An outbreak of measles in Albemarle delayed the trip, as Martha unsuccessfully "courted rather than avoided the infection" in hopes that her children would get it and thereby acquire immunity to the disease, which was much more dangerous for adults. Jefferson went home to Monticello to be with his family that summer and returned to Washington in early October.[14]

Finally, on 17 November 1802, the sisters set out for Washington, accompanied part of the way by Maria's husband, John Wayles Eppes. Martha brought her middle children, Jeff and Ellen, with her but left her oldest and youngest daughters with Tom in Albemarle; Maria's son Francis, born the preceding year, also remained at home. The journey to Washington took five days, though Jefferson typically made the trip in three. The president paid for the trip and also for hairpieces and other fashionable goods that Dolley Madison ordered from Philadelphia milliners so that the sisters would have the sort of things that were "universally worn" by ladies in society. Martha called this first trip "a flying visit only to shew that we are in earnest with regard to Washington." The expected briefness of their stay led her and Maria not to risk a journey "with a carriage full of small children," though they ultimately remained with Jefferson for nearly six weeks and returned home in early January.[15]

At first glance, Washington probably held few attractions for the sisters besides their father's company. Planned as early as 1791, the new federal city became the official seat of the U.S. government in November 1800. At the time, there were only 109 brick houses and 111 wooden ones in the territory that constituted the city of Washington; the approximately 500 families already in residence were joined by roughly 300 civilian officials, some of whom brought families with them. Still, the new capital boasted none of the amenities or amusements that were available in Philadelphia, or even in Richmond, which had a population of more than 5,000, along with theater, balls, and some "really good" society, at least according to one visitor from New England. Although the ambitious plan for the new federal city included vast boulevards and imposing buildings, none were fully completed by the time Jefferson's daughters arrived. Where roads had been cleared,

Washington in 1800. The new American capital was barely more than a country village when Martha Jefferson Randolph visited her father there in 1802. This view from the west front of the Capitol shows Pennsylvania Avenue as a tree-lined dirt road. Courtesy of the Library of Congress.

they remained unlit and unpaved. Two years into Jefferson's first term, a skeptical Philadelphian reported, "The Federal city is in reality neither town nor village. . . . There sits the President . . . like a pelican in the wilderness, or a sparrow upon the housetop."[16]

Living quarters, though much larger than Martha was used to at Edgehill or even Monticello, were less comfortable. John and Abigail Adams, the first presidential couple to inhabit the executive mansion (which was not yet called the "White House") moved there from Philadelphia in late November 1801. Abigail reported that "this great castle" was so big that it required a huge domestic staff of thirty and that the difficulty of heating and lighting such large rooms made them cold and dark. Worse still, only six rooms had been plastered, none was completely finished, and the main staircase leading to the second floor had not been built. The Adamses acquired some furniture with funds that Congress appropriated, but with so many rooms remaining empty, Abigail used "the great unfinished audience room" to dry her laundry. Only six chambers were "comfortable" during the Adamses' stay in Washington. Nevertheless, Abigail Adams praised the house's location near the Potomac as "a beautiful spot" with fine views, concluding that "when completed, it will be beautiful."[17]

Accommodations at the president's house improved somewhat after Jefferson's arrival, though parts of the building, including the spacious quarters on the second floor where Martha and her children stayed, remained unfinished or unfurnished when he left office eight years later. Workmen's huts, privies, and construction debris still occupied the grounds surrounding the house. And though most visitors commented favorably on the food and wine the president served at his dinners, often at his own expense, some Federalists and foreigners ridiculed the presence of a giant cheese, which measured more than four feet in diameter, in one of the public rooms on the ground floor of the house. In December 1801, Jefferson received the so-called Mammoth Cheese, which weighed 1,235 pounds, as a gift from some Massachusetts Baptists who admired his commitment to liberty of conscience and the separation of church and state. The cheese was on display in the presidential mansion for at least three years, though maggots infested parts of it by June 1802 and one visitor in early 1803 found that sixty pounds had been removed from the middle "in consequence of the puffing up and symptoms of decay."[18]

Although both Martha and Maria came home with happy memories of the time they spent in Washington, their surviving letters contain no specific information about how they passed their time. As young matrons, they probably took an interest in the daily running of the presidential household, which at most times employed a total of eleven servants, most of whom were free people. Jefferson brought only three enslaved workers from Monticello to Washington: Ursula Hughes, Edith Fossett, and Fanny Hern, all of whom were young women who worked as apprentices to Honoré Julien, the president's French chef. Another Frenchman, the maître d'hôtel and sometime cook Etienne Lemaire, became sufficiently friendly with Martha and Maria to share some culinary insights. Martha valued Lemaire's recipes for beef, mutton, "panne-quaiques," and bouilli so much that she passed them on to her own daughters, along with Julien's recipe for crème brûlée.[19]

Other sources indicate that the sisters made a good impression when they attended their father's dinners and other social functions. In November, they enjoyed a feast of venison and "profuse and extremely elegant" desserts when the architect Benjamin Henry Latrobe visited and dined with Jefferson and several of his political intimates, including James and Dolley Madison. A few weeks later, they took their places with their father at a dinner party of largely unfriendly Federalists, at least one of whom found Jefferson "very social" and clearly enjoying the company of his "well-accomplished . . . very delicate and tolerably handsome" daughters. The sisters' social skills probably received their greatest test on New Year's Day, however, when they attended their father's annual open-house reception, which, in one guest's estimation, attracted "every body" in Washington.[20]

Margaret Bayard Smith, the intelligent and sociable wife of the Republican newspaper editor Samuel Harrison Smith, liked both sisters but was especially effusive in her praise of Martha, whom she described as "one of the most lovely women I have ever met with." Smith admired Randolph's "intelligence, benevolence, and sensibility" and her "interesting" conversation. "Her manners," she declared, were "so frank and affectionate, that you know her at once, and feel perfectly at ease with her." Perhaps because of her years in Paris, the president's elder daughter was equally at ease with the city's cultivated women and foreign diplomats and visiting grandees.[21]

Martha and Maria also attended religious services at least once with Jefferson, and they socialized with a circle of well-informed women who stood at the forefront of Washington society. Both activities afforded them public exposure that reflected favorably on their father. By worshiping publicly with his daughters at services held in the Capitol—there were no churches yet in Washington—Jefferson, whom Federalists condemned as an infidel, could present himself as both a conventionally religious man and the father of virtuous daughters. By exchanging both informal and formal visits with the ladies of Washington, the sisters also may have eased Jefferson's relations with their politically influential husbands.[22]

Martha and Maria were away from home from late November 1802 until early January 1803. Two factors may explain the specific timing of their visit to Washington, for which Jefferson had lobbied for nearly two years before it actually happened. One involved Tom Randolph's ongoing attempts to get ahead in the world and shore up his troubled finances. The second, more politically salient, circumstance concerned a scandal that Federalists tried to use to undermine Jefferson's popularity and disrupt his administration.

Tom's discontent as a result of his depleted finances and overall lack of achievement may have been one reason why Martha finally left Albemarle. In the years after his father's death, Tom struggled to repay debts owed by his estate and meet the payments on a mortgage he had taken out on his Varina plantation. In November 1801, Martha confided to her father that she was playing what must have been an emotionally exhausting double role, nursing her sick children and consoling her increasingly troubled husband.

By October 1802, Tom's financial problems had worsened, and he wrote a pathetic, self-loathing letter to Jefferson in which he questioned his worthiness to be included in the "narrow circle" of excellent and accomplished people who were the president's intimates, likening himself to the "proverbially silly bird" who could not "feel . . . at ease among the swans" of Monticello. Given that Jefferson's daughters were the president's most beloved and accomplished "swans," it seems reasonable to conclude that Tom and Martha may have appreciated some time away from each other by the time she left for Washington a few weeks later.[23]

By then, Jefferson had more reason than ever for wanting his daughters to join him in the capital. On 1 September 1802, the Federalist *Richmond Recorder* published the following allegation against the president: "It is well known that the man, *whom it delighteth the people to honor*, keeps, and for many years has kept, as his concubine, one of his slaves. Her name is SALLY. . . . By this wench Sally, our president has several children. . . . The AFRICAN VENUS is said to officiate, as housekeeper at Monticello." More minor—and sometimes incorrect—details appeared in the press through mid-November. There is no way to know exactly how Martha, Maria, or the Hemingses reacted to this exposé. By December, with the sisters safely in Washington, Tom Randolph, motivated either by genuine outrage or by the desire to please his wife and father-in-law, considered publishing a defense of Jefferson or demanding either evidence or a public apology from the author of "those infamous stories," James Thompson Callender. As for Jefferson, he refused to comment publicly on Callender's allegations, some of which had circulated as rumors in Albemarle since he returned from Paris with the pregnant Sally Hemings in 1789.[24]

But the convenient arrival of Martha and Maria enabled the president and his daughters to project a public image that was, for many, at odds with the salacious one that Callender promulgated. Virginians and other southerners knew that planters' wives and daughters had little recourse but to accept white men's illicit sexual relationships with enslaved women. But Jefferson must have hoped that the presence of his devoted and accomplished daughters with him at public worship and official dinners would tacitly discredit Callender's charges, at least among those who knew little of the sexual dynamics and conventions of southern slave society. From the perspective of his elder daughter, who had worried that she and her children would be tainted by the scandal at Bizarre, defending her father's public image would have been essential. Protecting Jefferson's reputation, which historians have seen as the posthumous mission of his loving grandchildren and sympathetic biographers, actually began decades earlier when Martha and Maria went to Washington.[25]

❖ On 28 December 1802, Tom Randolph arrived in Washington to retrieve Martha, Maria, and the children. On 10 January 1803, they all reached Edgehill after a difficult five-day journey. Less than ten months later, Martha gave birth to another daughter, named for her sister, Mary Jefferson Randolph. Tom was not at Edgehill in November when Martha gave birth, attended by a midwife, a physician, and Maria, who was also pregnant. The preceding spring, perhaps seeking to achieve something that both he and Patsy could be proud of, Tom decided to run for Congress, but neither she nor her father were enthusiastic about his choice. For one thing, Tom ran against a steadfast supporter of the president's, Samuel Jordan Cabell, whom he defeated by a mere 13 votes out of some 1,800 cast. Another concern was that Tom's electoral victory required him to be in Washington by the time Congress convened in mid-October, despite his responsibilities at Edgehill, Varina, and Monticello. Maria's husband, Jack, who ran unopposed, was also elected to Congress for the first time that year.[26]

So Tom set out for Washington, where he and Jack boarded with Jefferson, leaving their wives and children at home. Altogether, Tom served two consecutive two-year terms in the House of Representatives. Congress met for one session each year, convening sometime between October and December and disbanding in March or April. Tom attended all four sessions, though he made only one significant speech in four years and his overall record as a member of Congress was not distinguished. Martha stayed in Albemarle during three of Tom's four legislative sessions, journeying to Washington again only in 1805.[27]

Although Martha, Maria, and their children could have gone to Washington with their husbands and resided in the executive mansion with Jefferson, staying home was more common among congressional wives at this time. Wives with grown children or who had daughters of marriageable age sometimes came to the capital for the social season, but the boardinghouse life of a member of Congress in a city with few amenities was not well suited to nurturing and educating youngsters. At least equally important were the costs of moving the whole family to Washington and maintaining two households, coupled with the loss of women's domestic productivity and oversight of the family's resources at home. For most congressional families, the disadvantages of coming to the capital outweighed the potential benefits. Thus, in 1807, presumably a typical year, only 9 of 164 members of Congress brought their wives with them to Washington.[28]

Economic concerns, along with the varied needs of six children ranging in age from twelve years to infancy, also made it logical for Martha to stay at Edgehill. These years, which began with both her husband and her father acknowledging their mounting financial problems, ended with Martha's exasperated observation, in 1808, that "the ruin of the family is still extending it self daily," as one by one her Randolph in-laws succumbed to insolvency. In any event, Martha never appears to have regretted or resented the decision to spend the bulk of her father's presidency, and her husband's congressional career, at home in Albemarle.[29]

An early measure of Martha and Tom's near-desperate straits in 1802, as he struggled to pay the mortgage on Varina, was his abortive plan to enter the lucrative cotton business in the Mississippi Territory. Tom had been interested in the West as early as 1801, but Jefferson persuaded him to consider Georgia instead because it was closer to Virginia and farther from "Indians who could be dangerous." Tom soon abandoned this plan, in part because South Carolina law prevented him from transporting his slaves through that state en route to Georgia.[30]

Although migration—westward, southward, and even northward to the nonslaveholding states of the Old Northwest—was the remedy many hard-pressed Virginia planters adopted to revive their declining fortunes, the Randolphs' flirtation with cotton planting was unusual in two respects. First, unlike the many southern planters who relocated their entire households, Tom intended to send his slaves to the cotton frontier, but he did not foresee settling his own family there. Perhaps he feared that both Martha and her father would strenuously oppose such a plan. Second, according to Tom, only he, Martha, and Jefferson knew the details of what he called "a plan . . . for the more profitable employment of my slaves." By March 1802, Tom had informed his slaves that, with the exception of "a few chosen domestics," they would all be moving to a cotton plantation that autumn in an attempt to "prepare their minds," but he did not reveal that the Randolphs themselves would not emigrate with them. Tom believed—and apparently Martha agreed—that this deception was necessary because his enslaved workers were "willing to accompany me any where. . . . Besides their attachment to Martha would make their departure very heavy unless they had a belief that she was to follow at some time."[31]

Motivated by financial considerations, Tom assuaged his conscience by professing a deep concern for "these persons, whose happiness fortune has thrown upon [our] will" even as he ignored the realities of enslaved people's lives. For one thing, though Tom's enslaved workers may, indeed, have regretted a move that separated them from their master and mistress, they were even more likely to resist leaving behind family and friends in the African American community in Albemarle and other parts of Virginia. While Tom and Martha may have tried to convince themselves that moving their slaves en masse prevented the breakup of black families, they surely knew that many of Virginia's enslaved people, including theirs, had spouses and children on neighboring plantations, in nearby towns, or even in other counties. The Randolphs also told themselves—and Jefferson—that "the culture of cotton is the least laborious of any ever practiced," though slave narratives and eyewitness accounts reveal that African Americans' lives on the cotton plantations were often brutal and not at all characterized by what Tom hypothesized was "gentle labor."[32]

Martha's apparent initial acceptance of this plan belied not only her own worries about the Randolph family finances but also a tendency, common among slaveholding women, to personalize her relationships with certain familiar slaves. Throughout her adult life, Martha appears to have experienced empathy for enslaved people she knew as individuals, even if, like many other southern whites, she was at best only vaguely critical of the institution of slavery and its impact on the lives of African Americans with whom she had no personal relationship. Given her constant interaction with the household staff at Edgehill, Martha must have been instrumental in preventing the removal of those "chosen domestics" to Mississippi or to Georgia, which she no doubt saw as giving preferential treatment to servants who earned her personal trust. At this point, Martha probably had little contact with her husband's fieldworkers, who were divided between two plantations, and so it was unlikely that she considered the pain that moving to Georgia would cause them.[33]

In addition to the financial incentive to make slavery more profitable by diverting enslaved workers to cotton production and abandoning tobacco in favor of grain on their Virginia properties, Martha espoused the conventional fear that slavery compromised the morals and manners of white people. Jefferson believed that young white Virginians learned to be despots by watching their parents interact with slaves. "The parent storms, the child looks on, catches the lineaments of wrath, puts on the same airs in the circle of smaller slaves, gives a loose to his worst of passions," he maintained, "and thus nursed, educated, and daily exercised in tyranny, cannot but be stamped by it with odious peculiarities." A generation later, Martha's sister-in-law Virginia, who spent much of her childhood and young adulthood in the Randolph and Jefferson households, likewise warned, "Children will exercise self-will . . . and the peculiarities of the domestic establishments of Virginia give free scope to this propensity." She, too, concluded that slavery fostered a "habit of despotism" that was especially incompatible with the "female temper." Virginia believed that because slaves were "by nature and habit the fosterers of moral evil," mothers must carefully monitor interactions between white children and those "unfortunate beings who surround our homes, and constitute a portion of every family." Martha spent many hours in the company of such "beings," whether her husband and father were at home or in Washington.[34]

Although the presence of slaves and the demands of domestic work were constant, Martha's life took three distinct forms during the years Tom served in Congress. If both Tom and her father were home, the Randolphs, along with the Eppeses, moved to Monticello. If Jefferson returned to Washington, as he sometimes did, when Congress was not in session, the Randolphs lived together with their children at Edgehill. But if Congress was in session and both her husband and father were in Washington, Martha generally stayed at Edgehill with the children, Tom's sister Virginia, and occasional guests, most of whom were female relations, such Tom's sister Jane, who had settled nearby with her "amiable" husband, Thomas Eston Randolph.[35]

In Tom's absence, Martha assumed his place as his overseer's on-site supervisor, and she also served as a conduit between the men in Washington and the overseers at both Edgehill and Monticello. Although she and Tom corresponded regularly, their letters have not survived. But those that she and her father exchanged were full of Randolph family news—the children's mumps, the replastering of some rooms at Edgehill, the coming and going of guests—as well reports from Monticello. For instance, in 1804 Martha informed her father that his overseer, Gabriel Lilly, had consulted her about the possible sale of Kit, a Monticello slave who had run away, had been caught, and now awaited his fate in the Charlottesville jail. Another letter concerned Lilly's apparent inability to control a slave named John, who the overseer feared would cause a rebellion at Monticello. Martha also shared with her father news of his grounds and gardens, reporting, for example, in spring 1805, that the weather would be good for his crops but that the "thorns" he had planted as a natural fence for his orchards were "certainly dead."[36]

In part because she was so busy and in part to further her children's education, Martha increasingly delegated letter-writing duties after Tom left for Congress. Because family members anxiously awaited the latest news about the health and well-being of distant loved ones and because writing letters was so time consuming and labor intensive, Jefferson systematically addressed letters alternately to Patsy and Polly and Tom—and urged them to take turns responding to his letters, too—when all three lived in Albemarle in the early 1790s. As he embarked on his second year as president, however, he asked Martha's older children to take up their duties as correspondents. "I shall now expect that whenever it is inconvenient for your papa and mama to write," he explained, "one of you will write on a piece of paper these words 'all is well' and send it for me to the post office."[37]

Although letters from Jefferson's grandson were infrequent and usually brief, the Randolph sisters, who unabashedly adored their grandfather, took their new epistolary duties seriously. Anne, who was nearly thirteen when her father left for Congress in late 1803, sent Jefferson the family news he requested, and she also wrote about gardening, the poultry she was raising as part of her domestic education, and a fire at Monticello. Ellen, who proved to be an even more dependable correspondent, also passed on family and neighborhood news, including a widespread but untrue rumor that their friend Elizabeth Trist, who had moved to Albemarle in 1798, was going to marry the governor. Like her sister, Ellen kept her grandfather up to date on her poultry and her gardening, but she also assiduously reported the books she read, which eventually included French texts and histories of the ancient world. In 1808, nine-year-old Cornelia, who had learned to read by age six, had not yet mastered writing but nonetheless dictated to Ellen a letter in which she informed Jefferson that each day she learned "a peice of poetry by heart and write a copy" and that she had not "begun arithmetic but I hope I soon shall."[38]

In Martha's letters, alongside family and plantation news, there were the usual accounts of illnesses and childrearing concerns. Tom's absence probably had little impact on Martha's performance of the maternal rites of watching over children and tending them when they were sick. In fact, Martha once complained that Tom was such an anxiety-ridden parent that she "had to act in the double capacity of nurse to my children and comforter to their father" when Ellen, Cornelia, and Virginia all suffered from whooping cough. In 1804, Martha reported to Jefferson that her sister-in-law and neighbor, Jane Cary Randolph, helped her tend to her nephew, Francis Eppes, who had "dreadful fits," which they feared might be "epileptick." Edgehill, she reported, was a hectic household, where her pregnant sister lamented the absence of her husband and "the noises and confusion of six children interrupted every moment."[39]

Although Francis gradually improved, his mother's condition worsened, despite Martha's care and her father's unwittingly hollow reassurance that "some female friend of your Mama's (I forget whom) used to say [childbirth] was no more than the knock of an elbow," so long as a physician was present to provide "scientific aid . . . if anything uncommon takes place." Maria gave birth to a daughter at Edgehill on 15 February 1804. The birth was probably premature, because when news of it arrived in Washington, a surprised Jack Eppes quickly left to join his wife in Albemarle. Maria, whose marriage was more demonstrably affectionate than her older sister's, called her husband the "best beloved of my soul," so his arrival was surely a comfort to her as she struggled with fever and the loss of her milk, leaving the comparatively robust Martha—who had given birth four months earlier—to nurse both her own infant and her newborn niece. Years later, Ellen Randolph remembered "the tender devoted care of my mother, how she watched over her sister, and with what anxious affection she anticipated her every want."[40]

Despite Martha's vigilance and a physician's ministrations, Maria's condition deteriorated steadily. In March, the family decided to move her to Monticello, where they hoped the mountain air and Jefferson's fine sherry might improve her health. Enslaved men carried the ailing woman's frail body on a litter for roughly four miles, across a stream and up the mountain, to spare her the pain and potential danger of a bumpy carriage ride. Although Maria rallied a bit after her father arrived on 5 April, she died twelve days later.[41]

The loss of her twenty-six-year-old sister, her sole surviving sibling, devastated the usually stoic Martha. The fact that both her mother and her sister died young as a result of complications due to pregnancy—a condition she herself endured so frequently—made the loss even more shocking. After Maria's death, Martha experienced cramps, spasms, and difficulty breathing, physical manifestations of grief that a distraught Tom called "hysterics" but which Martha attributed unconvincingly to "eating radishes and milk at the same meal both of which are unfriendly to my stomach." Shared grief also tightened the already strong bonds of affection and duty between Martha and her father. In the first letter she wrote to Jefferson after Maria's death, Martha reaffirmed her complete devotion in extravagant language that belied her thorough dedication to her children, if not to her volatile husband. "I do not hesitate to declare if my other duties could possibly interfere with my devotion to you I should not feel a scruple in sacrifising them. . . . It is truly the happiness of my life to think that I can dedicate the remainder of it to promote yours."[42]

Martha's physical ailments returned not long after Tom went back to Washington that November. By January, she admitted having "an hysteric fit," along with stomach pains, both of which she believed were "brought on by *cold*." Jefferson, fearing the loss of his only surviving child, urged her to do everything possible under the circumstances to regain her health. "Consider my dear Martha to what degree, and how many persons have the happiness of their lives depending on you," he wrote, "and consider it as a duty to take every care of yourself that you would think of for the dearest of those about you." Tom worried, too, about his wife's declining health. In an unusually emotional letter to Jefferson that January, he lamented leaving Martha at Edgehill while he attended Congress. "It is the hardest struggle I ever underwent to leave her, yet I must do it," he wrote, "indeed the regret I feel at having ever consented to be separated from her is so severe that it does not admit of any increase of painfull sentiment on that head."[43]

When Tom returned to Edgehill in April, however, he was able to report happily that Martha was fully recovered and that she had even regained much of the weight she lost while she was ill. A September visit from Dolley Madison must have lifted Martha's spirits. Dolley, who candidly admitted her emotional attachment to her own sisters, keenly appreciated the "Misery" that death of "a girl so young, so lovely" as Maria caused the family at Edgehill and Monticello. Martha also enjoyed the company of her sister-in-law Nancy, who arrived in May 1804, a month after Maria died, and left six months later. Finally banished from Bizarre by her sister Judith, Nancy was genuinely grateful for Martha's hospitality and kindness. "The Harmony in this house is never interrupted," she wrote contentedly from Monticello. "Never did there exist a more excellent woman," she observed, "than the one to whom my brother has the good fortune to be married."[44]

Although Martha and Tom were in bad financial straits, they were still arguably the most prosperous of the Randolphs, though Tom's obligations to his unmarried sisters, which he considered a "sacred duty," complicated their already precarious finances. In 1802, Tom had considered becoming a cotton planter in part to raise money to satisfy the debts on his father's estate so that he could pay his sisters the $6,000 each was to receive as her patrimony. Now, a few years later, the women needed the money. The two youngest sisters, Harriet and Virginia, both wed in 1805, choosing men with bleak financial prospects. When Harriet's husband, Richard Hackley, asked Tom to use his influence with Jefferson to get him the consulship at

Bordeaux, he became the first of a series of Randolphs or Randolph connections to seek government appointments through either Tom or Martha. Debt encumbered the property of the family of Virginia's husband, Wilson Jefferson Cary, much as it did that of the Randolphs. According to family tradition, Tom gave Virginia $5,000 when she and Wilson, a Fluvanna County planter, married at Monticello in August 1805.[45]

That December, when the new Congress met, Tom Randolph was again among its members, as was Jack Eppes. Jefferson, who began his second term as president in March, craved Martha's company, especially after the death of his younger daughter, but illness and unusually cold weather prevented her from joining him in Washington that winter. In the spring of 1805, however, Jefferson renewed his efforts to persuade her to come with all the children to Washington when Congress was in session. By October, Martha had decided to make the trip with Tom and the children, and because she was roughly six months pregnant, she expected to stay the entire winter. Mindful of the Randolphs' financial problems—and perhaps less so of his own—Jefferson sent Martha $100 for travel expenses and paid for the wigs, combs, shawls, veils, and handkerchiefs that Dolley Madison bought her in Philadelphia. He also rented a carriage for the family to use while they were in Washington. To ease her concerns about the mounting costs of their winter sojourn, Jefferson urged Martha to "consider every thing which your self or the family will want here as to be furnished by me so that the visit may not at all affect Mr. Randolph's pecuniary arrangements."[46]

The Randolphs and some unnamed servants left Edgehill sometime after 23 November. Traveling more slowly than usual because of Martha's advanced pregnancy and the large number of children in the carriage with her, they reached Centreville, in Fairfax County, as planned, by 30 November. Jefferson sent a carriage and driver to retrieve them, and the family arrived in Washington in time for dinner at four o'clock the next day, the day before Congress convened. After their long journey, the Randolphs joyously reunited with Jefferson and settled into the cavernous upstairs rooms of the president's house.[47]

❖ Some things in Washington had changed in the nearly three years since Martha's first visit. Though still a work in progress, the rustic village had become a small city, at least by American standards. In 1806, Washington had some 5,000 inhabitants, most of whom lived in the town's 700 houses. Made of brick and standing three stories high, most buildings now conveyed a sense of permanence and stability. Progress also had been made on public buildings, including the Capitol, where workers hoped to complete the south wing—the meeting chamber for the House of Representatives—in time for the next Congress. One visitor noted the presence of "two or three churches, three market-houses, and a jail," as well as artisans who made boots, shoes, hats, and other items "calculated for domestic consumption." Finally, and perhaps most important for Martha and her family, the president's house had more furniture and the Mammoth Cheese was gone.[48]

Partisan politics in the nation's capital, however, remained toxic, despite Jefferson's easy reelection to the presidency in 1804. Foreign policy concerns predominated in Jefferson's second term, as he doggedly tried to preserve American neutrality and freedom of the seas during the ongoing Anglo-French war. Federalists reviled Jefferson as cowardly and overly solicitous, while a faction within the president's own party also increasingly criticized him for supposedly making both the executive branch and the national government generally too powerful. Led by John Randolph of Roanoke, a Virginia congressman who was Tom's relation and the younger brother of the deceased Richard Randolph of Bizarre, this faction opposed the president on several key issues, including payment of restitution to defrauded land speculators in Georgia and the possible purchase of Spanish West Florida.

Jefferson remained enormously popular among his supporters, but his opponents ruthlessly vilified him in cartoons and newspapers. One notable print portrayed him as a cock or rooster (a symbol of revolutionary France) and Sally Hemings as a hen, doubly lampooning the president for his alleged partiality to both the French and his enslaved mistress at Monticello. Because some attacks on Jefferson concerned his personal life more than his policies, Martha sometimes felt that she herself "was in the very *focus* of political violence" during his presidency. "I was constantly exposed to see the most cruel slanders against my dear father," she recalled years later. In this caustic political environment, she believed, the "bad passion" of partisanship "like the jaundice, colour[ed] every object."[49]

Possibly the most troubling episode during this second visit to Washington involved a bawdy poem written by a young Irishman named Thomas Moore, which Jefferson's secretary, William Burwell, showed to Martha:

The patriot, fresh from Freedom's councils come,
Now plea'd retires to lash his slaves at home;
Or woo, perhaps, some black Aspasia's charms,
And dreams of freedom in his bondmaid's arms.

A Philosophic Cock, *ca. 1804. Martha must have known that her father's Federalist critics attacked and ridiculed him in the press and in political cartoons and caricatures. James Akin, who created this unflattering image of Jefferson and Sally Hemings, also produced another cartoon that portrayed the president as an emaciated dog coughing up gold coins at the foot of Napoleon, the French emperor. Courtesy, American Antiquarian Society.*

The poem, which portrayed her father as both a slave woman's lover and a cruel master, clearly upset Martha, who burst into Jefferson's study to show him the offensive verses. According to one account, the president "broke into a hearty, clear laugh" when he saw the poem. Martha interpreted her father's response as an implicit denial of his relationship with Hemings (the family's official story) or more plausibly as bitter recognition that he had been right all along in characterizing his political opponents—and party politics, in general—as demeaning and unsavory, in marked contrast to the virtues of domestic life.[50]

Martha and her children had come to Washington expressly to create a wholesome domestic refuge, away from the violence of party politics, a task at which they were sometimes successful. Margaret Bayard Smith recounted a visit to the president's house in the spring of 1806 on what must have been an ideal evening for Jefferson, who was in the middle of an acrimonious partisan debate over an appropriate response to British interference with U.S. shipping and commerce. When Smith arrived, she found the president and his daughter sitting together on a sofa with the "lovely children playing around them." One child stood on the sofa with her arms around his neck, while two others sat on his knees, playing. In this domestic environment, Smith observed, Jefferson "was in one of his most communicative social moods, and after tea, when the children went to bed, the conversation turned to agriculture, gardening, and the differences of both in different countries and of the produce of different climates." The time passed quickly, just as it might have at Monticello.[51]

The message of such a pleasing domestic tableau was not lost on Smith, who witnessed a similar scene when she visited Jefferson and his family a few years later in Albemarle. She and her husband were part of an unending stream of guests—including many strangers—who visited Jefferson after he retired from public life in 1809, when the Randolphs resided with him at Monticello. In her letters and, later, in her historical novel *A Winter in Washington* (1824), Smith portrayed Jefferson as a genial host and doting grandfather. Surrounding himself with family enabled Jefferson to burnish his public image as a respectable family man as a counterpoint to persistent rumors about him and Hemings. The shrewd but sympathetic Smith concluded as much when she visited the family, challenging those "whose envenomed calumny has painted him as the slave of the vilest passions" to see the former president among his grandchildren at Monticello, where "his life is the best refutation of all the calumnies that have been heaped upon him."[52]

As Jefferson's enemies disparaged him both personally and politically, he displayed his family to encourage the public—or at least Washington's official society—to see him in a more flattering light. Martha and the children were in Washington for the entire first session of the Ninth Congress—which convened on 2 December 1805 and adjourned on 21 April 1806—when Jefferson hosted a total of sixty-three dinners, as many as four in a single week. January, when the president hosted seventeen dinners and his annual New Year's reception, which was open to the public, was his busiest month, with four dinners each week, including one on the day that Martha gave birth to a son and another the following day. Born on Friday, 17 January, and named for his grandfather's friend and political ally, James Madison Randolph shared his name with the son born most recently to Sally Hemings, two days short of one year earlier at Monticello. In Washington, childbirth and its aftermath prevented Martha from attending some of her father's dinners. Her oldest daughter, Anne, who was now sixteen and attending balls during this visit, may have served as her grandfather's hostess while Martha was indisposed.[53]

Because Jefferson never included Martha or other family members on the "list of diners" that he carefully kept during his last four years as president, there is no way to know for certain how many dinners she attended. Martha surely was present at the thirteen dinners to which women were invited, though Jefferson significantly did not issue proportionately more invitations to mixed-sex dinners as a result of his daughter's presence in the capital. Other sources indicate that Randolph presided over dinners where the guests were all men, the first of which occurred on 9 December 1805, shortly after she and her family arrived in Washington. On that occasion, Jefferson gave a dinner for Sidi Suliman Mellimelli, a Tunisian diplomat, at which the other guests included Samuel Harrison Smith (Margaret's husband), John Randolph of Roanoke, and John Quincy Adams, who reported that "Mrs. Randolph, the President's daughter, and her daughter [Anne] were the only ladies" present.[54]

The fact that this dinner was politically significant and potentially contentious suggests that the famously nonconfrontational Jefferson deployed his daughter—and feminine influence generally—strategically to defuse political conflict. Mellimelli had come to Washington toward the end of four years of intermittent fighting between the United States and the Barbary pirates to negotiate a settlement for a Tunisian ship that the American navy had seized during its blockade of Tripoli. John Randolph of Roanoke, who would soon break completely with the Republicans, had already emerged as an important and sometimes virulent critic of Jefferson's administration.

Two incidents suggest that Martha occasionally used her charm and intelligence to soothe the bruised egos that sometimes resulted from Jefferson's pointed rejection of conventional ceremonial etiquette and diplomatic protocol, even as she largely conformed to his deliberately casual approach to official society. On the one hand, Martha's treatment of Elizabeth Merry, the wife of British minister Anthony Merry, corresponded to Jefferson's exasperatingly informal reception of the couple. When Martha arrived in Washington, Elizabeth Merry inquired whether she wished to be treated, in terms of status, as the daughter of the president or the wife of a member of Congress. Martha replied that she "claimed no distinction whatever, but wished only for the same consideration extended to other strangers"—a response that both flummoxed and outraged the aristocratic Englishwoman. On the other hand, when Jefferson snubbed Thomas Moore, a friend of the Merrys, Martha assuaged the sting by telling Moore's friend, Sir John Augustus Foster, who was also Anthony Merry's secretary, that Jefferson had "taken him for a boy" because of his "low stature and youthful appearance." Martha's effort to smooth relations with Moore probably occurred before he became known to her as the author of the poem publicizing her father's relationship with Sally Hemings. In any event, Foster, who heartily disliked Jefferson, praised Martha as "a very amiable woman."[55]

Attending dinners and exchanging visits and sitting with the other ladies, as was their custom, in the galleries of Congress, Martha renewed her acquaintance with some of the foremost women of in the republic. Dolley Madison, who lived nearby at Montpelier in Orange County when she and James were not in Washington, was a savvy political wife and a leader of fashionable society in the capital even before her husband succeeded Jefferson as president and she, in turn, invented the role of "first lady." Hannah Nicholson Gallatin, Dolley's close friend and the politically minded wife of Jefferson's secretary of the treasury, also became a friend of Martha's, as did the wife of the secretary of war, Dorcas Dearborn. Martha and her daughter Ellen enjoyed their reunion with Margaret Bayard Smith, who, besides being married to a newspaper editor, was a prolific writer in her own right and a leading organizer of charitable and civic efforts in Washington. The fact that Jefferson reassured Martha that her Washington friends would visit Albemarle that summer suggests that she enjoyed the company of such well-informed and accomplished women and that they, in turn, valued her friendship.[56]

Because politics often dominated the conversations of such women, Martha's five-month stay in Washington familiarized her more than ever with the issues of the day. The central debate in Jefferson's second term was how to oppose European depredations on American shipping, which led to the imposition of commercial sanctions against Great Britain, the chief offender, via the Non-Intercourse Act of 1806. When this law proved ineffectual, Jefferson prevailed on Congress to pass the Embargo Act, which closed American ports to all foreign traders in 1807. All Federalists and some dissident Republicans hated the embargo, but supporters of this controversial and ultimately disastrous policy embraced homespun cloth as an emblem of their patriotism, as their mothers had done during the revolutionary era. Between October 1807 and March 1808, Martha oversaw the production of 157 yards of homespun cloth at Edgehill and Monticello. Female slaves did the actual work, but Martha planned to clothe her own children in the homemade fabric, which eleven-year-old Ellen claimed she would "like . . . very well." Perhaps the Randolph women, like the "ladies" of Richmond and Goochland County, purposefully donned homespun dresses to attend that year's local Fourth of July festivities, publicly demonstrating both their patriotism and their Republican loyalties.[57]

If Martha left Washington with fond memories of her friends and a reinvigorated sense of patriotism, Tom's outlook was less sanguine. Not only did he come home to a house that still needed some new plaster and other repairs so that Martha and the children could stay there that winter; he also seethed with rage at his eccentric kinsman John Randolph of Roanoke (known within the family as "Jack"), who he believed had insulted him on the floor of the House of Representatives on the last night that Congress was in session. The two men disagreed on a substantive issue—the repeal of a salt tax—but their enmity was also rooted in the ongoing saga of Tom's sister Nancy. Jack Randolph increasingly blamed Nancy for his brother Richard's downfall and early death, eventually going so far as to accuse her of poisoning Richard in 1796. Jack resented Tom's kindness toward this woman whom he condemned as "a vampire" who "suck[ed] the best blood of my race." For his part, Tom probably worried that Jack and Judith's abandonment of Nancy would render her dependent on his own financially troubled family.[58]

Both Tom and Jack possessed what Martha had come to call "the Randolph character," which she defined as irritability, a propensity to jealousy and suspicion, and a tendency to "indulge mean and little passions." Jack, who was left beardless, frail, and with a high-pitched feminine voice as a result of a youthful illness, was understandably hypersensitive to insults, yet he also had an unshakably aristocratic faith in his own intellectual and moral superiority. He also believed that both Tom Randolph and John Wayles Eppes owed their political careers more to Jefferson's favoritism than to their own merit. For his part, Tom, too, had a hot temper and was increasingly prone to emotional outbursts. In 1804, he nearly engaged in a fistfight in the streets of an Albemarle village when a workingman called him a liar. Tom believed that honor "is the passion of pride" and that "shame is a . . . painfull sensation produced by the scorn or contempt of others whether real or imaginary." Although the man who insulted Tom, as he explained in a letter to his friend Peachy Gilmer, was "not one of those who fight duels," gentlemen like the Randolphs often vanquished shame and defended their reputations by seeking to avenge insults on the field of honor.[59]

So when Jack Randolph denounced the "contumely and hostility" of the House's wrangling over the salt tax, Tom took it personally. He retorted that his cousin had "made more noise than had been useful" during the session and that his use of obstreperous language was tantamount to hiding "behind the shield of the dignity of the house." While candidly admitting that Jack was his intellectual superior, Tom boldly asserted that "in the point of true patriotism he is my inferior." Tom acknowledged the potential impact of his words, hinting that he was amenable to a duel because he believed that "lead and even steel make very proper ingredients in serious quarrels." In effect, Tom accused Jack of cowardice and self-serving demagoguery, qualities that were at odds with prevailing ideals of masculinity in the early American republic. Jack responded immediately by sending his friend, Congressman James Mercer Garnett, to Tom with an ultimatum: He could apologize or they could duel. Tom returned to the House floor and almost inaudibly apologized for his "very severe and harsh language." But the issue was not resolved, in part because newspapers publicized the incident, leaving each man with cause to fear that his honor still needed to be avenged.[60]

Although adversaries resolved most affairs of honor without dueling and most duels ended without a casualty, the prospect of a duel must have chilled Martha, as it did her father. Indeed, they may have known that Elizabeth Schuyler Hamilton was now living in straitened circumstances with her eight children after the untimely death of her husband, Alexander, in a high-profile duel with Aaron Burr in 1804. When Samuel Harrison Smith's *National Intelligencer* ran an account of the Randolphs' altercation that was largely favorable to Tom, and the main Richmond paper, Thomas Ritchie's *Enquirer*, defended Jack, Jefferson worried that escalating rhetoric might lead to "a fatal issue." In a long letter to Tom, the president emphasized his son-in-law's responsibilities to Martha and the children, who depended "for all their happiness and protection in this world on you alone." Dueling and the code of honor, he declared sternly, were "not for fathers of families, or for those charged with other great moral concerns." Jefferson urged Tom to seek the advice of "rational and prudent friends," who he believed would agree that the happiness of his family "ought not to be sacrificed . . . for ever by the error of a single moment." Either Jefferson, his friends, or Martha herself must have persuaded Tom to drop the matter. The Randolph cousins did not duel, but politics and family issues prevented them from reconciling.[61]

When Tom returned to Washington to attend Congress that December, he found a new adversary, John Wayles Eppes, whom Jefferson continued to treat like a son after Maria's tragic death. The three men—Jefferson, Randolph, and Eppes—lived together in the president's house when Congress was in session. While Tom Randolph—in his daughter Ellen's words—was "morose, irritable, and suspicious" and became more so as his prospects worsened, Ellen remembered Jack Eppes as a "good-natured laughing man, inferior perhaps to my father in talent & cultivation, but of a much happier and more amiable temper." Jefferson, who interacted with his sons-in-law according to their respective temperaments, was often jovial with Jack and more reserved with Tom. Convinced that his father-in-law preferred Jack's company and his politics, Tom moved into a boardinghouse in February 1807. Jefferson objected, reassuring Tom that he loved him "as a son (for I protest I know no difference)" and declaring that "no man's republicanism can be better established." When Tom contracted a dangerous fever the following month, he nonetheless stubbornly stayed at the boardinghouse, despite Jefferson's entreaties. Ellen credited her grandfather's "forbearance and kindness," along with her mother's influence, with repairing the breach and restoring the family's unity.[62]

By the time Tom returned home in March, he had decided not to run for reelection, perhaps because of Martha's growing financial worries. Money problems were on her mind that winter, as she sadly detailed the mounting economic casualties among her husband's relatives. David Meade Randolph, having lost most of his Virginia property, had left for England to pursue "some mercantile scheme" while his wife, Mary, ran a boardinghouse in Richmond. Tom's brother William was ruined, as were at least two of his cousins. Tom's trials, Martha believed, "have been great," but she seemed cautiously optimistic about her husband's prospects, especially if he could resist his relatives' repeated pleas for help. Martha was increasingly out-spoken about the need to safeguard the financial interests of her immediate family, and her *"urgent entreaties"* sought to keep Tom "clear of all *new* engagements," at least until he could regain his own financial health.[63]

Related to the family's financial well-being were Martha's ongoing concerns about her children's education. When Tom returned from Congress in the spring of 1807, the Randolphs had seven children—five daughters and two sons—and by the end of the year Martha was again pregnant. First and foremost, Martha believed that morality and manners would help her offspring to make their way in the world as adults, but she also valued intellect highly. For that reason, and perhaps because her own education was such a great asset, both in social situations and as a resource for her children, she carefully monitored and vigorously encouraged their intellectual development. "Surely if they turn out well with regard to morals I *ought* to be satisfied," she observed, "tho I never can sit down quietly under the idea of their being blockheads."[64]

Despite the proliferation of schools and academies for girls and young women in Virginia and in the nation generally by the early nineteenth century, Martha remained entirely responsible for her daughters' education. Indeed, no one appears to have even considered sending the Randolph sisters away from home to be educated. Cost was certainly one factor that deterred Tom and Martha from enrolling the girls in school, but so, too, was Martha's superior education, which equaled and probably exceeded that of most proprietors of female academies. In Albemarle, the sisters also had access to their grandfather's library at Monticello, an impressive collection that at its peak included some 6,000 volumes, while Martha could monitor her daughters' behavior and, as they got older, teach them domestic skills and oversee their introduction to society.[65]

By all accounts, Martha's daughters were both well educated and well mannered. She taught them reading and writing—usually in that order—along with French and other modern languages. Although Martha struggled with Latin at the Panthemont, she evidently learned (and retained) enough to teach Ellen, who was reading Latin texts by 1808. The Randolph sisters studied music, mastering several instruments and becoming proficient harpsichordists like their mother and grandmother. They learned geography, history, and other subjects, reading widely in poetry, ancient history, and other genres. Martha guided her daughters' choice of books and taught them to read daily to keep their minds "in a constantly progressive state." Among authors of fiction, the Irish writer Maria Edgeworth was a favorite because her stories typically featured sensible and educated heroines who used their intellect to be model wives and mothers, an ideal that animated both Martha's and her father's approach to girls' schooling and echoed sentiments Tom expressed years earlier about his sisters' education. While Jefferson condemned novels generally for fostering "bloated imagination, sickly judgment, and disgust towards all the real businesses of life," he praised Edgeworth and a few other authors, who by "modeling their narratives, although fictitious, on the incidents of real life, have been able to make them interesting and useful vehicles of sound morality."[66]

In the postrevolutionary era, novels supplanted both conduct manuals and historical writing as guidebooks for correct behavior and values, especially for girls and young women. Female readers found fictional stories, many of which were penned by women authors, more engaging than prescriptive literature, much of which was the work of male clergy. They also found novels more relevant to their experiences—and hence more instructive—because female characters and their problems typically dominated the novels of the era, while women were generally absent from the pages of contemporary history books, which dwelt almost entirely on political and military topics. Novels taught female readers useful lessons about how to avoid seduction and ruin and how, conversely, to develop and use their abilities and intellects as respectable daughters, wives, and mothers.[67]

In 1808, for instance, Martha and her daughters read Edgeworth's novel *The Modern Griselda*, a parable about marriage and the proper role of women. Edgeworth's title character—whom Jefferson called "a perfect model of ingenious perverseness"—tried to dominate her husband by being, by turns, argumentative and submissive. Their marriage, which was miserably contentious, ended unhappily with Griselda's separation from the man she nonetheless claimed to love. By contrast, the novel's real heroine, Emma, won her husband's love and respect by being modest, reasonable, and intelligent. Their marriage was happy, and indeed, despite Emma's naturally self-effacing manner, it was a marriage of virtual equals. The story's lesson was clear: A wife's modesty, prudence, and intelligence were the best guarantors of her influence and happiness.[68]

Martha recognized the value of a good story in teaching lessons and providing moral exemplars. She was an accomplished storyteller who used characters and episodes from her own life to teach her daughters and other young people. Compared with other women of her generation, Martha had some unusual tales to tell, especially from the years she spent at the Panthemont in Paris. Martha fondly recalled her schooldays, and she often spoke

THE

MODERN GRISELDA.

A TALE.

BY

MISS EDGEWORTH,

AUTHOR OF PRACTICAL EDUCATION, BELINDA, CASTLE
RACKRENT, HISTORY OF IRISH BULLS, LETTERS FOR
LITERARY LADIES, POPULAR TALES, &c.

" And since in man right reason bears the sway,
" Let that frail thing, weak woman, have her way."

POPE.

LONDON:

PRINTED FOR J. JOHNSON, Nº 72, ST. PAUL'S
CHURCHYARD;

By Bye and Law, St. John's Square.

1805.

The Modern Griselda. *Like many postrevolutionary American females, Martha's
daughters learned much about the world and their place in it by reading novels.
Maria Edgeworth's moralistic stories and essays were extremely popular in the
United States. Martha and her daughters read this 1805 novel by Edgeworth, which
bore this epigraph from Alexander Pope: "And since in man right reason bears
the sway, / Let that frail thing, weak woman, have her way." Special Collections,
University of Virginia Library.*

of them, regaling her daughters with tales that, according to Ellen, "combined for us, all the interest of fiction with the force of truth. The facts were undoubted and the persons so far removed from us by time and distance that although we had . . . an intimate personal acquaintance with them, we could have no feelings personal to ourselves when they were held up before us as patterns and warnings."[69]

Martha's stories indulged her own nostalgia and her listeners' sense of adventure, but she also used her tales and their characters to teach, much as she might have used one of Edgeworth's novels, as Ellen's comment suggests. Martha's classmates, whose "names had become like household words," were also variously role models or cautionary figures. "The English Misses and French Mademoiselles became to us objects of emulation or warning as effectually as if they had been placed bodily before our eyes and observation," Ellen explained. Stories told with admiration for industrious, sweet-tempered, principled, and well-bred young women from Martha's past inspired her daughters to cultivate those attributes, while equally compelling tales of schoolgirls who were "idle and dirty" or "selfish & greedy" made them ashamed "to resemble persons so disagreeable and disgusting." One of Ellen's cousins agreed, describing Martha as one who "knew how to bring back past events and portray the characters connected with them," and who especially enjoyed sharing stories with young people.[70]

Lest her daughters find themselves unprepared to fulfill their destiny as American wives and mothers, however, Martha mixed stories of her life in what Ellen called "the gay circles of Paris" with practical lessons and skills that she believed would be useful to them in their future lives. Perhaps recalling her own uninitiated plunge into the world of housewifery, Martha had her older girls raise poultry, tend gardens, and assist her with routine housekeeping. Jefferson encouraged these efforts, which he believed to be ultimately even more important than intellectual pursuits (for females at least), stressing the value of "the good housewife, one of whom is worth more than a whole family of muses." As her oldest daughters became young women—Anne was seventeen in 1808—Martha clearly fretted about their futures. Jefferson, who urged them to live simply and avoid debt, shared her worries. But all she could do to prepare them for the future was to equip them with the necessary domestic skills and other knowledge they could use and then pass on to their own children and hope that they would marry prudent and sensible men.[71]

Educating sons was more complicated, and often more costly, because men had more choices about how to spend their adult lives. At the same time, there was also great pressure on them to succeed, both economically and in terms of their public reputations. For that reason, Tom Randolph had hoped that profits from a cotton plantation would enable him to give his son, Thomas Jefferson Randolph, a first-rate education in the United States and Europe. When the cotton plantation (and its expected earnings) did not materialize and when it became apparent that Jeff, who had proven through his studies with Martha and at a series of local schools that he was not an apt student, the Randolphs scaled back their plans for educating their eldest son.[72]

In 1808, Martha explained her reservations about sixteen-year-old Jeff's abilities when she declined her father's offer to pay the youth's expenses to study science at the University of Pennsylvania. "With regard to Jefferson our objections were incurring so great an expense with out any certain benefit," she declared bluntly. "His education is too back ward I am afraid to enable him to profit by any instructions conveyed by *lectures* and his indolence so great as to render it doubtfull whether he can be trusted to himself as much as he would be" away from home. Concerned about her father's financial well-being, as well as the uncertain future of her other children, Martha forcefully asserted that "it would be *wrong* to incur a certain evil for a very uncertain benefit and perhaps the danger of giving expense for one who certainly has very little prospect at present of any thing more than bare competency."[73]

While Jeff's parents saw him as a future planter and Jefferson envisioned his eldest grandson and namesake as an educated man of science, the larger issue here, for Martha at least, was economic. For the second time in six months, she questioned her father's financial priorities and reminded him that even his expenditures on behalf of herself and her children could be damaging in the long run. Lamenting the expense of her family's recent trip to Washington, she urged Jefferson to put his own financial needs ahead of "the maintenance of our large family. . . . Secure your tranquility and ours will follow." Now she worried that investing in Jeff's education would be more money "wantonly squandered." In this argument between a practical-minded mother and an optimistically benevolent grandfather, the latter prevailed. Jeff left Edgehill that October, stopping at the president's house before continuing on to Philadelphia.[74]

❖ Jeff's departure for Philadelphia was one of four family milestones that occurred during Martha's last year as the daughter of the president. A month before Jeff left home, Martha's oldest child, seventeen-year-old

Anne, married Charles Lewis Bankhead at Monticello. If Martha or Tom or anyone else in the family thought that Anne was too young to marry or that she chose hastily or unwisely, such misgivings are not evident in the family correspondence. Two months before Anne's wedding, Martha gave birth to her ninth child, Benjamin Franklin Randolph, at Edgehill. Dolley Madison reported that her friend, who was now thirty-six years old, hoped that this "fine . . . but cross" child would be her last. Although Martha did not get her wish, another woman in the family concluded her childbearing career that May: Sally Hemings gave birth to her last child, a son named Thomas Eston Hemings. This child bore the name of Jefferson's friend and cousin Thomas Eston Randolph, who had married Tom's sister Jane. Light-skinned and said to possess a striking resemblance to Thomas Jefferson, as an adult Eston Hemings, like his siblings Beverley and Harriet, passed as white.[75]

chapter 5   { # Return to Monticello

About a week after James Madison succeeded Thomas Jefferson as president, Martha Jefferson Randolph and her daughters went to Monticello to prepare for the homecoming of the country's most famous living citizen. Traveling first by carriage and then on horseback, Jefferson arrived at Monticello on 15 March 1809. "The people of the County" had asked to accompany the retiring president on the final leg of his journey so that they might, as his daughter informed him, have one "last opportunity . . . of giving you a public testimony of their respect and affection." When that ceremonial reception proved too difficult to organize, local people instead drafted a welcoming address, which Jefferson acknowledged with "inexpressible pleasure" as he "gladly lay down the distressing burthen of power."[1]

For Jefferson, retirement from public life meant returning to his farms, his gardens, his library, and his family and friends in Albemarle, but for Martha, her father's retirement posed both opportunities and potential problems. On the one hand, she looked forward to spending more time with Jefferson once he returned to private life. She truly enjoyed his company, and despite the cramped sleeping quarters her family occupied on Monticello's upper floor, they probably appreciated the house's comparative spaciousness overall. On the other hand, Thomas Mann Randolph, who had farms of his own to tend, came to resent the removal of his family to Monticello, though he did not seem to mind that arrangement at the outset. Guided by a sense of obligation and affection, Martha divided her time between her children, her father, her husband, and her domestic duties, which now included extending hospitality to the many guests who flocked to see the famed patriot and former president. Whether at Edgehill or Monticello, her daily routine alternated between extreme busyness and the dull seclusion of rural life.

❖ As the wife of a former congressman and the daughter of a former president, Martha watched both men struggle to attain solvency after they returned to private life. Although she and her daughters defensively attributed Jefferson's financial problems mainly to his years of public service both before and during his time as president, at least he received an annual salary of $25,000 during his two presidential terms. Jefferson used that salary to pay his living expenses in Washington and to finance his official dinners, but he also paid for the Randolphs' trip to the capital, his grandson's education in Philadelphia, and the continuing construction at Monticello. Thomas Mann Randolph received much less compensation for his four years in Congress—only $6 a day, plus travel expenses—and though he lived cheaply in his father-in-law's house during most of his tenure in Washington, his financial situation was precarious even before he entered public life.[2]

Tom had debts to pay, both in his own name and in his capacity as executor of his father's estate. To keep up with the payments due to his creditors, he relied on his income from rents on land in Henrico, Albemarle, and Bedford counties, which he leased to tenant farmers, and from his yearly crops. In the summer of 1805, however, he had lost his wheat crop to the Hessian fly, a voracious insect so named because it arrived in America with the European armies in the 1770s. The destruction of his wheat prevented Tom from paying down his debts that year. The fact that his creditors gave him extensions helped, but only temporarily. By 1807, he had to borrow more money to meet his obligations, using a deed of trust on Edgehill as his security.[3]

When Tom returned to Albemarle after completing his second term in Congress, he devoted himself to the business of farming. Always a committed student of agriculture, Tom as a young man kept a memorandum book full of information and observations on crops, planting, and plowing. In Albemarle, he was an agricultural reformer and a leading advocate of scientific farming. As early as 1793, he had experimented with plowing furrows horizontally, rather than straight downhill, to prevent soil erosion, and he invented a hillside plow to do the job more effectively shortly after he left Congress. In 1817, Tom was among the founders of the Agricultural Society of Albemarle, whose avowed purpose was to "promote the interests of Agriculture and Domestic Economy in general" primarily by studying farmers' chronic problems—such as insects and soil depletion—and experimenting with new techniques to solve them. Tom was an active member of the society and served for many years as one of its officers.[4]

With Martha and the children firmly rooted in Albemarle, Tom first attempted to reduce his debts by selling assets elsewhere. By early 1809, he had decided to sell Varina, the valuable but heavily mortgaged plantation in Henrico that had been in his family for generations. Jefferson approved, doubtlessly echoing Martha's sentiments when he suggested that Tom would not want one of their sons to settle in remote, unhealthy Henrico. He counseled his son-in-law to sell Varina and, if possible, to retain the land in Bedford County that he gave to Martha when she married. "My idea is that your lands & mine adjacent to one another in Albemarle & Bedford will ensure a competent provision to all the children," he observed, adding, "If by selling our detached parcels we can clear ourselves of debt it will enable us to enjoy an easy situation in tranquility."[5]

Well aware of her husband's financial obligations, Martha shared her father's vision of her grown children settled together in agricultural clusters in Albemarle and Bedford, but she was sufficiently clearheaded to see that her family's mounting debts jeopardized the attainment of that happy goal. Consequently, when Tom found no buyer for Varina and he considered instead disposing of Martha's portion of the Poplar Forest tract in Bedford, she acquiesced, believing that crops alone would not pay his debts and that selling land was both economically and morally preferable to selling slaves. She hoped that selling the Bedford land, by enabling Tom to pay his debts, would save Edgehill and her father's remaining lands in Albemarle and Bedford for the younger generation. In February 1810, Martha and Tom therefore sold 840 acres in Bedford County to Anne Moseley for $10 an acre, for a total of $8,400. That October, their conveyance of the 160 acres they retained at Poplar Forest to their son-in-law, Charles Bankhead, for the nominal fee of five shillings, amounted to a belated marriage settlement for their eldest daughter.[6]

Tom worked hard at Edgehill, and for a while at least, it seemed like his efforts were paying off. In February 1810, after heavy rains damaged most of the fields in Albemarle, only Tom's horizontal furrows remained intact, according to Jefferson, who praised his son-in-law's system, which some of his neighbors soon adopted. By the end of the year, Elizabeth Trist, who was visiting Monticello and who now saw Martha on a regular basis, happily reported that Tom was "surmounting his difficulties and appears much more happy," in part due to the "excellent crops" he produced for two years running. Martha must have breathed a sigh of relief when Tom avoided the temptation to become a candidate for the state senate because, in his words, the "urgency of private business" made him reluctant to leave Edgehill. Tom himself expressed both satisfaction and relief when Joseph Carrington Cabell agreed to run for the seat, fearing that he would have felt obliged to serve if no suitable candidate had come forward.[7]

At both Edgehill and Monticello, diversification was part of the long-term plan to attain solvency. After 1809, Jefferson expanded his vegetable gardens, orchards, and vineyards, mostly to supply his own table; he also erected a gristmill at Shadwell in 1807 and a sawmill at Monticello a few years later, and he increased the production of nails, barrels, and cloth on his home plantation. Spurred initially by the Embargo Act of 1807, Tom began a cloth-making operation at Edgehill, which Martha managed. By 1811, Tom had also taken over the lease on his father-in-law's gristmill, in partnership with a miller named Finney. Together, father- and son-in-law oversaw the construction of a sluice to facilitate access to the mill and the shipping of its grain on the Rivanna River, which intersected the James River and connected Albemarle to Richmond, which had become an important commercial center.[8]

Martha's involvement was essential to the cloth-making ventures at Edgehill and Monticello. She was knowledgeable about spinning, had a spinning jenny of her own, and may have spun herself from time to time, though she mostly supervised the work of others. Martha had overseen the spinning and weaving at Edgehill during the embargo, but her husband and father sought to manufacture cloth on a larger scale in 1811 when they hired William McClure to establish a small-scale "factory" at Legos, across the river from Monticello. McClure's task was to build spinning and weaving machines and to teach enslaved women and girls to run them. By the time he left Albemarle in 1814, McClure had at least four spinning jennies running ninety-six spindles, which would ideally produce enough homespun to clothe the enslaved workforce at both Edgehill and Monticello.[9]

By 1815, when Jefferson informed a friend that "a few women, children & invalids who could do little in the farm" were producing 2,000 yards of cloth a year to replace what he had previously imported from Britain, the spinners and weavers had left Legos and were working under Martha's watchful eyes at Monticello. Ellen Randolph recalled how "after the introduction of the spinning Jenny we had a sort of manufacturing establishment in an out building at Monticello, where work used to be weighed out in her [mother's] presence and partly with her own hands." Comparatively speaking, work in the textile factory was not onerous, and it was one of the few skilled occupations open to female slaves. One enslaved spinner described the atmosphere in the factory as somewhat rowdy and less regimented than some other work environments on the plantation, even when "mistress" was on the premises. That Harriet Hemings worked as a spinner for a while reflected the comparatively privileged status of that occupation in Monticello's slave community.[10]

As both a productive enterprise and a gathering place, Monticello was the headquarters of the Jefferson-Randolph family after 1809. When Jefferson took a census of his property in 1810, he counted not only Martha, Tom, and their nine children among its "inhabitants," but also their son-in-law, Charles Bankhead, Tom's sister Harriet Randolph Hackley and her children (who were there temporarily), and sixteen of Tom's slaves. In fact, Tom went to Edgehill every day, and he and Martha lived there during the busy harvest season. But Monticello was the Randolphs' primary residence—so much so that in late 1810 some local gossips believed that Jefferson would move to Poplar Forest and cede Monticello entirely to Tom Randolph and his family. That rumor was groundless, but there were several reasons why, from Martha's perspective at least, it made sense for the Randolphs to take the relatively unusual step of living mainly at her father's home.[11]

First and foremost, the accommodations at Monticello were much expanded and improved since Anna Maria Brodeau Thornton arrived there with her husband in 1802 and entered an "irregular and unpleasant" parlor through "a large unfinished hall, loose plank forming the floor, lighted by one dull lantern." At that point, a small, steep ladder led to unfinished sleeping quarters on the upper floor, and the grounds, too, were a work in progress. Although she enjoyed the company of Jefferson, his daughters, and the other guests, Thornton disliked the "general gloom" of Monticello, and she deemed the house's setting "something grand & awful . . . but far from convenient or in my opinion agreeable." Monticello, she concluded, was "a place you wou'd rather look at now & then than live at."[12]

By contrast, when Jefferson retired from the presidency in 1809, the house was virtually complete, aside from the porticoes and their columns, which would not be erected until the early 1820s. Even Thornton was impressed when she visited again in 1806, four years after her first trek up the mountain. Now her carriage proceeded up an "excellent road" to a house and grounds that were "amazingly improved." Thornton praised Monticello overall as "quite a handsome place." Work continued, and by 1808, less than a year before her grandfather returned permanently to Albemarle, thirteen-year-old Ellen Randolph informed him that "the hall, with its gravel coloured border is the most beautiful room I was ever in, without excepting the drawing rooms at Washington." According to Ellen, the dining room was also "greatly improved," the house's exterior was fine, and though the flower gardens and lawn were still "rather dismal" and the "mean little" sheep were eating the orange trees, Jefferson's large new terrace was nearly finished.[13]

The newly completed house and the vast space it afforded, therefore, was one compelling reason for the Randolphs' removal to Monticello. Jefferson's private quarters—his bedroom, adjoining study, and library—were generally off limits, but the Randolphs had access to the large entry hall, parlor, dining room, and tearoom, plus two other rooms downstairs and a total of ten rooms in the house's upper stories. Designed to appear smaller, Monticello was, at 11,000 square feet, enormous by contemporary standards. The house at Edgehill, though bigger than an average Virginia farmhouse, must have seemed extraordinarily crowded for a large and growing family, plus their servants, and especially for a family who at times had occupied far more spacious quarters. The comparative dimensions of Edgehill and Monticello might have seemed particularly salient when Martha became pregnant yet again in early March 1809, around the time her father left the presidency. Monticello's proximity to Edgehill, Martha and the children's devotion to Jefferson, and the former president's congenial working relationship with Tom, whose agricultural expertise he valued and praised, made the prospect of sharing Monticello's large space even more appealing.[14]

The Randolphs' residence at Monticello also made sense from the perspective of its master, who needed someone to oversee his household staff and act as his hostess. Nancy Randolph, Tom's oldest unmarried sister at the time of their mother's death, played these roles at Tuckahoe for her widowed father before he remarried, and Martha, of course, had done so often at Monticello. Jefferson might have entrusted Sally Hemings, who lived in the house and knew its staff well, with housekeeping duties, but placing Hemings in the role of mistress or hostess would have conferred legitimacy on their relationship, a step that Jefferson's white family, friends, and others would have found intolerable. In early 1809, Jefferson proposed asking his youngest sister, Anna Scott Jefferson Marks, to be his housekeeper, but Martha protested that her aunt had "neither head nor sufficient weight of character to manage so large an establishment as yours will be." Martha added that she, by contrast, would "devote my self to it and with feelings which I could never have in my own affairs."[15]

Both Martha and her father also must have recognized that the Randolphs' presence allowed Jefferson to enjoy the domestic environment he professed to value and, in the process, to enhance his public image as a respectable family man and discredit persistent rumors about him and Hemings. When Margaret Bayard Smith and other visitors came to Monticello, they saw a benevolent gentleman in the midst of his adoring "children & grand children," and one who divided his time between his books and gardens when he was not with his family or conversing with his guests. Smith, whose visit produced a detailed account of family life at Monticello that she intended for a public audience, portrayed the former president as "truely a Philosopher, & truely a good man," whose virtuous domesticity belied "all the misrepresentations and calumnies" that his enemies had heaped upon him. "I looked upon him, as he walked, the top of this mountain, as a being elevated above the mass of mankind," she opined, "as much in character as he was in local situation. . . . After forty years spent on the tempestuous sea of political [life,] he had now reached the secure haven of domestic life." Without the presence of Martha and her children, such stirring domestic performances would not have been possible.[16]

Finally, both Martha and Tom must have believed that their children would benefit by living at Monticello. As a devotee of Enlightenment ideals, Tom would have embraced the notion that humans learn by experience and that, more often than not, they were products of their environments. Martha must have looked on her father's books, artwork, and scientific specimens as practical resources that she could use to advance the education of her offspring. Jefferson certainly saw his Indian artifacts, fossils, classical statuary, Houdon busts, and paintings of biblical scenes and historical figures in that light. At a time when museums of any sort were scarce in the United States, Jefferson left some rooms at Monticello—the hall, the parlor, and possibly the dining room—accessible to the public when he was away from home as a sort of educational museum. Eighteen-year-old George Gilmer of Georgia came to see the "Statuary, fine paintings, and a collection of Indian works" during Jefferson's last months as president. He found the statues "very beautiful" and the Indian artifacts "singular," but he remarked that the "paintings did not at all equal the expectations which my scholastic reading had excited."[17]

After 1809, the flow of interesting and learned people who visited the former president exposed his grandchildren to ideas and social experiences that were available to few, especially in rural America. In the first years of Jefferson's retirement, for instance, visitors who brought political news from Washington included Margaret Bayard Smith and her husband, the editor of the *National Intelligencer*; Hannah and Albert Gallatin; and President and Mrs. Madison. Elizabeth Trist came often, armed with her sharply Republican political opinions and greetings from old friends in Philadelphia. Tom's sister Harriet brought stories about the "horrors of war" in Europe and life in Cádiz, where her husband was U.S. consul. David

Entrance Hall at Monticello. The young Randolphs learned from their grandfather's books, art, and artifacts, as well as from the steady flow of guests who passed through Monticello. Among the highlights of the house's entrance hall were historical busts and paintings, maps, Native American artifacts, and specimens from natural history. Monticello/Thomas Jefferson Foundation, Inc.

Baillie Warden, an erudite Irish immigrant who obtained a consulship in Paris, visited and became friendly with Martha, to whom he sent magazines and books and for whom he offered to procure goods from Europe. The Portuguese scholar and diplomat the Abbé Correa de Serra made the first of his many visits in 1813. Years later, Ellen Randolph recalled that this "learned" man was "always a welcome guest [who] passed some weeks of each year" with them for several years running. On its best days, life at Monticello thus combined the most appealing qualities of a wholesome rural environment with those of genteel cosmopolitan society.[18]

Martha's daily routine at Monticello rarely varied. The family and their guests rose early and had breakfast at 8:00. After breakfast, Jefferson retired to his library, Tom usually went to work at Edgehill, and guests were left on their own to read, walk, or ride horses, while Martha and her daughters did some light housework before taking up their books. Margaret Bayard Smith found that "excepting the hours house-keeping requires [Martha] devotes the rest to her children whom she instructs." The children, in turn, "seem never to leave her for an instant, but are always beside her or on her lap." Mother and children passed the day together until 4:00 or 5:00, when the family assembled for dinner. Smith found the dinner table "plainly, but genteelly and plentifully spread" with meat, vegetables, and fruit produced at Monticello or Poplar Forest and "a costly variety" of French and Italian wines, along with Madeira and some "sweet ladies wine." Martha sometimes took part in the family's favorite after-dinner activities—conversation, strolls through the gardens and grounds, and music—but often she tended to various household tasks while Jefferson, who loved to play with his grandchildren, kept the youngsters occupied. She returned to the group for tea, a light meal at 9:00, which typically featured fruit from the orchards on Jefferson's estate.[19]

Martha's days were busy. She was not her father's guest, but rather, she played an active and essential role in the daily functioning of Monticello. Edmund Bacon, who was Jefferson's overseer from 1806 until 1822, knew Martha well and saw her frequently, in part because she often made decisions related to matters on the estate. In his memoirs, Bacon explained that sometimes Jefferson "would refer me to her, or she would refer me to him, a half dozen times in a day." Bacon praised Martha's pleasant demeanor as well as her industry. "I never saw her at all out of temper. . . . As she was attending to her duties about the house, she seemed to be always in a happy mood," he wrote, adding, "She was always busy."[20]

The mistress of Monticello exuded an aura of cheerful competence, even in times of crisis. In the summer of 1809, Margaret Bayard Smith and her husband visited Monticello at a particularly bad time. About three weeks earlier, Martha's oldest daughter, Anne, had given birth to her first child. The baby, born one month prematurely, had died. Anne, who did not inherit her mother's vigorous constitution, was still "confined" and "delicate" when the Smiths arrived. At the same time, one of Martha's younger sons was also seriously ill, and Martha herself, at age thirty-seven, was midway through another pregnancy. The sympathetic Smith observed that Martha and Tom "sat up every night" with their sick children and that Martha also spent much of her day nursing them, even as she continued to teach their healthy siblings and attend to other domestic responsibilities. Still, she managed to show her guests "a smiling face" and "kind & cheerful man-

*Martha Jefferson Randolph's Notebook. In this small, leather-bound notebook,
Martha kept track of the Monticello silverware ("18 dessert spoons, 2 soup ladles . . .")
and other household matters that kept her constantly busy as the mistress of a large
family on a working plantation where long- and short-term guests were common.
Monticello/Thomas Jefferson Foundation, Inc.*

ners," retaining her good cheer even after she herself became ill a few days
into the Smiths' stay. Most visitors who came to Monticello, like Smith, marveled at the beauty of the place, the unpretentious hospitality of its master, and the charm of his affectionate family circle. But Smith—who was
herself an accomplished hostess and mother of four children—also recognized Martha's role in creating a domestic environment that featured timely
meals, well-behaved children, and sociable moments that made their idyllic visits possible.[21]

❖ Some scholars have seen the Randolphs' removal to Monticello as a decisive turning point in the deterioration of Martha's relationship with her husband. Often cited in support of this contention are Martha's inevitable suffering as a result of the "knowledge that her husband was contributing almost nothing financially for their upkeep" and Tom's equally inevitable resentment of what amounted to the "public display of the failure of his marriage and his inadequacies as a provider." The decision to live with Jefferson, according to this argument, was either a cause or a consequence of the unavoidable estrangement between husband and wife.[22]

In fact, the Randolphs' marriage, though troubled, was remarkably resilient. On the one hand, Tom's occasional outbursts—his assault on an Albemarle County man in 1804, his near-duel with Jack Randolph, and his fallout with Jack Eppes—had been more frequent in recent years, and Martha's increasingly vocal concerns about his financial problems must have heightened tensions between them, though she also recognized that her husband's economic woes, at least, were neither unique nor especially shameful. On the other hand, Tom must have conceded some of the advantages of having his large family live at Monticello, where he and Martha had spent extended periods every year since they married. The change, though dramatic in retrospect, may not have seemed so at the time. The Randolphs returned to Edgehill each year at harvest time, and Martha and Tom still enjoyed some happy times. Tom's biographer, who described the months following Jefferson's retirement as "very much like other summers," did not consider the move worth mentioning as a watershed moment in his subject's life.[23]

That said, Martha's place in her father's house was satisfying and well defined, but Tom's position was less clear. As the owner of Monticello, father or grandfather of its most privileged residents, and master of 122 others, Jefferson was the patriarch in this household. A patriarch, by definition, was a man who had authority over his dependents, who included his wife and children, as well as servants or slaves. By the postrevolutionary era, Americans (especially slaveholding southerners) increasingly emphasized the gentler aspects of patriarchy, maintaining that good patriarchs were obliged to provide material sustenance and protection to their dependents and show paternalistic benevolence as they exercised their powers. At Monticello, Jefferson provided food and shelter for both his family and his enslaved workforce. He also made the rules for the house—most notably protecting the privacy of his library and living quarters—though he was openly affectionate to his white family and humane to his African American dependents.[24]

By contrast, Tom's status at Monticello was ambiguous but at the same time vitally important, because postrevolutionary Americans associated both manliness and citizenship with patriarchal autonomy and power. Whether Tom qualified as a patriarch depended on his legal and customary authority over and responsibilities toward dependents in a household. To be impoverished, childless, or even unmarried compromised one's masculinity. Men without property could not vote or hold office in Virginia and most other states, and "old bachelors," though not disenfranchised, were often ridiculed and politically suspect.[25]

Tom clearly possessed some of the most important qualifications for patriarchy, manhood, and citizenship. He had a wife, many children, and extensive property in land and slaves. Like Jefferson, he was reputed to be a kind master. In addition, Tom's position as an officer in the county militia, his two terms in Congress, and his viability as a possible candidate for the state senate in 1810 all indicate that his neighbors still considered him one of the leading men in Albemarle. The fact that Martha and the children returned to Edgehill to live periodically, mostly when Jefferson went to Poplar Forest or when she and Tom provided the customary harvest feast for their enslaved workers, also allowed Tom to present himself on occasion as the head of a more typically patriarchal household.[26]

At the same time, Tom's status in his own family was at best poorly defined and at worst dependent on Jefferson, if not on Martha. Unlike his wife, Tom had no specific responsibilities at Monticello and played no obvious role. Jefferson provided food, shelter, and amusement for Tom's wife and children, and he paid for the schooling of his eldest grandson. Years later, Martha recalled that her children received "every thing in the way of a luxury, their books, their trinkets, their watches, and even their equipment for riding" from their grandfather. In 1823, Jefferson hired James Westhall Ford, a young itinerant artist, to paint a portrait of his then-fifty-one-year-old daughter to hang at Monticello. As both he and Tom must have known, commissioning and displaying the portrait of a married woman was typically the prerogative of her husband.[27]

During this period, Tom tacitly ceded his parental prerogative to name his children to his father-in-law, who chose names to honor his own political associates and friends. Tom probably shared his father-in-law's esteem for James Madison and Benjamin Franklin—whose Randolph namesakes

James Westhall Ford, Martha Jefferson Randolph, *1823. This portrait shows Martha Jefferson Randolph as a matronly mother of eleven living children and mistress of her father's household. Jefferson paid the seventeen-year-old artist $50 for two portraits: this likeness of Martha and one of her oldest daughter, Anne Cary Randolph Bankhead. Monticello/Thomas Jefferson Foundation, Inc.*

were born in 1806 and 1808, respectively—but Jefferson's later choices were more personal. In January 1810, at Monticello, Martha gave birth to her fourth son, named Meriwether Lewis Randolph for an Albemarle neighbor who served as her father's private secretary and then led the famous Lewis and Clark expedition to explore the Louisiana Purchase. In July 1811, Martha suffered a miscarriage during the fourth month of her next pregnancy, but in 1814 she gave birth to a seventh daughter, Septimia.[28] The Randolphs' youngest child, who was born at Monticello in March 1818, bore the name George Wythe Randolph to honor Jefferson's legal mentor. Of the eleven Randolph children who survived to adulthood, only Anne Cary and Virginia—who was probably named for Tom's youngest sister, though her middle name was Jefferson—received names that acknowledged important influences or relationships associated specifically with their father.

In general, then, Martha and her father attended to the household, the plantation, and the family at Monticello, while Tom went off to work at Edgehill. Property ownership, which afforded political rights and at least the potential for economic self-sufficiency, differentiated Tom's status at Monticello from that of Jefferson's sister, Anna Scott Jefferson Marks, who had joined the household after her husband died in 1811. Tending the farm at Edgehill also gave Tom a respite from his large and noisy family, where someone was usually sick and four or more children were constantly "chattering." While Martha's bookish and somewhat unsociable husband probably appreciated the chance to get away, his incongruous status as a putative patriarch living in another man's house was a source of occasional and eventually increasing tension between husband and wife.[29]

Jefferson tried to be tactful toward his volatile son-in-law, but the older man's well-known aversion to confrontational behavior must have made Tom feel at times like a youngster forced to abide by the standards of his elders. One particular problem was Tom's bitter hatred of John Wayles Eppes, with whom Jefferson desired to remain on good terms even after Eppes remarried in 1809. By then, the daughter Maria bore shortly before her death had also died, leaving Francis as her only surviving child. Jefferson wanted this grandson to come to Monticello to be educated, but Jack Eppes adamantly opposed his son's "forming attachments" in the Randolph family circle, from which he himself felt excluded because of Tom's hostility. Jack refused to visit Monticello or to bring his son there, despite his affection for the rest of the family, including Martha, whom he considered "the dearest of sisters." Eventually, Jefferson must have prevailed on Tom either to keep his criticism of Jack to himself or to avoid interacting with Francis, because Jack relented and Francis spent much of 1809 and 1810 at Monticello. A year later, when he wrote to Jefferson, Francis closed his letter with "love to aunt Randolph and all the children" without mentioning Tom.[30]

Tom's ambiguous status and Jefferson's authority over him, however understated, must have caused some discord between him and Martha, though there is no evidence of specific altercations immediately following Jefferson's return to private life. Visitors to Monticello without exception praised Martha as gracious and amiable, but they also noted Tom's presence as a member of Jefferson's congenial family circle. Margaret Bayard Smith portrayed Martha and her husband as devoted parents who sat up together to nurse their sick children. Elizabeth Trist, who was closer to the family than most guests and therefore more likely to see the Randolphs when they were not on their best behavior, described Tom as a man of "industry and goodness of heart."[31]

Soon, however, a crisis in American foreign policy gave Tom an opportunity to seek distinction outside his father-in-law's household. Despite the best efforts of Jefferson and Madison to avoid involvement in the war in Europe, Congress declared war on Great Britain, at the president's behest, in June 1812. Although Federalists vehemently opposed this second war with Britain, stalwart Republicans in Martha's circle strongly supported it. Jefferson believed that Britain's continued depredations on U.S. shipping ultimately made war unavoidable; he observed optimistically that he had "known of no war entered into under more favorable auspices." Elizabeth Trist was less circumspect. An adamant proponent of war even before it was declared, she professed feeling "a little of the old sperit of Seventy Six when I hear of [Britain's] daring outrages," and she playfully advocated "the Use of the Guillotine to extirpate every Villian" who opposed going to war to defend American rights. So, too, did Tom Randolph desire war with Britain, which he saw as the "natural enemy" of the United States, mistakenly believing that Americans would receive military support from the French, their old revolutionary allies.[32]

Tom had harbored both military ambitions and a deep and vocal hostility toward Britain since at least 1807. When a British warship, the HMS *Leopard*, fired on the USS *Chesapeake* that June, Tom, who was by then a colonel in the Albemarle County militia, asked the governor's permission to raise a company of riflemen and march them to Hampton Roads to attack the *Leopard*, which remained off the Virginia coast. The governor refused, but in 1812 Tom was still a militia colonel awaiting a call to action. None came.

In March 1813, however, nine months after the declaration of war, on the recommendation of William A. Burwell, a congressman from Virginia and one of Jefferson's former secretaries, President Madison nominated Tom for a military commission. Congress confirmed his appointment, giving Colonel Thomas Mann Randolph command of the Twentieth Regiment of Infantry. Aside from participating in local militia musters, Tom had no prior military experience. Nevertheless, President Madison and other "friends" expressed confidence in the new colonel's "superiority in the talents and military acquirements so much needed in our army."[33]

Madison expected the response of Tom's family to his military commission to be at best "mingled," but he also accurately gauged what Jefferson called his son-in-law's "military fever." Tom was now forty-five years old and feeling the effects of disillusioned middle age, and his reasons for seeking military service were both public spirited and self-regarding. He had come of age during the American Revolution, and for years afterward, as Jefferson's disciple and protégé, he had ingested a steady diet of anti-British politics. He truly believed that Britain was the "natural enemy" of the American republic and that the republic was worth defending. At the same time, however, Tom probably viewed the war as an opportunity for an honorable escape from the daily grind of family and plantation duties, perhaps most especially after the British naval blockade of the Chesapeake Bay prevented him from shipping his flour to northern markets in the spring of 1813.[34]

If being the family breadwinner was one way to prove one's manhood, military service was an even more time-honored way for a man to show his virility and worth. The fact that Jefferson had never won glory on the battle-field—and, indeed, the fact that Martha knew that his enemies still mocked his supposed cowardice as Virginia's wartime governor—afforded added incentive to Tom, who ardently hoped to excel in an arena that his wife's beloved father had not already conquered.[35]

Tom was not the only middle-aged civilian who took up arms for the first time as an officer during the War of 1812. The fact that the United States had not fought a full-scale war in the decades since the Revolution, coupled with the smallness of the country's peacetime army, meant that many of the 341 men who held the rank of major or higher during this second war with Britain were comparatively inexperienced. Tom was one of 166 men appointed to such a rank whose only prior military service was marching and drilling with the county militia. At age forty-five, he was slightly older than the typical newly commissioned senior officer—the average age for colonels, lieutenant colonels, and majors was thirty-nine—but significantly younger than some of them. Like Tom, most of his fellow officers came from society's upper strata. While most were men of either state or local prominence, Tom was one of 14 high-ranking officers who had held political office, all as members of Congress, at the national level.[36]

Although there is no direct evidence that Martha pressed her husband to reject the commission that the president and Congress offered, clearly she would have been happier if Tom had remained at home. For one thing, although the battlefield casualties in the War of 1812 were relatively light, war always brought the possibility of death, either by wounds sustained in battle or, more commonly, as a result of the diseases that typically ravaged military encampments. Tom decided to accept the commission as soon as it was offered, and after discussing with Martha the possibility of his dying in service and the likelihood of her remarrying, he drafted his will on 16 March 1813. Unlike many formulaic wills of the era, Tom's was apparently heartfelt. He began by expressing "full confidence in the understanding, judgment, honour and impartial Maternal feeling of my beloved wife Martha," who had assured him that she (like increasing numbers of middle-aged widows of means) would not remarry in the event of his death. Tom recommended that Martha sell Varina to satisfy his financial obligations and that she give Jeff a large portion of Edgehill and divide the rest among the younger boys. But he ultimately left the disposition of his property in her trustworthy hands, "to distribute among her children and certain for her own use as she may think fit after paying all my debts."[37]

For five anxious months, Martha and Tom waited while Tom recruited soldiers for his regiment. In March, around the time her husband made his will, Martha again became pregnant. By May, perhaps sharing his daughter's apprehensions with an old and trusted friend, Jefferson confided to Elizabeth Trist that Tom's impending departure would "be a great loss to his family" because his "affairs" would suffer tremendously in his absence. Around the same time, it became evident that the British blockade would prevent Tom from selling not only his own wheat crop but also the extra 23,000 bushels he had purchased and ground into flour, hoping to make big profits in a market where grain was scarce due to the return of the Hessian fly and an unusually cold winter. As Tom waited impatiently to receive his orders, he worried about his financial "embarrassment" and contemplated his "numerous family which I am about to leave perhaps forever." By June he was decidedly ambivalent about leaving, confiding to a friend that he sincerely hoped that the United States and Britain could compromise their differences. But he also declared that he would "be unhappy for life" without the opportunity to participate in at least one major battle.[38]

Another growing concern for Martha and Tom during the spring and summer of 1813 was the steadily deteriorating situation of their daughter Anne, who had married Charles Bankhead, the handsome son of one of Jefferson's closest friends. For a few years, the young couple seemed to be happy. After losing her first baby in 1809, Anne gave birth to a son, John Warner Bankhead, in December 1810. When Charles, who initially studied law with Jefferson at Monticello, decided instead to become a planter, he received "a good many" slaves from his father and bought Carlton, a nearby farm, in 1811. Anne assumed the duties of a plantation mistress, using skills she had learned by tending poultry and gardens and keeping the household accounts at Monticello for three years before she married, but the Bankheads did not prosper. Charles produced inferior tobacco, which he could not sell. Though it is not clear how quickly his fortunes declined, by 1814 he was drinking heavily and selling slaves to raise money, and he became the subject of local gossip. Elizabeth Trist declared ruefully that "Bankhead has turn'd out a great sot always frolicking and Carousing at the Taverns. . . . Poor Ann I feel for her."[39]

In the summer of 1813, Tom's imminent departure evoked strong feelings in both him and Martha. Whatever problems afflicted their marriage, they still retained enough mutual affection to regret their separation and to worry about each other. Husband and wife seemed to fear the prospect of each other's impending death. Tom had second thoughts about leaving Albemarle because this time Martha's pregnancy was uncharacteristically difficult. She was depressed, and Tom believed that her overall prognosis was "unfavorable." In a wave of emotion, Tom fervently promised his ailing wife that he "would do any thing rather than continue to live separately from [you] for any length of time" after he returned from the war. As for Martha, Dolley Madison reported that she was "miserable at parting with Mr R."[40]

Finally, in August, after six months of waiting, Tom received orders to proceed with his regiment to Sackets Harbor on Lake Ontario to rendezvous with other troops for a planned invasion of British Canada, which the hawkish colonel claimed was "long a favorite object with me." By early November, Tom's Twentieth Regiment had completed its northward march and joined the main army. After the assembled forces divided to mount an ill-fated two-pronged assault on Montreal, Tom's regiment participated in the successful seizure of the lightly defended Fort Matilda, but then it missed the much more important battle at Crysler's Farm, where a combined army of British regulars, Canadians, and Native Americans defeated the U.S. forces. With that, the fighting ended for the winter, as the armies retreated to their respective camps and waited to return to the field in the spring.[41]

As the army settled into its winter encampment, family concerns preoccupied Tom, who missed his children and fretted about Martha's health. By mid-November, as the family at Monticello waited anxiously for news from Canada, Colonel Randolph requested and received leave to return home for the winter, while the army was idle. Traveling southward via New York, Philadelphia, and Washington, he arrived in Albemarle by mid-December. Martha gave birth to a daughter, Septimia Anne Randolph, on 3 January at Monticello, but she recovered from her ordeal more slowly than usual. "Our Martha has had a poor time since the birth of her new daughter," Jefferson observed that February, when his daughter uncharacteristically suffered from dangerously "lingering fevers which have greatly debilitated her."[42]

Meanwhile, during her husband's absence, Martha had moved boldly to promote her family's solvency and safety, despite her ill health. After Tom left Virginia with his regiment, she angled to get him a federal appointment that would bring guaranteed income for the family and keep him safe at home. Martha knew that her friend Dolley Madison sometimes acted as an intermediary between her husband and those seeking favors or patronage positions. Martha and her father visited the Madisons at their Orange County home, Montpelier, in early September, about one month after Tom's departure. That visit afforded Martha a prime opportunity to present her request, with Jefferson's support, to Dolley and perhaps also to James.[43]

The Madisons, who knew of both the Randolphs' financial problems and Martha's distress at Tom's departure, were willing and able to help. At this particular moment, the federal government needed to enlist men of local prominence to collect the temporary taxes Congress had imposed to pay for the war with Britain. Given his stature in Albemarle and its environs, Tom seemed to be an ideal choice to collect taxes in the area, so Madison appointed him collector of the federal revenue for the congressional district that included both Edgehill and Monticello. Tom did not learn of his appointment until he passed through Washington on his way home to Albemarle in December 1813. Whatever influence Jefferson wielded in getting him the post, Tom believed that Martha had raised the issue with the Madisons and that she was primarily responsible for his appointment. Because the government would abolish the wartime taxes not long after the restoration of peace, Tom's employment would be short term, but he estimated that serving as tax collector for the year would net him almost $4,000.[44]

Tom was torn between taking the job he received, as he put it, "on application of my Wife" and continuing his quest for distinction on the battlefield. He was still the commander of the Twentieth Regiment, he was popular among his men, and he derived genuine satisfaction from military life. On learning of his new civilian appointment in December, Tom confessed to President Madison his strong desire to return to his military post. Declaring that he would bear "the risk, the suffering, and toils" of another Canadian campaign "with pleasure," he expressed "great mortification" at the prospect of having to resign his command to take a significantly less appealing job that he received mainly because the Madisons felt sorry for his wife. To make matters worse, a tax collector was in some ways the antithesis of the martial ideal that Tom found so appealing. Soldiers wielded arms, but laws were the tax man's weapon of choice. While many Americans lionized soldiers as virile, brave, and independent, they disdained tax collectors as dependent (and sometimes rapacious) government functionaries.[45]

Yet Tom had promised Martha that he would not prolong their separation, and he genuinely missed his family during his time away from home. In addition, as he conceded to a friend in late December, "the wellfare of my family, indeed the preservation of what estate I enjoy" required him to accept the collectorship. Both Martha and her father certainly took that position. As Jefferson observed in a letter to Elizabeth Trist in February, Tom had already done his patriotic duty. As the parent of young children during the Revolution, Jefferson sometimes had put his family first and suffered criticism because of his desire to spend more time attending to his wife and children. Now he believed that his son-in-law should do likewise and resign his commission, because even one military campaign "was a great undertaking for a man with so large a family."[46]

For a few months, Tom sustained his military ambitions but tried to pursue them closer to home by seeking a vacant command in the Virginia state militia, which would have stationed him in Norfolk, approximately 150 miles from his family but still much closer than Canada. Tom asked his friend Joseph C. Cabell to nominate him for the command, indicating that he would sacrifice "all other hopes, even all other duties" in order to get it. "I feel myself impatient to risk honour, fortune, life in . . . the defense of [Norfolk]," he wrote. When Tom expressed confidence in his ability to command, his choice of words indicated a true affinity for military life, despite its dangers and costs. "My confidence in myself has never been blind," he observed with telling understatement. "Indeed I have scarcely ever in my life felt confidence before." Nevertheless, Tom declared that the Norfolk post was "the only command I want," perhaps because any battlefield glory he achieved in defense of Virginia would powerfully enhance his reputation with his family and friends and among the inhabitants of his native state generally.[47]

When Tom did not secure the Norfolk appointment, he remained ambivalent about resuming his command in Canada. The odd sequence of events that led to the end of his brief career as a professional soldier suggests that while Tom was unwilling to defy his family's wishes, he also refused to allow Martha and her father to dictate his course of action. In late February, in response to orders to report to Leesburg in northern Virginia to begin recruiting for the new campaign, Tom requested more time at home, and in mid-March he indicated that he preferred to go directly to the encampment instead of participating in the recruitment efforts. When Tom implied he would rather resign his commission than go recruiting, his superiors accepted his resignation. This maneuver allowed Tom to save face by making his resignation the result of a conflict with his superiors rather than of the meddling of his wife and father-in-law. Martha was reportedly "well and happier" once Tom resigned his commission and began to fulfill his duties as the local tax collector. By April, he was reassessing his financial prospects and planning to sell both Varina and his Albemarle gristmill to satisfy his debts.[48]

Tom was one of many officers who resigned their commissions before the war ended. More than one-third of the high-ranking officers recruited during the war's early years were not in uniform when the conflict was over. Resignations were especially common among officers who, like Tom, lacked prior military experience. Some departures resulted from conflicts over rank or precedence, but other men explicitly cited family obligations as the reason for resigning their commissions. Although Tom offered his superiors no specific explanation for his leaving the army, aside from his aversion to recruiting, at least one of his colleagues concluded that his family's circumstances had been decisive.[49]

Like most of the able-bodied white men in Virginia, however, Tom was still a member of his county's militia, as was his son Jeff. Martha again endured the absence of her husband as well as her twenty-two-year-old son in the summer of 1814, when British activity in the Chesapeake led the governor to call up the militia to defend the state. Stationed at Camp Fairfield outside Richmond, the militia prepared to defend the capital to avoid a repetition of not only the state's abysmal performance during the Revolution, when Jefferson was governor, but also the recent British attack on Washington, which destroyed much of the undefended city and occasioned Dolley Madison's famous rescue of an iconic portrait of George Washington from the flames of the president's house. By late September, as it became apparent that the British would not proceed to Richmond, the troops began to disperse. Jeff Randolph went home, but Tom returned to Albemarle only when he received the official order to disband the militia. By December, diplomats had hammered out a preliminary peace treaty. Although American forces attained an impressive victory at the Battle of New Orleans in January, the war was essentially over.[50]

Tom's military service did not bring him the glory and adventure that he craved, but his performance won him the respect and esteem of like-minded men in Albemarle and beyond. David Campbell, a native of western Virginia who was Tom's second in command with the Twentieth Regiment, admired his character and abilities, valued his advice, and regarded their friendship as "one of the greatest pleasures of my life." Soldiers generally respected Tom as an approachable commander who willingly shared their crude living conditions and sympathetically received their requests for winter leave so that they, too, could go home. One described Tom as "an attentive, industrious officer." For these reasons, Tom's neighbors in Albemarle relished the opportunity to serve in the militia under his command. In urging him to lead the unit that marched to Richmond in the summer of 1814, Martha's cousin Peter Carr claimed to speak for "every person" when he exhorted Tom to seek the command and "give us an opportunity, of serving under a man, whom we *know*, whom we love, and whom we are convinced, will lead us, to honor and glory." Tom's military service, a source of so much grief at home, was for him a path to public success, respect, and honor.[51]

The constant tension between military ambition and family duty made the war years stressful for Tom, but they were at least equally so for Martha. Whereas friends and guests typically described her as cheerful, sociable, and energetic, during Tom's military service they found her miserable, anxious, and sickly. Martha feared for Tom's life because he was her husband of twenty-three years and the father of her children. In addition, as Jefferson often noted, Tom's family depended on him to oversee the crops, slaves, mills, and other assets that they hoped would secure the future of the next generation. In 1813, Jefferson was seventy years old and had financial troubles of his own, while his grandson Jeff was still unproven in the business of agriculture. Whatever his shortcomings, Thomas Mann Randolph was the most likely candidate to keep his family's fortunes afloat. So when Tom went off to war, Martha reasonably worried that her husband's life was at stake but so, too, was the already precarious economic and social well-being of her daughters and sons.

Wartime anxiety and stress took such a toll on Martha's normally cheerful demeanor that some observers believed that she was "turning religious" to cope with her difficulties. Although Martha, like her father, believed in God and took comfort in the funeral and wedding rituals performed by the local Episcopal minister, religion did not figure prominently in her daily life. Martha's daughters probably read the Bible as part of their studies, but their letters, which often mentioned books, rarely referred to Scriptures or devotional writing. The Randolphs' daughters were baptized in the Episcopal Church, but their sons—except for the youngest—were not. Years later, Martha regretfully blamed this omission on her deist "friends," which certainly included Tom and perhaps also her father, given his considerable influence in matters concerning the Randolph offspring. By the early nineteenth century, however, many elite Virginians were shedding their deism or their sedate and formalistic Episcopal worldview in favor of a more emotional, biblically based, Protestant evangelicalism. People experienced religious conversion for all sorts of reasons, but many gentry embraced evangelical religion, and the eternal salvation it offered, as a balm for the disorder and instability that undermined their status, wealth, and confidence in the postrevolutionary decades.[52]

Martha disavowed the rumor that she "had become very religious," though evangelicalism made inroads in the Randolph family. Her sister-in-law Judith, the unhappy and impoverished widow of Richard Randolph of Bizarre, became a zealous Presbyterian. Her sister-in-law Jane, with whom Martha was particularly close, experienced a religious conversion in 1814 as she grappled with illness and struggled to maintain her large family in the face of her husband's mounting financial problems. "My health requires some respite from family cares, which I feel at times so oppressive, that no principle under Heaven but Christianity could support me," Jane explained to a friend in 1814. "Christianity," she declared, "is truly the religion of the poor & sorrowful."[53]

As her country struggled to affirm its freedom and independence via a second war with Britain, did Martha act patriotically? Was she politically engaged? Despite her concerns about the well-being of her family, Martha shared her husband's and her father's warm support for the War of 1812. Moreover, like Jefferson, who promoted spinning and weaving at Monticello as part of a broader initiative to attain commercial independence from Britain, and like those men who toasted women's domestic production of homespun at local Independence Day celebrations and praised them in the press, Martha must have interpreted her involvement in cloth-making at Edgehill and Monticello as patriotic and politically relevant.[54]

As part of a politically minded household, Martha also followed elections. In 1815 she even tried to influence the outcome of a congressional race between the incumbent Republican John Wayles Eppes and Jack Randolph, a vocal opponent of the war with Britain and sworn enemy of Martha's husband and father. In 1814 Jack Randolph had unleashed his vitriol against Martha's sister-in-law Nancy, who had overcome her scandalous past and married Gouverneur Morris, the wealthy New Yorker whom Patsy Jefferson had met years earlier in Paris. Unwilling to let Nancy live happily in the serene comfort of Morris's riverfront mansion, Jack penned a diatribe accusing her of seducing and poisoning his brother Richard, having sex with slaves, and bearing a bastard child whom the unwitting Morris recognized as his son and heir. Nancy refuted these charges and vilified her accuser as hotheaded, selfish, mendacious, and dishonorable. She sent twenty copies of her own manifesto to Virginia, where she hoped her friends would use its contents to discredit Jack in the upcoming campaign. Dolley Madison received one of Nancy's letters; Martha apparently did not. Nevertheless, she clearly read the letter, which she summarized for Elizabeth Trist, whom she expected to repeat her own denunciation of Jack's "infamous falsehoods" and "the morality of a district who can choose such a man to represent them."[55]

❖ In the years immediately following the restoration of peace in 1815, the Randolphs sought to secure the future of their nine unmarried children, who ranged in age from infancy to adulthood. Tom struggled to recoup his fortunes and to repay his debts. Martha oversaw the entry of her elder daughters into society, in Washington and Richmond, in hopes of their finding suitable husbands. In both cases, their efforts were for the most part unsuccessful.

Tom's finances suffered from a combination of bad crops and his inability to find a buyer for Varina, the Henrico plantation he still hoped to sell to pay his debts. In 1815 and again in 1816, Tom assured his creditors that he would sell some slaves and hire out others to raise cash, though it is unclear whether those promised transactions ever occurred. In 1817, he took out yet another loan, from the Richmond branch of the Bank of the United States, which he could ill afford to repay. Except for Nancy, Tom's siblings were even worse off and in no position to help. In 1817, Tom gratefully accepted two barrels of corn seed that Nancy sent from New York, observing that he had "nothing to offer you for your kindness but thanks." In 1818, as a last resort, Tom raised $500 by selling Maria, a slave girl who had been born at Edgehill and lived there with her mother, Iris, to Edmund Bacon, Jefferson's overseer at Monticello.[56]

The only bright spot in the Randolphs' financial future was their eldest son, Jefferson, who, after a disappointing academic career, was turning out to be a capable businessman and plantation manager. After returning from a lackluster year at the University of Pennsylvania, Jeff studied natural philosophy and mathematics for a time at Louis H. Girardin's school in Richmond, where he stayed at the boardinghouse run by his aunt Mary Randolph. Perhaps because he preferred boardinghouse society to the company of his tutors, by 1811 Jeff was back at Monticello. When Thomas Mann Randolph went off to war two years later, twenty-one-year-old Jeff assumed responsibility for the gristmill, which he managed well, according to his grandfather. Indeed, a combination of the grandson's apparent aptitude and the grandfather's old age and growing physical debilities led the latter to entrust Jeff, in 1815, with the management of his properties at Monticello and elsewhere.[57]

Tom Randolph increasingly resented his father-in-law's perceived preference for Jeff over himself, in part because Jefferson's appointment of his eldest grandson to oversee his estate gave Jeff the path to manly independence that his father could not. Jeff owned a small plot of land and a few slaves, but his resources were not sufficient to support a family, and he did not own a house. Jeff was ready to marry. He had fallen in love with Jane Hollins Nicholas—and she with him—despite the initial reservations of women in both their families. Jane's mother disparaged Martha Randolph as "a very vulgar-looking woman" and called Jeff's sister Anne "a poor stick," though the underlying issue for her was plainly economic. Peggy Nicholas, whose father had been a Baltimore merchant and who hoped that her daughters would use marriage as a means to escape Virginia and its seemingly bleak economy, knew that Jeff had little property. The Randolph women, especially Anne Bankhead, understandably resented Nicholas's criticism and chafed at her (probably unexpected) suggestion that her daughter Jane was too good to marry into their family.[58]

By 1815, Jeff's work ethic and his candid appraisal of his financial situation eventually swayed his future father-in-law, Wilson Cary Nicholas, a family friend who was also Virginia's current governor. "My prospects from my father I consider as blank, from my grandfather as not very cheering," Jeff explained to Nicholas, adding that Jefferson's estate was "large, but unprofitable and unless judiciously managed will probably consume itself." For the time being, Jeff offered Jane only "a bare competency and a most enthusiastic and devoted attachment," but he pledged to deploy his "industry and perseverance" to improve his circumstances. Jefferson's arrangement gave Jeff a job and enabled him and Jane to live at Monticello, where the family promised to welcome Jane "as a member of our family with very great pleasure and cordiality." In March 1815, twenty-two-year-old Jeff married seventeen-year-old Jane Hollins Nicholas, and Martha welcomed her new daughter-in-law to the family at Monticello.[59]

Having Jeff and Jane close at hand was a boon to both Martha and her father. Not only did Jeff shoulder increasingly more responsibility for the estate of his aging grandfather, but Jane became a beloved member of the Jefferson-Randolph family circle, as she assisted her mother- and sisters-in-law with their assorted household labors. Within two months of the wedding, Martha praised Jane as "a lovely little woman." Jeff and Jane's marriage was exceptionally happy, and the newlyweds worked purposefully—and with Martha's full support—to ease whatever tensions remained between their families. Jane and Jeff, who had thirteen children in all, named their first two, both daughters, Margaret Smith Randolph and Martha Jefferson Randolph, for their respective mothers. By the time Martha bore her last child, George Wythe Randolph, in March 1818, Peggy Nicholas was sufficiently mollified to ask Jane to convey her "prayers for her speedy and happy recovery" to her "most excellent mother-in-law." Two months earlier, Jeff had taken a five-year lease on his grandfather's farm at Tufton, where he and Jane established their separate household in close proximity to Monticello.[60]

Jeff's initially cool reception by his prospective in-laws foreshadowed the more serious problems his sisters encountered as they reached adulthood. Unlike them, Jeff could be more or less a free agent in the marriage market, making the case that his industry and prudence, along with his affection for Jane, could compensate for his initial lack of property. His sisters' circumstances were entirely different because law and custom made wives by definition dependent. The economic value of white women's domestic work was grossly underestimated, and the financial assets a woman brought to marriage were assessed solely in terms of property transmitted from her father (or sometimes from another relation) to her prospective husband. Although Charles Bankhead received 160 acres when he married Jeff's older sister, Anne, the Randolphs' mounting debts meant that their younger daughters would receive no property at all when they married. In 1815, Ellen was nineteen years old and Cornelia was sixteen, just one year younger than her brother's new wife. A chagrined Martha understandably doubted whether her daughters, with their "promised *30 cents* per annum," would be able to find husbands.[61]

Along with Virginia and Mary—ages fourteen and twelve, respectively, in 1815—Ellen and Cornelia spent most of their time helping their mother with housework or accompanying their grandfather on his frequent trips to Poplar Forest, where Jefferson began building an octagon-shaped house in 1806. Initially, Jefferson journeyed there with John Hemings, his master woodworker, and Burwell Colbert, his personal servant, but by 1816 he considered the still-unfinished eight-room house sufficiently comfortable for female members of his family. In 1816, Martha and her daughters Virginia and Mary accompanied Jefferson and his servants on the three-day trek by carriage to Bedford, leaving Ellen and her father in charge at Monticello. Although Ellen told her mother that "the family without you, is completely a body without a soul," she also praised her father's efforts to assist her "in doing the honors of the house" when uninvited guests arrived to gawk at the former president's home. "Papa," she added, "has taken good care of us since you went away, he has paid great attention to our comfort." Later that year, and again in 1817 and 1818, Martha stayed home while Ellen and Cornelia went with their grandfather to Poplar Forest, where they took advantage of the quiet seclusion and the comparative lack of domestic chores to devote themselves to reading. Ellen also played chess with Jefferson, and the artistic Cornelia learned mechanical drawing from him.[62]

The unhappy precedent of Anne Bankhead's increasingly tragic marriage must have troubled Martha as she pondered the future of her younger daughters. In May 1815, Martha bemoaned Anne's "hard fate" in a letter to Elizabeth Trist, without mentioning any specific details, aside from Charles's insolvency. In October, however, Jefferson reported that Charles "committed an assault on his wife of the greatest violence," forcing Anne to "take refuge for the night in her mother's room." By 1816, Charles Bankhead was drinking heavily, and he seems to have become increasingly abusive toward his wife. Martha responded angrily when Charles beat Anne in her presence at Monticello, sharply suggesting that the best way to deal with her son-in-law would be "to hire a keeper for him to prevent him from doing mischief, and let him finish him self at once" by drinking himself to death. In fact, both she and Anne were powerless against Bankhead, who as a husband claimed unfettered authority over his wife and children. State law, as well as the most common interpretation of Scripture, largely supported these claims.[63]

Although Tom Randolph assumed his son-in-law's debts, which he could ill afford, and Jefferson transferred some property from Charles to Anne to shield it from his creditors, neither man was willing to intervene to protect Anne by challenging the authority of her husband. In the postrevolutionary era, as American law insulated families from governmental or judicial interference, a husband's treatment of his wife was increasingly regarded as a private matter and patriarchal power was deemed a manly right. Accordingly, the most Jefferson believed he could do was to persuade Charles's father, his old friend Dr. John Bankhead, to let the troubled couple live with him at his home in Caroline County. Unwilling to violate the precepts of patriarchy, Anne's deeply saddened grandfather hoped that Dr. Bankhead's benevolence would supersede his son's malevolent power.[64]

In part because of Anne's travails as a married woman, Martha was understandably ambivalent about the prospect that Ellen, her second oldest daughter, might not marry. Like most mothers, Martha wanted her children to succeed as adults, and she was the product of a culture that made marriage, for women especially, a prerequisite for success. At the same time, however, as she considered Anne's unhappy fate, Martha admitted that "I almost wish she never may [marry]." Ellen's temperament, she feared, was "too acute for her own happiness." In that respect, Martha confided to Elizabeth Trist, this daughter was "very much like her Father but with out his temper, and such are not calculated for this selfish world."[65]

Beginning tentatively in 1814 and proceeding more aggressively in the coming years, Martha actively promoted her daughters' prospects, using her contacts and limited resources to help Ellen and her sisters meet men in respectable social venues. Tom's sister Mary Randolph and Martha's friend Dolley Madison, neither of whom had daughters of their own, facilitated their introduction to society. Madison invited Ellen to enjoy the "large & enlighten'd society" of Washington during her husband's presidency. Mary Randolph's popularity as hostess and proprietor of a fashionable Richmond boardinghouse gave her nieces a comparatively safe and inexpensive place to stay, as well as an entrée to the balls and parties of Virginia's increasingly sociable capital. Although Mary Randolph's boardinghouse was a hotbed of anti-Jeffersonian sentiment after her husband, the Federalist David Meade

Randolph, lost his official post to a Republican appointee in 1801, "Aunt Randolph" reconciled with her kin at Edgehill and Monticello after Jefferson left the presidency. Martha and Tom's son Jeff had been the first of their offspring to lodge in her house, when he began school in Richmond in November 1809.[66]

In 1814, eighteen-year-old Ellen made her first foray into Richmond society. During her two months away from home, she wrote to both her parents. While her letters to Tom have not survived, Ellen described for Martha the people she met, the beautiful clothes she wore (and saw others wearing), and the "large & brilliant" parties she attended, usually with her aunt, who enjoyed shepherding her niece around town. In her letters, Ellen also acknowledged her parents' financial investment in what was at least partly a preliminary husband-hunting venture. When she spent $40 on a piece of fine linen for a dress, she declared, "My conscience reproaches me. . . . I wished to get some that was a good deal coarser but Aunt Randolph would not permit me." Ellen also dutifully reported that her "charms have thawed [the] icy heart" of the handsome, wealthy, and well-educated Mr. Barksdale, whom she disdained as one whose "habits of indolence . . . make him the victim of languor & ennui" and therefore utterly unattractive.[67]

Two years later, when Ellen was twenty years old and still unmarried, Martha accepted Dolley Madison's standing invitation for her accomplished and attractive daughter to visit Washington when Congress was in session. Martha doubtless believed that Ellen's Jefferson lineage would be more bankable in the nation's capital, where Republican ranks included some prosperous men and where the Randolphs' financial problems were less widely known. But Washington had become far more fashionable since Martha's last visit, and the normally unflappable Ellen was unprepared for the constant visiting, crowded parties, and sumptuous balls of the capital's social season. On arriving in Washington, she defensively professed "loathing and disgust" for this "dissipated" style of living, while also admitting her confusion about how to behave and her "anxiety *to be admired*." Within weeks, Ellen was more comfortable in her surroundings but still deeply aware of their novelty. "My visit to Washington," she informed her mother, "will give me a portion of that experience which before I came I was not conscious of wanting."[68]

Martha might have felt vicarious pleasure in her daughter's successful assimilation into the highest levels of American society, but Ellen's sojourn in Washington, as she herself acknowledged, cost her family dearly. Ellen's second letter from Washington, in which she confessed that she bought a beautiful—and expensive—shawl that proved to be too thin to keep her warm and too long to wear safely, must have irked Martha as she struggled to keep her household solvent. Ellen knew that her family's finances were precarious, and she claimed to worry incessantly about the problems of her "poor father." She decried her own "selfish gratifications," while at the same time accepting an invitation to accompany the family of her new friends, George and Matilda Dallas, the son and daughter of Madison's secretary of the treasury, on a trip to Baltimore and Philadelphia. Ellen feared what her parents would think of this plan, though she was certain that her grandfather would approve—and, indeed, the imprudently generous Jefferson provided $100 to pay for her junket. By the time she returned home in May, however, Ellen was broke, in part because she bought "a thousand little articles of dress indispensable in Philadelphia."[69]

Perhaps recalling her own expensive sartorial preparation for a season in Washington, Martha forgave Ellen's extravagance, but she would have been justified in regretting that her daughter's expensive adventure did not produce the desired outcome. Ellen enjoyed listening to debates in the House of Representatives, attending fancy balls, and seeing the opulent homes of Philadelphia's elite, but she disparaged nearly all of the men she met during her travels. Washington, she opined, could "boast of no first rate beaux." Ellen dismissed Mr. Logan as "not brilliant" and Mr. Milligan as "cold and formal." She described Mr. De Roth as "an insignificant little creature." Although she expressed mild interest in Mr. Forney, a North Carolina congressman, she informed Martha that it would be difficult to get to know him because he seldom went out. Martha apparently had high hopes that Ellen would hit it off with Mr. Pederson, but her daughter informed her that this gentleman left Washington in mid-February. Ellen reported that Mr. Daschkoff admired her more than any other woman he had seen in America, but she found this Russian diplomat and his attentions "very disagreeable."[70]

Ellen evidently enjoyed her adventures in urban society, and for the time being at least, she apparently did not intend to trade those pleasures for a settled married life. At the same time, possibly to satisfy her mother, she praised one man, albeit one who was already safely married. Ellen described John Forsyth, a Republican congressman from Georgia, as "very intelligent, gay, handsome, and . . . the most agreeable man in Washington." Because Forsyth was married, however, Ellen felt obliged to avoid him for fear of receiving "any attention from a husband which is to give pain to his wife." By praising Forsyth, Ellen showed her mother that her standards, though high, were not impossible to meet and that she took her search for a spouse seriously. Nevertheless, like many other unmarried women, she seemed eager to prolong that search, which temporarily freed her from her domestic responsibilities as a daughter and enabled her to delay taking on much more demanding duties as a wife.[71]

In September 1817, while Ellen and Cornelia were at Poplar Forest with Jefferson, sixteen-year-old Virginia had the unexpected pleasure of accompanying her "Aunt Randolph"—along with her younger sister Mary and a female cousin—to the Virginia springs. At this well-known venue for flirtation and courtship, she enjoyed "the luxury of that delightful bath" but found no beaux. Ellen and Cornelia spent the following winter with their aunt in Richmond, though Virginia remained at Monticello.[72]

Once again, the Randolph sisters' venture into the world of balls and parties netted them no serious suitors. This calamity at least one observer attributed to Martha's "system of education," which left her daughters fluent in several foreign languages but unwilling or unable to make engaging small talk with their peers in social settings. Even by her own account, Cornelia Randolph was painfully shy, had "country" manners, and wore her clothing unattractively loose because she "prefer'd comfort to good looks." Peggy Nicholas, who saw the sisters often in Richmond, noted sympathetically that Cornelia was "as new to the world as a girl of sixteen," though she was two years older. Had Martha allowed her daughters to socialize more with their respectable neighbors in Albemarle, Nicholas maintained, Cornelia would have been more at ease in Richmond. By contrast, though Ellen was handsome and stylish, Nicholas believed that her "tell-tale countenance" showed prospective suitors that "she feels her superiority." In fact, Ellen had good things to say about only two men she met in Richmond that winter, neither of whom was husband material. The Jewish Mr. Mordecai was, in her opinion, "the only creature who is not stupid or a puppy" among her aunt's boarders; Mr. Nivison was a "very charming beau," but he was already engaged.[73]

Martha never enumerated the qualities she deemed desirable in a prospective son-in-law, but she knew that marriage was risky under any circumstances. An educated man who treated his dependents humanely and whose property or talents were sufficient to support a wife and family and perhaps attain public honor might seem like an ideal mate, but her own marriage to Thomas Mann Randolph, if nothing else, showed how the passage of years could dim the brightest prospects. Indeed, if Martha was anxious to see her younger daughters wed, the events of 1818 show that she tried to prevent them from marrying young.

Perhaps reflecting on her own experiences as a teenaged bride and certainly thinking of her daughter Anne's continuing troubles, Martha responded to eighteen-year-old Nicholas Trist's request to propose marriage to her daughter Virginia with a combination of wisdom and warmth. Martha knew Nicholas well, and she expressed both "esteem and affection" toward Elizabeth Trist's beloved grandson, who had lived at Monticello for the past year while he studied law with Jefferson and whose departure for the military academy at West Point was now imminent. Nevertheless, she counseled him and seventeen-year-old Virginia that they were "both too young to be entangled by an engagement which will decide the happiness, or wretchedness of your lives." Nicholas respectfully accepted Martha's advice to delay his formal proposal of marriage until he returned from West Point. He promised to "remain silent . . . cherishing the hope that on my return, I may find the heart of Miss Virginia as free as mine shall be devoted, and that I may one day be entitled to the appellation of your Son."[74]

❖ The fact that Nicholas addressed his request to Martha, not Tom, reflected not only his esteem for her but also his perception that in the Randolphs' division of labor she, not Tom, was primarily responsible for decisions that affected the future of their children, especially their daughters. Martha wielded that authority in part because she took the initiative in such matters, but also because the negotiation of marriage settlements, typically the domain of fathers, would not be part of the process when the Randolph daughters married because their father's property (as well as their grandfather's) was increasingly encumbered by debt.

In March 1818, when she was nearly forty-six years old, Martha gave birth to her last child at Monticello. Early marriages and frequent pregnancies gave rise to the peculiar demography of southern planter families, which the Randolphs exemplified. The infant, George Wythe Randolph, was twenty-seven years younger than his oldest sibling, Anne Cary Randolph Bankhead; he was also younger than his nieces and nephews, Anne's children and those of his oldest brother, Thomas Jefferson Randolph. As for Martha, when she experienced childbirth for the last time, she was already a grandmother several times over. If she did not know that her childbearing days were over, that would have been a happy surprise, but much more unhappiness was in store for her and her family during what would be their final decade at Monticello.

chapter 6 | Decay and
Dissolution

On 1 February 1819, Charles Bankhead stabbed his brother-in-law Thomas Jefferson Randolph in the courthouse square in downtown Charlottesville. The two had been on bad terms for years. Bankhead, the abusive husband of Jeff's sister Anne, had previously threatened violence against Jeff and not long before had sent an insulting letter to Jane, his wife. Now Randolph sought an apology. Having ridden into town, he carried his horsewhip, and Bankhead, possibly anticipating the humiliation of the sort of public whipping normally reserved for slaves, shoved his brother-in-law, who fell to the ground. The men scuffled, and Bankhead, who had a knife, stabbed Randolph twice, above the hip and across his left arm. The wounds were serious. Jeff spent several days under a physician's care in Charlottesville before he could return home.[1]

Although some of Jeff Randolph's relations hoped that such a violent outburst in this public place would land Bankhead in the state penitentiary, others worried that his imprisonment, however well deserved, would be scandalous for them all. Most agreed "that Villain Bankhead," one way or another, should be separated from his long-suffering wife, who bore the brunt of his rage. Instead, he was released from the sheriff's custody on bail and inexplicably never stood trial. Charles and Anne continued to live together as husband and wife.[2]

Although no surviving letters document Martha's reaction to the altercation between her beloved son and this reviled son-in-law, years later she might have considered the episode a fittingly symbolic start to her second decade as the mistress of Monticello. Beginning in 1819, her family's problems proliferated. Martha, however, strove to maintain her customary facade of competence and good cheer as their economic woes became increasingly intractable, her own health and that of her aging father declined, and conflicts within the family festered and multiplied. The brawl between Jeff Randolph and Charles Bankhead was the first of a series of episodes that would bring Martha and her family personal pain and public dishonor, culminating in the eventual dispersal of the family and the loss of Monticello.

❖ Unlike most women of her time, who experienced their worst physical ailments during their childbearing years, Martha's health problems began later. In May 1819, roughly a year after Martha bore her last child, Tom observed that his wife was "really ill." Her unspecified sickness either lasted several months or came and went over the course of the spring, summer, and early autumn of 1819. In mid-September, when Elizabeth Trist stayed at Monticello, she found its mistress so "unwell" that she remained in bed for three days, despite the presence of many guests besides Trist, including two sisters-in-law with their daughters and a friend of Ellen's from Richmond. The following year, Martha was "indisposed" when Dolley Madison visited in April. She was "very unwell" and "look'd Pale" in July when Elizabeth Trist again saw her.[3]

By 1820, Martha was experiencing menopause, and the change apparently hit her hard. Mostly she suffered from debilitating headaches, which she may have initially regarded as a hereditary ailment akin to the excruciating headaches that afflicted her father in times of stress. Eventually, however, she came to attribute her headaches, along with "violent palpitations of the heart, spasms in my limbs and back, and frequent fevers" to menopause. In the summer of 1821, Martha felt so miserable that a worried Tom considered sending her on a sea voyage, possibly to see his sister Nancy in New York, in hopes that the ocean air would restore her health. Financial considerations probably led her to travel instead with Jefferson to Poplar Forest, where the cool mountain air alleviated her discomfort in the short term. But recurrent headaches, body pains, fevers, and stomach problems took their toll on Martha's normally buoyant personality. In 1824, when a particularly painful attack confined her to bed for a week, one physician concluded that Martha had gout, which, unlike menopause, could be a life-long malady, a worrisome prospect for both her and her family.[4]

"For more than two years I have been in that state between comfortable feelings, and positive illness," she explained to her sister-in-law Virginia Randolph Cary in 1822, "which necessarily induces apathy, listlessness, and all those idle propensities that unfit us for the proper discharge of our duties." That year, possibly because she was spending more time upstairs, away from the family, Martha finally prevailed on her father to allow her to rearrange her room in Monticello's crowded upstairs living quarters—which housed her entire family as well as their houseguests—by converting her alcove bed, one of Jefferson's pet space-saving innovations, into a closet. Martha's octagonal room, which measured approximately 225 square feet, was a space that was in no way comparable to her father's suite of rooms downstairs, but accomplishing this practical renovation was an important act of self-assertion by which she claimed it as her own.[5]

Martha's health problems, along with her daughters' increasing maturity, altered the division of labor at Monticello and changed her role somewhat in this crowded household. Although the Randolph sisters were avid readers who clearly favored intellectual pursuits, they now spent more time on domestic matters, in part to help Martha but also to prepare for their presumed destinies as household managers. By 1818, Ellen, Cornelia, Virginia, and Mary—who ranged in age from twenty-two to fifteen—acted as housekeepers on a rotating basis. They oversaw the enslaved workers who cooked, cleaned, and did other domestic work, and they kept the keys to the pantries, dependencies, and other locked storage areas. Tom Randolph composed an affectionate verse that humorously contrasted the approaches of two of his daughters to food and kitchen management:

> While frugal Miss Mary kept the stores of the House
> Not a rat could be seen, never heard was a mouse,
> Not a crumb was let fall,
> In kitchen or Hall:
> For no one could spare one crumb from his slice
> The rations were issued by measure so nice
> When April arrived to soften the air,
> Cornelia succeeded to better the fare,
> Oh! the boys were so glad,
> And the Cooks were so sad,
> Now puddings and pies every day will be made,
> Not once in a month just to keep up the trade.[6]

Whatever its advantages, this new system of shared housekeeping duties did not entirely please any of the female members of the Randolph family. Their new responsibilities alternately overwhelmed or irritated the sisters. In 1820, Cornelia worried about the "numberless variety of orders & directions to be recollected & given" to the domestic staff and complained of the "bodily labour" of putting away books and other items. Virginia also dreaded her time in charge, lamenting that her "few months of housekeeping badly done" were not serving their pedagogic ends and left her without even "one useful acquirement, not even the regular & industrious habits which would enable me to spend my future life more profitably." All four sisters regretted that domestic work prevented them from pursuing their studies. "I had rather *read* than *sew* or *keep-house*," Virginia emphatically informed her future husband, Nicholas Trist. Ellen cherished her time at Poplar Forest, where, released from domestic cares, she could be a full-time student, like "a man studying chiefly for present gratification and because he finds it the most agreeable way of passing his time."[7]

Martha appreciated her daughters' assistance and recognized the necessity of their becoming adept at housekeeping, even as she resisted relinquishing control of the domestic routine at Monticello. Martha owned a copy of *Le Cuisinier Royal*, a cookbook and guide to wines that was published in Paris in 1817. On the book's endpapers and on its opening pages, she added an extensive glossary of cooking terms—from aspic to zest—along with some recipes, notes, and other instructions. Jefferson purchased this book in 1819, possibly at Martha's behest. Notwithstanding her ambivalence about surrendering her housekeeping responsibilities to her daughters, the timing of the purchase, along with her painstakingly detailed inscriptions, suggests that Martha was assiduously preparing them to oversee Monticello's domestic staff and to instruct their own slaves or servants in the future, or perhaps even to prepare meals by themselves.[8]

While Martha's "rebellion against the management of her daughters," like her continuing efforts to raise poultry and do other domestic work, may have taxed her physically, ceding control of the household exacted a high psychic cost. An idle Martha felt lethargic and sometimes downright useless. "There is nothing more certain than that the less occupation we have, the less we are disposed to execute that little," she confided to her sister-in-law Virginia Cary in 1822. "During the period when my eyes opened with the dawn upon the toilsome drudgery of the day," she recalled, she had accomplished much. But now that her work consisted of only some occasional light cleaning or menu planning, which was "done in a very small space of time," she found herself "absolutely too lazy" to do much else.[9]

During these years, though Martha continued to indulge her "taste for reading," she curtailed or possibly even ceased the instruction of youngsters at Monticello. In the past, Martha had taught her older children and occasionally offered French lessons to other members of the family or to family friends. Four of her five youngest children, however, were boys. She may have taught them the basics of reading, writing, and arithmetic, but then, on Jefferson's insistence, they, unlike their sisters, attended local schools, for which their grandfather apparently paid. Martha may have taught her

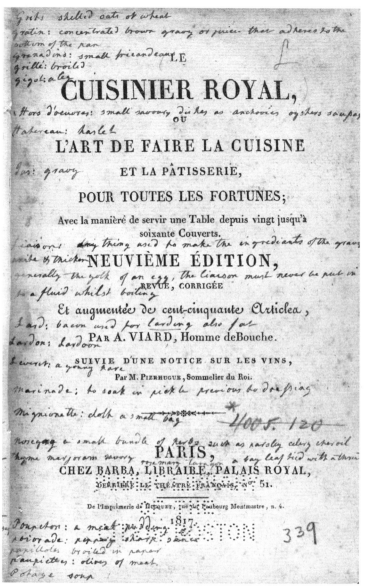

LE
CUISINIER ROYAL,
OU
L'ART DE FAIRE LA CUISINE
ET LA PÂTISSERIE,
POUR TOUTES LES FORTUNES;

Avec la manière de servir une Table depuis vingt jusqu'à
soixante Couverts.

NEUVIÈME ÉDITION,
REVUE, CORRIGÉE

Et augmentée de cent-cinquante Articles,

PAR A. VIARD, Homme deBouche.

SUIVIE D'UNE NOTICE SUR LES VINS,

Par M. PIERHUGUE, Sommelier du Roi.

PARIS,
CHEZ BARBA, LIBRAIRE, PALAIS ROYAL,
DERRIÈRE LE THÉÂTRE FRANÇAIS, N° 51.

De l'Imprimerie de Fiquet, rue du Faubourg Montmartre, n. 4.

1817

Handwritten annotations:

Grits: shelled oats of wheat
Gratin: concentrated brown gravy or juice that adheres to the bottom of the pan
Grenadins: small fricandeaux
grillé: broiled
gigot à la

Hors d'œuvres: small savoury dishes as anchovies oysters sausages
Haterau: harslet

Jus: gravy

Liaisons any thing used to make the ingredients of the gravy unite & thicken generally the yolk of an egg, the liaison must never be put in to a fluid whilst boiling

Lard: bacon used for larding also fat
Lardon: Lardoon

Leveret: a young hare

Marinade: to soak in pickle previous to dressing

Mignionette: cloth a small bag

Rosegag a small bundle of herbs such as parsley celery chervil thyme marjoram savory rosemary &c a bay leaf tied with a thread

Poupeton: a meat pudding
Poivrade: peppery sharp sauce
papillotes: broiled in paper
Paupiettes: olives of meat
Potage soup

4005. 120

339

Le Cuisinier Royal. *Martha's glossary of cooking terms and other notes cover the blank endpapers and title page, shown here, of this French cookbook. Her notes, mostly translations of French cooking terms into English, also include definitions for some common ingredients in Virginia cooking, such as grits (incorrectly described as "shelled oats of wheat") and lard. Martha used this book, which Ellen later inherited, to teach her daughters how to plan and prepare fine meals, though Jefferson's enslaved kitchen staff did the cooking at Monticello. Courtesy of the Trustees of the Boston Public Library/Rare Books.*

youngest daughter, Septimia, but it is more likely that her studious and accomplished older daughters did so for the most part. In the mid-1820s, Virginia and Cornelia oversaw "the childrens copies," which must have included the schoolwork of their youngest siblings, Septimia and George, who were born in 1814 and 1818, respectively.[10]

Martha's responsibilities as Monticello's hostess and her father's gatekeeper increased, however, as growing numbers of Jefferson's admirers and colleagues trekked to Albemarle to see the aging statesman, who, aside from his visits to Poplar Forest, rarely left home. Those seeking access to Jefferson approached him through Martha. In 1819, for instance, Benjamin Vaughan wrote Martha a long letter about science, seeds, and architecture because he supposed that her ailing father was "averse to receiving letters which he may think that he must answer." Vaughan did not expect Martha to respond to his musings, but rather he hoped that she would communicate his observations and sentiments to her father and let him know whether Jefferson "recovered his usual state of health." Six years later, when James W. Wallace feared that a forthcoming biography of Richard Henry Lee would be overly favorable, he asked Martha to get a statement from Jefferson assessing Lee's conduct during the Revolution. Martha also mediated visitors' access to the aging Jefferson at Monticello. "I *recieve* his company," she explained to her sister-in-law Nancy Morris, "and where the case will admit excuse him for not appearing."[11]

The social routine at Monticello also changed somewhat to reflect Martha's growing role as her father's gatekeeper and the corresponding lessening of her maternal responsibilities. When Margaret Bayard Smith visited Monticello in 1809, she found that Martha devoted her entire day to childrearing and other domestic concerns, joining her houseguests only for breakfast at 8:00 and then for dinner at 4:00 or 5:00; after dinner, she often returned to her work and then rejoined the company for tea at 9:00. In the 1820s, by contrast, Martha occupied herself with her children and with "domestic affairs" only during the hours between breakfast and noon; after lunch she "returned to her own rooms" to read or rest. At 3:00, she and her father joined the family and their guests in the drawing room, and they "remained with their guests for the rest of the afternoon & evening except for a short time when Mr. Jefferson returned to his own rooms." In earlier times, Jefferson was the primary host in the afternoon and evenings, while Martha attended to her various household responsibilities. Now, with her daughters to assist her and her elderly father in need of more time to rest in his rooms, Martha spent proportionately more time acting as hostess to the many guests who visited Monticello.[12]

All of these changes unfolded against a backdrop of economic distress that deepened as Jefferson became a prominent casualty of the Panic of 1819, a financial crisis caused by the proliferation of banks, credit, and inflated paper currency in the boom years after the War of 1812. On retiring from public life, the former president had begun to address his financial problems, selling land as well as his cherished library (which became the core of the Library of Congress) to raise funds. But Jefferson was still in debt in 1818, when Wilson Cary Nicholas asked him to serve as guarantor for a $20,000 bank loan. Nicholas was Jeff Randolph's father-in-law and an important Virginia Republican who used his banking contacts to help Jefferson get credit when he needed it, so he now felt obliged to return the favor. Within a few months, however, American credit markets crashed and the bank summoned Nicholas to repay part of what he owed. An alarmed Martha Randolph wrote to her father at Poplar Forest, where he and his granddaughters absorbed the ominous news and anxiously waited to see if Nicholas's own property would cover the loan. It did not. Nicholas died penniless in 1820, leaving Jefferson liable for the $20,000, along with some $1,200 in annual interest, which he could not repay.[13]

Like many other Americans, especially outside the commercial Northeast, members of the Monticello family blamed the banks for the financial crisis and the suffering it caused, especially for rural people. Although they were willing to accept credit from banks when they needed it before the crash, now Martha and her father condemned lenders for encouraging extravagance and debt by creating artificial wealth. The banks' system of easy but unstable credit, they observed disapprovingly, was tantamount to gambling. By bringing financial ruin to individual citizens and their families, overreliance on credit and speculation, they feared, would "ruin the country." In Jefferson's case, the bank required payment of the Nicholas debt within two years, so Jefferson had to sell the land he had hoped to bequeath to his grandsons to raise the necessary funds. Yet Virginia land prices were so low that Martha worried that her father might not be able to meet the bank's demands, even if he liquidated most of his landholdings.[14]

Everywhere, Martha and her circle saw portents of Virginia's bleak economic outlook. Peggy Nicholas, wife of the ruined Wilson Cary Nicholas, observed that many recently affluent men were now worth "thousands worse than nothing." Elizabeth Trist saw hundreds of distressed planter families leaving Virginia for Alabama, Missouri, or some other new territory, taking their slaves with them. She sternly advised her grandson Nicholas to "live on bread and water," if necessary, to avoid debt. In Albemarle, people gossiped about the money problems afflicting so many of their neighbors. Martha bemoaned the decline of her "dear native state," fretting about not only her father's sudden financial crisis but also her husband's ongoing problems. Still unable to find a buyer for Varina, in 1819 Tom sold a second Edgehill slave, Edy, to Edmund Bacon and took out small loans from both Bacon and his mother. In 1823, Tom went to New York, seeking to borrow money on his Henrico property. He wanted $10,000 but got only half that, along with some sobering advice from Henry Remsen, a sympathetic New York merchant. The economic downturn, coupled with the sale of western lands by the U.S. government, Remsen surmised, "had the effect . . . of reducing the value of lands generally."[15]

In these distressed circumstances, Tom Randolph made the seemingly incongruous decision to return to politics, perhaps seeking to enhance his reputation by winning public acclaim and honor. Tom's involvement in the civic-minded Agricultural Society of Albemarle may have revived his interest in public service. Certainly he was a strong supporter of Jefferson's effort to establish a public and wholly secular university in Charlottesville. Tom announced his candidacy for the state assembly in March 1819 and was elected to fill one of Albemarle's two seats the following month. When the legislature convened in December, a majority chose him as Virginia's next governor, a post he retained for three consecutive one-year terms, the legal maximum.

As an officeholder at the state level, Thomas Mann Randolph was progressive by Virginia gentry standards. As governor, he championed education, canals, and fuller political representation for the state's growing western counties. Reacting to rumors of a possible slave rebellion and acting on his own deep reservations about the slave system, he proposed a plan to abolish slavery incrementally by manumitting enslaved people as they reached adulthood, whereupon they would be forced to leave the state. After his time as governor, Tom also served two one-year terms in the general assembly. Altogether, he spent many months in Richmond, away from home, in the early 1820s.[16]

Although Jefferson and some other previous governors had brought their families with them to Richmond, Virginians did not think of the governor's wife as their "first lady," and they did not expect her to perform ceremonial or social functions. The governor's mansion, completed in 1813, was an elegant neoclassical house with four spacious downstairs rooms for family living and public functions and four upstairs bedrooms, but it was probably less convenient for a large family than the house and grounds at Monticello. Tom missed Martha and especially his daughters when he was away from home. Indeed, soon after his election to the legislature, he confided to a friend, "I cannot live apart from my family, without the absolute and unlimited power to rejoin them whenever I deem it proper for their own and my happiness." Fortunately, Richmond was near enough to Albemarle that he could leave after supper on Saturday and, riding all night, arrive at Monticello by daybreak to spend Sunday with his family.[17]

These considerations, along with the expense of maintaining a separate establishment in Richmond, deterred Martha from joining Tom there, at least initially. Martha knew the costs Jeff's in-laws had incurred by living in Richmond during Wilson Cary Nicholas's recent tenure in the governor's mansion. Elizabeth Trist probably echoed Martha's own sentiments when she expressed her fervent hope that Tom would "cut his coat according to his cloth" and live within his means during his governorship. Nevertheless, as Jefferson's experience in Washington had shown, sociability could be used to promote goodwill and nurture political alliances. During his first term, Tom socialized little and became unpopular in some circles as a result of his antislavery proposal and his candid insistence that religion had no place in the new state university. Facing reelection, Tom persuaded Martha to come to Richmond. She arrived in early December 1820, about a week before the legislature was scheduled to choose a new governor. Although neither the legislators nor the Richmond newspapers publicly acknowledged her presence, she was surely in the gallery that was "crowded with spectators" when the legislators elected Tom to a second term by a comfortable margin.[18]

Much as Martha had reflected favorably on her father during his presidency, she was a "very popular" addition to Richmond society, an asset whose presence helped to soften the hard edges of the irascible governor. In the course of accepting a second term, however, Tom ignited a major political controversy by urging the legislature to augment the governor's powers at the expense of those of his privy council. If Tom thought that Martha's attendance at dinners and other functions would advance his legislative program, he was sadly mistaken. The legislators enacted virtually none of his proposals, though they did elect him to a third term in December 1821.[19]

Overall, Martha enjoyed her time in Richmond. When she arrived at the governor's mansion, she found "every thing in disorder, windows unwashed, carpets unshaken," which she attributed to Tom's having lived as a bachelor during the previous year. Within a week, however, she was writing excitedly to her daughters, describing the parties and dinners she attended and the uncharacteristically fashionable clothes she wore. "The dinner at the Marxes yesterday was elegant," she wrote to Virginia, who was with Jefferson and Ellen at Poplar Forest. "Can you figure to yourself *me*, my dear Virginia, in a beautiful white crape *robe*, a lace turban and ruff, fashionably drest and looking like a *lady*?!!" Perhaps she also enjoyed some of the educational and cultural activities that Richmond, like other American cities, increasingly offered. While Martha was in Richmond, newspaper notices beckoned "Ladies and Gentlemen" to lectures on topics ranging from chemistry to Virginia history. Readers were also alerted to a traveling exhibition that featured not only a jaguar—America's "most formidable animal"—but also the "only male [elephant] in America," whose keeper promised to put his head in the mouth of this huge but docile animal.[20]

As the weeks wore on, however, Martha seemed to tire of her hectic social schedule. When David Campbell, a western legislator and a former army associate of Tom's, visited the governor's mansion in mid-January, he found that she received him coldly while her husband withdrew and "invites no social intercourse." Perhaps Campbell, who admired Tom, was ill disposed toward Martha because he blamed her for thwarting her husband's promising career in the army. In any event, his uniquely critical description—he found her "*vain*, and *sarcastic*"—suggests that by the end of her month in the capital, she was ready to go home.[21]

From Monticello, Martha followed the politics of her husband's final term as governor, approving his policies while regretting his lack of charm and political savvy. With regard to the most contentious issue of his governorship, the abortive attempt to enhance the powers of the executive, she asserted that Tom's "construction of the constitution was unquestionably the true one." Loyally defending her husband as a conscientious and public-spirited leader, she nonetheless conceded that his temperament undermined his effectiveness in office. "Self-command . . . was never his characteristick virtue," she observed glumly in a letter to Nicholas Trist in 1822.[22]

Although Tom earned a total of $10,000 for his three years as governor, his salary did not enable him to repay the debts he owed. Indeed, his family's expenses continued as usual and probably even increased. Daughters Ellen and Virginia had serious dental work—including, in Virginia's case, the luxury of "gold plugs"—done in Richmond in 1819, when Cornelia joined them in the capital for the spring social season. By then, twenty-six-year-old Ellen

Governor's Mansion. Thomas Mann Randolph was the fourth Virginia governor to live in this splendid house, which was completed in 1813. Martha lived here with her husband during the winter of 1820–21. The governor's house, shown here in an 1865 photo, is situated on Richmond's Capitol Square, within sight of the neoclassical state capitol that Jefferson designed. Courtesy of the Library of Congress.

confided to Martha that she felt it was time for her "to retire a little to the background, and let my sisters have their shares of those pleasures, which must be purchased with money," though she returned to Richmond the following spring. In 1820, Ellen spent five months in Washington. She stayed with her aunt Mary Randolph, who had closed her Richmond boardinghouse and moved to the nation's capital, where she resided with her son.

Ellen was said to have many "beaux," including New York's Senator Martin Van Buren, a wealthy widower, who saw her again when he visited Monticello. Cornelia and Virginia spent the winter of 1821–22 with their father in Richmond, where they attended balls and parties. Cornelia attracted at least one suitor, a man named Frederick Gibbon, who, according to Virginia, was "violently in love."[23]

A season in Richmond or Washington was supposed to give young people—and especially marriageable young women—opportunities to acquire and master social graces and, in the process, find prospective spouses. Whatever progress the Randolph sisters made toward that first objective, the time they spent at balls, parties, and other genteel social gatherings brought them no lasting romantic attachments. The fact that neither their father nor their grandfather could provide them with property must have deterred at least some potential suitors. Maybe, as Peggy Nicholas suggested, the many years they spent cloistered with their family and books at Monticello made them less adept in social situations than some of their competitors.

As it turned out, two of Martha's middle daughters married men they met at Monticello. In the spring of 1824, Joseph Coolidge, a Harvard graduate who had recently completed a grand tour of Europe, visited Monticello to meet Jefferson and fell in love with his granddaughter Ellen. They were married a year later. By then, Virginia and Nicholas Trist, who had remained steadfastly devoted to each other, had also wed. Both marriages pleased Martha. Although Nicholas had little property and could not support a wife and family, Martha loved him like a son. Nicholas's decision to study law with Jefferson and serve as the old man's private secretary ensured Virginia's continuing residence at Monticello. Ellen, by contrast, took the more traditional path, relocating to her husband's home state of Massachusetts once she married. Martha admired Joseph's intelligence and his good manners. She rejoiced that Ellen, at age twenty-nine, had found such a loving and prosperous husband.[24]

❖ Martha was decidedly ambivalent about the departure of Ellen and Joseph for the six-week wedding trip that would end at their new residence, the Coolidge home in Boston. Although she surely regretted the loss of the company of her daughter—the first of her offspring to leave Virginia— she was nonetheless relieved that at least one of her children had escaped their seemingly doomed family. The Randolphs suffered both materially and emotionally, especially after Tom retired from public life and returned home to live more or less full time with his wife and children in Albemarle. Martha pointedly contrasted newlywed Ellen's circumstances with those of her sister-in-law, Jane Randolph, who had married her son Jeff a decade earlier. Ellen's prosperous in-laws could help her and Joseph financially and ease their entry into Boston society. By contrast, Martha mused, "instead of smoothing [Jane's] path and assisting her in her difficulties, we make a frightfull addition to them, and to the daily privations and sacrifices evident to their connection with us, which she bears with the affectionate resignation of a *child*."[25]

Ellen was not the first member of the Monticello household to leave Albemarle. In 1822, Jefferson allowed twenty-four-year-old William Beverley Hemings (known as Beverley) and his twenty-one-year-old sister, Harriet, to escape from slavery by running away from Monticello. The oldest son of Sally Hemings and Thomas Jefferson, Beverley was a gifted musician who played his violin at parties the Randolph sisters gave at Monticello. Harriet was his only sister. The light-skinned siblings traveled together northward and assimilated into white society, shedding their Albemarle identities as enslaved Hemingses. Their uncles, Robert Hemings and his younger brother, the Paris-trained chef James, both of whom received their formal manumissions in the 1790s, were the only other Monticello slaves whom Jefferson freed during his lifetime.[26]

Not long after the departure of the Hemings siblings, Thomas Mann Randolph completed his three terms as governor and returned to Monticello. Although Tom would serve two more years as one of Albemarle's elected delegates to the general assembly, Martha expected him to spend less time in Richmond now that he was no longer governor. In late 1822, perhaps anticipating that Tom would want to indulge his taste for scientific and intellectual pursuits after three contentious years in politics, Martha prepared a room for him at Monticello where, according to Elizabeth Trist, "he may be in Peace and quietness."[27]

Whatever difficulties she and Tom had experienced in the past, Martha still had little reason to fear that their marriage was headed for irrevocable disaster in the early 1820s. While in Richmond, Tom had yearned for the company of his family, and Martha expected him to return to their domestic circle when his tenure as governor was over. Tom remained openly affectionate toward his daughters, and he enjoyed a cordial and fatherly relationship with his future son-in-law Nicholas Trist. Tom wrote to the young man about family and military matters, as well as his objections to "the new morality which tolerates the perpetuity of slavery," which he discerned among southerners in debates leading to the Missouri Compromise of 1820. Nicholas responded with candid but respectful letters about his studies and career prospects and his continuing affection for Virginia. Martha joined their conversation, reassuring Nicholas that her husband would help him whenever he could and that both she and Tom would "never cease to love" him. Jefferson's overseer, Edmund Bacon, who knew of Tom's financial difficulties, nonetheless considered him a "favorite and valuable" connection.[28]

Martha and Tom exchanged letters when they were apart, but none survive, so it is difficult to recapture the tone of their relationship. In letters to others over the years, Tom had admired Martha's diligence as a mother and worried about her health; she had praised him as an affectionate father and a conscientious public servant and expressed anxiety for his safety as he went off to war. In characterizing her beloved daughter Ellen as "very much like her Father but with out his temper," Martha acknowledged Tom's intellect, his love of family, and his sometimes troubling combination of pride and insecurity—all qualities that Ellen seemed to inherit from him—while also conceding her husband's less appealing attributes. The Randolphs, as the overseer Bacon put it, "were all strange people." As Tom aged, his mercurial temper surfaced more often in the form of depression or rage, neither of which made him good company. Tom's rage had resulted in a near-duel with his kinsman John Randolph of Roanoke in 1808 and an assault (with an iron poker) on his noxious son-in-law Charles Bankhead about a decade later. After the latter incident, Martha tried to keep the two men separated, sending for Bacon instead of Tom when Bankhead became dangerously drunk.[29]

Sharing decades of common experiences and profound affection for their children, Martha and Tom survived the bad times and enjoyed the good—one of which appears to have occurred in early January 1824. Tom hurried home from Richmond for a one-day visit, perhaps to celebrate Septimia's tenth birthday. He arrived bearing gifts for his family and news from Richmond, which included the arrival of a Unitarian minister and an Egyptian mummy, both of which became sources of interest and merriment at this family gathering. Virginia reported cheerily to Nicholas Trist that "our going to hear [the Unitarian minister] will depend on Grand-Papa's wishes," though "Mama objects because she thinks it will scandalize our neighbours, with whom we already stand suspected" for spurning more conventional religion. Martha herself disliked what she called religious "ranting" and avoided evangelical meetings and revivals. As the Randolphs joked about their religious foibles, Virginia reported, "Papa set us mad upon the subject of the mummy . . . by suggesting the idea that it would pass thro' this neighbourhood." In sum, Tom's brief visit offered a playful respite from the usual routine of life at Monticello.[30]

This comparatively joyous occasion, however, also signaled an ominous turning point in Martha's relationship with her husband. Long concerned about what she called the "derangement of Mr. Randolph's affairs," Martha learned the full extent of their financial debacle in early January 1824, probably on the same day that Tom regaled his family with stories about the minister and the mummy. Tom had amassed more than $33,000 in debt, which he had little hope of repaying, even if he became postmaster of Richmond with an annual salary of $2,000—a position he avidly pursued without success. When he returned to Richmond, Tom penned a plaintive letter to Henry Remsen, his creditor in New York, offering to "add all the slaves I possess" to the security for his debt and promising that the expected profits from his farms would easily enable him to pay what he owed. "The industrious father of a numerous family who has formerly worked through heavier difficulties," he declared wistfully, "cannot lose hope while the means of rising above them again are left in his powers for he is encouraged by the best affections of the heart." By April, however, in an effort to satisfy the creditors and preserve at least part of the family property, Jeff Randolph assumed his father's debts in exchange for a deed of trust for Edgehill, Varina, and the enslaved people who resided on those properties. This arrangement quickly turned father and son into enemies, leaving Martha to choose sides.[31]

Jeff and his father had never been close, and as grown men they had little in common. Tom Randolph was well educated, bookish, and ambitious for public acclaim. Despite his knowledge of and professed love for agriculture and its methods, he never succeeded as a planter overall, as his mounting debts showed. By contrast, Jeff lacked his father's intellectual gifts as well as his studious habits, but he was hardworking and keenly focused on supporting his large and rapidly growing family. Jeff's solid competence made him a natural choice to manage Jefferson's resources and, later, his father's. Reflecting the practical, self-improving bent of the generation who inherited the Revolution and thus never doubted the survival of the American republic, Jeff privileged private success over public honor. While Tom Randolph had been Jefferson's ideological and political protégé, Jeff was supposed to be his financial savior.[32]

Even before the crisis of the 1820s, relations between Jeff and his father were sometimes rocky. One early source of tension may have arisen from Jeff's conduct as a private in his father's militia company in 1814. While Tom stayed in camp until the unit was formally disbanded, Jeff had been one of many men who, "tired of waiting for the British," asked (and received) permission to go home. He returned to the business of running his grandfather's mill, thereby demonstrating that his father's priorities were not his own. Keenly self-conscious about his rough manners and weak intellect, Jeff, who never excelled at school, nonetheless blamed his father's neglect and insolvency for his lack of learning and cultivation. Years later, Jeff recalled, "My grandfather, my Mother, and my Wife, were my earthly Trinity," while he remembered his father as distant and "prodigal."[33]

Conversely, Tom resented his father-in-law's growing respect for and reliance on Jeff at a time when his own status at Monticello was ambiguous at best. Tom's insecurity coupled with the conspicuous decline of his prospects as his son's rose was a recipe for an explosive rivalry between a failed father and his more successful son. Tom's bitterness toward Jeff turned violent at least once, sometime before 1822, when Edmund Bacon recalled seeing Randolph beat his adult son with a cane—a form of assault intended to inflict both humiliation and physical injury. Jeff later denied this story, which made him appear unmanly, but on one occasion he described his father as "more ferocious than a woulf and more fell than a hyena" when enraged.[34]

After April 1824, as Jeff assumed control of his father's remaining assets, the growing estrangement between father and son resulted in what ultimately became an irreparable rupture between husband and wife. Although it is unclear whether Martha was party to the initial decision to empower Jeff to manage Tom's property, she wholeheartedly supported his plan to liquidate Tom's estate in order to meet the creditors' demands promptly. "I see no advantage in putting off the evil day for come it must, and with accumulating interest for every day that it is delayed," she wrote drearily to Nancy Morris. Martha considered the efforts of her "dear Jefferson" the family's sole hope to regain solvency. She challenged her son's judgment only once during this difficult period, when she offered "steady support" to her daughter Virginia, who wished to order a new piano from Boston, which Jeff and his wife considered "a most foolish *extravagant* act at this very time." An exasperated Jeff acquiesced, however, and Virginia rejoiced that the piano would be "a source of pleasure to Nicholas as well as myself, & to Mama."[35]

Tom himself believed that Martha's support for Jeff's decision to sell

Edgehill and his other property dealt a fatal blow to a marriage he still professed to value. At "one critical moment," he opined, his wife of more than three decades abandoned him because "she had been artfully persuaded that if I were completely sacrificed, her father could be saved." Tom naively hoped to retain some of his assets, which would have preserved his status as a property holder and the resulting rights—held by adult white men in Virginia who owned fifty acres—to vote and hold political office. He understandably resented what he perceived as Martha's and Jeff's desire to save Monticello instead of Edgehill. But rage and paranoia informed his mistaken belief that malice lay at the root of Martha's choice, given his own abysmal stewardship of the family's finances.[36]

During the autumn of 1824, Tom gradually but emphatically distanced himself from his family. In September, he was still living at Monticello, where he and Martha continued to play their customary roles when visitors came to call. The Reverend Horace Holley, a Unitarian minister and president of Transylvania College in Kentucky, described Tom as "very taciturn, though speaking well and agreeably when he speaks at all," while he praised Martha as a "well educated" woman who "converses with great intelligence and ease." Tom's status in Albemarle remained sufficiently high to warrant his being chosen to chair the committee that orchestrated the local reception of the Marquis de Lafayette when he came to Virginia as part of a grand tour of the United States to celebrate a half-century of American independence. By early November, however, when the old revolutionary hero arrived in Albemarle, Tom had left Monticello, and he participated in neither the formal activities the welcoming committee had planned nor the more intimate gatherings at Jefferson's house.[37]

Martha, by contrast, played a role second only to her father's in the moving scene that unfolded on that sunny November afternoon when Lafayette rode with Jeff Randolph in Jefferson's landau up the mountain to Monticello. The fifty-three-year-old matron stood beside her elderly father as he reunited with his old friend, the veteran of two revolutions. "The *General* was led up the steps by *Mr. Jefferson*, & introduced to *Mrs. Randolph*, whom he remembered as a school girl . . . and then as the mistress of her father's house in Paris," recalled one observer, who saw Lafayette kiss Martha's hands and speak "many kind words" as she graciously welcomed him to her home. Peter Fossett, the ten-year-old son of Monticello's head blacksmith and cook, remembered that Monticello was "in gala array" to welcome the marquis and that "Mrs. Patsy Randolph . . . received Lafayette with grace and dignity befitting a queen." Martha occupied center stage in the tableau performed on Monticello's columned portico, with some 400 people—slaves, neighbors, militia, and curious Albemarle residents—looking on in silence as the two old men "burst into tears as they fell into each other's arms."[38]

Despite the gravity of her family's problems, Martha serenely presided over a genteel and emotionally moving celebration. After welcoming Lafayette to Monticello, about twenty "ladies & gentlemen," including several of Martha's daughters and nieces—but not her husband—enjoyed a fine dinner indoors. Jefferson sat next to Lafayette at one end of the table in Monticello's spacious dining room; George Washington Lafayette, son of the marquis, sat at the other end, between Martha and her daughter Ellen. Three other Randolph daughters and several of their "young lady relatives," along with Nicholas Trist, Joseph Coolidge, and two members of the governor's council who had accompanied Lafayette from Richmond to Albemarle, constituted the remainder of the company. The marquis's secretary, Auguste Levasseur, had retired early due to illness. James Madison arrived to join the group as dessert was being served. As the old revolutionaries renewed their acquaintance, feelings of warmth and nostalgia filled the dining room as the "glory of the setting sun shone from behind the many tinted mountains behind which it was sinking."[39]

The family received more visitors during Lafayette's eleven-day stay, most notably Frances and Camilla Wright, Scottish sisters whom Lafayette regarded as "adopted daughters" and who, on Jefferson's invitation, followed the marquis to Monticello a few days after his own festive arrival. Twenty-nine-year-old Frances Wright was the published author of two plays, a highly regarded travel account of the United States, and a fictionalized treatise on Epicurean philosophy. An enthusiastic admirer of American republicanism and of Jefferson, Wright had sent him a copy of her book on Epicurus, which he praised as "a treat . . . of the highest order." Like Lafayette, Wright found slavery abhorrent, but she respectfully entertained Jefferson's assertion that the races could not live peaceably together if enslaved people were freed.[40]

Martha, like her father, probably enjoyed the company of this educated and thoughtful woman, who left Monticello with her esteem for Jefferson intact after what she later called, in a note of appreciation to her hostess, the "most interesting [days] of my life." Four years later, Wright became infamous among Americans as the first woman to present a public lecture to an audience that included both women and men. In so doing, she flouted convention by inverting the standard cultural hierarchy in which men instructed women (and never vice versa). Wright acted boldly on her radical impulses, pursuing a controversial agenda that included antislavery and women's rights. The Scotswoman's radicalism led Ellen Randolph, among others, to disparage her, but if Martha shared her daughter's outrage, she never said so in writing.[41]

By the time Lafayette returned to Monticello for a final, brief, and much more private farewell in August 1825, relations between Martha, Tom, and Jeff had deteriorated precipitously. Tom returned to Albemarle after the legislative session ended in early February, but he lost his bid for reelection in April. By then, Jeff was trying in earnest to sell his father's properties in order to save his own. Although Tom readily accepted the sale of Varina in July, he still vehemently opposed Jeff's efforts to sell Edgehill, as well as his rumored plan to pay the rest of the family's debts by growing tobacco and breeding slaves. Jeff scheduled the sale of all of Edgehill for early August, refusing to allow his father to keep even a modest hillside tract, on which Tom proposed to put a vineyard and a sawmill. Embittered by what he perceived to be his son's "coldblooded avarice," Tom sought and received a court order to delay the sale until December. Martha again opposed her husband, preferring to sell the property and pay their debts as soon as possible.[42]

Martha and Tom never lived together again as husband and wife. During the troubled summer of 1825, Tom spent his days in the nearby town of North Milton, where he owned several lots and a small house. Sometimes he went to Monticello at night to see Martha. Those visits must have been exceptionally tense, given her support for Jeff's plan to sell Edgehill and her belief that Tom would never reconcile completely with her beloved eldest son. "Decency of deportment is all the most sanguine can expect," she observed sadly to Ellen, who had left recently for Boston. As Tom faced poverty and humiliation, Martha tried to empathize, but she nevertheless rejected his judgment in favor of her son's.[43]

Years later, reflecting on her parents' marriage, Ellen indicated that her mother was sometimes the target of her father's rage. A daughter's stubborn affection tempered Ellen's indictment of her father, who she believed "loved & honored her [mother] to the last," as, indeed, Tom himself asserted both on his deathbed and in a letter to his daughter Septimia in 1827. But because "a man's wife is too near to him not to suffer from whatever defects most influence his conduct in private," Ellen believed, Martha's exposure to Tom's "unfortunate temper" was nearly inevitable. Characterizing his behavior toward Martha as "fluctuating," Ellen recalled that her usually cheerful mother "suffered greatly from my father's sullen moods and angry fancies." According to Ellen, Tom "hated" some of her mother's "best friends," and though he was "uniformly kind" to his daughters, he often made Martha "unhappy by his treatment of her sons."[44]

What Ellen called her father's "paroxysms of rage" were probably common occurrences in 1825, as Tom attempted to navigate the most stressful period of his life. Although Ellen recounted no specific instance in which her father vented his rage on her mother, given Tom's penchant for angry rhetoric, it seems likely that he subjected her to verbal abuse for heeding Jeff's counsel. At the same time, circumstantial evidence suggests that Tom did not follow the example of Charles Bankhead by physically abusing his spouse. The fact that Ellen remembered her father fondly suggests that he was not a wife beater, and Jeff Randolph, who had every reason to revile his father and who portrayed him unfavorably in his memoirs, never accused him of mistreating his beloved mother. Tom's daughters remembered him fondly, and the oldest and youngest—Anne and Septimia—each gave his name to one of her sons.[45]

Even more compelling is the fact that Jefferson, who had hoped that Anne and Charles Bankhead could live separately, repeatedly tried to persuade Tom to rejoin his family at Monticello. In June 1825, Jefferson reassured his son-in-law that his financial problems were no cause for embarrassment and that with his "varied education and the resource of books" Tom might happily return to his intellectual pursuits and agricultural experiments. Six months later, Jefferson renewed his invitation, urging Tom to "resume the calm so necessary to your own happiness, and that of your family and friends" by returning to Monticello. Jefferson apparently conveyed his daughter's sentiments, as well as his own, when he tried to persuade Tom to make Monticello his full-time home.[46]

In late December 1825, a notice titled "GREAT SALE" appeared under Tom's name in the Richmond and Petersburg newspapers, announcing the upcoming sale of his land, slaves, and livestock. The sale would occur in Charlottesville on 2 January, when more people than usual would be in town to attend the quarterly meeting of the Albemarle County court. The language Tom used to describe his Albemarle property conveyed an emotional attachment to it that the practical-minded Martha probably never truly appreciated. Edgehill, he wrote, had "the healthiest climate of the whole earth, sheltered by the mountains from the westerly winds of winter, and enjoying the cool breezes inevitably descending from wooded crests in summer nights to replace the rarefied air of the open country, [and] heated during the day by the direct rays of the sun." The land boasted "30 perennial springs of the purest water" and plentiful forests of "oak, . . . hickory, walnut, locust, and ash." Tom praised his enslaved workforce as "the best trained farm servants anywhere to be found." In an attempt both to increase their selling price and to prevent the dispersal of Edgehill's slave community, he emphasized the usefulness of even the elderly, who, he maintained were "qualified to instruct young negroes in all sorts of work." Edgehill's enslaved workforce also included "many valuable tradesmen" as well as Martha's "domestics," whom Tom deemed "as likely and as well taught as any in the state."[47]

While Tom suffered the emasculating social and psychic costs of dependence, Martha experienced as a personal tragedy the sale of the family's slaves. The first to go was Susan, one of Jeff Randolph's house servants at Tufton, who, according to Martha, was "so bad a *servant*, so negligent, so heartless, and of a family of such bad dispositions generally, that there was no probability of her mending." Despite her supposed shortcomings and their own dire need for cash, the Randolphs were loath to part with Susan, and they resisted doing so until she arranged the sale herself. Susan asked to be sold away from an abusive father, who "beat her most unmercifully." After objecting to one prospective purchaser, who offered to buy her for $600, Susan decided to go with a planter from Mississippi who had come north to purchase slaves. Martha admitted that selling this slave helped Jeff to keep more desirable workers, and she took some satisfaction in the fact that Susan expressed her devotion to her mistress before she left. Nevertheless, Martha interpreted the loss of Susan as an ominous prelude to the wholesale liquidation of her family's enslaved workforce. "The discomforts of slavery I have borne all my life," she wrote tellingly to Ellen, "but its sorrows in all their bitterness I never before conceived."[48]

The sale of Edgehill's slaves proceeded as planned in Charlottesville in early January. Martha noted distastefully that "the country is over run with those *trafickers* in human blood, the *negro* buyers." She worried that an advertisement for a general sale of slaves would attract traders who would transport their chattel to the cotton frontier and who cared nothing about preserving black families and communities. "How much trouble and distress y[ou] have been spared . . . by your removal," she wrote to her daughter Ellen in Boston, "for nothing can prosper under such a system of injustice." Martha was both unwilling and unable to take practical action against the "injustice" of Virginia's slave system, but she did attempt to shield some of the most vulnerable of her family's slaves from the worst consequences of

GREAT SALE.

BY decree of Staunton Chancery court with consent of parties: both real and personal estate.

On the 2d January 1826, Albemarle court day, all the negroes belonging to the subscriber heretofore advertised will be sold in Charlottesville for cash. He appeals to the neighbourhood when he declares that they are for the most part the best trained farm servants any where to be found, the elderly being qualified to instruct young negroes in all sorts of work. There are many valuable tradesmen among them, and the domesics belonging to the subscriber, and are as likely and as well taught as any in the state. When the sale of the negroes is over, the estate called EDGEHILL, five miles from Charlottesville, lying between the Rivanna and the foot of the South West chain of mountains, the whole having a South East aspect, will be sold on a credit of one, two, and three years without interest, security to be given upon the land itself. The tract is divided into five parcels, each making a well watered, well wooded, fertile farm of 3, 4 or five hundred acres in the healthiest climate of the whole earth, sheltered by the mountains from the westerly winds of winter, and enjoying the cool breezes invariably descending from wooded crests in summer nights to replace the rarified air of the open country, heated during the day by the direct rays of the sun. There are 30 perennial springs of the purest water within the estate. The timber with which about one half the land is still covered consists of oak of various kinds, mixed with hickory, walnut, locust and ash, but little pine or chesnut, yet enough for all useful purposes of farms. A large stock of cattle, horses, hogs and sheep, with abundance of coarse provender, a couple of hundred barrels of corn, and 9 or 10,000 lbs of beautiful Tobacco unprised, with carts, &c. for the oxen and horses; ploughs, axes, hoes, &c. will be sold at the same time upon six months credit. The whole property will be put into the hands of the Marshal of the Chancery Court on the day preceding the sale, which is made for the benefit of Thomas Jefferson Randolph.

TH: M. RANDOLPH.

Dec. 20, 1825.   68—tds

The Editors of the Petersburg Intelligencer will publish the above till day of sale.

"GREAT SALE." In December 1825, Tom Randolph placed this advertisement in the Richmond Enquirer to announce the imminent sale of his plantation, Edgehill, along with its slaves and livestock. The loss of Edgehill, necessitated by the gravity of his financial situation, was an irreparable blow to Tom, if not to Martha. The Library of Virginia.

Tom's insolvency. She stopped the sale of three aging domestics and eight young girls, three of whom were daughters of Jefferson's body servant and companion, Burwell Colbert (who was also a nephew of Sally Hemings), and his deceased wife Critta, longtime nursemaid to Martha's own children at Edgehill and Monticello.[49]

Martha's retention of these eleven bondswomen, whom she owned outright in fee simple and therefore could dispose of as she wished, reflected a combination of sentiment and hardheaded economics. On the one hand, Martha dreaded "the sorrow of seeing these my house *servants* and their children sold out of the family." She had known the older women, two of whom were married to members of the Hemings family, for her entire adult life. Priscilla, wife of John Hemings, Jefferson's talented woodworker, served as nurse to Martha's younger children, who called her "Mammy." Betsy was married to Peter Hemings, Sally's youngest brother. If these women were roughly the same ages as their husbands, they were in their fifties and would have sold for relatively low prices, so keeping them allowed Martha to protect servants toward whom she felt a sense of duty and affection without much cost to her family or herself. On the other hand, the young girls whom Martha kept, whatever their personal connection to her, would appreciate as they matured, and as they bore children they, too, would increase the value of Martha's holdings overall. By hiring out these girls and, eventually, their children, Martha could generate much-needed income without having to work for pay herself.[50]

Martha was fully aware of the economic benefits of this arrangement, which she herself helped orchestrate. Jeff had planned to save some of his mother's favorite servants by bidding on them at auction, but she suggested this alternate arrangement. Thus she saved Jeff the cost of buying the slaves and spared these women and children the horror and humiliation of standing on the auction block before a gawking crowd in downtown Charlottesville. Insolvency was endemic among the Randolphs, and Martha recalled that when Tom's younger brother William lost his property, his wife Lucy received one-ninth of his estate to support herself and her children before the rest of the family property was sold. Giving these assets to Lucy in fee simple shielded them from William's creditors. Martha, having learned from her sister-in-law's experience, now sought a similar arrangement "in consideration of My relinquishment of dower [rights]," or the life use of one-third of a husband's estate that the common law afforded to widows. In effect, Martha gave up future claims against Tom's estate, if he managed to acquire more property before he died, in exchange for the immediate emotional and financial benefits of retaining these eleven slaves. A prudent financial choice, this decision also showed how little confidence Martha now had in her husband's ability to regain solvency.[51]

As for Tom's landholdings, his creditors allowed him to keep the house in North Milton, but Edgehill was sold at auction. The buyer was none other than Jeff Randolph, his estranged son. At Jeff's suggestion, the property was subdivided into five parcels on the assumption that smaller, less expensive plots would sell more readily. Tom believed that the division of Edgehill into narrow strips made the farms less workable and therefore undermined their appeal to potential buyers and lowered their selling price. He accused his son of scheming to "get possession of his property for half price and turning him adrift in his old age"—a charge that, in his eyes, seemed justified when Jeff acquired all five parcels, some 1,500 acres in all, for $23,000. Martha, by contrast, deemed her son blameless. She saw Jeff's bid of $17 per acre as a boon to the family because he offered a dollar more per acre than anyone else would pay. Besides, Jeff still owed money on his father's account because the combined proceeds from the sales of land and slaves were insufficient to pay Tom's entire debt.[52]

Shortly after the sale of Edgehill, Martha sympathetically assessed her husband's options in a letter to Nancy Morris. "I am afraid of his health's failing from excessive anxiety of the mind," she observed, adding that "dear father wrote most kindly and pressingly to him to live with us altogether, for of late years he has spent most of his time at [Edgehill], but his independence of spirit will not permit him to stay [at Monticello] where he could do nothing for his family." Tom was, in Martha's opinion, dispirited and "completely overwhelmed." The only potentially bright spot was his plan to form a partnership with a man who owned a press to publish a newspaper and a magazine in hopes of retrieving his fortunes. Martha believed that if Tom saw any chance of success in this "new career," he would be "happier than he has been for years past," when he lived in anticipation of his "approaching ruin." Yet the fact that Tom's prospective partner was the son of his mother's former housekeeper was a stunning measure of how far this Randolph of Tuckahoe had fallen in the perilous postrevolutionary era.[53]

Throughout this travail, Martha and her younger children remained at Monticello, where another financial crisis was brewing even as the Jeff took steps to settle his father's affairs. Nearly eighty-three years old, Thomas Jefferson sought to get his own affairs in order in the hopes of being able to leave at least a modest legacy for Martha and her younger children. The old man intended to raise cash by selling land, but because the market for land was so depressed, he decided to hold a lottery, despite his well-known disapproval of gambling and other forms of financial speculation. Jefferson's plan was to sell tickets throughout the Union to admiring citizens who wanted to help a venerable statesman who had devoted so many years to public service to the detriment of his personal finances. Either because he wanted to protect Martha or because, as she put it in a letter to Ellen, he "never speaks of his affairs" to anyone save Jeff, Martha did not know about the lottery until she saw a newspaper notice about it. Jefferson may have thought that the lottery would not affect Martha and her children directly. At least initially he believed that by raffling off his other substantial landholdings, he could preserve his family's ownership of Monticello.[54]

Such a lottery required the approval of the state legislature, but when Jeff Randolph went to Richmond in January 1826 to lobby on his grandfather's behalf, he found many legislators opposed to the scheme, either on religious or moral grounds or because they feared it would reflect badly on Jefferson. In February, however, both legislative houses authorized the lottery and the sale of $60,000 worth of tickets on the condition that the prize offered was worth the equivalent of that sum—which meant that the prize would have to include the house and grounds at Monticello.[55]

A friend reported that Jefferson "turned quite white" when he learned of that condition, which meant that the family would necessarily lose Monticello. Although the old man would be able to stay in his house until he died, Martha and the children would have to leave no more than two years later. Having no viable alternatives, Martha became resigned to the eventual loss of her childhood home. With her husband ruined and her father declining both physically and financially, she had no choice but to trust Jeff, her "dear and excellent son," to oversee a lottery that she hoped would raise enough money to pay her father's debts and provide "a maintenance for the family, the means of educating the boys, and a *home* for my self and children . . . and last tho not least, the undisturbed possession of Monticello during [Jefferson's] precious life."[56]

❖ Jefferson's advanced age and frailty made Martha increasingly preoccupied with his mortality, just as the old man worried more and more about his daughter's apparently weakened health. In June 1826, when Jeff returned from a trip to Boston, New York, and Philadelphia to promote the lottery, he found his grandfather "in agony" about Martha, who he believed was "sinking every day under the sufferings she endures" and "literally dying before his eyes."[57]

The old man's somber mood owed as much to his own sickness and to his daughter's woes as to the recent death of a close family member. On 11 February, Martha's firstborn child and Jefferson's firstborn grandchild, Anne Cary Randolph Bankhead, died at the age of thirty-five. Anne, who remained bedridden at Monticello after the premature birth of a son in mid-January, died of complications due to childbirth. In her seventeen-year marriage, she had been pregnant twelve times but had only four children who survived infancy. For the last five years of her life, Anne had kept a diary that chronicled both her deep religious devotion and the physical debilities that came with what she called her "advancing age." Her life was sad and ultimately tragic, though if her diary entries are any indication, her husband, Charles, may have reformed himself after he eluded prosecution for assaulting Jeff Randolph in 1819. In her diary, Anne described herself as an "affectionate wife & mother" who hoped that her husband and children would read the Bible and other "good religious books" after she was gone.[58]

Anne routinely prepared for death as she approached childbirth. This time, though Martha initially believed that her daughter was "doing well" after delivering her baby boy, her condition soon deteriorated. On 11 February, Cornelia, who was attending Anne's sickbed with her mother, scribbled a note to her sister Mary informing her that there was no hope for Anne and that "grandpapa" should be told how ill she truly was. Jefferson's own delicate condition had prevented him from seeing Anne for several days, but that morning he heeded Cornelia's warning and went to the sickroom, where he found his granddaughter "speechless and insensible." She died a few hours later. Anne was buried with her grandmother and her aunt, Maria Jefferson Eppes, in the family graveyard at Monticello.[59]

Anne's death devastated the entire family. Martha mourned her daughter deeply. Both she and Cornelia attributed the death of their "lost saint" to overmedication by "ignorant" physicians, which both Martha and Anne herself had opposed. The belief that Anne's death had been avoidable heightened Martha's anguish and her determination to care for her daughter's surviving children. A loving father to his daughters, Tom took Anne's death especially hard, perhaps because he felt that he had not done enough to protect her. According to one young relative, Tom vented his despair and rage over his daughter's fate on Martha, which aggravated her own distress. He also became increasingly possessive toward his youngest children, twelve-year-old Septimia and eight-year-old George, whom he prohibited from visiting Tufton, the home of Jeff Randolph, who was himself in "dreadful spirits" after Anne died.[60]

One immediate consequence of Anne's death was the addition of two of her four children to the Monticello household. Sensing his responsibility as the oldest surviving sibling and putative head of the family, to ensure the well-being of his sister's children, Jeff Randolph reconciled with Charles Bankhead. Jeff persuaded Charles to leave his only daughter, thirteen-year-old Ellen, and her infant brother, William, with Anne's mother and sisters at Monticello, though the older boys stayed with the Bankheads in Caroline County. Virginia and Cornelia oversaw their niece's education and cared for the baby, who they believed resembled their own father. The premature infant eventually thrived with the help of breast milk provided by Anne Hughes, the nineteen-year-old daughter of Wormley Hughes, who, as Monticello's head gardener, had shared his love for and knowledge of plants and flowers with the child's dead mother.[61]

Another consequence of Anne's death was Cornelia's departure for Boston, where Ellen awaited the arrival of her first child and was eager to have someone from her own family with her. Even before Anne died, Joseph Coolidge had asked his mother-in-law to allow Cornelia to come to Boston to be with Ellen. Martha was receptive to the idea, though she worried about the cost of the trip and the need to find a suitable escort to accompany her daughter on the journey north. After Anne died, as she apprehensively monitored the health of her daughter-in-law Jane, who had recently given birth, and that of her daughter Virginia, who was "indisposed" during her own first pregnancy, Martha became "more anxious . . . than ever" that Cornelia should go to Ellen. So in late March, when Jeff Randolph traveled northward to solicit support for his grandfather's lottery, Martha prevailed on him to take his sister to Boston. Ellen gave birth before her siblings arrived, but Cornelia stayed with the Coolidges after Jeff left, providing invaluable assistance to the new mother.[62]

In the spring of 1826, Ellen Coolidge and Virginia Trist each gave birth to a daughter, and reflecting the affection and respect the sisters felt for their mother, each hoped to name her infant daughter Martha. Although Ellen deferred to her husband's wish that their first child bear her own name, Virginia and Nicholas named their daughter Martha Jefferson Trist. When Ellen learned of the Trists' choice, she declared, "How I envy you the privilege of calling your daughter Martha, a name dearer to my heart than any other."[63]

Meanwhile, as Jefferson's conditioned worsened, he wisely revised his will to shield Martha and her children from the demands of Tom's remaining creditors. As Jefferson's sole surviving child, Martha would inherit his entire estate, but because she was married, the law would vest control of that property in Tom, whose creditors could seize it in compensation for his still-outstanding debts. To avert that catastrophe, Jefferson stipulated that, after his own debts were satisfied, the remainder of his estate was to be settled on Jeff, who would hold it "in trust, for the sole and separate use . . . of my dear daughter Martha Randolph" until Tom died, after which the property would go to Martha herself. Jefferson's objective was not to offend Tom but, rather, to protect Martha and her children in the event of his death. He also wanted to make sure that Jeff—whom he considered "the greatest of the god-sends which heaven has granted to me"—knew how he planned to dispose of his property and to give others written directions about how to proceed if he died while Jeff was gone. Jefferson named his trusted grandson as his sole executor, a logical choice that nonetheless further infuriated Tom.[64]

To placate his "friend and son-in-law," Jefferson addressed Tom's situation explicitly in a codicil he added just one day later. One purpose of this codicil was to dispose of some personal items, such as a silver watch he gave to Jeff, a walking staff for James Madison, and books he earmarked for the library at the University of Virginia. Another was to manumit Burwell Colbert, John Hemings, and Joe Fossett and to stipulate that his younger children by Sally Hemings, Madison and Eston—whom Jefferson identified only as their uncle John Hemings's "two apprentices"—should receive their freedom when they reached the age of twenty-one. But the codicil also made explicit Jefferson's reason for his formal exclusion of Tom from his will and from the administration of his estate, as well as his hope that his son-in-law would nonetheless benefit from whatever property he left. "I have made no specific provision for the comfortable maintenance of my son in law . . . because of the difficulty and uncertainty of devising terms which shall vest any beneficial interest in him which the law shall not transfer to the benefit of his creditors," he wrote, adding that "property placed under the executive right of my daughter . . . as if she were a femme sole . . . will be a certain resource against want for all." Tom accepted neither this rationale nor the reality that Jefferson bore him no ill will. He never again visited his father-in-law, even after the older man's health worsened decisively that summer.[65]

On 24 June 1826, not long after Jeff returned from Boston, optimistic about the lottery's prospects, Jefferson summoned his trusted physician, Dr. Robley Dunglison, to Monticello. At that point, Dunglison later recalled, Jefferson knew that he was near death. That day, he wrote a letter politely declining an invitation to celebrate the fiftieth anniversary of American independence with the "citizens of the city of Washington"; the next day, he addressed his last letter to a Baltimore merchant to arrange for the payment of duties on a shipment of imported wine. From 26 June on, Jefferson remained bedridden, and on 29 June he received his last visitor from outside Albemarle. When Henry Lee, son of the revolutionary hero and Federalist partisan "Light-Horse" Harry Lee, arrived for a prearranged interview, Martha told Lee that her father was too ill to receive him, but Jefferson insisted on seeing his guest, who was revising his father's memoirs. Mindful of his historical reputation, the dying man hoped that Lee's revisions would include a more sympathetic account of his still-controversial tenure as Virginia's wartime governor. Always hospitable, Jefferson invited Lee to stay for dinner. For Martha, who presided over the meal in the absence of her ailing father, Lee later professed "the most exalted esteem."[66]

For nearly two weeks, Martha spent her days sitting at her father's bedside as his health declined steadily. Family members and servants came and went throughout the day in Jefferson's sickroom, but Martha, Jeff, Nicholas Trist, and Burwell Colbert were the dying man's near-constant companions. Granddaughters Virginia and Mary visited during their respites from child care and housekeeping, respectively. Jeff spent the nights in his grandfather's room, along with Colbert and some other servants—probably Sally Hemings, who, with Colbert, cared for Jefferson and his room, and possibly other male Hemingses with whom he had long been on familiar terms. Worried about the toll that his illness and her other travails were taking on his daughter's health, Jefferson made Martha retire to her own room each night for some much-needed rest.[67]

Martha was too busy and too distraught to write to family and friends during her father's two-week deathwatch. At the end of June, Virginia informed Cornelia that their grandfather's condition was grave and that she, Ellen, Joseph, and the baby should come immediately if they hoped to see him before he died. On the morning of 4 July—the fiftieth anniversary of American independence—Jefferson still lingered, but Nicholas Trist wrote to Joseph Coolidge that his death was imminent. "You will be too late," he wrote, "yet, I hope you'll be on your way before this reaches Boston. The presence of [Ellen and Cornelia] is of *inexpressible* importance to *Mother*." Joseph received the letter the next day, which was Wednesday, and he promised to try to leave Boston by Saturday. In Boston, Joseph added hurriedly, the "bells are now tolling for the decease of President Adams," who "died yesterday, July 4th at Quincy" in the afternoon. By then, Adams's fellow revolutionary and successor as president had died at Monticello.[68]

Two days earlier, a tearful Martha had had her last substantive conversation with her father. Although Jefferson left his grandson Jeff completely in charge of the disposition of his property, part of his conversation with Martha may have concerned the fate of Sally Hemings, whom Jefferson had not formally emancipated in the will he wrote months earlier. Mentioning Sally Hemings by name in his will—a public document that would be certified by the local courts—would have drawn public attention to their private relationship, embarrassing Martha, her children, and perhaps Hemings herself. Virginia law, moreover, required that slaves who received their freedom had to leave the state within a year. Though the four male slaves Jefferson formally manumitted in his will were either skilled enough to secure the legislature's permission to remain in Virginia or young enough to leave and begin new lives elsewhere, Hemings was fifty-three-years old, and her most notable skill was sewing, a near-universal feminine accomplishment. After Jefferson died, Sally Hemings and her sons simply left Monticello to live in de facto freedom in nearby Charlottesville. Martha later made this arrangement official in her own will, directing her children to give Hemings "her time" if Martha predeceased her. Legally, Martha Randolph owned Sally Hemings, who nonetheless lived as a free woman until she died in 1835.[69]

On Sunday, 2 July, Jefferson also gave Martha "a little casket" of souvenirs that included a handwritten verse, which he called his "death-bed Adieu." The poem attested to Jefferson's abiding love for Martha as well as to his comforting and surprisingly conventional vision of the afterlife as a family reunion, where he at long last would rejoin his two "Seraphs," his beloved wife and his younger daughter Maria:

Life's visions are vanished, it's dreams are no more.
Dear friends of my bosom, why bathed in tears?
I go to my fathers; I welcome the shore,
Which crowns all my hopes, or which buries my cares.
Then farewell my dear, lov'd daughter, Adieu!
The last pang of life is in parting from you!
Two Seraphs await me, long shrouded in death:
I will bear them your love on my last parting breath.[70]

Jefferson was buried in the small family graveyard at Monticello at 5:00 P.M. on Wednesday, 5 July. John Hemings made his coffin, and Wormley Hughes dug his grave. At Jefferson's request, the funeral was simple. The Reverend Frederick Hatch, the local Episcopal minister whom Jefferson received not as a clergyman but, rather, as a "kind and good neighbor" during his final illness, read the funeral service to the family and a crowd of uninvited mourners, who trudged up the mountain from Charlottesville despite bad weather. Among the latter were the students of the University of Virginia whose riotous behavior less than a year earlier had profoundly disappointed Jefferson. They now assembled, grief-stricken and reverent, to pay their last respects. Tom Randolph was also among the mourners, but far from rendering him circumspect or repentant, his father-in-law's death made him even more truculent. At least one family friend believed that Tom hypocritically "pretended to mourn exceedingly," even as he quarreled with Jeff over who should tell Hatch when to begin the funeral service as a "dreadfully distressed" Martha looked on.[71]

After the funeral, Tom, who still resided alone in his house in North Milton, continued to fume about Jefferson's decision not to make him at least coequal with Jeff as coexecutor of his estate. Because executorships usually devolved on heads of families, Tom interpreted his exclusion as a profound insult that marked him as inferior and subservient to his son, whom Jefferson chose to succeed him as the family's head. Tom wrote a letter, which he intended to publish, vilifying "the Executor" and possibly criticizing his late father-in-law, but he withdrew the letter—which has not survived—before it appeared in print because its contents upset Martha. At the same time, however, Tom emphatically informed his son-in-law Nicholas Trist that he no longer considered himself "a member of the family at all" and that he could not return to Monticello. In addition, though he "stopped the letter which has thrown Mrs R into such agitation," Tom defiantly asserted that henceforth he did not "feel myself bound to consult with any member of [the family] upon what I do, or what I write or what I say."[72]

Perhaps Martha took some temporary comfort in the many heartfelt tributes to her father. Thousands of people attended public eulogies in Richmond and other cities, and mourners of every sort addressed personal letters directly to Martha. Friends James Madison and James Monroe sent condolences and offers of assistance. The writer Lydia Sigourney, who had once enjoyed the hospitality of Jefferson's family at Monticello, sent a poem describing her sadness on learning of his death. Edward Everett, a Harvard professor who became a famed orator, extended his sympathy to Martha and her family on behalf of the American Academy of Arts and Sciences. A. H. Hubbard, who owned a Connecticut paper factory, wrote to praise

Jefferson and suggest that his "sayings" be collected and published "for the support of liberty." The citizens of Germantown, Pennsylvania, the site of a revolutionary battle, wrote a polite note. From France came an anonymous ode, "Sur La Mort De Thomas Jefferson," and a missive from Lafayette, declaring his esteem for his much-loved friend.[73]

At age fifty-four, Martha had lost her husband to rage and her father to death, and it became increasingly clear that she would lose her home as well. When Jefferson died, he still owed more than $100,000. Martha attributed her father's insolvency not to bad management or to extravagance but, rather, to his years of public service and his generosity toward others. He was, she believed, "kind and liberal in the extreme [and] his heart and purse were always alike open to those who had any claims even the slightest upon them, and often . . . to those who had none but their distresses." Martha predicted—correctly, as it turned out—that her father's estate was not sufficient to cover his debts and that the lottery, which many of his admirers had supported expressly to help the venerable statesman, would not succeed once he was dead. Within months of his death, she therefore faced the grim reality that Monticello, her childhood home and that of her children, would be sold. "I am sick now, but shall be well again," she confided to her daughter Ellen, despite the "bitter anguish of seeing his abode rendered desolate, the walls dismantled, and the sanctuary of his bed room violated by the auctioneer."[74]

Jefferson's death marked another pivotal moment in the downward spiral of the Randolphs' marriage, though no one said so explicitly. While the old man lived, Tom had an open—and often-extended—invitation to return to the family at Monticello. Jefferson cared for Tom, sympathized with his financial predicament, and perhaps believed that his at least occasional presence was essential to Martha's respectability and happiness. Once Jefferson died, those invitations to resume his place in the family stopped coming. At the same time, Tom's aloofness during Jefferson's final illness and his bizarre behavior at the funeral undermined whatever affection Martha still felt for her troubled spouse. When Martha assessed her options for the future immediately after Jefferson's death, she rarely mentioned Tom.

The anticipated loss of Monticello and the ultimate collapse of the Randolphs' marriage necessarily raised the issue of where she and her younger children would reside once the house was sold. Jeff, whose large family lived in a small house at Tufton, proposed to build a house at nearby Shadwell for his mother. But Martha worried that her son—who, as Jefferson's executor, was now responsible for his debts—could not afford the expense.

Jefferson Lottery Ticket. Thomas Jefferson hoped that a public lottery would raise enough money to pay his debts and enable his family to keep Monticello at least during Martha's lifetime. Though authorized by the state legislature, the lottery never took place, in part because those who would have purchased tickets to help the penurious statesman were unwilling to support the lottery after he died in 1826. Princeton University Library.

Instead, she considered renting a house somewhere in Albemarle so the family could "all remain together." She also pondered opening a school with her daughters Virginia, Cornelia, and Mary to generate much-needed income. Because of her superior education and accomplishments and her unique status as the daughter of Thomas Jefferson, she noted, "I am told that my number [of students] will only be limited by my power of accommodating them." Martha's Parisian schooling and the learning and manners she passed on to her daughters were now arguably her family's most valuable assets. After the settlement of their financial woes, she confided sadly to Nancy Morris, "for *me*, nothing will remain but an education given in happier days and for very different purposes."[75]

Martha's children pressed her to visit Ellen in Boston, where they hoped she could regain her health and enjoy a temporary respite from both the family's money problems and her estranged husband. Jeff, in particular, urged his mother to go to Boston, wishing to spare her the pain of witnessing the sale of Monticello and its enslaved workforce, which he expected to accomplish in her absence. Martha reluctantly left for Boston in mid-October, taking her two youngest children with her. Jeff escorted them on a trip that included a stop in Baltimore, where Martha contrasted the wealth and luxuries she saw with "the discomfort in which I had left all that I loved most on earth" at home. Although she planned to spend only the coming winter in Boston, Martha did not return to Albemarle until May 1828.[76]

❖ Debt and death had destabilized Martha's world at Monticello and left her future and that of her family in an uncomfortably unsettled state. Within months of Jefferson's death, she was living with the Coolidges in Boston, her separation from Tom seemed to be permanent, and the daughters who remained in Albemarle—Virginia, Cornelia, and Mary—were planning their eventual departure from Monticello. Mary purposefully prepared for the expected opening of their school, studying "those things which will best fit me for bearing my part of it." Cornelia, by contrast, wondered where the family would live, preferring to leave the state "but whether to Louisiana or Vermont, to the west or to the east, when people's inclinations are so different & yet all wish to hang together, is hard to say." In Boston, Martha emerged from the New England winter "still in a miserable state," despite some improvement in her health. "Every thing before me is gloom and uncertainty," she lamented to Jeff in March 1827. "I have really suffered so much that I can not comprehend the possibility of better days."[77]

chapter 7 | Honorable
Poverty

   In the five years after her father died, Martha lived in four places—Boston, Cambridge, Albemarle, and Washington—but she never had a home that was entirely her own. Although she relied on her older children for living quarters and financial assistance and advice, Martha counted sixteen people for whom, in turn, she felt a certain sense of responsibility after her father's death and her husband's ruin and self-imposed exile.[1] There was her daughter Virginia and her well-educated but unemployed husband, Nicholas Trist, and their young daughter, Martha's namesake. Of the three unmarried Randolph sisters, Cornelia, the oldest, was twenty-seven when her grandfather died; Septimia, the youngest, was twelve. In addition, in 1826, Martha had four younger sons, who ranged in age from twenty to eight, none of whom was married or settled in a career. She also saw herself as a surrogate mother to her four Bankhead grandchildren, whose father soon remarried. Finally, there were the two elderly widows: Martha's childless aunt, Anna Jefferson Marks, who had lived at Monticello since 1811, and their old friend Elizabeth Trist, who was also a frequent houseguest, especially after her grandson Nicholas wed Virginia Randolph in 1824.

 Money was a constant problem that Martha and her relatives addressed with a hodgepodge of old-fashioned and modern strategies. On the one hand, in a manner reminiscent of the personal and influence-laden politics of the colonial era, which her father excoriated but nonetheless practiced to some extent, Martha gratefully accepted—and sometimes even sought—official assistance in the form of subsidies, land grants, and political or military appointments (for her sons or son-in-law) from national or state governments.[2] On the other hand, in this age of democracy and self-improvement, she also did her best to give her sons the education they needed to become self-made men and to increase her daughters' chances to meet prospective spouses, even as she pondered new ways to generate income for her troubled family. Like many Americans, the Randolphs were on the move by the 1820s, in search of new opportunities. But the social, economic, and geographic fluidity that for many brought upward mobility signified a seemingly downward spiral for Martha. Her children, unlike her, would begin their adult lives without property in a world where their famous grandfather and once-enviable gentry lineage would be less tangible assets than curiosities.

❖ In the months and years after Jefferson's death, a broken marriage and the expected sale of her beloved home forced Martha to weigh her options. She could resolve her differences with Tom and they could try to live on whatever modest income she received from her father's estate, or they could make their separation permanent, with or without formal legal sanction. If Martha were to live on her own without her estranged husband, she could either reside with her adult children or some other relations, or she might attempt to maintain her own household. She could be financially dependent on her family—mostly likely relying on Jeff or son-in-law Joseph Coolidge—or she might try to earn additional money, either by hiring out her slaves or by running a school. Martha ultimately experimented with most of these options.

In the short term, however, the dispersal of the family, which began with Tom's removal to North Milton, continued after Martha journeyed to Ellen's house in Boston with Septimia and George in October 1826. Jeff and Jane and their growing family continued to live at Tufton, though by spring Jeff had demolished most of Tom and Martha's small house at Edgehill and was busily erecting "a handsome . . . square building with a long portico" in its place. Cornelia and Mary divided their time between Tufton and Monticello, where Virginia and Nicholas Trist watched over the emptied house whose contents had been auctioned to raise money, though many items were sold cheaply as keepsakes to Jefferson's relatives. James Madison Randolph returned to the university his grandfather founded in Charlottesville, where he soon completed his studies only to decide to become a farmer. His younger brothers, Ben and Lewis, headed off to schools in Amelia and Spotsylvania counties, respectively. Meanwhile, in January 1827, Thomas Mann Randolph left Virginia for Georgia, where he was to be a member of a federal commission charged with surveying the boundary between that state and Florida.[3]

Competent and intelligent, the Randolph women recognized the problems inherent in a social system that, by law and custom, rendered them dependent on men who were not always willing or able to fulfill their patri-

Edgehill. Thomas Jefferson Randolph bought his father's plantation and replaced his parents' house there with larger and more genteel living quarters, where Martha and her unmarried daughters often stayed. Fire demolished Jeff Randolph's house at Edgehill in 1916, though the exterior walls were saved. This photograph, which shows the rebuilt house with some modern alterations, is from the early twentieth century. The Library of Virginia.

archal roles. Although she never criticized either her father or her grandfather directly, Ellen Coolidge noted the "melancholy" tone of her sisters' letters, declaring that "for those, who from sex or age are condemned to a passive endurance of whatever may happen, I cannot help hoping that better brighter days are in store." Her sister Cornelia, who ardently desired "to make money for my friends," half-seriously proposed two plans of action that tellingly juxtaposed men's autonomy and women's constraints in times of crisis: She could either "put on men's cloths, go to Louisiana, make a fortune, die of yellow fever & leave it to you" or "marry a horrid old man here . . . if he would give me his immense fortune to divide among you." More pointedly, Martha herself told the story of the "confirmed sot" Miles Cary, who died leaving "his wife pregnant, [with] a very large family, one . . . horribly deformed, and his fortune totally gone." Undoubtedly seeing parallels between that poor widow's predicament and her own, Martha declared that if Cary "had died 10 years ago his wife had so much energy of character that I have no doubt she would have retrieved their affairs." Instead, he "lived till he spent everything," leaving his family in grave distress.[4]

Martha never directly criticized her husband for his insolvency, nor did she blame her father for his inability to retain the land, slaves, furniture, and other familiar possessions that she had known since childhood, which would have ensured her comfort in old age, regardless of Tom's problems. While her attitude toward Tom evolved from empathy to pity, Martha strongly defended Jefferson, even as it became increasingly clear that there would be little left for her and the children after Jeff paid off his massive debts. In 1826, Ellen Coolidge met one of her grandfather's admirers, who wanted to defend the recently deceased Jefferson against the insinuations of those who wondered "how it came that having received from his father a large property, marrying an heiress & receiving for many years a regular salary from the public Treasury, he should have in his latter years fallen into the distress which induced him to apply for permission to sell his estate by lottery." When Ellen inquired about the "causes of the embarrassment of his pecuniary affairs," her mother responded with a long letter in which she attributed Jefferson's financial woes to four factors: the assumption of debts incurred by others, his generosity and openhanded hospitality, Virginia's economic problems and especially its reliance on enslaved labor, and the many years he devoted to public service, during which his personal financial interests necessarily suffered.[5]

While Martha had gently criticized her father's extravagance while he lived, that was not part of the official story she told to explain his ultimate financial ruin. Indeed, by 1828, she recounted an even simpler story that attributed her father's "embarrassment" almost completely to his patriotism, and by virtue of her own inheritance of his misfortune, she claimed a share of that public virtue as her own. "I never had, and never shall have the folly to be ashamed of an honorable poverty," she explained to her old friend Margaret Bayard Smith, because "it is the fruits, and the price we have paid, for a long and useful life devoted to the service of his country." Martha believed that because a "slave estate" in Virginia's "precarious" economy needed constant monitoring, her father's frequent absences made his financial failure virtually inevitable. Still, she stoically declared, "I never regretted the sacrifice he made . . . and if a few must suffer for the advantage of the many it is a melancholy necessity."[6]

If Martha's status as the self-sacrificing daughter of an American patriot was uniquely "honorable," she nonetheless joined the growing numbers of mature women in her own extended family who, having little or no property, faced the prospect of dependence. Widows and single women without property typically lived as dependents in their fathers', sons', or brothers' households, just as Anna Jefferson Marks had lived with Jefferson, and Cornelia and Mary eventually became wards of their brother and brothers-in-law. When it became clear that Monticello would be sold, Martha, who expected to receive at least a small annual income from the proceeds of the sale of her father's property, moved in with her prosperous son-in-law, Joseph Coolidge, in Boston. Although that arrangement was temporary, living with the Coolidges or with Jeff in Albemarle would have been a reasonable option for Martha if she and Tom did not reach some sort of reconciliation.

At the same time, three of her Randolph sisters-in-law, whose husbands also fell on hard financial times, offered Martha more proactive models for her future life. Mary, the oldest Randolph sister, ran a boardinghouse in Richmond for many years before moving to Washington. There she lived with her son and wrote the first American regional cookbook, *The Virginia House-Wife*, which went through many editions after its first publication in 1824. Harriet Randolph Hackley opened a successful school in Richmond in 1818 and moved to Norfolk in 1826. According to Martha, Hackley soon was "doing very well" with her "very large school of 50 scholars," while her husband did a brief stint in debtors' prison in New York. Jane Randolph, who was Martha's friend and neighbor in Albemarle, moved to Lynchburg after her indebted husband lost his property. She, too, opened a school in her small house before moving to Norfolk to work with Harriet Hackley and her daughters. Although coverture prohibited these women, as wives, from controlling property, they worked around the law to become the main breadwinners in their families.[7]

Hackley's example might have inspired Martha to consider establishing a school with her own daughters in Albemarle. On 4 December 1826, exactly five months after Jefferson's death, Martha, aware that the lottery had not succeeded, decided to support herself and her children "by the profits of a school which I shall open immediately" after her return from Boston. Jeff encouraged his mother's plan and pressed his sisters to issue a public announcement of the school's opening, but they delayed, in part because they needed time to review the subjects they would teach. Cornelia, Mary, and Virginia wrote cheerful letters to their mother, whom they expected to teach Italian, introductory French and music, and perhaps some natural history.

Martha's responses to their letters were equally cheerful, though her enthusiasm for the project waned. By March 1827, she confided to Jeff that she dreaded the "frightful responsibility" of being a schoolmistress. Writing even more frankly to her sister-in-law Nancy Morris, Martha declared that she would do anything to avoid "the horrors of keeping a boarding school," which she believed would be "a very severe trial in my feeble state."[8]

Although teaching her own children had been one of the great joys of Martha's life, several factors led her to recoil from the prospect of teaching other people's daughters. Tending school and taking in boarders especially would be hard work and unrelenting responsibility for a woman who believed that she already had plenty of both. In addition, because many parents sent their daughters to school for only a few years, most of the lessons Martha and her daughters taught would have been rudimentary and therefore not intellectually satisfying. Finally, despite the income-generating activities of her Randolph sisters-in-law, Martha believed that her status as Jefferson's daughter—the attribute that Jeff and others assumed would attract students in droves—rendered her working for wages as somehow disreputable. Cornelia, who as early as 1825 wished she could "do something" to support herself, sadly concluded, "I suppose not until we sink entirely will it do for the granddaughters of Thomas Jefferson to take work in or keep a school." This idea came not from Jeff, who was eager for them to start a school, but from Martha.[9]

In the months following Jefferson's death, Martha and her children assessed other options for generating income, at least until Jeff found a suitable buyer for Monticello. As early as January 1827, Joseph Coolidge was urging his brother-in-law to consult Jared Sparks, the highly regarded historian and editor, about the publication of his grandfather's manuscripts. Because of the growing popularity of biographies and writings of revolutionary heroes, Joseph expected Jefferson's papers to bring at least $5,000, if Jeff found a reputable editor and handled the negotiations wisely. Since she no longer had a household of her own, Martha hired out her slaves, while Jeff oversaw the sale of the bulk of Monticello's enslaved workforce. Jeff refused an offer from a Georgia man in hopes of keeping Monticello's enslaved community more or less intact, and the prices of some slaves were set low to enable family members to purchase them. Mary Randolph convinced herself—though there was no way she could have known for certain—that "*the negroes* with one exception I believe, are all sold to persons living in the *State*, many of them in this neighbourhood or the adjoining counties." Mary, who did not attend the sale herself, nevertheless found the ordeal of the five-day auction painful, just as the sale of Edgehill's slaves had repulsed her mother a few years earlier.[10]

Public appointments, gifts, or stipends were a final source of possible income for Martha and her family. In fact, Tom's appointment as a member of the boundary commission in Georgia was the result of successful efforts by Martha's "friends" to persuade Secretary of War James Barbour to offer her husband the position to assist Martha and demonstrate the "Gratitude common to every American for [her] illustrious father." Not long afterward, the state legislatures of South Carolina and Louisiana each allocated $10,000 in bank stock for Martha's support and maintenance in tribute to her father's patriotism and public service. Although neither Martha nor her relatives had solicited these tributes, they truly appreciated such honors and optimistically anticipated that others might follow. When no more gifts materialized, some of Jefferson's grandchildren became bitter. Cornelia complained that despite her grandfather's "sixty years of devoted services . . . his children were left in beggary by the country to whom he had bequeathed them," while her cousin Francis Eppes ranted that "the liberality and generosity, and patriotism of the Old Dominion" especially had vanished under the influence of "Yankee notions, and Yankee practices." Martha was more circumspect, but by 1828, she, too, wondered why Jefferson's "own state which has most benefited by his talents and virtues has given him a grave, and left to others to give bread to his children."[11]

These expectations were unrealistic and, in light of Jefferson's stated preference for limited government, a bit ironic. State governments were generally not in the business of honoring famous individuals or their families with monetary gifts. They gave pensions to impoverished petitioners, especially old soldiers or their widows, and in 1818, Congress finally enacted a national pension law for Revolutionary War veterans. Individuals who could prove their military service and were living in "reduced circumstances" received modest pensions, though in 1820 Congress added a means test and required applicants to take a pauper's oath to show that they were in the "lowest grade of poverty." Proponents of this pension system saw payments to poor veterans as a form of social justice insofar as military service left many veterans disadvantaged while their sacrifices fostered opportunities for their countrymen to thrive and prosper. Jefferson's descendants apparently saw his sacrifices as analogous to those of the old soldiers, though neither Congress nor the states ever considered granting pensions to civilian officeholders. Some Americans openly criticized the special stipends that South Carolina and Louisiana gave to Martha. Jefferson, unlike the soldiers, received a substantial salary during his eight years as president, and Martha was not his widow but, rather, his adult daughter. Nor were she and her children indigent, unlike the military pensioners.[12]

In the spring of 1827, an uncertain future weighed heavily on Martha as she languished amid the comforts of Ellen's Boston home. On leaving Virginia, she recalled, she had experienced a "complete prostration of health, strength, and spirits" that still afflicted her six months later. To Jeff, she confided that she was so depressed that she could not imagine "the possibility of better days." Although Monticello had not been sold, Martha resigned herself to abandoning the house on both emotional and financial grounds. "I see no use in returning to Monticello as we shall have to leave it again," she wrote to Jeff in early March, adding that the house would "require so much more furniture and so many more servants to keep it decent than a smaller house." Looking ahead, Martha believed that her annuity from the South Carolina and Louisiana gifts would be sufficient for her "to rent a house some where," allowing her to avoid both dependence on her older children and the unpleasantness of keeping a boarding school.[13]

In the meantime, she waited, passing her time in Boston enjoying her young granddaughter, awaiting the birth of Ellen's second child, reading, walking, and "mix[ing] in society." Eliza Quincy, the wife of Boston's mayor, observed that like her daughter Ellen, Martha was much admired by those in her social circle. "Mrs. Randolph," she declared emphatically, "must always command the respect of all who know her." While Septimia and George attended school, first in Boston and then in Cambridge, and Jeff sorted out the family's affairs at home, Martha nervously contemplated her unsettled future. Although Jeff optimistically assured his mother that her eventual income would be "very abundant," he also advised her that the "continued uncertainty as to the definitive result of our affairs render it impossible for me to put your mind at ease relative to your future home."[14]

❖ Martha's stay in Boston, which ultimately lasted eighteen months, was her first taste of urban life since she visited Richmond when Tom was governor. This trip marked the first time she left Virginia since her father was president, as well as her first foray north of the Potomac since, as a girl, she traveled to Philadelphia. Twelve-year-old Patsy Jefferson had spent a little more than two weeks in Boston in 1784, awaiting the departure of the ship that would carry her and her father to Europe. Forty-three years later, she returned to a city that had roughly tripled in size and boasted an active cultural life and a diverse and expansive economy. The 1830 federal census found more than 60,000 people living in Boston, making it the fourth largest city in the United States (after New York, Baltimore, and Philadelphia) with roughly four times the population of Richmond, the largest city in Virginia.[15]

Founded by Puritan settlers in 1630, nearly two centuries later Boston was emerging as a modern urban center. By the 1790s, the city's merchants had rebounded from the violent upheaval of the Revolution and the postwar depression to resume their trade with the West Indies and Europe and expand into new markets, pioneering an especially lucrative trade with China. The city and its surrounding region also developed an industrial base—becoming a leading producer of textiles especially—during and after the War of 1812.

Commercial and industrial prosperity, in turn, funded many civic improvements. By the time Martha arrived in Boston, three bridges spanned the Charles River, and efforts to eradicate unpleasant odors and promote public health by removing trash and improving public sewers had begun to good effect. Boston's grandest public building, the New State House, with its massive coppered dome designed by Thomas Bulfinch, opened in 1799, one year after the completion of the smaller neoclassical capitol in Richmond, which Jefferson designed to represent his own more democratic political values. In 1826, Bostonians began shopping at the newly expanded Faneuil Hall Market. Two massive granite warehouses flanked the Greek Revival market house with its austere classical facade that, despite the building's huge dimensions—it was more than five hundred feet long—was stylistically reminiscent of Jefferson's capitol. The new market, like Bulfinch's State House and so many other things in Boston, conveyed a sense of prosperity and stability.[16]

Anne Newport Royall, who traveled throughout the United States in the mid-1820s and was often critical of what she saw, nonetheless reported that "Boston, rising up as it were, out of the water, makes a fine display [from] whatever point it is approached." Royall disliked the narrow streets in Boston's older sections and decried the supposed crudeness of the city's lower classes. But she praised the generosity and public spirit of genteel Bostonians, whose efforts resulted not only in the erection of fine public buildings but also in the proliferation of public schools and various cultural and philanthropic associations. The Maryland-born Royall described the city's "ladies" as intelligent, polite, and benevolent. They "possess all the yielding softness of southern ladies, with warmer hearts, minds improved by travel-

Boston, from the Ship House, West End of the Navy Yard, *1833. By the early 1830s, Boston was a prosperous commercial city with many impressive public buildings. This engraving by W. J. Bennett shows Boston's busy port, along with its attractive skyline, which included many church steeples and the recently completed State House with its massive dome, which appears here on the far right. Courtesy of the Library of Congress.*

ing," she wrote, combined with "irresistible sweetness . . . the utmost grace of gesture and harmony of voice."[17]

Ellen's own early impressions of Boston, where she settled with Joseph in 1825, probably helped prepare Martha for what she would find there. While Ellen had experienced boredom and discomfort as her aunt's guest in Virginia's rural Fluvanna County, where the locals were excessively pious and expected their "fashionable" visitor to "shew myself like a wild beast," she readily assimilated into Joseph's urbane Boston social circle. Although she missed her home and family in Albemarle and sometimes wished that Bostonians "were a little more sentimental & roma[ntic]" like Virginians, Ellen admired New Englanders as "enlightened . . . liberal, and public spirited" and wondered "how their character has come to be so misunderstood at the South." Ellen's letters portrayed Bostonians as hardworking, educated, and benevolent. She reserved her highest praise, however, for what she called "the domestic economy of the north," observing that "no where are the women better *house-keepers* & managers."[18]

When Martha arrived in Boston, possibly the first thing she noticed was the absence of slavery and the relative invisibility of the city's free African American population. Aside from the time she spent away from Virginia during the 1780s, Martha had been surrounded by African Americans, most of whom were slaves, her entire life. Albemarle County had more black than white residents by the 1820s, and enslaved people had outnumbered whites by at least a six-to-one ratio at Monticello. Martha had long-term personal relationships with some members of Monticello's enslaved community, and according to her children, she spent many Sundays "receiving colored visitors from all [Jefferson's] other plantations that were within walking distance." These slaves came "to ask small favors, or complain of small grievances, to see and talk to Mistress," and to visit their family and friends. By contrast, in Massachusetts, the Supreme Court had abolished slavery outright in 1780. Though most of the state's African Americans resided in and around Boston, they accounted for only about 2 percent of the city's population overall. Most black Bostonians lived near the Coolidge residence, which was located on the newly fashionable south side of Beacon Hill. Reflecting the growing trend toward residential segregation in American cities, however, developers devised street plans to minimize contact between this lower-class precinct and Ellen's affluent neighborhood.[19]

Martha probably shared Ellen's ambivalence about the dearth of African Americans in her new northern home. Ellen commiserated with her family in Virginia as they sorrowfully sold the Randolph and Jefferson family slaves, and she concurred with Martha's observation that she and her children would be spared "much trouble and distress" by living in a state that had abolished "such a system of injustice." In 1825, shortly after Ellen left for Boston, Martha reflected on the slave sales and perhaps also on her family's complicated relations with the Hemingses, lamenting that she had borne "the discomfort of slavery . . . all my life." But Ellen also found that New England ladies did much more housework than their Virginia counterparts and that the servants they had were—at least from a mistress's standpoint—mostly lazy, insolent, and unreliable, in part because hired servants could leave their employers for higher wages or better treatment elsewhere. Not long after Martha arrived in Boston, Ellen complained that she had had three cooks in the past six months and that the loss of her two domestics—one to marriage and the other to a rival employer—was imminent. Nancy

Morris encountered similar difficulties finding and keeping white servants at her New York home. Although neither she nor Ellen ever wished for a return to the slave system, both preferred having servants whose movements and behavior they could control more fully, and both tried unsuccessfully to hire free black women from Virginia to be servants in their northern households.[20]

A second difference between Albemarle and Boston, which Martha would have noticed immediately on arriving at Ellen's new home in Bowdoin Square on Beacon Hill, was the wealth of the city's merchants and their predilection for spending money on their houses to make them both impressive and comfortable. Early nineteenth-century urban merchants built houses and chose furnishings to showcase their wealth and refinement to outsiders, but they also valued the home as a refuge from the bustling city, a place where they could immerse themselves in the ameliorative comforts of family life. Whatever its charms, Monticello had few comfortable spaces, aside from Jefferson's own library and sleeping quarters, and most of its furniture was threadbare and outdated by the 1820s. The Coolidges, by contrast, lived in a three-story Federal-style house among their prosperous and well-educated neighbors. Joseph cherished the "tranquility" of his home, which he regarded as "necessary." He himself carefully chose its furnishings, aiming for both "unostentatious elegance" and domestic comfort.[21]

Boston's prosperity, rendered tangible in the sumptuous homes of the city's leading merchants, awed Thomas Jefferson Randolph when he visited for the first time in 1826. At Ellen's house, Jeff reported to his wife, he washed his feet "in a plain basin that cost $30 [and] had the water deep enough I might have taken a swim." The bed in which he slept cost $120, though it was "*a plain* bedstead alone without ornament." Other houses he visited were even more opulent. "A man who is worth $50,000 had $10,000 of it in furniture," he reported incredulously. In Boston, Jeff dined at tables piled high with "cut glass & silver." His detailed accounts of the luxurious and well-appointed homes of the "mercantile men of Boston" belied his vehement assertion that he "coveted nothing" he saw in the northern cities, where he clearly felt out of place. In Philadelphia, where he stopped on his return journey, Jeff marveled at "fine broad streets . . . so clean that I felt ashamed to spit tobacco juice on them."[22]

Martha had seen more of the world than her comparatively sheltered son, but even she must have appreciated the beautiful homes and public buildings and the social opportunities they portended for both her children and herself. Exchanging social visits was easier in cities than in rural areas, especially when genteel householders boasted such welcoming formal parlors. Elite Bostonians, who self-consciously modeled their city on Athens and who aspired to intellectual leadership in the young American republic, surrounded themselves with literature and the arts. They were justifiably proud of their local schools, where Septimia and George were soon doing well, though Joseph disliked his young in-laws' "want of manners, their frequent bickerings, their absence of all subordination . . . which is not permitted to children of their age at the north." Just weeks shy of her fourteenth birthday, Septimia was "pronounced the prettiest girl in the room, & one of the *best dressed*" at one of several Christmas dances she attended. Indeed, even Christmas was different in Boston, where the holiday was increasingly family oriented and commercial—in effect, modernized—by the 1820s. White southerners, by comparison, continued to see Christmas primarily as an occasion for heavy drinking and an opportunity for slaveowners to foster peace on their plantations by providing food, drink, leisure, and other seasonal treats to their bondpeople.[23]

Finally, in terms of both the quantity and the quality of religion and religious institutions, Boston differed dramatically from Albemarle. Organized religion came to Boston with its founders, and nearly two centuries later Anne Royall counted some seventy steeples in the city's skyline. Albemarle was home to two Anglican parishes during the colonial period, but it was not until 1826 that the first house of worship, an Episcopal church, was consecrated in its largest town of Charlottesville. Before that, members of the Monticello family sometimes went to Charlottesville on Sunday to attend religious services conducted on a rotating basis by Episcopal, Presbyterian, Methodist, and Baptist ministers in the county courthouse or the courthouse square. The family retained its loose, comfortable affiliation with the Episcopal Church, in part because of their preference for rational religion. The Reverend Frederick Hatch, Charlottesville's Episcopal minister in the 1820s, was a good classical scholar, an accomplished gardener, and a friend of Jefferson's. Although the trend in rural Virginia was toward emotion-laden evangelicalism, Martha and her family regarded Hatch as their clergyman, and they gravitated toward his practical, moralistic—and, in their view, nonfanatical—version of Christianity.[24]

Although Ellen chafed at the Federalist politics of her Boston neighbors, she heartily approved of their religious beliefs and habits. As she observed in a letter to Martha, there was "something in the very air of New England which produces or increases a religious tendency in the mind, for I feel a stronger confidence in the doctrine of an immediate providence, & greater trust in its interference with the affairs of men, than, I think, I used to feel." Part of the appeal of the Bostonians' religion was the local clergy, who were highly educated and, in Ellen's opinion, "very respectable & excellent men" who preached learned and nondogmatic sermons that emphasized the power of human reason and the importance of practical Christian morality. The overwhelming majority were Harvard-educated Unitarians. After nearly two years as a regular churchgoer in Boston, Ellen offered a glowing assessment of the city's religious culture. "I consider it as the greatest advantage of my change in situation, that it has placed me where Religion is to a great degree divested of mummery & intolerance," she declared, "& the Clergy from their talents, learning, irreproachable lives & *gentlemanly manners* [are] qualified for diffusing a respect for their profession, & confidence in themselves, through all classes of society."[25]

Following Ellen's lead, Martha, too, attended religious services far more frequently during her time in Boston for at least three reasons. First, churches and clergy were much more readily accessible. The Coolidges generally attended King's Chapel, an old Episcopal church that now had a Unitarian minister, Francis William Pitt Greenwood; this church was located conveniently less than half a mile from their house in Bowdoin Square. Second, Martha, like Ellen, appreciated the message and demeanor of Boston's Unitarian clergy, which differed markedly from the increasingly emotional, anti-intellectual style of many Virginia preachers. As Joseph Coolidge observed triumphantly in January 1827, "Mother is quite spoiled by the Boston preaching, and dreads the necessity of listening to Mr Hatch after Greenwood, & Ware, & [William Ellery] Channing," the reform-minded Christian humanist generally regarded as the most important and influential of the Boston Unitarians. Finally, like her sisters-in-law in Virginia, who embraced Protestant evangelicalism as their family's problems reached crisis proportions, a distraught Martha may have sought solace in this rather different sort of Christianity.[26]

In April 1827, as she emerged from her deep depression, Martha wrote her son-in-law Nicholas Trist a remarkable letter in which she implicitly contrasted the tedium and futility of life in economically troubled rural Virginia with the easy sociability of her current life in Boston. "Land and Negroes in Virginia are to nine persons out of ten *certain ruin*, and to *all* certain expense, uncertain profit, and trouble, and vexation of the spirit, that wearies one of life," she wrote, as she pondered her own future and that of her family. Although Martha did not explicitly express a preference for Boston's urban amenities, she informed Nicholas that her recent outings had included two trips to the theater, several visits to the homes of nearby Coolidge family members, and attendance at a party given in her honor by the Parkmans, a prominent Boston family who were among the Coolidges' closest friends. Martha reported that for the party "two rooms were thrown open . . . one a beautiful oval drawing room with paintings, silk damask curtains, carved mahogany chairs," in which guests enjoyed costly and delicious foods ranging from oysters and lobster salad to ice cream and "every variety of cake in silver baskets." Social life improved Martha's "strength and spirits" overall, despite some occasional "*black* days."[27]

Although Martha had expected to spend only the winter in Boston, she stayed much longer, not only to evade the dreaded prospect of becoming a schoolmistress, but also because Ellen enjoyed her family's company. Martha also believed that the move afforded her youngest children significant educational and social benefits. In May, Joseph rented part of a house in nearby Cambridge, dispatched George to boarding school, and persuaded the family to send Cornelia north as company for her mother and sister in hopes that—in Joseph's words—they could "marry her here to some good fellow." Everyone remained in Cambridge through September so that Ellen, who was again pregnant, could "get rid of housekeeping in town . . . and morning visits" and enjoy the "country air and quiet." By October, the Coolidges were back in Boston with the recently arrived Cornelia, while Martha stayed in Cambridge with Septimia. "The plan is that one of the three shall always be with us," Joseph informed Nicholas Trist, explaining, "Cornelia is now here; and, on her return, Tim, or her Mother will follow." This system prevented the Coolidges' house from becoming overcrowded and spared them from George and Septimia's constant bickering. "It is strange that behaving so well as they do at school," Ellen mused, alluding to her family's famous temper, "they should resume all the Randolph as soon as they get home."[28]

Martha spent roughly ten months in Cambridge, a village that Anne Newport Royall praised as uniting "every thing that can be called great and beautiful," from riverfront views and rolling lawns to the "lofty halls" and "grand squares" of Harvard. Martha made friends in this college town, where she lodged in an "apartment" in the home of John Farrar, a widower, who was a professor of mathematics and natural philosophy at Harvard. She remained in Cambridge until Christmas, when she and Septimia joined the Coolidges and Cornelia in Boston, where they stayed until at least the end of January, in part because Cambridge was less sociable in winter. By late February, Martha had returned to Cambridge with Cornelia. In April,

Jeff arrived in Boston, bearing some of Jane's Virginia hams as gifts for Ellen, ready to take his mother and sisters back to Albemarle.[29]

Martha had stayed with the Coolidges for approximately a year longer than expected, despite the fact that her family in Virginia missed her terribly. "A year's separation from Mama is a sad thing, as you know by experience," Virginia Trist observed to her sister Ellen, though she conceded that "none of us can say that we regret it on the present occasion because there are so many reasons why it is best She should be absent from home now." Two reasons for Martha to delay her return to Albemarle were her family's still-precarious financial circumstances and Jeff's inability to find a buyer for Monticello. Even more compelling, however, was her difficult relationship with Tom, who, after completing his work in Georgia, returned home in June 1827.[30]

Tom attempted to reestablish his ties to Martha and his daughters during his time away from Albemarle, writing a long letter to his daughter Mary and at least one letter to his wife. Although Tom's letter to Martha has not survived, Ellen described it as including information about his accommodations in Georgia and the "delicious climate" of that southern state. To Mary, he sent three densely written pages in which he recounted in great detail his trip southward, the difficult working conditions as he and his co-workers surveyed a boundary through wilderness, and his arrival in Darien, Georgia, where he lodged with Thomas Spaulding, a boundary commissioner and wealthy cotton planter who shared Tom's interest in experimental farming.[31]

When Martha passed on news about Tom to his sister Nancy Morris, she neither praised nor disparaged her husband. By contrast, she was extremely critical of Tom's youngest brother, John, who had gone with him to Georgia. In Martha's view, John, who had failed as both a physician and a planter, was an "irrational helpless being." Once in Georgia, Martha reported, John quarreled with Tom and by his "folly and . . . ill temper" lost a job that paid $5 a day, forcing him "to return to his unfortunate family," who might, she believed, "do better without him."[32]

Martha proceeded cautiously and ambivalently in her relations with Tom, but Joseph Coolidge plainly detested his father-in-law and adamantly opposed any sort of reconciliation between him and Martha. Joseph had met Tom only briefly during two short visits to Monticello, but he nonetheless concluded that the older man possessed all the bad qualities and none of the good ones that he grudgingly conceded to his brother-in-law Jeff. Joseph privately ridiculed Jeff Randolph, whom he considered "altogether and entirely a Virginian—exclusive and uncompromising; and full of strange and erroneous opinions, arising probably from the mode of life he has led" and especially from his lack of education. At the same time, Joseph admitted that Jeff's "noble qualities" included courage and a willingness to sacrifice for the good of his family, neither of which were qualities he found in his father-in-law. Despite Ellen's continuing affection for her father, Joseph reviled Tom Randolph as "that animal" whose presence, if he returned to the family circle, "would torment [them] to death."[33]

When news of Tom's return to Albemarle reached Boston in mid-July, Joseph mounted a concerted effort to have Martha and her children remain permanently in Cambridge, writing letters to Jeff, Virginia, and Nicholas to persuade them of the wisdom of his plan. To Virginia, he explained that Martha was "well and cheerful" in Cambridge, where Mary and Cornelia could also settle, and he contended that his mother-in-law had "neither heart nor spirit to encounter what she will unavoidably be called on to endure if again under the same roof" with her estranged husband. Joseph's letters to his brothers-in-law also addressed his concerns about Martha's safety and happiness and examined her legal and economic options. Because the little property Martha had was explicitly vested in her, not Tom, by virtue of her father's will, the main issues were whether she would seek a legal separation or even a divorce, where she would live, and most important, whether she or Tom would have custody of their minor children.[34]

Joseph's surprisingly frank and utterly unsentimental assessment of Martha's situation eschewed legal formalities in favor of delay tactics. Although he never said so explicitly, Joseph must have known that Martha could not get a divorce, even in a comparatively liberal state such as Massachusetts, where the statutory grounds for divorce were consanguinity, bigamy, impotence, and adultery. She might have obtained a legal separation in either Massachusetts or Virginia on the grounds of cruelty or desertion, but in both states most wives who successfully applied for legal separations typically claimed that their husbands' offenses included adultery, which Tom's did not. Moreover, because the Randolphs had few assets and because Martha's property already was secure, the only benefit of a legal separation would have been the possibility of obtaining a court ruling giving Martha custody of Septimia and George. But Joseph believed that so long as the children remained with Martha in Massachusetts, Tom could not compel them to leave. He was even willing to hide the youngsters "with some friend at a distance" if their father came north to take them. Eventually, Martha would be free of Tom because "every day lessens the only hold *he* has upon her by adding to the age of George and Septimia," who were nine and thirteen years old, respectively.[35]

Above all, Joseph sought to prevent Martha from returning to Virginia. If she went, he argued, Tom would get the children "into his own hands," and if he proved unwilling to give them up, she would be forced to remain there with him. Conversely, if Martha stayed in Cambridge, he contended, she would be free of Tom and able to continue to be "independent, and devoid of all care of housekeeping" responsibilities as a boarder in a genteel household. Septimia and George could continue their education in the "admirable" schools that they were already attending.[36]

Although Martha agreed that a legal separation was "out of the question," she still felt a sense of duty and perhaps compassion toward her estranged husband. She communicated her plan for Tom to him indirectly in a letter she wrote to Nicholas Trist in August 1827. On the one hand, Martha believed that Tom had a right to expect both kindness and respect from his wife and children, and she affirmed that she would never feel "absolved from affording him support so long as I have a shilling in the world." On the other hand, she did not intend to live with him, in part because she believed that his "unsocial habits and hatred for the necessary restraints of civilized life would . . . make him prefer a little establishment of his own in some sequestered spot of Monticello."[37]

Martha's concerns about her children and a judicious assessment of her own legal status as a wife also impelled her to treat Tom cautiously, rather than adopting Joseph's more blatantly antagonistic approach. True to its English origins, American law historically deemed children marital property—and hence, in effect, the husband's chattel—which meant that fathers typically got custody of their offspring in the event of separation or divorce. Although nineteenth-century American courts gradually came to weigh the children's best interests against patriarchal rights, fathers were still awarded custody much more often than mothers, especially in southern states like Virginia, where patriarchal attitudes were most heavily entrenched. Consequently, Martha took the possibility of losing Septimia and George far more seriously than Joseph did. Declaring that she "would make any sacrifice" for her children, Martha acted kindly, if firmly, toward Tom, in part to avoid provoking him into an ugly and painful assertion of his legal rights. The law of marriage, she believed with some justification, "puts me completely in his power," despite the fact that "*he* is destitute."[38]

Just four days after Martha wrote to Nicholas, a distraught Tom communicated his sentiments to Martha through a letter to his youngest daughter.

Although Tom began his letter with the salutation "My dear Septimia," its outer cover was addressed to "Mrs. Martha Randolph," suggesting that Tom intended the contents for his wife as well as for his daughter. Tom's letter vindicated Martha's fears that he would try to take the children from her if they formally separated. Correctly believing that Martha would never try to turn his children against him, Tom nevertheless promised to assert his presumptive right to custody of Septimia and George if Martha succumbed to "the fatal belief that she can deprive me of [them] by law." Martha may have been surprised to learn that Tom still professed to love her deeply and that he cherished the prospect of "spending some happy years yet, in the decline of life, with her." He unfairly blamed Joseph, Nicholas, and especially Jeff and his in-laws, the Nicholases, for turning her against him.[39]

After decades of marriage, Tom feared the loss of his family, which, however dysfunctional, was all that remained of the once-enviable prospects he had enjoyed as Tuckahoe's heir and Jefferson's son-in-law, and which was the sole remaining vestige of his masculinity. "I have loved your mother, and only her, with all my faculties for 35 years next December," he wrote poignantly to Septimia, adding, "I have loved her most when she was sick, as she herself must confess." At the same time, Tom was drinking heavily, and he seemed unwilling to accept responsibility for either the deterioration of his personal relationships or the collapse of his finances. Instead, he blamed his father for the loss of Tuckahoe, his rightful inheritance, and maintained that he suffered additional losses as a result of Jeff's mismanagement of his property and Jefferson's financial problems. Martha, he believed, also contributed to his downfall, as well as to their strained relationship, when she "at one critical moment" aligned herself with Jeff instead of him. Nevertheless, Tom now conceded that he would willingly abandon his vendetta against Jeff in deference to Martha's wishes and in hopes of their reconciliation.[40]

In the coming months, with Martha still in Cambridge, Tom took some tentative steps toward self-rehabilitation. In September, he wrote letters to his daughter Mary, inquiring about the family's circumstances, offering to bring them a cow for meat, and discoursing eloquently on the recent appearance of the aurora borealis, which he believed was "unquestionably an Electrical phenomenon and will someday lead to the discovery that Electricity and Magnetism are the same natural agents, under different forms." In early October, buoyed by a recent letter from Martha, Tom decided to move from North Milton to Charlemont, an Albemarle farm belonging to the Bankhead family, where he planned to rent some acreage and cultivate it on a "small scale." In late October, the Agricultural Society of Albemarle chose Tom as its president. He also continued to work at his newest "employment," translating foreign agricultural literature into English for publication and sale to southern farmers. By early November, Tom hoped that the sale of his translations and his return to farming would net him "some little property again." To maintain his independence, Tom turned down Nicholas Trist's kind invitation to return to Monticello.[41]

In December, Ellen gave birth to her third child, a son, in Boston, and for reasons that are not entirely clear, Martha began planning a spring return to Albemarle soon thereafter. Although she later claimed that she was reluctant to leave Massachusetts, her letters suggest that her stance toward Tom had mellowed in some respects, either because he seemed intent on changing or because she feared losing Septimia and George. Now Martha evidently was willing to live with Tom in Albemarle, though she insisted that their reunion would be on her terms. "In my correspondence with him I have been very frank," she explained to Jeff in late February 1828. "I have told him it was best to come to an understanding at once as to the future, and better for both of us to drop a curtain over the past." Martha vowed that she would never give up her children and that her "friends" would always have a "cordial reception" wherever she lived. She was content to live simply, and she desired to live peaceably. For her, the key question was not whether she and Tom "had mind enough to keep our hearts warm" but, rather, whether they had "self control enough to repress what would chill them, that upon such subjects as we could not agree we must be silent."[42]

Tom apparently accepted these terms, which potentially offered him the semblance, if not the substance, of marriage and family life. His negotiations with the Bankheads for the rental of the farm at Charlemont had fallen through, and though he still had his small house in North Milton, his funds were getting "too low" for him to continue to buy his food in taverns. Martha's impending return and her stated intention to reside at Monticello gave Tom the impetus he needed to swallow his pride and pen a brief note to Nicholas Trist, asking that he be allowed to occupy the house's North Pavilion. Writing in the third person, Tom made it clear that "Mr R means to live entirely in his own room, at his own charge, making no part of the family, & receiving nothing from it in any way whatever." Nicholas responded immediately, accepting his father-in-law's terms but also expressing his wish that he would socialize with him, Virginia, and other members of the family. Within a day, Virginia Trist had prepared the North Pavilion for her father. Although she and her sister Mary went to visit him in his room every morning, Tom took his meals alone and rarely interacted with anyone else. Virginia reported to her sister Ellen that their father was feeble and that he complained constantly of stomach pains, which he believed were caused by gout.[43]

News of Tom's illness probably strengthened Martha's determination to go to Virginia, despite the persistent opposition of Joseph Coolidge, who feared the consequences of her reuniting with her husband. Despite her kindness toward her father, Virginia, too, had some reservations about her mother's apparent resolution to reside with him at Monticello. "Mama . . . must recollect that her children cannot see things return to their former state," she observed, adding, "if her rest is broken, I think we shall have a right to interfere" to protect "her whose . . . life, health and happiness is the very breath of our lives."[44]

Early on the morning of 1 May 1828, reluctantly leaving ten-year-old George behind at school, Martha left Boston with Jeff, Cornelia, and Septimia. After an eighteen-hour sea voyage, they arrived in New York City. They visited Nancy Morris, who lived just north of Manhattan, and then returned to the city, where Cornelia and Septimia went to the theater that evening. Leaving New York the next day, they made their way home by way of Philadelphia, Norfolk—where they saw Harriet Hackley and her daughters—and Richmond. There they boarded a stagecoach that sixteen hours later deposited them at Jeff's new house at Edgehill.[45]

Not long after their arrival, Martha and her daughters went to Monticello to visit Tom. Either because he sought to reconcile with Martha or because illness dulled his ordinarily sharp temper, Tom received his wife and daughters calmly and cordially. Cornelia believed that her father had "softened towards every body," but she also worried about his health, which was much worse than they had expected. "I was so shocked when I saw him looking so pale & haggard that I forgot every thing for the moment but the filial feeling I used to have so warmly," she wrote to her sister Ellen, adding, "*We* never have seen him look as he does now." Martha and her daughters went to see Tom every day in his room in Monticello's North Pavilion. His condition deteriorated steadily, however, and by mid-June Martha was spending entire days and evenings at her husband's bedside. On 20 June 1828, sixty-year-old Thomas Mann Randolph died at Monticello. His entire estate consisted of some $600 worth of books, most of which he had obtained from Jefferson, and a horse appraised for $20.[46]

The fact that it took ten days for Martha to write to Ellen and George to give them the unhappy news suggests that Tom's unexpected demise shook her, while her detailed descriptions of her husband's last days reveal her conviction that he had experienced what was known as a "good death." Tom had died in his own bed of natural causes. He reconciled with God, affirming his faith as "a unitarian Christian," a religious stance he declared—perhaps for Martha's benefit—he shared with his revered father-in-law. Finally, and perhaps most important in view of his recent history, Tom died surrounded by his family, having made a special effort to reconcile with his eldest son. Even before it was evident that he was dying, Martha had pressed her husband to meet with Jeff. Finally, by Monday, 16 June, after a particularly "wretched" night, Tom, who believed that death was imminent, sent for Jeff because, according to Martha, "he would not die for the world without making friends with him." Tom asked for and received his son's forgiveness, after which Jeff, his younger brothers, and Nicholas Trist tended the dying man at night, while Martha, her daughters, and Jeff's wife, Jane, spent their days at his bedside. The reunification of the family was a great comfort to Tom, his children, and most especially to Martha.[47]

As was customary, the Randolphs sought to extract emotional gratification from the deathbed scene as it unfolded. Although Tom remained argumentative and temperamental during his illness, Martha took comfort in the fact that he "spoke of me as his adored wife, and his children with great affection generally," thereby validating those often strained family relationships. As Martha explained to Ellen, "All was forgotten but the sufferings, and repentance of the sufferer" as Tom "died in peace with every body." Cornelia, too, believed that "it was a great comfort to us that he died among us all . . . & it was a comfort to him to be surrounded by his family, his wife administering to him, his daughters around his bed fanning him through the day & his sons through the night. . . . Chiefly did we thank god that he was at peace with all the world."[48]

Tom's death resolved the problem of the Randolphs' troubled marriage, as Martha herself observed. A month into her widowhood, she wrote a letter to Ellen in which she again noted Tom's happy reconciliation with his family and his resulting transformation from "an object of terror or apprehension" into "one of deep sympathy." At the same time, however, she intimated that her husband's death, unlike her father's, had no long-term impact "after the first burst of grief was over." Because Tom had been estranged from his family since his removal to North Milton nearly three years earlier, his death created no gaping void in the Randolph family circle. "No chair at a table recalled him at meals, no part of the house was associated with his ideas," Martha observed, "and we could not but acknowledge that all was for the best." While in death Tom healed old wounds and reunited his family "in commiseration and kind feeling," his recovery, Martha predicted, "would have brought with it the same passions and jealousies." Though she still had no home and few financial resources, becoming a widow in some important ways simplified her life.[49]

❖ Not long after Tom died, Margaret Bayard Smith, Martha's old friend from Washington, visited her at Monticello. Although Smith found the grounds in ruins and the house itself "bare and comfortless," Martha welcomed her with "sweetness, dignity, resignation, [and] cheerfulness" and informed her that she would move to either Philadelphia or Washington after the family vacated her father's house. Martha favored Philadelphia, a city she associated with happy memories and one that was located midway between Ellen in Boston and Jeff in Albemarle. She gave her son-in-law Nicholas Trist the task of finding a job and a house in one city or the other. The plan was for Martha and her unmarried daughters to reside with the Trists and to share household expenses with them. Martha believed that an urban residence would be "most advantageous to her children," including Nicholas, who, after a brief and unprofitable stint as co-owner and co-publisher of a newspaper in Charlottesville, hoped to find work either teaching law or doing legal research.[50]

For more than a year, Nicholas had considered moving to Washington, but now he dutifully explored the possibility of employment in Philadelphia. He wrote to James and Dolley Madison and to Attorney General William Wirt, whom he had met at the Virginia springs, to solicit their advice and patronage. Wirt offered Nicholas a job collecting and translating land laws in Florida, which he rejected, partly because he knew that neither his wife nor his mother-in-law would want to move there. The Madisons advised him to jettison Philadelphia in favor of Washington, where, according to Dolley, "people in straightened circumstances enjoy greater advantages of society than they do elsewhere." From Boston, Joseph Coolidge agreed that Washington offered Nicholas a better opportunity to use his personal connections and his status as a member of "Mr Jefferson's family" to good effect.[51]

Fluent in French and Spanish, educated at West Point and Monticello, and esteemed by Madison and other political luminaries, Nicholas had many assets, the greatest of which proved to be his mother-in-law's connections in the capital. Martha's recently deceased sister-in-law, the cookbook author Mary Randolph, had a son who worked in the Navy Department. Out of sympathy for Martha, he offered Nicholas a job that paid $800 per year. Nicholas turned down that post, but he accepted another offer from Secretary of State Henry Clay, who learned of the family's predicament from Margaret Bayard Smith. A longtime Washingtonian with many powerful friends, Smith ardently hoped that Martha would settle in the capital, but she knew that her friend would go wherever Nicholas found acceptable employment. Smith sprung to action, and Martha believed that her influence was decisive. Clay offered Nicholas a clerkship with an annual salary of $1,400. "A strong motive . . . in tendering you this appointment," he explained, "is that I have reason to believe it may contribute to the personal comfort of Mrs. Randolph, your mother-in-law." A jubilant Martha thanked Smith for her "very efficient exertions," which afforded her "the promise of a life of ease, *leisure*, and charming society" in Washington instead of "the fatigue, anxiety, confinement, and bustle of a school" in Albemarle.[52]

Nicholas accepted the position and left for Washington in late November 1828, but money problems detained Martha for almost a year in Albemarle. Jeff calculated that his mother's annual income—about $2,300 after paying for George's expenses in Cambridge—would be insufficient to support her and his sisters in Washington, so they were forced to delay their move until the following October. In the meantime, Jeff hoped to raise money by selling the published volumes of Jefferson's papers, which were nearing completion; by disposing of his grandfather's remaining books and paintings; and most especially by finding a buyer for Monticello. At Jeff's insistence, Martha, Virginia Trist, and the three unmarried Randolph sisters moved in with his own large family at Edgehill. The normally imperturbable Jane Randolph, by now the mother of eight, was "a little bit mortified at there not being one word of commiseration for all the trouble I am to have" accommodating her in-laws, whom she nonetheless resolved to make "comfortable and happy whilst they are with me."[53]

To relieve Jeff and Jane from "the burthen of our large family" and to ease the malaise she felt on leaving Monticello, Martha spent much of the ensuing months visiting friends and relatives. She, Virginia, and Virginia's newborn son, Thomas Jefferson Trist, saw the Madisons at Montpelier in late December, then passed much of January and February with Virginia Randolph Cary and her family at Carysbrook in Fluvanna County. Martha's youngest sister-in-law, who had spent her girlhood at Monticello, was widowed in 1823 and, a few years later, followed the example of her oldest sister, Mary, by writing for publication to make ends meet and pay her family's debts. Cary's first book, *Letters on Female Character Addressed to a Young*

Lady, on the Death of Her Mother—in which she idealized the authority of benevolent men and invoked both Scripture and natural law to argue that women should be subordinate to men both at home and in society— appeared in print shortly before Martha visited Carysbrook. Although she did not comment on the contents of her sister-in-law's treatise or its central argument, Martha was clearly impressed by Virginia Cary's ability to sell the book's copyright for $1,000 and by her publisher's request that she write more.[54]

As mistress of Monticello, Martha had been the hostess, not the guest. But now the tables had turned, and as she put it, she felt "no scruples in returning visits now that I am without a home to those who . . . received so many my self as long as I had a house to receive them in." At Carysbrook, Martha and "the girls" celebrated their hostess's forty-third birthday with rounds of toasts, prompting Virginia Trist to reassure her husband that, though she was tipsy when she wrote him last, she was not "getting into *habits* of *intemperance*." According to Virginia, Martha regained her health and spirits at Carysbrook, away from Monticello and "the scene of so much suffering she has endured in that neighborhood."[55]

By spring, however, Martha and her daughters were back at Edgehill, hard at work as they awaited their upcoming removal to Washington. Hannah Stearns, an acquaintance from Boston, had come south to oversee the Randolphs' new school, and Martha informed Ellen that she had "a certain number of scholars" who paid $30 apiece for a five-month course of study. During these months, Martha and her daughters helped with the school and spent hours poring over Jeff's edited copies of his grandfather's manuscripts, whose publication was imminent. Martha estimated that she, Cornelia, and Mary each devoted between five and eight hours a day to this project, while Jeff spent two to three hours reviewing their work. Martha and her daughters contributed at least as much as Jeff to the eventual publication of this first collection of Jefferson's writings, the contents of which were carefully selected and heavily edited to present the great man in the most flattering possible light. Nevertheless, only Jeff's name appeared on the title page of the four volumes he self-published via the press of the *Virginia Advocate*, the Charlottesville newspaper that his brother-in-law Nicholas formerly co-owned.[56]

In Washington, Nicholas had arranged to rent J. H. Handy's two-story house, which had four rooms on each floor, besides two large garret rooms, "an excellent kitchen," and a pleasant yard and garden. The house was only two blocks from the president's house, near the homes of Dolley Madison's niece Mary Cutts and Martin Van Buren, who succeeded Henry Clay as secretary of state in 1829 when Andrew Jackson became president. The first year's rent would be $300, after which it would increase to $400. Following Martha's advice, Nicholas scoured local auctions for bargains on furniture, while she sent him money to defray the costs and, with her daughters, packed up the remaining pieces from Monticello. Martha instructed Nicholas to economize, noting not only their limited means but also the "impropriety of a family who have been held up as objects of *charity* launching out in to any thing like show or expense." She and her daughters also sewed busily, aware that that they could not afford to buy fashionable new clothes but nonetheless fearful that their "straightened funds had reduced the wardrobes of the whole family to a style not admissible in any society" in the capital.[57]

As Martha prepared to leave Albemarle, she saw family and friends, some of whom she might have reasonably expected never to meet again. In fact, death and departures had already thinned the local ranks of her extended family. Her aunt Anna Jefferson Marks died at Monticello in July 1828, leaving a will in which she expressed gratitude for "the manifold and unceasing kindnesses and services which I have received . . . at the hands of my dear and beloved niece." In December, Martha sat at the Monticello deathbed of her longtime friend and Nicholas's grandmother Elizabeth Trist. The family's departure from Monticello in January resulted in the dispersal of their few remaining slaves, including "Mammy" Priscilla Hemings, whom Martha allowed to live with her husband, John, whom Jefferson had freed. Many of Martha's white relatives were leaving Virginia. Her friend and sister-in-law Jane Randolph dreaded her imminent departure for Florida, which was part of a larger exodus that included the family of Francis Eppes, who condemned Virginia's exhausted soil and its citizens' ingratitude to Jefferson. "I see no ties," he observed bitterly, "which should bind any descendants of our grandfather to this state."[58]

For Martha and her daughters, leaving was painful, though they expected to return to spend summers in their old neighborhood, where Jeff had a large and growing family and his younger brothers James, Ben, and Lewis farmed and studied medicine and law, respectively. Cherishing fond memories of Monticello, they knew that the pangs of sadness they experienced on emptying the house would be more profound once Jefferson's estate was finally sold. Virginia Trist believed that she could "never be comforted at losing" her "dear, dear home." Martha's sense of loss was understandably even greater. Her last visit to Monticello, and especially to her

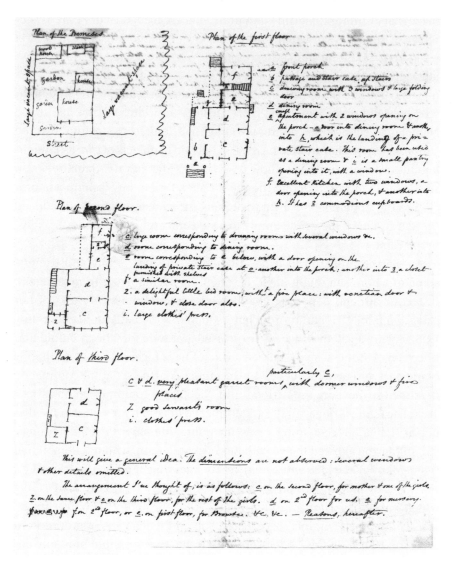

Floor Plan of Martha Jefferson Randolph's First Home in Washington. Nicholas Trist sketched these diagrams on the back of a letter he wrote to his wife, Virginia. In the upper left corner, he drew the "premises," in which he showed a house surrounded by gardens and adjacent to a vacant lot. Other sketches show plans of the first, second, and third floors. Trist expected Martha to share the large front room (c) on the second floor with "one of the girls." *Southern Historical Collection, Wilson Library, University of North Carolina at Chapel Hill.*

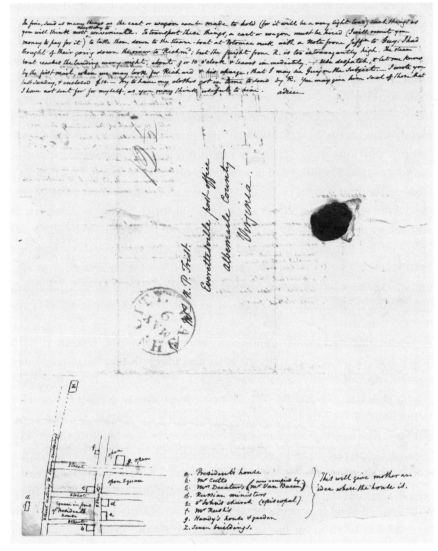

Location of the Trist-Randolph House. Nicholas Trist drew this map of his family's future neighborhood in Washington to "give mother an idea where the house is." Martha moved into the house in the upper right corner of Trist's map ("Handy's house & garden") in November 1829. Both the president and the secretary of state— whose houses Trist designated respectively as "a" and "c"—lived within walking distance of the house. Southern Historical Collection, Wilson Library, University of North Carolina at Chapel Hill.

father's rooms, resulted in melancholy and stomach pains, afflictions she now increasingly suffered in times of stress or sorrow.[59]

In mid-October, Virginia and Cornelia traveled to Washington via Richmond. A few weeks later, Richard and his wife, Ellen (two enslaved domestics who would reside with the family), followed, as did Martha, Mary, Septimia, and the Trists' two young children. Martha was to occupy the large front room on the second floor of the rented house. She furnished her room mainly with pieces from Monticello. Her prized possessions included two or three portraits of her father, some family silver, a mahogany chest of drawers that had belonged to Elizabeth Trist, a sewing table, and a dressing table that was her mother's. Behind the house, Martha planted a flower garden, along with pomegranates and other fruit- or vegetable-bearing plants and herbs, though fresh produce was available in Washington's city markets. Martha, her three unmarried daughters, the Trists, and the servants lived together in this crowded urban household. Martha arrived in Washington in November 1829 and resided in the capital until May 1831. She left only during the latter half of 1830 to be in Boston with Ellen when she gave birth to twin sons.[60]

Washington had grown significantly since Martha had lived there with her father. The ninth largest city in the United States, the capital now boasted a population of nearly 19,000. The federal city also was home to at least fifteen churches, including two African American congregations and St. John's Episcopal Church, where most presidents worshiped. St. John's was only two blocks from Martha's new residence on Seventeenth Street NW, near Lafayette Square. Shops were also plentiful. Margaret Bayard Smith, who published two novels about Washington society in the 1820s, created female characters whose daylong shopping expeditions would have been impossible during Jefferson's presidency, when Martha had relied on Dolley Madison to shop for her in Philadelphia. By the 1830s, milliners and other local retailers provided fashionable goods to ladies and gentlemen who participated in the city's increasingly elaborate social season.[61]

The well-connected Smith saw Martha nearly daily during her first months in Washington and helped her to navigate the politically charged waters of capital society, which had become even more treacherous with Andrew Jackson's recent defeat of the incumbent president, John Quincy Adams. Jackson's raucous inauguration in March 1829 culminated in a near-riot of "rabble, a mob, of boys, negros, women, children, scrambling, fighting, romping," who nearly suffocated the new president in their eagerness to shake his hand, portending the ascendance of what Smith and her

City of Washington, 1834. The American capital grew significantly in the time between Jefferson's presidency and that of Andrew Jackson. This view is from the south bank of the Anacostia River, looking to the northwest. The president's house is the large white rectangular building near the center of the print. To the right is the enlarged Capitol with its original copper dome. Courtesy of the Library of Congress.

genteel friends feared would be a disorderly and vulgar new democracy. Not long after Martha arrived, Smith held a party for her. Guests included not only the families of her friends Nicholas Biddle and Albert Gallatin—both of whom, like the Smiths, were ill disposed toward the new administration—but also that of John M. Berrien of Georgia, a member of Jackson's cabinet. Smith also guided Martha through the capital's complex visiting rituals, lending her carriage for trips beyond walking distance. After Emily Donelson, the wife of Jackson's nephew, who served as hostess for the recently widowed president, paid Martha the signal honor of visiting her first, Smith accompanied her old friend when she reciprocated by visiting Donelson at the president's house.[62]

By spurning elitism, Jackson, like Jefferson, ultimately became extraordinarily powerful, not only during his presidency but also as an enduring symbol of democracy for subsequent generations. But the sea change in

American politics that ushered in what became known as the "Age of the Common Man," which elicited vehement criticism from Smith and others, had to attain legitimacy by grafting new democratic rhetoric and practices onto more conventional ideals and values. Under these circumstances, Martha Randolph thrived, in part because her status as Jefferson's daughter made her a link to the founding era and one of its most revered statesmen. Moreover, even as the avowedly populist Jacksonians criticized women's political activism, Martha benefited because she—unlike her friend Margaret Bayard Smith, for instance—had not acted as a political free agent in the nation's capital.[63]

According to Smith, Martha was "very much affected" when she returned to the executive mansion, now commonly called the "White House" because of the paint applied to its exterior after the British burned it during the War of 1812. Walking through the house with her friend, her daughters, and her hostess, Emily Donelson, Martha pointed mournfully to "my dear Father's cabinet . . . his favorite sitting room . . . my chamber and . . . [her daughters'] nursery." Near-constant reminders of happier times took both a physical and an emotional toll on Martha, especially during her first months in Washington, when her social schedule was heaviest. In late December, Smith found Martha briefly bedridden because "the round of company in which she has been involved lately has made her sick," in part because the people she met routinely introduced her—and honored her— as the sole surviving daughter of Thomas Jefferson. As a result, Smith noted, her father's image was "seldom absent from her mind." Even in her bedchamber, Martha could not escape the past. Her bedding, which had been on Jefferson's deathbed, included the coverlet he had used for forty years at Monticello.[64]

While decades earlier Martha had been a validating accessory for her sometimes controversial father, now the deceased Jefferson was her ticket into the highest social circles in the capital. Shortly after Emily Donelson visited Martha, the president himself called on her with Martin Van Buren, the Randolphs' old acquaintance, who now was their neighbor and, as Jackson's secretary of state, Nicholas Trist's new superior. Van Buren's admiration for Jefferson and respect for Martha, whom he regarded as "one of the worthiest women in America," probably helped her son-in-law to retain his clerkship, despite the change in administration. Nicholas's talents, his pro-Jackson politics, and the perceived importance of awarding patronage to Van Buren's Virginian supporters no doubt were also contributing factors.[65]

Both Van Buren and Jackson assiduously courted Martha, inviting her to formal dinners, where she invariably took precedence over all the other women in attendance. Martha occupied the "seat of honor" to the right of her host at the White House and at Van Buren's in December 1829, while the Trists and the unmarried Randolph sisters sat at the opposite end of the long table. According to Virginia Trist, her mother was the center of attention, while she and her sisters were "*little fish* . . . and do not approach her foot stool . . . only getting a peep at Mama through the platinum ornaments every now & then."[66]

Martha knew that both Jackson and Van Buren could be sources of preferment for Nicholas and for her own sons, too, and she probably surmised that they, in turn, hoped that her friendship could help confer legitimacy on the new president's already tumultuous administration. In the months following Jackson's inauguration, his administration, his party, and Washington society in general were in a furor over the appointment of his friend John H. Eaton of Tennessee as secretary of war. Eaton had married a tavern-keeper's daughter who many believed engaged in illicit sexual relations with him (and others) before their nuptials and who, as a result, had never been "admitted into good society." The ladies of Washington, including Margaret Bayard Smith, detested Margaret O'Neal Timberlake Eaton (known derisively as "Peggy"), as did the wives of Vice President John C. Calhoun, most other cabinet appointees, and many members of Congress. So did Emily Donelson. The women snubbed Margaret Eaton and prevailed on their husbands to do likewise. Jackson, whose own wife had been slandered mercilessly during the presidential campaign and died shortly thereafter, championed Margaret Eaton. The widower Van Buren defended her, too, and his singular loyalty strengthened his relationship with Jackson.[67]

Washington's official social season began with the president's dinner for his cabinet and their families, followed by dinners given by each cabinet member in order of precedence, beginning with the secretary of state. Hoping to avoid a public rupture, Jackson held no formal dinners for his cabinet during his first nine months in office, thereby depriving Eaton's enemies of the opportunity to snub his wife. Jackson knew that he could not forgo entertaining entirely, but he hoped that by delaying his invitations he could avoid bringing the issue to a head until either his critics backed down and accepted Margaret Eaton or his own authority as president was sufficiently entrenched to withstand a confrontation with them.[68]

But both Jackson and Van Buren believed that the convening of Congress in December forced the president to act, in part because dinners with members of Congress, which could only come after the cabinet dinners, were important for building and maintaining political alliances in Washington. Accordingly, Jackson issued invitations for his first cabinet dinner, which was held in the East Room of the White House on Thursday, 26 November 1829. All of the cabinet members and their wives attended, but all but Van Buren and Postmaster William T. Barry and his wife snubbed Margaret Eaton. The "splendid" but excruciatingly formal affair ended early. Van Buren, who was due to host the next dinner, noted the president's "mortification."[69]

Although Van Buren expected most of his cabinet colleagues to decline his invitation in order to embarrass both him and the Eatons, Martha's presence in Washington offered him a way to fulfill his social and political obligations without losing face. The highest-ranking woman on Van Buren's prospective guest list was Deborah Ingham, wife of the secretary of the treasury. Van Buren correctly expected her to decline his invitation, but he was "not disposed to make the vacancy . . . conspicuous by filling it with a lady of inferior rank," so he turned to Martha. "I waited on her in person," he recalled years later, "and informed her of my desire to invite the Cabinet to dine with me and of my desire to combine with that official ceremony an act of respect towards her which had been already too long delayed." Van Buren asked Martha to choose the date "if she was willing to do me the honor to attend," and she "cheerfully agreed."[70]

Van Buren, who liked parties and enjoyed the company of women, was planning what contemporaries called "a ladies' dinner," and to offset the expected absences of the cabinet wives, he invited several military officers and their spouses, all of whom attended. Martha's presence at the dinner was a big attraction for many attendees, who, Van Buren believed, "reverenced her almost as much as I did." Ultimately, all but one member of the cabinet accepted Van Buren's invitation, but none of their wives attended, though the secretary counted the affair a success at least insofar as his guests enjoyed themselves and Martha "manifested the greatest gratification" at the public accolades she received at his elegant house.[71]

Martha's presence conferred both moral and political legitimacy on an administration under fire for embracing the allegedly immoral Peggy Eaton and for ushering in what many feared would be an era of democratic despotism. Martha was a dutiful daughter of a revered patriot and mother of a large and demonstrably respectable family, and her public image was that of a paragon of virtue whom even the rabidly anti-Jeffersonian John Randolph of Roanoke praised as "the sweetest woman in Virginia."[72] Tall, thin, and fair with graying red hair, Martha bore a striking resemblance to her father. That physical resemblance and her willingness to share stories about

Decatur House. This 1822 watercolor by a woman known only as "E. Vaile" shows
a house designed by the architect Benjamin Henry Latrobe for the Decatur family.
After Stephen Decatur, a celebrated military hero, died in 1820, his widow rented
the house, which was located near the White House, to various prominent tenants,
including three successive secretaries of state. The Decatur house was the site of the
elegant dinner that Martin Van Buren gave to honor Martha Jefferson Randolph in
1829. Courtesy of The National Center for White House History at the Decatur House,
a National Trust Historic Site.

him at gatherings Van Buren and Jackson hosted allowed them—and Jackson's Democratic party in general—to present themselves as political descendants of the Sage of Monticello and the new standard-bearers of Jeffersonian ideals and values.

Although Martha did not mention either Margaret Eaton or Jackson's divided cabinet in any of her surviving letters, her friendship with Margaret Bayard Smith and Nicholas Trist's increasing familiarity with both Van Buren and Jackson kept her sufficiently well-informed to weigh the potential benefits and drawbacks of becoming the star attraction at events that Eaton herself attended. Perhaps Martha believed, as did Jackson, that Eaton was blameless, or maybe she remembered her father's admonition to show kindness toward Nancy Randolph, another woman embroiled in scandal who eventually became a respectable wife and mother. Equally important, Martha and her daughters liked both Jackson and Van Buren. Cornelia described the president admiringly as "no common man" and as one "who has character & decision enough to do any thing however great," while her mother praised the "warm hearted old gentleman" for showing her "much friendly attention." The Randolph women, who had known Van Buren for nearly a decade, esteemed his intelligence, manners, and easy sociability.[73]

Martha publicly acknowledged her respect and affection for Jackson in late December 1829, when she presented him with a walking stick that had belonged to Jefferson. The president acknowledged her gift with a heartfelt note, thanking her for "the cane she has had the goodness to present him with feelings of deep sensibility, as a testimonial of her esteem, derived from the venerated hands of her father."[74]

Besides improving her social life and bringing her daughters into the highest circles of Washington society, Martha's cordial relationship with Jackson afforded her family other, more tangible benefits. In 1831, Martha credited the president with securing an appointment for her youngest son, thirteen-year-old George, as a midshipman in the U.S. Navy, despite his youth and competition from older boys. George embarked on a three-year Mediterranean cruise during which he attended naval school and was expected to earn as much as $1,000. Martha bemoaned George's departure as "a *dreadfull* sacrifice and one that I shall not immediately recover," but she concluded that his was a "desirable situation," much better than the army, which would have sent him to "some fort to the westward to waste his youth in the most detestable manner." Around the time George received his appointment, Nicholas Trist became the president's private secretary, as a direct consequence of his—and his mother-in-law's—support for Jackson during the Eaton controversy. Emily Donelson's intractable opposition to visiting Margaret Eaton, which amounted to a public repudiation of the president's authority, ultimately resulted in her return to Tennessee. Emily's husband, the president's nephew Andrew Jackson Donelson, was his uncle's private secretary. When Donelson left Washington with his wife, Jackson chose Nicholas to fill this important post.[75]

At least one of Jackson's political adversaries may have recognized the symbolic value of Martha's friendship and, coveting the respectability it conferred, attempted to cultivate it for himself. George Poindexter of Mississippi, a native Virginian, was elected to the Senate as a Jacksonian in 1830, though both Jackson and Van Buren distrusted him from the start. In fact, the senator soon broke with the administration over issues of patronage and then sided with Calhoun and other radical states' rights advocates in the protracted political controversy that began with the enactment of a tariff in 1828—which some southerners sought to nullify—and culminated in the Nullification Crisis of 1832–33. The Jackson–Van Buren wing of the

Democratic party asserted the primacy of the Union and rejected the idea that states could nullify acts of Congress. Perhaps because the nullifiers also looked to Jefferson as their ideological forebear, Poindexter sought to curry Martha's favor by introducing a bill in the Senate that would have awarded her western acreage in recognition of her father's years of public service. As Poindexter explained when he visited Martha in early 1831, he believed that "it would be easier to obtain a grant of land from Congress than a small sum of money." The bill was eventually defeated in a nonpartisan vote in June 1832, with both Virginia senators voting against it.[76]

Martha was ambivalent about Poindexter's effort on her behalf. On the one hand, as she informed Ellen, when a Washington newspaper reported that the senator introduced his bill, apparently without her knowledge, Martha and her daughters were horrified. On the other hand, after Poindexter met with her and indicated that the bill was a "popular measure," she hoped for its success, in part because she believed that she could sell the land and use the proceeds to save Monticello. By spring, however, the Twenty-First Congress had adjourned with Poindexter's bill in committee, and Martha, Cornelia, Mary, and Septimia returned to Albemarle.[77]

❖ Not much had changed since Martha and her daughters left nearly two years earlier. The publication of Jefferson's papers, which did not sell well, in part because of Jeff's choice of a small-time Charlottesville printer, did little to help the family finances. There was still a school at Edgehill, where Martha resumed giving music lessons to students not long after she returned. One happy development concerned her middle sons, Ben and Lewis, who moved further along the road to self-sufficiency, their education financed by the hiring of two of Martha's slaves, Lavinia and Charlotte. In 1831, Ben graduated from the university his grandfather founded. "He is now *Doctor Randolph*," Martha proudly informed Ellen, while confiding that Lewis, who was doing less well with his studies at the university, considered moving to Florida. A more bittersweet moment occurred that summer when Jeff finally found a buyer for Monticello. "There is some prospect of selling Monticello but I do not wish the thing spoken of yet," she wrote sadly to Virginia. "I thought I had made up my mind upon that subject," Martha confessed, "but I find when it comes to the point that all my sorrows are renewed and that it will be a bitter bitter heartache to me its going out of the family."[78]

During the five years after his death, Jefferson and his legacy continued to shape his family's life. The disposal of Monticello and the manuscripts, the two most valuable and cherished remnants of a once-sizable estate, preoccupied the family both emotionally and economically. In Washington, Martha's unique status as the daughter of an American icon was a source of both sadness and privilege. Her grace and virtue helped to shield her father from public opprobrium while he lived, but now the deceased Jefferson was his daughter's aegis as she navigated the challenges of life away from Monticello.

chapter 8

NO Longer a Home for the Family of Thomas Jefferson

In September 1831, Martha spent her fifty-ninth birthday at Edgehill. As she began her sixth decade, maybe she counted her considerable blessings. Of the twelve children she bore, eleven had survived to adulthood, and all but Anne were still living. Although two daughters, Cornelia and Mary, seemed destined to spinsterhood, Ellen and Virginia had married happily, Jeff had a loving wife and family, her younger sons were either independent or on the road to self-sufficiency, and the prospects of Septimia—who was pretty and popular in society—seemed bright. Martha truly loved her children and they, in turn, adored her. As Virginia put it, "She is *our sun* and when she thinks how many live in her *light* & *warmth* she must guard [her health] carefully."[1]

Still, in some ways the early 1830s were tough times for Martha and her family. The sale of Monticello was painful, though all agreed that disposing of the decaying property was necessary, and Martha's now-official homelessness had little practical impact on her daily life. Her financial circumstances did not improve, and for the next five years, as she had for the preceding five, she divided her time between the households of her married children, Jeff, Ellen, and Virginia. Martha's health deteriorated, and her family increasingly scattered, as a younger generation left home to look for opportunities. Her inability to keep her children together especially saddened Martha, who saw the disintegration of her family and its prospects as emblematic of the decline of her native state. Once the home of patriots and presidents, Virginia seemed to slide into a mediocrity that belied past glories, while thousands of its people abandoned the Old Dominion to try their luck elsewhere.[2]

❖ The sale of Monticello to James Turner Barclay of Charlottesville made Martha physically ill, occasioning a severe attack of the symptoms that now routinely surfaced in stressful times. She had a fever for a few days after Jeff received Barclay's initial offer in late June, and she suffered intense stomach cramps for at least two weeks before the parties concluded their negotiations in mid-August. Martha perceived a connection between her physical pain and the emotional trauma brought on by the impending sale of Monticello. At one point in August she believed that she was near death and that her excruciating pain would "have terminated my earthly cares if there had been no laudanum in the house." After weeks of negotiating, Martha received only $7,000, all of which went toward repaying the estate's debt to Jeff, who mistakenly had hoped that the property would bring him three times as much.[3]

Even after its sale, Monticello remained an important place for Martha and her family. Jefferson's descendants still owned the family burial site there, and they continued to visit the grounds of the estate. Once Barclay took possession of the property, Jefferson's grandchildren worried that he would "disfigure that sacred spot" by adding decorative "gingerbread work," which the classically minded Jefferson would have hated. They also criticized the new owner's destruction of old trees and cherished gardens in order to plant corn. Lewis Randolph went so far as to wish that "my eyes may be gladdened with the sight of the House wrapped in flames, and . . . every vestige of the building swept from the top of the Mountain," rather than subject it to Barclay's supposed plan for a "Gothic barbarian" renovation. In 1834, Barclay sold the house and grounds to Uriah Levy, an ardent admirer of Jefferson's with whom the family had better relations, despite his clumsy (and probably not entirely serious) attempt to become a "complete Jeffersonian" by courting and marrying one of the great man's granddaughters. Even without a Levy-Randolph union, Monticello remained a monument to Jefferson's stature—and by extension that of his family—in Albemarle and beyond. The loss of Monticello, in turn, symbolized the family's declining status and their changing identity. "The truth is we have been people of consideration in the world," mused Cornelia, "& now are poor & neglected."[4]

However powerful Monticello remained as a focal point of family identity and nostalgia, Martha was ready to let go. In October 1833, just months after Barclay purchased the house and grounds, a "Mr. Hart" visited Martha at Edgehill and told her that he was leading an effort to raise money to reclaim Monticello for her and her family. Martha balked, insisting "that it would be of no use to *me*. . . . Not only could I not afford to live there, but . . . I could not afford the necessary repairs requisite for immediate use." When Hart promised to raise additional funds to enable her to maintain the house properly, Martha listened to "his wandering babble" but remained uninterested. Hart's fund-raising trip included a stop that spring in Boston, where Ellen tried to dissuade "crazy Mr Hart" from "tormenting the natives to subscribe for the purchase" of Monticello. Martha and her daughter might have been more receptive to Hart's ill-fated scheme had they truly desired to re-establish family ownership of the estate.[5]

If anything, events that occurred in Virginia between the sale of Monticello and Hart's visit to Edgehill made full-time residence there less appealing to Martha. Most important, on 22 August 1831, an enslaved man named Nat Turner led an insurrection in Southampton County that resulted in the violent deaths of at least fifty-five white people. The largest slave uprising in Virginia's history, Nat Turner's insurrection elicited a swift response from white authorities. In Southampton, militia killed hundreds of African Americans, most of whom were not involved in the conspiracy. Courts tried and executed eighteen conspirators and banished fourteen others. Motivated by both vengeance and fear, legislators imposed draconian new regulations on the conduct of slaves and free blacks.[6]

The bloody insurrection made white Virginians across the state apprehensive of the spread of unrest and the possibility of future slave uprisings. In Albemarle, where enslaved people accounted for slightly more than half of the county's inhabitants, authorities sent out nightly patrols to intimidate local blacks and reassure panicky whites. A meeting of "gentlemen" convened in Charlottesville to determine where to shelter local women and children in case of an attack and to decide the signals they would use to summon the county militia if needed. Among the Randolphs, Jeff's wife, Jane, was most palpably terrified by what she called the "Horrors of Southampton" and the prospect of violence closer to home. For months Jane, who lived among her family's thirty-six adult slaves and their offspring at Edgehill, miserably pondered the specter of insurgency and pressed Jeff to move the family to some nonslaveholding territory.[7]

Believing that Albemarle was safe, Martha and her daughters did not share Jane's terror, though they viewed Nat Turner's insurrection as a watershed in terms of both the history of slavery in Virginia and their own family's history as slaveholders. A week after the violence occurred in Southampton, Cornelia reported to Ellen that Martha and her daughters—Mary, Septimia, and "perhaps Virginia"—agreed with Jane that it was time "to leave the slaves states." Only Cornelia preferred to stay in Albemarle because she was "accustomed to this state of things & attached to our own slaves." But Cornelia's admission that the institution of slavery was "unjust & tyrannical" and her "fervent prayer . . . that we may be rid of them" showed that she,

HORRID MASSACRE IN VIRGINIA·

The Scenes which the above Plate is designed to represent, are—Fig 1, a Mother intreating for the lives of her children.—2. Mr. Travis, cruelly murdered by his own Slaves.—3. Mr. Barrow, who bravely defended himself until his wife escaped.—4. A comp. of mounted Dragoons in pursuit of the Blacks.

Horrid Massacre in Virginia, *1831. Written accounts of Nat Turner's insurrection and images such as this one fanned the fires of white vengeance and increased fears of slave rebellion. Here, a white mother begs for the lives of her children, sword-wielding African American insurgents attack a gentleman, and another white man takes on an ax-bearing black while his wife and child escape. The print's lower panel shows a company of "mounted Dragoons in pursuit of the Blacks." Courtesy of the Library of Congress.*

too, was not content with the status quo. Mary, who leaned toward leaving, worried about the future when, she believed, black Virginians would vastly outnumber whites, thereby enabling enslaved people to mount a more successful offensive. "They say that the people of this state are opening their eyes to the truth," Mary observed in a letter to her sister Ellen. "I wish it may be so & that they may continue to keep their eyes open after the excitement of the present moment is over & until they have taken measures to remove the evil."[8]

The perceived "evil" was not only slavery but also African Americans, both enslaved and free. The main thrust of antislavery sentiment in nineteenth-century Virginia derived from three essential points Jefferson made decades earlier in *Notes on the State of Virginia*: Slavery was evil, it was detrimental to whites as well as blacks, and the two races could never coexist peaceably as free people. Despite their professed attachment to individual African Americans, Martha and her children shared this perspective overall, as did surprisingly large numbers of white Virginians, who hoped that their state's population would become progressively whiter. To that end, many antislavery Virginians, who insisted that emancipation be coupled with the deportation of freed African Americans, supported the American Colonization Society (ACS), which sought to resettle both emancipated slaves and free blacks in the West African colony of Liberia. While some colonizationists simply sought to rid the state of its free black population, others genuinely opposed slavery on moral grounds and believed that enslaved Virginians would prosper as free people in Africa.[9]

The ACS was an eminently respectable organization whose members included James Madison, Henry Clay, and John Marshall, as well as women from some elite Virginia families, most of whom were Christian evangelicals. Martha was not a member of the ACS, but she shared the organization's antislavery sentiments and objectives. Like many white Virginians, she blamed incendiary abolitionist literature from the northern states—chiefly David Walker's *Appeal to the Colored People* and William Lloyd Garrison's newspaper, *The Liberator*—for inciting Virginia slaves to revolt, and she regretted white Virginians' vengeance in the aftermath of the Turner insurrection, which brought suffering to many blameless blacks. Most important, Martha saw emancipation and colonization as the best hope for the future of both races. "Our own safety," she maintained, "requires that exportation must be the consequence of emancipation." While restive blacks waited anxiously for freedom, however, their "every struggle, necessarily ineffectual, will but rivet their chains faster" as fearful whites withdrew their "numerous little privileges" and imposed increasingly harsh rules and punishments.[10]

After the insurrection, some white Virginians looked to their state government to strengthen slavery, while others hoped that the legislature would act to end it. Martha was unequivocally in the latter camp. Her son Jeff was among its standard-bearers, elected to the legislature as a self-described "unflinching advocate of abolition." In January 1832, Jeff Randolph presented to the legislature a plan for gradual emancipation that in some ways resembled ideas his grandfather professed but never championed publicly. Jeff proposed that all slaves born on or after 4 July 1840 would become state property when they reached adulthood, whereupon the state would hire them out and use the money they earned to pay for their eventual expulsion from the United States. In an attempt to allay concerns about slaveholders' potential financial losses, the plan stipulated that masters could sell underage slaves to buyers outside Virginia to avoid state confiscation. The end result would be the same, at least for whites whose primary goal was to decrease Virginia's black population. Although Jeff was sympathetic to enslaved people and hoped most would be emancipated and colonized, he made their liberty and welfare at best secondary considerations. Instead, to make his plan more politically viable, he stressed how it might promote and protect the interests of white Virginians.[11]

In the wake of Nat Turner's insurrection, Virginia's governor and major newspapers supported gradual abolition, and the state legislature was uncharacteristically willing to devote months to debating slavery's future in the commonwealth. Despite these seemingly fortuitous circumstances, the legislators rejected Jeff's plan by a vote of 73 to 58. Antislavery forces achieved what many considered a signal victory later in the session, however, when a coalition of abolitionists and moderates amended a largely conservative committee report by adding a preamble that declared slavery "evil" and asserted the desirability of its eventual eradication. "Friends of abolition," Jeff rejoiced with stunning naïveté, "have gained all they asked." Martha, too, concluded that "Virginia seems to be disposed to take seriously the subject of liberating her slaves," and she proudly reported to Nancy Morris that Jeff "came forward . . . very boldly in the cause." Martha complained that her father's "political enemies" assailed her son with "sneers & ridicule . . . and malice," including innuendo about Jeff's having inherited "the sins of his Grandfather"—presumably a reference to Jefferson's relationship with Sally Hemings. Nonetheless, Martha hoped that, with Jeff's help, "the cause of justice and mercy will finally prevail, and that the fears of the people will at least counteract their avarice if their sense of justice cannot do it."[12]

Although the legislature appropriated some funds for the colonization of free blacks, which abolitionists saw as a prelude to the emancipation and deportation of enslaved people, these legislative sessions of the early 1830s were the high-water mark of state-sponsored antislavery in Virginia. Nearly 500 free African Americans left the state voluntarily after Nat Turner's insurrection; many fled the Southampton area, fearing reprisals from local whites. Some slaves left for Liberia in the 1830s and 1840s, freed and funded by their well-meaning masters and mistresses.[13] But despite many citizens' continuing misgivings about the existing system, Virginia remained a slave state.

However emphatically the Randolphs identified with Virginia and its storied past, they did not see themselves as members of a cohesive community of southern slaveholders. In 1833, as it became apparent that the victory of Virginia's antislavery forces was more rhetorical than real, the Randolphs reexamined the prospect of leaving. Unlike their relatives who went to Florida to use slave labor to grow cotton, Jeff and his family intended to join the steady stream of Virginians who migrated instead expressly to escape the economic and moral dilemmas—and now the physical dangers—of slavery. Jeff first considered resettling his family in the Cincinnati area, but land there proved too expensive. He then contemplated moving to Indiana. By September 1833, however, Jeff had selected a new destination, Missouri, though it, like Virginia, was a slave state. Martha believed that her son picked Missouri because of his "tenderness for his negroes," whom he did not want to sell and whom he could not emancipate in Virginia without their being banished from the state. By taking his slaves to Missouri, Jeff reasoned, he could keep them together, while Missouri's proximity to the free states would enable them to "disappear by degrees without danger or violence" when they were ready to take their freedom.[14]

Martha, who considered following Jeff to the West once he settled there, believed that the family had good reason to go. Besides the "constant dread of insurrection," which affected them all, she perceived a "hostile spirit" toward Jeff among Virginia's political leaders as a result of his prominence in the antislavery initiative (an effort popular mainly among westerners and poorer whites) and his subsequent support for President Andrew Jackson during the Nullification Crisis. Martha's denunciation of Jeff's enemies showed pride in her political lineage and drew implicit parallels between religious dogmatism and political fanaticism, both of which she found distasteful. She condemned Virginians' "mean spirit of jealousy towards those whom the world considers superiors" and their "presbiterian and methodistical prejudices" against her son specifically. The lack of civility in Virginia politics led both mother and son to conclude that the state was "no longer a home for the family of Thomas Jefferson." With the likes of the proslavery legislator Benjamin Watkins Leigh emerging as the state's leading presidential candidate for 1836, Martha surmised that "the days of [Virginia's] glory are gone."[15]

In the end, however, Jeff Randolph and his family did not abandon Edgehill for Missouri or anywhere else. Perhaps the low selling prices of Virginia land made moving impractical. Or maybe Jeff realized that carrying his slaves en masse to Missouri, while preserving some families, would fracture others, because enslaved people sometimes lived separately from spouses or children who worked for different masters.[16] Jeff owned slaves until the Civil War brought emancipation to Virginia. For the rest of her life, Martha, too, continued to own slaves and to benefit from their labor.

Because she no longer presided over a household of her own, Martha hired out her slaves to generate income, so her main impact on them as a mistress involved deciding where and for whom they would labor. As one who professed "friendly feelings" toward enslaved people, Martha self-consciously strove to place her bondpeople in households where they would be "kindly treated" and live in close proximity to their families. "I could never reconcile it to my conscience to tear a human creature from his wife and children to send him off to a distance where he would never again see or hear from them," she wrote in response to the proposed hire of an enslaved man named Israel, which Martha opposed unless Israel's prospective master agreed to employ his entire family. Like many white southerners, Martha believed that owning slaves made her responsible for their well-being, and she took her stewardship seriously. "I feel myself bound by the most sacred of all duties to protect them," she explained, "and guard them from the misfortunes incident to their situation as much as possible."[17]

It was difficult to live up to these high ideals. Slavery, which attempted to turn people into property, sometimes led even well-meaning mistresses and masters to inflict pain and anguish, as Harriet Beecher Stowe later showed dramatically in *Uncle Tom's Cabin*, her enormously influential antislavery novel. Like Stowe's kindly and well-meaning Kentucky slaveowners, when forced to choose, Martha put the financial interests of herself and her children ahead of the happiness of her slaves. In 1836, for instance, she pondered the fate of Martha Ann Colbert, an enslaved female who currently resided with her son Ben in Albemarle. Martha believed that Martha Ann, who was one of four daughters of Burwell Colbert, Jefferson's companion and body servant, would make an ideal "gift" for her son Lewis and his new wife, who were moving to Arkansas, but she also acknowledged that separating Martha Ann from her family would be "an evil." Yet even as she reiterated the "awful responsibility" she felt toward her slaves, Martha affirmed that her own children's interests were the "first and dearest objects of my life." Though she admitted that she had "no right to sacrifice the happiness of a fellow creature *black* or *white*," she ultimately decided to give Martha Ann to Lewis. Because Martha knew that this news would devastate the enslaved woman and her family, she instructed Ben to tell them soon so "that it may not fall like a clap of thunder upon her at the moment of separation."[18]

The master-slave relationship, as Martha's father once observed, was "a perpetual exercise of the most boisterous passions, the most unremitting despotism on the one part, and degrading submissions on the other." Although most masters and mistresses on large plantations preserved a veneer of benevolence by employing overseers or drivers to whip and otherwise discipline their bondpeople, maintaining discipline was more difficult in cities like Washington, where enslaved people sometimes lived apart from their masters and always mingled with comparatively large numbers of free blacks. The problem of slave discipline was hard to evade for small-scale urban slaveowners. Their bondpeople did mostly domestic work and were therefore subject to constant scrutiny of masters and mistresses who, having no overseers, either disciplined errant slaves themselves or secured the services of outsiders to inflict punishment for them. White residents of Washington could send troublesome slaves to local authorities for "correction," which Martha and her daughters did on at least one occasion in 1833, when they dispatched a slave girl named Sally to the constable to be flogged. When Sally later stole a pair of stockings, Martha and her daughters decided not to return her to the constable, fearing that they would get a "bad reputation," either as cruel mistresses or as slaveowners who could not control their bondpeople.[19]

In August 1833, Martha whipped Sally in the basement of the Trists' house in Washington. The tone of Cornelia's description of the incident, which she addressed to her absent sister Virginia, and the fact that she thought that the whipping was newsworthy, suggests that corporal punishment was uncommon in their household. Using forced humor to defuse her anxiety over what must have been an unpleasant situation for everyone, Cornelia recounted how Martha "inflicted the flagellation pretty seriously" while she and Melinda Colbert Freeman, a free black Hemings relation who lived in Washington and who may have been employed by the Trists, restrained the unfortunate Sally. "What disciplinarians we have turned out to be," Cornelia observed wryly, even as she defensively informed her sister that Melinda Freeman judged Martha's whipping "not enough" to reform the intractable slave.[20]

Martha herself never mentioned this incident, which may have been her first and only experience directly inflicting corporal punishment. At Monticello, her father, who saw himself as a benevolent master, left the whipping to his overseers, as Tom Randolph probably did at Edgehill, though Jeff sometimes wielded the whip himself. When Martha lived with the Trists, Nicholas or Virginia probably administered most punishments or sent offending slaves to the constable to be whipped. On this occasion in August 1833, however, the Trists were in Virginia, leaving Martha as mistress of the Washington house. Perhaps she found being alone in Washington with a houseful of children and servants overly stressful. In the same letter in which Cornelia described the whipping of Sally, she also noted that her mother gave her grandson Willie Bankhead "a nice trimming," which meant either a scolding or a beating. Yet there is no evidence that either she or Tom had used corporal punishment to discipline the Randolph children at Edgehill or Monticello.[21]

For some, the fact that white women whipped their servants epitomized the evils of slavery. Martha's sister-in-law Virginia Randolph Cary believed that slavery encouraged a "habit of despotism" among slaveholding whites and had an especially "pernicious" effect on "the female temper," which she idealized as naturally nurturing and pliant. Reflecting on what she had seen in seemingly genteel and respectable Virginia households over four decades, Cary lamented that slavery often turned a civilized and virtuous Christian lady into a cruel tormentor of her "poor abject dependant." In the wake of Nat Turner's insurrection, Cary addressed an antislavery petition (from "the female citizens of the county of Fluvanna") to the state legislature, decrying slavery as "a blight . . . [on] our national prospects, and a cloud [that] dims the sunshine of domestic peace throughout our state." Martha surely shared this perspective. Indeed, her experience with Sally in that Washington basement shows that even the most thoughtful and sympathetic women sometimes wielded the slaveholder's fearsome and corrupting power.[22]

❖ Martha had left Edgehill in November 1831. She followed the ensuing debates on the future of slavery in Virginia from Washington. Although she had hoped to rent a small house of her own in the capital, she instead rejoined the Trists' household. They had moved to a larger and newly renovated house to accommodate a family that now included Martha's son Lewis, along with Anne Bankhead's children, whose father had remarried and who now sought to escape their new stepmother. Martha liked the house's large, "chearful pleasant rooms with beautiful fireplaces," but she regretted its distance from their old neighborhood and their city friends. They were now "entirely out of the world," Martha informed her daughter-in-law Jane somewhat ruefully. "We shall have to travel half a day to get to our old haunts," she observed, though the length of their "visiting list" dictated that "the journey *can* and *must* be performed occasionally."[23]

Once it became clear that Jeff and his family would stay at Edgehill, Martha expected to live primarily in Washington and spend summers in Albemarle. As it turned out, however, for the next five years she divided her time roughly equally between Washington, Edgehill, and Boston, where she had two lengthy stays with Ellen and her children when Joseph's mercantile business required his presence in China. In July 1832, Martha left Washington for Boston, where she stayed for ten months before returning to Washington. Then, in August 1833, she went to Edgehill, where she remained until December 1834. After spending seven months in Washington, Martha traveled to Boston in July 1835. This time, she stayed with Ellen and her children for roughly a year before going back to Virginia.

Martha and her unmarried children especially continued to enjoy Washington society. The most notable social event of 1832 was a costume ball, which Lewis, dressed in a green coat and cap and carrying a bow and arrows, attended as Robin Hood, while his three sisters and Ellen Bankhead went as "the four parts of the day." With Martha's help, the "girls"—who ranged in age from eighteen to thirty-three—based their costumes on a dictionary article on iconography, which described how female images had been used artistically to represent dawn, noon, evening, and night. Septimia wore "saffron," Mary dressed in "poppy," Cornelia appeared in white, and Ellen Bankhead was attired in black; but Martha proudly reported that "nothing . . . has been bought but the poppy coloured gause" and some "gold & silver tinsel" to make the four ensembles. Martha believed that her daughters had become accustomed to the balls and parties of Washington and that, after several seasons in the capital, they now knew enough people and received "the necessary degree of attention to make a party agreeable."[24]

In Washington, President Jackson's administration also continued to look kindly on Martha and her family. Twenty-one-year-old Lewis received a government clerkship in 1831. In 1834, Lewis became engaged to Elizabeth Martin, Emily Donelson's pretty niece, which made him part of the president's extended family. Jackson appointed Lewis secretary to the governor of the Arkansas Territory in 1835. Lewis, who considered the president his "best friend & benefactor," named his firstborn son Lewis Jackson Randolph. So, too, did Nicholas Trist benefit from the patronage of Jackson and Edward Livingston, an old mentor from Louisiana who succeeded Van Buren as secretary of state in 1831. The administration chose Nicholas to be the new American consul in Havana in 1833, though he did not leave for Cuba until the following year. Martha regretted the eventual departures of her son and son-in-law, but she acknowledged the prestige and value of both appointments. She also continued to admire Jackson and felt sufficiently comfortable in the company of the "old gentleman" (who was only five years her senior) to ask him how he liked "*Yankee land*" after he returned from a trip to the northern states, where he denounced nullification.[25]

Because of her loyalty to Jackson and her consciousness of her father's role in creating the Union, Martha solidly supported the president during the Nullification Crisis of 1832–33. In Virginia, Jeff Randolph lost his seat in the state legislature in the spring of 1832, largely because of his staunch support for both antislavery and Andrew Jackson. His mother backed the president but recoiled from the specter of disunion that South Carolina's embrace of nullification—and Jackson's firm response—seemed to augur. Martha could not forget the generosity of South Carolinians, whose "gratitude & reverence" toward Jefferson "had given bread to his children" in their time of need. She desired a peaceable conclusion to the crisis, not least because she hoped she would "never live to see any child of mine turn his sword against [South Carolina's] fostering bosom." She presumably breathed a sigh of relief when the crisis passed.[26]

Martha expressed no reservations about Jackson's other policies, which were arguably at least equally controversial. Although she never said so explicitly, at least in writing, like most Virginians she probably supported the president's refusal to approve the rechartering of the Second Bank of the United States. People like Martha, who distrusted banks generally, were most hostile to this distant and privileged national bank, which Jackson condemned as the monopolistic servant of special interests, aristocracy, and foreign influence. Like most southerners and westerners, Martha also likely supported the president's policy of Indian removal, by which the U.S. government forcibly dispossessed five southeastern Indian nations to open their lands to white settlement. Unlike Jefferson, who met Indian leaders, studied their cultures, and posited that native Americans had the intellectual and moral potential to be integrated into white society, Martha had little firsthand knowledge of Indians, but she apparently detested them nonetheless. In 1836, at a time when Jackson's government was forcing Indians to move westward and fighting the Second Seminole War, Martha described native Americans as "murderers" who "make war like tigers and hyenas, and in our own defence must be treated as such, [and] *exterminated.*" She concluded that "our own people must be protected from the inroads of such ruthless savages."[27]

Martha's Jacksonian political views did not damage her friendship with Margaret Bayard Smith, who was a close friend and admirer of Jackson's archnemesis, Henry Clay, and whose husband had left the newspaper business and became president of the Washington branch of the Bank of the United States. In 1835, Smith invited Martha and Ellen, who was visiting from Boston, to her home to meet Harriet Martineau, the famous English reformer and writer. According to Smith, Martha, who often "disregards her toilette," looked dignified and handsome on this occasion, though she had difficulty conversing with the nearly deaf Martineau, who used a long ear trumpet to help her hear. Martineau spoke disapprovingly of the debauched state of London's poor and the dependence of American women. Martha and Ellen must have enjoyed the visit because an envious Virginia Trist reported to Nicholas that she desired nothing more than "to meet [Martineau] at a party and sit in hearing of her conversation," which Margaret Bayard Smith praised as "rich in most interesting illustrations of manners, facts, and opinions."[28]

Martha's eight-month sojourn in Boston, beginning in July 1832, occasioned her return to the society of old friends and introductions to others. Her most notable new acquaintances during this visit were John James Audubon and his wife, Lucy Bakewell Audubon, both of whom she met aboard the steamboat en route to Boston. Born in Haiti of French parents, Audubon had immigrated to the United States as a young man and settled in Kentucky and then in Louisiana, where he taught art, dancing, fencing, and French. Lucy, too, was a teacher. In the 1820s, John James Audubon devoted himself increasingly to art. He collected and painted various American bird species and produced *Birds of America*, the first of several celebrated books, in 1828. Four years later, prominent Bostonians welcomed the Audubons, purchased subscriptions to the artist's colorful folio volume, and exhibited his drawings in their city's leading cultural institution, the Boston Athenaeum. Martha enjoyed the company of "Madame Audubon," and she especially relished watching her husband and son "painting & working on their birds" when she visited.[29]

While in Boston, Martha had an active social life, in part because Ellen had sent her children to the countryside to protect them from the cholera epidemic that spread southward from Canada into the northeastern United States in 1832. Although some Bostonians believed that cholera afflicted only "filthy wicked people," the Coolidges were among those who saw disease as the work of microbes, not divine vengeance. They took precautions to protect their children, whom they considered particularly vulnerable, especially after their five-year-old daughter, Elizabeth, died that summer. While the children were away, Martha saw her Boston friends, attended at least one concert, and helped Ellen to move into a new, smaller house, located farther south on Beacon Hill, near Park Street Church. The Park Street congregation sympathized with the moderate antislavery objectives of the ACS, but their church nonetheless was the site of the first public lecture of the radical abolitionist William Lloyd Garrison in 1829. Martha pronounced Ellen's new house "much more pleasant though less stylish" than the old one. "With Mr Coolidges beautiful furniture in it," she reported to Septimia, "it will look very well." [30]

When she returned to Washington in June 1833, Martha, too, moved into a new house. After consulting his mother-in-law, Nicholas purchased a spacious two-story house on H Street NW, not far from the White House and near their original lodgings in Washington. Martha and Nicholas both contributed funds toward the purchase and cosigned the necessary bank loan for it. They considered the house a bargain at $6,000, because a few years earlier it had cost nearly twice as much. Surrounded by a high brick wall, the property included a large garden with fruit trees, stables, a carriage house, and a smokehouse; the house itself had enough room for the "17 grown persons including servants, and six children black & white" that Martha counted as members of their household. Of her own children, she expected Virginia, Cornelia, Mary, Septimia, Lewis, and George—recently returned from his first naval cruise—to live with her, and she hoped that Ellen would visit occasionally while Joseph was in China. According to Martha, Nicholas expected to be able to sell the house "at any time for more than he gave" if it proved expensive to maintain after he and his family left Washington for Havana.[31]

Martha and her extended family had occupied the new house for less than a month, however, when it became apparent that their financial prospects were entirely less rosy than they had hoped. When Nicholas accepted the consulship in Havana, he lost his clerk's salary, and because he delayed his departure for Cuba, he received no pay at all until the following winter. Without Nicholas's salary, "dire necessity" led Martha to sell two slaves in June 1833, in hopes that the proceeds would "with my *interest* due the first of July, pay off my bank debt & all the bills," leaving only Lewis's modest rent to support the family for the next six months. To generate additional income, Martha rented the house to Senator William Cabell Rives, a family friend from Albemarle, and she and Septimia went to Edgehill, where Virginia and Cornelia joined them after Nicholas left for Cuba. In January 1834, Rives resigned from the Senate rather than comply with instructions from the Virginia state legislature to oppose Jackson's removal of government funds from the Bank of the United States, a strategy by which the president aimed to eviscerate the bank even before its charter expired in 1836. Rives's support for Jackson meant the loss of a paying tenant, though Lewis secured another, Martha's would-be benefactor Senator Poindexter of Mississippi, as a short-term replacement.[32]

Meanwhile, another family crisis unfolded involving Martha's youngest daughter, Septimia, who sometime in 1832 had developed a "predilection" for Roman Catholicism, which Martha attributed to the influence of a cousin and a friend, both of whom were recent converts. Mother and daughter discussed Septimia's desire to become a Catholic before Martha left for Boston, and Martha subsequently wrote a series of letters to dissuade her from converting. To Septimia, she confessed her own youthful attraction to Catholicism, a faith that she now characterized as irrational and "almost as far removed from the religion of Christ as the Mahomedan." Martha's efforts to keep her daughter faithful to what she called "our own church" apparently succeeded. In the process of constructing her critique of Catholicism, moreover, Martha jettisoned her customary reticence in matters of faith and doctrine, articulating more clearly than ever her own religious views.[33]

Martha's mature religious orientation wedded the rational morality of Unitarianism to the familiar and comforting rituals of the Episcopal Church, which she had known since childhood. An irregular churchgoer when she resided in rural Albemarle, Martha attended services routinely in Washington and Boston, where churches were nearby and where her daughters were also regular attendees (though her son-in-law Nicholas remained a steadfastly nonchurchgoing deist). When in Boston, Martha attended Unitarian services with Ellen, though she much preferred "the forms of the Episcopal church" over those of other denominations. Yet Martha took issue with the doctrine of the Holy Trinity, which, like other traditional Protestants, Episcopalians accepted. Taking the Unitarian position on this key issue, Martha asserted that the idea of the Trinity came not from Scriptures but, rather, was invented by an ancient Catholic council to support transubstantiation, which she deemed "the most *monstrous* article of their creed." Martha rejected as "not only absurd, and disgusting, but absolutely blasphemous" this Catholic belief that Christ "would transform himself into a little bit of wafer to be *eaten*," so "like cannibals, we might *eat* our God." More generally, she maintained that Catholics had "added so much" to their religion that it bore little resemblance to the "simple doctrines of Christ."[34]

Although Martha conceded the virtue of individual Catholics, including most priests and nuns, she urged Septimia to cultivate rational religion and practical piety. Drawing on her own experiences, she advised her daughter to "devote a short time every day to some little exercises of [rational religion] and also . . . offering up a little prayer . . . and still oftener thanks for the pleasures & comforts with which we are surrounded." Reflecting the increasingly pious temper of the times and perhaps a growing awareness of her own mortality, by the 1830s Martha occasionally punctuated her letters (and presumably also her conversations) with religious sentiments, which were rare in her earlier writings. Yet, as her advice to Septimia shows, Martha wore her piety lightly, condemning neither those whose beliefs differed from hers nor those who, like her son-in-law Nicholas, lacked religious faith entirely. Her uncharacteristically harsh critique of Catholicism derived mostly from what she saw as the bigotry of the Roman Catholic Church in its denial of salvation to all non-Catholics. How, she asked, "can any rational being believe that a just . . . [and] merciful God can condemn so great a portion of creatures that he has called into existence?" Martha was intolerant toward Catholicism because she believed that the Catholic Church itself was ruthlessly intolerant.[35]

Martha must have leaned heavily on her religious faith during the devastating winter of 1833–34, which she spent with Jeff's family at Edgehill, where snow engulfed their crowded house. She worried endlessly about her finances. Though she took out yet another bank loan to pay her bills in Washington, her situation was so bad that Virginia offered to hire out Ellen, the longtime family house servant and her children's nurse, and recommended that her mother delay her return to Washington until fall "on account of the great embarrassments she is under for money." More grievous pain arose from the unexpected and sudden death of Martha's second oldest son, twenty-eight-year-old James Madison Randolph, on 23 January 1834. James, who lacked both his father's intellectual gifts and his older brother's business acumen, had recently lost his small farm and had come to live temporarily at Edgehill. A man of quiet, gentle manners, he was remembered as "patient, disinterested & affectionate . . . innocent and helpless like a lamb." James's death profoundly affected Martha, who blamed herself at least in part for her son's demise. "He was too good for this world," she confided to Nancy Morris, "and I too poor to have shielded him from the blight of poverty which had nipped him in his early youth" and would have "crushed his gentle spirit" had he survived the loss of his "little farm."[36]

Virginia Trist believed that her mother's depression in the wake of James's death and her continuing financial woes aged her considerably. In March, Virginia described Martha's health as "far from good" and "so delicate [that] the least trifle . . . gives her a fever." Her sixty-two-year-old mother's constitution, she observed, was "broken down" and showing "the infirmities of age." Although they could do nothing to allay their mother's sorrow over James's death, Virginia and her sisters vowed to "economize" and "never deal on credit again" to relieve Martha's anxiety about her ongoing money problems. The first step they took was to dismiss the governess at Edgehill, Miss Elliott, and have Cornelia take over the school there, while Virginia and her mother taught the younger children by themselves.[37]

By June, Martha seemed to be better. She rejoiced at the abundance of meat, vegetables, milk, butter, and "everything that a rich & well managed farm can supply" at Edgehill. Jeff and Jane, she observed gratefully, were kind and competent, and their children were intelligent and helpful. When Ellen and her family came to Edgehill in the fall, eight adult Randolphs— Martha, Jeff, Jane, Virginia, Cornelia, Septimia, Ellen, and Mary (who had come from Boston with Ellen)—were reunited, with Martha's Randolph, Trist, and Coolidge grandchildren making a total of twenty-five in all, besides the family servants. That fall, Ben, who lived nearby, married Sally Champe Carter, whom Martha described as "a good economist and an excellent manager."[38]

Martha thoroughly enjoyed being surrounded by her children and grandchildren, and she looked forward to the prospect of having nearly her entire family with her in Washington during the coming winter. From December 1834 through the spring of 1835, she and all of her surviving children except Jeff and Ben lived in the "beautiful house" on H Street. Soon, however, they went their separate ways. Martha, Mary, and Septimia went back to Boston with Ellen and her family, though Septimia later returned to Edgehill before embarking on a trip to Louisiana and Florida to improve her health. Virginia and Cornelia, who were preparing to join Nicholas in Cuba, first went to Philadelphia to consult a specialist about the Trists' young son, Thomas Jefferson Trist, who was deaf. George departed on his second naval cruise. Lewis went to Tennessee, married Betty Martin, and moved with her to Arkansas, where he took up his duties as secretary to the territorial governor.[39]

Before the family scattered, however, they came together as Martha suffered her most serious illness yet, which Virginia Trist chronicled in letters to her husband. Martha became ill during the unusually cold and snowy early months of 1835. By March, with the temperature still far below freezing, she was "very feeble" and suffering from "frequent fevers followed by . . . heavy perspirations." Three weeks later, Martha was well enough to pen a newsy letter to Nancy Morris, apparently the only letter she wrote during this seven-month stay in Washington. Around that time, she also visited Margaret Bayard Smith, one of the very few times she went out since her return to Washington in December. By mid-April, however, Smith found that her friend was again indisposed. "I wish I could be there with her in her illness," Smith observed, "but with her five daughters around her, I fear there will be no room for me."[40]

By Friday, 17 April, Martha had been seriously ill for nine days with some unspecified "disease," and Virginia reported that the family "await the crisis with the alternations of hope and fear which are natural." By two o'clock on Saturday morning, Martha, believing that she was near death, summoned Virginia to her bedside to discuss "the division of her little property among her children, and some other arrangements," declaring her need to attend to these matters at once while her head was "perfectly clear." Martha then dictated a brief will by which she divided her small holdings in cash and stock among her five daughters and bequeathed certain items that had belonged to her father to her son Jeff and her sons-in-law Nicholas and Joseph. Ben and Lewis received "the two negroes now in Benjamins possession." Two other slaves, the sisters Emily and Martha Ann Colbert, were to be emancipated. Martha directed her children to give Sally Hemings, her niece Betsy, and Wormley Hughes "their time," which meant that though they would remain legally enslaved, they could come and go as they pleased, live where they wanted, and keep any wages they earned for themselves. All three were Monticello slaves who had lived as free people since Jefferson's death, but Martha knew they would be obliged to leave Virginia if she freed them outright.[41]

The enslaved people whose lives were so closely intertwined with those of Jefferson and his descendants preoccupied Martha in this moment of distress, but protecting her father's reputation remained her chief priority. When her sons arrived from Albemarle, expecting to attend their mother's deathbed, Martha broached the topic of Sally Hemings and the persistent rumors that Jefferson had been the father of her daughter and three sons. According to family tradition, Martha, believing that her death was imminent, summoned Jeff and George to her bedside and asked the elder if he remembered when "_____ Henings (the slave who most re-

Will of Martha Jefferson Randolph, 1835. An ailing Martha dictated this will to her daughter Virginia in Washington. Slaves, both as people and as her most valuable property, dominated the contents of Martha's will, which she was too weak to sign. Special Collections, University of Virginia Library.

sembled Mr. Jefferson) was born." Jeff said he could find the date in Jefferson's farm records. Martha then told her sons that Thomas Jefferson and Sally Hemings "were far distant from each other" for fifteen months before the boy was born. She instructed them to "remember this fact, and always to defend the character of their grandfather." Jeff, who, like all his siblings, consistently disavowed the relationship between Jefferson and Hemings, later remembered this episode as the only time when Martha ever spoke to her children about the subject.[42]

Although subsequent research would show that Jefferson and Hemings were, in fact, both at Monticello when she conceived all four of her surviving children, this purposeful family cover-up that originated in Martha's sickroom endured into the late twentieth century. Jeff, who admitted that there were mixed-race Hemings children at Monticello who strongly resembled his grandfather, later fingered Jefferson's nephews, Peter and Samuel Carr, as their fathers. Perhaps Martha herself first implicated the Carrs as part of her last-ditch effort to discredit the "Dusky Sally stories," which Jeff later claimed she took "much to heart."[43]

Not long after her children gathered at her bedside, Martha's health improved unexpectedly. On 24 April, Jeff informed Jane that his mother's voice was stronger and her pulse was slightly better, though she still had a fever, lacked an appetite, and was "excessively weak" overall. He worried that her forehead appeared wrinkled in a way that reminded him of his grandfather's "last moments." Two days later, Jeff reported that Martha's fever had diminished, but he still believed that her "age and debility" would prevent her complete recovery. In the coming weeks, Martha improved significantly, though her children agreed that she would never again be strong enough to keep house on her own. With the impending liquidation of the Trist household, Ellen and Joseph persuaded Martha to live with them for a while in Boston. The Coolidges left Washington in early June, and Martha, Mary, and Septimia, accompanied by Ben, started their journey to Boston at the end of the month, when Martha's physician advised her that she was fit to travel.[44]

The trip from Washington to Boston took nine days, including brief stops along the way. Martha and her children stopped in Baltimore to visit Robley and Harriette Dunglison—Jefferson's physician friend and his wife—and they saw Harriet Randolph Hackley, who recently had left Norfolk to open a new boarding school in Philadelphia. This brief visit was Martha's first to Philadelphia since her girlhood days a half-century earlier. This trip also marked her first encounter with railroads, which were a new but increasingly important mode of transportation in the United States in the 1830s. Martha, Ben, Mary, and Septimia traveled by rail on the final leg of their trip, from Providence to Boston. According to Mary, they were initially "crowded into a little car next to the engine," where they were showered with sparks, which singed their clothes. Then they had to move to another train because of a break in the tracks and a change in gauge—a common problem with early railroads—and there they found seats in a "comfortable car" and "finished the ride very pleasantly." Martha must have enjoyed the trip because Mary reported that she "gained strength on the road" and was better when she arrived in Boston than when she left Baltimore. But travel was tiring, and the effects of the journey, along with Martha's determination to help with various household tasks, made her sick not long after she arrived at Ellen's.[45]

Martha's health fluctuated during the year she spent in Boston, and her surviving letters reveal her generally dispirited outlook. For one thing, she was clearly upset by the sudden rise of radical abolitionism, with its massive postal campaign in 1835, when antislavery activists flooded the slaveholding states with pamphlets and broadsides, which incited a riot in Charleston, South Carolina, and protests throughout the South. Although she disliked slavery, Martha abhorred abolitionist demands for immediate, uncompensated emancipation, and she regarded radical abolitionists variously as knaves, madmen, and fools. At the same time, Martha numbered many Bostonians and other residents of the free states among her friends (and family); contrary to the strident assertions of proslavery extremists in South Carolina and elsewhere, she insisted that northerners generally did not demonize slaveholding whites. As she explained in a letter to Nicholas Trist, most Bostonians, while opposing slavery in principle, were "doing us the justice to say that it had been forced upon us by [Great Britain] and that circumstances had not been such as to enable us to free ourselves from it." Although elite Bostonians probably handled the slavery issue with particular diplomacy in her presence, Martha was essentially correct insofar as radical abolitionists constituted only a small and unpopular minority of the inhabitants of the northern states.[46]

Another more profound and personal source of sorrow for Martha was the continuing dispersal of her family. Despite the presence of Ellen, Mary, and Septimia with her in Boston, Martha missed her other children, especially her daughters, more than ever before. Shortly after her arrival in Boston, she confided to Virginia that she had neither the strength nor the spirit to survive "the repeated separations I seem doomed to experience," adding that her "heart was sad and I feel no interrest in the present or hope for the future." In December, according to Mary, Martha "made herself sick by her grief at parting with Septimia," who was going south for her health. Lewis's unexpected arrival in Boston that February cheered Martha, who nonetheless worried that his impending departure for Arkansas would "see him cut off from his friends and family and thrown amongst strangers in such a state of society [which] looks infinitely more to me like a melancholy exile than what it really is."[47]

Despite Jeff's status as the family's financial steward and nominal head, Martha held herself responsible for keeping her family intact, and her inability to do so hurt her deeply. As her precarious health augmented her desire to be surrounded by her "dearest children," financial problems undermined her ability to prevent the scattering of her offspring, whom she and her father had once envisioned happily settling together on family lands in and around Albemarle. Martha was a third-generation Albemarle resident; her husband had been the great-grandson of the first master of Tuckahoe plantation, where he himself grew to manhood and expected to spend his life. In her later years, Martha bemoaned the apparent rootlessness of the rising generation, which she considered "as painful as it is mortifying."[48]

Being housebound during the long and unusually harsh New England winter compounded Martha's depression and further undermined her health. Although she did not partake of the carriage rides and sightseeing adventures to Mount Washington and nearby manufacturing towns that Mary and Septimia enjoyed in late summer and early autumn, in good weather Martha took walks, which her daughters believed revived her spirits and her health. In November, however, the snow began to fall, and the winter weather—which Ellen claimed was the coldest in her ten years in Boston—lasted until April. Midway through that difficult winter, though Martha was in what she called her "ordinary state of health," she again prepared her will, but this time she wrote it herself. She began by attesting to her homelessness, identifying herself as "Martha Randolph formerly of Albemarle but now a temporary resident of Boston." The main difference between this will and the one she wrote in Washington nine months earlier involved the fate of Martha Ann Colbert. She was to be emancipated under the old will, but now she was to become the property of Lewis, who intended to take her to Arkansas, though Martha hoped that Lewis (and Martha Ann) would eventually return to Virginia.[49]

The long winter took a heavy toll on Martha, who left the house only twice between early November and mid-April. She herself concluded that her "infirmities" had been "greatly increased by the absence of warm weather," which caused her to live as a "close prisoner" in Ellen's house for so many months. By mid-April, Mary reported to her sister Virginia that their mother was bedridden and suffering from a recurring cough and fever. Martha hoped to travel to Albemarle in May, but Mary believed that she would be too feeble to make the trip. As it turned out, Martha recovered sufficiently to leave Boston in mid-May and arrived at Edgehill two months later.[50]

❖ In early March, writing from the depths of what she called Boston's "shocking winter," Martha prepared for her return trip to Edgehill. She intended to stop for a week to ten days in Philadelphia, where she looked forward to seeing Virginia and her two children, as well as her sister-in-law Harriet Hackley and her family. Martha planned another stopover of a week or so in Baltimore to see her friends there. After "perhaps . . . one or more days" in Washington and then a visit with the Madisons at Montpelier, she and Mary would go on to Edgehill, where Martha expected Virginia, Septimia, and perhaps Ellen—whose husband had returned to China—to join her. Although the Trists had tried to persuade Martha to go with them to Havana, she preferred instead either to live with Harriet Hackley in Philadelphia or to rejoin Ellen and her children in Boston that fall when Nicholas, Virginia, and her unmarried sisters left for Cuba. Martha enjoyed the social life of cities, and she seemed to envy her widowed sister-in-law Virginia Cary, who had recently left Fluvanna County for Norfolk and thrived in the city, where she "has something to do with, or for, all the charitable schemes on foot in town." In this urban milieu, Martha observed, she could "spend her leisure time abroad with propriety."[51]

On her way to Edgehill, Martha enjoyed a four-week stop in Philadelphia, where she visited the Hackleys and had her portrait painted at her daughter Virginia's behest. The artist who executed this commission was Thomas Sully, one of America's premier portrait painters, who had visited Monticello in 1821 to produce a likeness of Jefferson. The artist and his new subject shared another mutual acquaintance, John James Audubon, who had studied oil painting briefly with Sully. Although Martha was initially reluctant to spend the time and effort sitting for this portrait, she enjoyed Sully's company once the process was underway. Virginia informed Nicholas that at the start of their first session, Martha looked "pale and languid, and uncomfortable," but that her mother was "animated, her eyes sparkling and her colour heightened, and her whole countenance lit up" by the time it was over. Sully began his work on 27 May and completed the painting eleven days later at a cost of $150.[52]

Although Virginia Trist believed that the portrait made her mother look significantly younger than her sixty-four years, Sully's Martha was thin, frail, and much altered since James Westhall Ford had painted her thir-

Thomas Sully, Martha Jefferson Randolph, *1836. Martha traveled from Boston to Edgehill in 1836, stopping on the way in Philadelphia, where she sat for this portrait by one of the nation's leading portrait painters. At sixty-four, Martha appeared thin and subdued, though her children believed the artist made her look younger than she did in real life. Sully's portrait also captured Martha's strong resemblance to her father, which contemporaries often noticed. Monticello/Thomas Jefferson Foundation, Inc.*

teen years earlier at Monticello. Jefferson had considered the Ford portrait a good likeness of his daughter, whom the artist portrayed as still round-faced and robust at age fifty-one. Ford's Martha has dark hair and looks nothing like Jefferson, though contemporaries often described her as a female version of her father. This discrepancy suggests that Jefferson admired the Ford portrait more for capturing his daughter's personality and spirit than as an exact physical likeness of her. In Ford's portrait, Martha's gaze engages viewers confidently and directly, perhaps welcoming them as mistress of Monticello. Sully's portrait conveys a sense of Martha's less capacious spirit as an elderly woman. In 1836, her gaze was less direct and more contemplative, and her face and figure were comparatively gaunt. But her children liked the finished product in part because, as Virginia observed, Sully's auburn-haired Martha bore a strong resemblance to Jefferson. Virginia informed Nicholas that Sully painted a "fine" portrait, and Jeff and Ellen later purchased copies of the original.[53]

Although Martha did not accompany Virginia, Mary, and their cousins on their outings to see the sights of Philadelphia, her health was somewhat better during her time with the Hackleys, and her weeks there passed quickly and pleasantly, despite the chronic pains in her stomach. By mid-June, Septimia, who had returned from her southern tour, joined Martha and Mary in Philadelphia, and the three set out for Baltimore. The day was hot, the steamboat was crowded, and Martha arrived in Baltimore exhausted and dreading the next leg of their journey, which would take them to Washington. "Travelling," she uncharacteristically grumbled, "is certainly a horrid business for most people, & particularly for the old and infirm." Martha and her daughters were in Washington for a few days, and they arrived at Montpelier some time after James Madison died on 28 June at age eighty-five. Septimia recalled that a distraught Dolley sent for Martha, her "much loved friend," and they went to comfort her at once. Like Martha, Dolley would confront poverty in widowhood. Unlike her, however, she would sorely miss the company of her devoted and genial husband.[54]

By 25 July, Martha and her daughters had left Montpelier and arrived at Edgehill, where Martha seemed to enjoy unusually good health, despite the torrential rains that sometimes flooded Jeff's house. "We have become perfectly amphibious and minds damp & wet, as . . . the mud eels and tortoises," she wrote cheerfully to Ellen about a month after her arrival, adding, "I have never in my life been so free from colds." The society of family and friends kept Martha occupied during the summer and early fall. Besides Jeff and Jane and Ben (who lived nearby), Mary, Cornelia, and Septimia were with her initially at Edgehill. Septimia soon left to visit friends in Washington, but later Virginia and her children joined the family circle, arriving in early October. Surrounded by children and grandchildren, Martha met her newest granddaughter, the first child of Ben and his wife, Sally. When she heard that the new parents had named the infant Isaetta Carter Randolph, Martha reacted with mock horror. "Really people have not a right," she chortled, "to entail such a name upon a poor helpless child not old enough to raise her voice against it."[55]

Less happily, Martha navigated a final contretemps with her Randolph in-laws. While she remained on friendly terms with Tom's sisters, Martha appears to have lost contact with her surviving brother-in-law, William, whose financial ruin antedated Tom's own. Now, however, William wrote to Jeff Randolph, his nephew, seeking the support of him and his siblings (as the heirs of Thomas Mann Randolph) for a legal challenge to the will of John Randolph of Roanoke, who had died, unmarried and childless, in 1833. Jack Randolph's will divided his land, livestock, and personal property among his relations, one of whom was St. George Randolph—the sole surviving child of Tom and William's sister Judith and Richard Randolph of Bizarre—but it also provided for the emancipation of his 383 slaves, who were to be given land and resettled in Ohio. Some of Jack's legatees decided to challenge his will in order to retain his valuable slave property. William, who was St. George's only living uncle and his closest blood relation, hoped to become the custodian of the property of his adult nephew, who was both insane and deaf.[56]

On receiving his uncle's proposal, Jeff dutifully deferred to Martha, whose response exhibited the moral scruples and economic sense that typically characterized her complicated and sometimes self-contradicting approach to slavery. On the one hand, Martha insisted that she would never support any effort to keep Jack Randolph's slaves "in bondage," and she encouraged her children to follow her example in that regard. On the other hand, she also acknowledged that if William's effort succeeded, the payoff would be minimal once all the relatives divided "the plunder" and paid the lawyers they had hired to challenge Jack's will. Although Martha believed that William thought "he had discovered a gold mine," she feared that the main product of his scheme would be "the odium attached to a scramble for property." Ultimately, Martha persuaded her children to inform their uncle that they did not wish to be involved in the lawsuit, which was not resolved until 1845, when the slaves got their freedom and some land and St. George Randolph inherited property worth some $50,000.[57]

"From the house of Col. Jef. Randolph, Edgehill, 1844." This drawing by Russell Smith, a Pennsylvania artist, shows the view from Edgehill. On the low hill in the foreground was Jefferson's birthplace (marked with an asterisk) and the mill at Shadwell, which Martha's husband and son had once operated. To the right, atop a hill in the distance, a small circle marks the site of Monticello. The Library of Virginia.

Martha and her family spent a bittersweet late summer and early fall at Edgehill, where Martha could see Monticello in the distance and ponder the fact that Nicholas Trist's consulship in Havana, Ellen's loneliness in Boston, and her own fragile health—along with the financial concerns that still plagued them all—made the permanent dismemberment of her family unavoidable. By early October, Martha had begun to prepare for her return to Boston. Septimia was already in Washington with Nicholas, who would move his wife, children, and sisters-in-law to Cuba with him around the time Martha planned to leave Albemarle with Mary, who would go with her to Ellen's.

On 9 October 1836, Martha was bedridden with a headache, the most severe she had experienced since her arrival at Edgehill. The family attributed her illness to the fatigue caused by packing and otherwise preparing for her departure, and to the stress and sadness caused by the prospect of her impending separation from so many members of her family. Cornelia, Mary, and Virginia tended their mother, whose pain increased over the course of the day and whose headache was eventually accompanied by nausea. When night came, the sisters went to bed because their mother's symptoms, though troubling, were not extraordinary. Years later, Mary remembered that her mother "passed a bad night but this was so usual a thing in these indispositions" that the family believed there was no cause for alarm.[58]

The next morning, however, Martha's pain was so intense that Cornelia sent for her brother Jeff, perhaps intending to ask him to call a doctor. Moments after Jeff entered the room, Martha experienced what her children called a "spasm," after which she fell limply forward, her face having turned "a blue shade," Virginia later recalled. Jeff believed that his mother "died of apoplexy caused by the rush of blood to the head." When a blood vessel ruptured, Martha experienced "one momentary spasm and her sufferings were over." Surrounded by her daughters, her daughter-in-law Jane, and probably some of her older grandchildren, she "expired almost instantly" in Jeff's arms.[59]

Because Martha's death was so sudden and unexpected, her children took it especially hard. A stricken Virginia described the "bitter . . . pangs of parting" to Nicholas, whom she charged with communicating the news to Septimia, who was with him in Washington. Martha's youngest daughter collapsed when she learned of her mother's death, and then she and Nicholas wept for half an hour, clinging to each other. Her youngest son, eighteen-year-old George, responded in disbelief when Jeff sent him the sad news. "Even now, I can hardly realize that I am without a mother," he wrote mournfully, two days after receiving his brother's letter. "So accustomed am I to think of her," he mused, "that there is a blank in my very existence which I can't fill up." The news also shocked Ellen, who never suspected that Martha's "sweet parting smile," which she saw as the train left the station in Boston the preceding spring, would be her last glimpse of "one who loved me better than any other being on earth." No other love, she opined, is "like that of a mother."[60]

Jeff Randolph penned an epitaph for his mother, who was buried in the family graveyard at Monticello two days after she died. In his brief summation of his mother's life and virtues, Jeff included the customary dates and genealogical information, but he also praised Martha's superior intellect, along with the other more conventional feminine attributes that contemporaries valued. "She possessed a mind strong and cultivated; mild and gentle temper; warm affection," Jeff wrote; he also noted that she was "disinterested and self-sacrificing in the discharge of her duties." Women's lives, he knew, were replete with personal obligations toward their parents, husbands, children, enslaved people, and others—all of which, in Jeff's view, his mother amply honored.[61]

Jeff's sister Ellen memorialized her mother in similarly glowing terms but with a keener appreciation of the constraints that gender inflicted on women in both Martha's generation and her own. Like Jeff, Ellen admired her mother for her "deep affection, her high principles, her generous & magnanimous temper, her widely diffused benevolence, her sound judgment and glowing imagination, her highly cultivated understanding and fascinating manners." Reflecting on Patsy Jefferson's experiences in the "gay circles of Paris" and her marriage so soon after returning to Virginia, however, Ellen knowingly exclaimed that the young Martha could not have imagined "a greater contrast between her single & her married life!" Ellen noted that her mother "bore the change with true female heroism, which is made up of resistance to small evils and cheerful courage and patient endurance under domestic grievances." In bearing these burdens and other "calamities," she was "equal to all." Although Ellen may have been alluding in part to her parents' difficult marriage, she did not mention her father, whom she, in fact, remembered fondly. In Ellen's view, Martha's experiences in Paris and at Monticello may have been extraordinary, but her sacrifices and difficulties were unexceptional for a woman of her place and time.[62]

❖ For an era in which published obituaries increasingly celebrated the conventional virtues of elite women as mothers, wives, daughters, and mistresses, the notice of Martha's death, which appeared in newspapers in both Charlottesville and Richmond, was oddly perfunctory. "Died, suddenly, at the residence of Thomas Jefferson Randolph . . . Mrs. Martha Randolph, the widow of the late Thomas Mann Randolph, and the daughter of Thomas Jefferson," began her two-sentence obituary, which initially appeared in the *Charlottesville Republican*. "The character of this distinguished lady," the brief notice concluded, "must be drawn by an abler hand than ours."[63]

Epilogue

Perhaps no one provided a more substantial obituary because Martha's virtues—her "perfect temper," her intelligence, competence, dignity, and compassion for others—were already so widely known that she could be a female exemplar without a detailed published obituary, much less a biography of the sort that increasingly idealized famous men to provide role models for new generations of Americans. Implicitly acknowledging the absence of women in both written and remembered history, Ellen Coolidge lamented that her mother's virtues and achievements would be lost to both. "It may be told for a while in the neighborhood of her and her father's home, that a daughter of Thomas Jefferson sleeps by his side in that neglected burying ground at Monticello," she wrote sadly, "but of who or what she was, otherwise than the daughter of Thomas Jefferson, a well known statesman & great political leader, no tradition will after one generation remain."[1]

Ellen Coolidge died in 1876, probably believing that her fears were fully realized. Unlike her friend Dolley Madison, who became a symbol of hospitality and fashion, Martha never became an American icon, and to the extent that history remembered her at all, it was, indeed, as an accessory to her famous father. In 1857, Henry Stephens Randall's three-volume biography of Jefferson, the first to include accounts of his personal and family life, featured flattering descriptions of Martha as her father's companion and housekeeper and hostess at Monticello. In 1871, *The Domestic Life of Thomas Jefferson*, by Sarah Nicholas Randolph, Jeff Randolph's youngest daughter, described Martha's Paris school days and her devotion to her father and her children, though the main purpose of her book, as she herself stated, was to vindicate Jefferson's "private character," which had been "foully assailed . . . and . . . wantonly exposed to the public gaze" in his lifetime and after death. Randolph recounted stories of Jefferson's family life, with Martha often at their center, in hopes of giving her readers "a tithe of that esteem and veneration which I have been taught to feel" for her famous great-grandfather by her own beloved father, much the same way that Jefferson and Martha herself had assembled the family to create a domestic tableau seemingly at odds with his enemies' portrayal of him as an énslaved woman's debauched lover.[2]

Six years later, however, Sarah Randolph published a short biography of her grandmother in a collection titled *Worthy Women of Our First Century*, a project inspired by sentiments similar to those her aunt Ellen Coolidge expressed years earlier, when she regretfully noted the disappearance of the life stories of exemplary women. According to its editors, *Worthy Women* sought to memorialize "the lives of women of weight and mark, whose influence was felt for good in their own circle, whether a wide or a narrow one; who had thought and acted for themselves, either in decisive public issues or in the even tenor of public life."[3] It was understood that such women, almost by definition, would be white, of middling social status or better, and probably connected to great men. Martha Jefferson Randolph, whose biography was the first of only six that appeared in this volume, filled all these criteria admirably.

In her carefully crafted biography, Randolph portrayed her grandmother, who died three years before she herself was born, as a "loyal wife and devoted and attentive mother," a "kind and thoughtful mistress," and her father's closest companion until his death caused "the great agony of her life." Randolph chronicled Martha's social triumphs in Paris and Washington, but she emphasized that her most important challenges and accomplishments were "hidden from the world" as mistress of a crowded and welcoming household where "her good sense, her spirit of self-sacrifice, and her bright, happy temper bore her in triumph through every trial." Thomas Mann Randolph played at best a shadowy role in this family narrative. Sarah Randolph described her volatile grandfather as a "suitable husband" whose companionship helped to ease young Patsy Jefferson's reentry into Virginia's "primitive country life," and, with some justification, she attributed Tom's financial ruin to his generosity toward others. Never mentioning the estrangement between husband and wife, however, she noted simply—and somewhat disingenuously—that Martha was "saddened by her husband's death" in 1828.[4]

Although the broad outlines of Sarah Randolph's account were accurate, her grandmother's life and the context in which her life story unfolded were, of course, more complex. Sarah Randolph would have agreed that Martha Jefferson Randolph was an intelligent, competent, patriotic, and sometimes sentimental woman who strove to live up to prevailing expectations for females of her time, place, and social stature. In fact, she would have heartily celebrated the aspects of her grandmother's story that marked her as a conventional daughter, wife, and mother. She was less willing to acknowledge (or at least to share with her readers) Martha's struggles to keep her family together and viable—emotionally, socially, and financially—and her ongoing and often difficult, even thankless, efforts to reconcile her conflicting personal obligations by balancing the competing needs and interests of her father, children, husband, slaves, and others. Those sometimes conflicting responsibilities, in turn, led occasionally to difficult choices or unconventional behavior—such as when Martha deterred her husband from moving west, sought and obtained employment for Tom and other family members, and (despite her professed good intentions) acted less than benevolently toward her family's slaves.

People who knew Martha as an adult invariably emphasized her intelligence, sociability, and dedication to her children. Peachy Gilmer, a friend of Thomas Mann Randolph's, was in some respects a more objective observer than Martha's sons, daughters, nieces, and nephews, who universally remembered her with a veneration that—in the words of one admiring niece—"would seem exaggerated or partial to those who did not know her." But Gilmer, too, believed that Martha was "decidedly the most accomplished woman I have ever known." Although "her person" was "tall, large, loosely made, and awkward" and "her face not what would be esteemed beautiful," he wrote in his memoirs, an "expression of intelligence always animates her countenance," and her "frankness and eloquence far above . . . any other person of her sex, give a charm to her manners" unlike those of any other. Martha's "exemplary life, her devotion to the instruction of her children, and everything in her history," Gilmer believed, made her "one of the most interesting persons of the age."[5]

That "age" was a transformative one politically, socially, and economically. Born as a subject of King George III, Martha died as a self-conscious citizen of an independent American republic. In a few respects—her disdain for evangelical religion, distrust of banks, and lack of involvement in the women's associations that were increasingly prominent in American communities—Martha did not readily embrace change. But her criticism of slavery and the slave trade, her support for Jacksonian democracy, her stoic willingness to let her children make their own way and find their own spouses, and her creative strategies for dealing with her own increasingly unhappy marriage reveal a woman who was sufficiently flexible to question the pieties of the past and cautiously fashion pragmatic solutions to vexing problems. Martha did not divorce Tom, but she did live separately from him. Neither she nor her relations freed their slaves en masse, but by preventing their dispersal to the cotton states, the Randolphs tried (at least in their own minds) to ameliorate the terms of their enslavement. Martha never claimed political rights for women, but she occasionally intervened in politics to advance her interests and those of her family. Nostalgically lamenting the demise of her family's wealth and influence, she prepared her children as best she could to thrive in an increasingly challenging world in Virginia and beyond.

The newspaper that carried Martha's obituary in October 1836 offers a window onto the Virginia of her later years and suggests how much had changed during her lifetime. For starters, the quantity and breadth of Virginia's homegrown print culture had expanded dramatically. While the colony of Virginia had only two newspapers, both based in Williamsburg, when Martha was born in 1772, Virginians in at least seventeen cities produced a total of at least twenty-six newspapers by 1820. In 1836, when the *Richmond Enquirer* printed Martha's obituary, it was one of at least three secular newspapers in the city, which was also home to a growing religious press.[6] Virginia presses also produced books, ranging from popular novels to legal treatises to advice manuals, including some by women authors, such as Mary Randolph's *The Virginia House-Wife* and Virginia Randolph Cary's *Letters on Female Character*.

Politics and partisanship fueled the growth of newspapers, which focused overwhelmingly on state and national politics to mobilize voters for closely fought elections. In October 1836, the main political story was the presidential election, in which Martha's old friend Martin Van Buren ran for the Democrats against the Whigs' William Henry Harrison. Virginia Whigs portrayed the New Yorker Van Buren as sympathetic to radical antislavery, while local Democrats similarly accused Whigs of being soft on abolition and presented Van Buren, the eventual victor, as the political heir to the heroic Andrew Jackson. Albemarle County's Democratic delegate to the Electoral College, which formally chose the ninth president, was Samuel Carr, one of two cousins who Martha's children would later claim sired the mixed-race Hemings children at Monticello.[7]

Newspaper advertisements and public notices signaled important changes in Virginia's society and culture during Martha's lifetime. Among the most notable was the increased demand for—and availability of—education for girls and young women, which had penetrated even the state's most rural areas. In remote Prince Edward County, a "Ladies' Seminary" offered a three-year course of study that included not only reading, writing, and polite accomplishments (for an extra fee) but also algebra, geometry, botany, geology, logic, and modern and ancient history. Still, a sentimental poem titled "Woman," which the *Enquirer* published a week before Martha's obituary appeared in its pages, revealed few changes in the way men idealized what they considered the best of the female sex, whom they praised primarily for the comfort and moral improvement their beauty, virtue, politeness, and selfless devotion brought to men.[8] Although Virginia women were becoming authors, educators, and leaders of religious and benevolence groups by the 1830s, few people envisioned women's education as preparation for anything other than marriage and domesticity. In that sense, little had changed since Thomas Jefferson enrolled Patsy at the Panthemont.

Other advertisements and public notices offered glimpses into Virginia's changing economy. Items announced the progress of subscriptions for the Richmond, Fredericksburg, and Potomac Railroad, which would operate between Richmond and Fredericksburg beginning in 1837 and be completed to the Potomac River five years later, and the chartering of the Louisa Railroad Company, which eventually provided the first rail service to Charlottesville.[9] An advertisement promising "constant employment" to a "good Tailor . . . at the New Store, in Amelia county" evidenced a growing demand for finished retail goods beyond the state's major towns and cities.[10] Richmond dry goods merchants offered an array of merchandise from London and from northern cities. Although Jefferson's lottery had been controversial a decade earlier, now three lottery companies—Hoyt's, Bigger's, and Dixon's—sold tickets for $20 and awarded prizes as large as $60,000 to their lucky winners.

Despite the proliferation of commerce, lotteries, and banks—many of which would crash in the Panic of 1837—agriculture remained at the heart of Virginia's economy and culture. Many people clung to the Jeffersonian agrarian ideal, lauding agriculturists for their supposed self-reliance and independence. A poem called "The Farmer," which appeared in the *Enquirer* three days before Martha's death, praised those who till the soil and

> never fawn, nor fib, nor fain
> To please old Mammon's fry;
> But independence still maintain
> Of all beneath the sky.[11]

Virginia planters still placed newspaper advertisements to sell land and slaves and to offer rewards for the return of runaways; like their colonial predecessors, they were dependent on markets and credit and were typically encumbered by debt. While Georgia and Florida had been prime early destinations for Virginia planters seeking to improve their fortunes, in 1836 advertisers beckoned prospective migrants farther west, to Mississippi and Alabama especially.

Although none of Martha's children followed Francis Eppes and his family to the cotton frontier, her death accelerated the breakup of her family. Lewis had left for Arkansas in 1835, and he died there of malaria two years later. After Martha died, Nicholas Trist returned to his consulship in Cuba, taking Virginia, the children, and Cornelia and Septimia to Havana, while Mary went to Boston to stay with Ellen. By 1838, however, Ellen had gone, first to London and then to Macao, to be near Joseph, leaving her daughter with family in Boston and sending her sons to school in Switzerland with a family friend. Around the same time, Virginia took her younger son, Browse, and her daughter, Patty, to France to be educated—Patty, like her grandmother, attended a convent school—while the Trists' older son, Jeff, studied at a school for the deaf in Philadelphia. Cornelia and Mary settled at Edgehill, where they worked for many years in the Randolphs' family school. Septimia stayed behind in Havana, where she married Dr. David Scott Meikleham in August 1838.[12]

Unmarried or joined to landless men, most of Martha's daughters lived peripatetic lives. Nicholas Trist, who would be best known for negotiating the treaty that ended the Mexican-American War in 1848, moved his family from Havana to Washington and then to Philadelphia; he finally settled in Alexandria, in northern Virginia, where he was appointed postmaster in 1871, in part because of his loyalty to the Union during the Civil War. Cornelia and Mary eventually joined Virginia and her family in Alexandria. After several years in Macao, the Coolidges spent nearly a decade in Europe, returning to Boston only in 1850. Septimia settled in New York and then spent her widowhood in Virginia, Maryland, and Washington. In the 1880s, a New York congressman spearheaded an abortive effort to get the impoverished Septimia a congressional pension on the grounds that she was the "sole surviving grandchild of the author of the Declaration of Independence" and thus the "grandest link that connects the infancy of our Republic with its maturity."[13]

The surviving Randolph brothers, by contrast, remained in Virginia, and all three, with varying degrees of enthusiasm—or, in Jeff's case, outright reluctance—supported their state's eventual secession from the Union in April 1861. George Wythe Randolph, the youngest, left the navy to study law at the university his grandfather founded. Eventually he moved to Richmond, where he developed a successful practice; he later served briefly as the Confederacy's secretary of war. Unlike their younger brother, both Jeff and Ben stayed in Albemarle. Ben, the physician, acquired 642 acres and eighteen slaves by virtue of his marriage to Sally Carter, in addition to the two enslaved men he received from his mother. Jeff, of course, had Edgehill, an estate of some 1,500 acres that was home to his own large family of unmarried daughters, the students at the Edgehill Academy, and an enslaved workforce that numbered forty-six people over age twelve, plus children, making him, in 1840, the county's fifth largest slaveholder.[14]

As she advanced in years, Martha had regretted the loss of Monticello and other circumstances that resulted in the dispersal of her family. Because her own identity—as Jefferson's daughter, as the mistress of a household, and as the mother of a large and respectable, if troubled, family—was so deeply rooted in the hills of central Virginia, she doubtless would have been pleased to learn that her children returned to their ancestral home from time to time. From Edgehill, the land that their father and now their brother owned and cultivated, they could see Monticello in the distance, reminisce about the past, and visit the family graveyard with its crumbling markers, where Jeff, Cornelia, Mary, and George would join their siblings Anne and James, and their parents and grandparents, in due time.

❖ Martha Jefferson Randolph's nineteenth-century admirers sentimentalized her as an exemplar of the feminine ideals of their era, but modern readers should view her in a somewhat different light. For us, Randolph's story as the daughter of an American icon yields new insights into how women could be political long before suffrage and how the manners and mores of domesticity could infiltrate and influence sociability and public life. It also shows how Martha was complicit in—and, indeed, essential to—the construction of Jefferson's public image, even before his death, and how that image became, along with her Paris education, a tangible asset for her and her family.

At least equally important, however, were the more routine aspects of Martha's life, which made her in many respects representative, at least among elite women of her place and time. As a slave mistress, she recognized the injustice of slavery but was rarely either willing or able to do much about it. Devoted to her family but often torn between her conflicting obligations as a daughter, wife, and mother, she sometimes criticized her father, sought autonomy in marriage, and prepared her children as best she could to inhabit a world far different from her own. For the most part conventional, she was neither passive nor selfless. Martha's gracious manners and her "perfect temper," which her nineteenth-century admirers praised so mightily, masked the challenges, dilemmas, and disappointments of a privileged but often troubled life.

Notes

Abbreviations
The following abbreviations are used in the notes.

ANB	*American National Biography Online*, http://www.anb.org/articles/03/03-00500.html
APS	American Philosophical Society, Philadelphia, Pa.
Coolidge Collection	Coolidge Collection of Thomas Jefferson Manuscripts, Massachusetts Historical Society, Boston
DMDE	Holly C. Shulman, ed., *The Dolley Madison Digital Edition* (Charlottesville, 2004), http://p8080-rotunda.upress.virginia.edu.mutex.gmu.edu/dmde/default.xqy
DNB	*Oxford Dictionary of National Biography*, http://www.oxforddnb.com.mutex.gmu.edu/index.jsp
EWR	Ellen Wayles Randolph
EWRC	Ellen Wayles Randolph Coolidge
Family Letters	Edwin Morris Betts and James Adam Bear Jr., eds., *The Family Letters of Thomas Jefferson* (Columbia, Mo., 1966)
FLDA	Thomas Jefferson Foundation, Inc., *Family Letters Digital Archive* (transcripts), http://retirementseries.dataformat.com
ICJS	International Center for Jefferson Studies, Monticello, Charlottesville, Va.
LC	Library of Congress, Washington, D.C.
LVa	Library of Virginia, Richmond
Memorandum Books	James A. Bear Jr. and Lucia Stanton, eds., *Jefferson's Memorandum Books: Accounts, with Legal Records and Miscellany*, 2 vols. (Princeton, 1997)
MHi	Massachusetts Historical Society, Boston
MJ	Martha Jefferson
MJR	Martha Jefferson Randolph
NcD	Perkins Library, Duke University, Durham, N.C.
NcU	Southern Historical Collection, University of North Carolina, Chapel Hill
NPT	Nicholas P. Trist
Papers	Julian P. Boyd et al., eds., *The Papers of Thomas Jefferson* (Princeton, 1954–)
Papers: Retirement Series	J. Jefferson Looney et al., eds., *The Papers of Thomas Jefferson: Retirement Series* (Princeton, 2004–)
TJ	Thomas Jefferson
TJR	Thomas Jefferson Randolph
TMR	Thomas Mann Randolph Jr.

VHi	Virginia Historical Society, Richmond
ViU	Small Special Collections Library, University of Virginia, Charlottesville
ViWM	Swem Library, College of William and Mary, Williamsburg, Va.
VJR	Virginia Jefferson Randolph
VJRT	Virginia Jefferson Randolph Trist
Writings	Paul Leicester Ford, ed., *The Writings of Thomas Jefferson*, 10 vols. (New York: G. P. Putnam's Sons, 1892–99)

Introduction

1. Smith, "Carysbrook Memoir," 74–75, ViU.

2. Ibid., 23–24.

3. The most important of the traditional accounts is Malone, *Jefferson and His Time*. The first critical assessment of Jefferson's personal relationships was Brodie, *Thomas Jefferson*. Other influential works that in some respects build on Brodie's insights include Burstein, *Jefferson's Secrets*; Jan Ellen Lewis, "The White Jeffersons," in Lewis and Onuf, *Sally Hemings and Thomas Jefferson*, 127–60; Kukla, *Mr. Jefferson's Women*; Wayson, "Martha Jefferson Randolph"; Gordon-Reed, *Hemingses of Monticello*; and Scharff, *Women Jefferson Loved*. Scharff devotes chapters to Jefferson's mother, wife, mistress, daughters, and granddaughters, focusing primarily on their relationships with him and how their connection to Jefferson entailed both costs and benefits. Gordon-Reed's thoughtful and deeply nuanced study understandably tells Martha's story primarily from the perspective of the Hemingses and her relations with them and is generally more sympathetic to Jefferson than most other recent accounts.

4. Recent biographies of these iconic Founding Mothers are Holton, *Abigail Adams*, and Allgor, *Perfect Union*.

5. VJRT to Laura Carter Holloway, [ca. 1870], in Holloway, *Ladies of the White House*, 150.

6. Classic texts on the value and purpose of women's history include Lerner, "New Approaches"; Scott, "Gender"; and Kerber, "Separate Spheres." Some important studies of southern patriarchy include Fox-Genovese, *Within the Plantation Household*; Bardaglio, *Reconstructing the Household*; and Wyatt-Brown, *Southern Honor*.

7. On Cary, see Cynthia A. Kierner, "Cary, Virginia Randolph," in Bearss et al., *Dictionary of Virginia Biography*, 3:115–17.

8. Smith, "Carysbrook Memoir," 83, ViU; Allgor, "Margaret Bayard Smith's 1809 Journey to Monticello and Montpelier"; Jan Ellen Lewis, "The White Jeffersons," in Lewis and Onuf, *Sally Hemings and Thomas Jefferson*; Burstein, *Jefferson's Secrets*, chap. 8.

9. For the earlier literature, see, most notably, Kerber, *Women of the Republic*, esp. chap. 9, and Lewis, "Republican Wife." The most important recent work includes

Branson, *These Fiery, Frenchified Dames*; Zagarri, *Revolutionary Backlash*; and Allgor, *Parlor Politics*.

10. The most careful statement of this position is Gordon-Reed, *Hemingses of Monticello*, 603–4.

11. Weiner, *Mistresses and Slaves*, chaps. 3–5; Lebsock, *Free Women of Petersburg*, 137–45; Varon, *We Mean to Be Counted*, chap. 2. Elizabeth Fox-Genovese's work is representative of that of scholars who argue, conversely, that slaveholding women identified so fully with their class (and hence with the hegemony of white male patriarchs) that gender was not a mitigating factor in their relations with female slaves; see *Within the Plantation Household*, esp. 22–27, 129–45.

The literature on Jefferson and slavery is enormous. Although most scholars who consider the issue agree that Jefferson was a relatively humane master, interpretations of his attitudes toward slavery and the extent to which he actively opposed (or supported) it politically and personally vary widely. Some important interpretations include Cohen, "Thomas Jefferson and the Problem of Slavery"; Finkelman, "Thomas Jefferson and Antislavery"; Lucia C. Stanton, "'Those Who Labor for My Happiness': Thomas Jefferson and His Slaves," in Onuf, *Jeffersonian Legacies*, 147–80; Gordon-Reed, *Hemingses of Monticello*, esp. 112–13, 141, 347, 477, 567; and Burstein, *Jefferson's Secrets*, chap. 5.

12. "The Memoirs of Madison Hemings," in Gordon-Reed, *Thomas Jefferson and Sally Hemings*, 246; MJR to EWRC, 2 Aug. 1825, Coolidge Correspondence, ViU. The literature on this debate is immense, but see the articles in Lewis et al., "Forum," for scholarly opinion after the DNA testing, and also "Report of the [Monticello] Research Committee on Thomas Jefferson and Sally Hemings," which includes a "Minority Report" and the committee's response, 2000, at http://monticello.org/plantation/hemingscontro/hemings_report.html (17 Mar. 2010).

13. Gordon-Reed, *Thomas Jefferson and Sally Hemings*, 78–98; Henry Randall to James Parton, 1 June 1868, in ibid., 254–55.

14. On the hostility of Jefferson and his partisans toward politically minded women, see Allgor, *Parlor Politics*, chap. 1; Zagarri, *Revolutionary Backlash*, 149–52; and Kukla, *Mr. Jefferson's Women*, esp. chap. 7. See also MJR to EWRC, [1826], Martha Jefferson Randolph Letter, VHi, and MJR to Ann Cary Randolph Morris, 1 May 1832, Smith-Houston-Morris-Ogden Family Papers, APS.

15. On Jefferson's antipathy toward women, see, for instance, Lockridge, *On the Sources of Patriarchal Rage*, chap. 3, which focuses mainly on Jefferson's resentment toward his mother, and, more generally, Kukla, *Mr. Jefferson's Women*. A gentler critique is Scharff, *Women Jefferson Loved*.

16. MJR to Margaret Bayard Smith, 10 Nov. 1828, Henley Smith Papers, LC.

Chapter 1

1. TJ to TMR, 19 Oct. 1792, *Papers*, 24:501; Malone, *Jefferson the Virginian*, 153–55; Rutman and Rutman, *Place in Time*, 91; "George Gilmer," in *Thomas Jefferson Encyclopedia* at http://wiki.monticello.org/mediawiki/index.php/George_Gilmer (12 Aug. 2009); Stanton, *Free Some Day*, 33.

2. Glassie, *Folk Housing in Middle Virginia*, 65; Isaac, *Transformation of Virginia*, 73–79; McLaughlin, *Jefferson and Monticello*, 157–70.

3. Malone, *Jefferson the Virginian*, chaps. 2–3; Kern, "Material World of the Jeffersons."

4. Isaac, *Transformation of Virginia*, chaps. 5–6; Sydnor, *Gentlemen Freeholders*, chaps. 5–6.

5. Smith, *Inside the Great House*, chap. 4; Cripe, *Thomas Jefferson and Music*, chap. 1; *Memorandum Books*, 1:36; TJ to Thomas Adams, 1 June 1771, *Papers*, 1:71; lines copied from *Tristram Shandy* by Martha and Thomas Jefferson, [before 6 Sept. 1782], *Papers*, 6:196–97.

6. Burstein, *Inner Jefferson*, 30, 42; Scharff, *Women Jefferson Loved*, 61–109; Kukla, *Mr. Jefferson's Women*, 68–70; Malone, *Jefferson the Virginian*, 162–63, 435–42; Main, "The One Hundred," 354–84. Main's study was based on tax lists for 1787 and 1788, on which Jefferson was assessed for 12,050 acres in 6 counties and a total of 149 slaves in the counties of Albemarle and Bedford.

7. *Virginia Gazette* (Purdie and Dixon), 24 Sept. 1772, 1 Oct. 1772. On early Virginia newspapers generally, see Robert M. Weir, "Newspaper Press in the Southern Colonies," in Bailyn and Hench, *The Press and the American Revolution*, 109–13, 131–34, 146–47, and Meyers, "Old Dominion Looks to London."

8. On the effects of the credit crisis on Virginia planters, see Breen, *Tobacco Culture*, 127–28, 198–203, and Ragsdale, *Planter's Republic*, chap. 5. On Wilkes, see Maier, *From Resistance to Revolution*, 162–69, 203–4.

9. *Virginia Gazette* (Purdie and Dixon), 24 Sept. 1772; Hemphill, "John Wayles Rates His Neighbors," 305; Breen, *Tobacco Culture*, 208–9.

10. For evidence of social tensions in Virginia generally, see Holton, *Forced Founders*.

11. Kierner, *Beyond the Household*, 59–67; Kerrison, *Claiming the Pen*, 13–17.

12. *Virginia Gazette* (Purdie and Dixon), 24 Sept. 1772.

13. Ibid., 1 Oct. 1772.

14. Peckham, *Toll of Independence*, 130; Mayer, *Belonging to the Army*, 126, 129, 132, 133, 138; Norton, *Liberty's Daughters*, 196–224.

15. "Reminiscences of Th. J. by MR, copied by Mary and Caryanne," [ca. 1826], Edgehill-Randolph Papers, ViU. See also Randolph, *Domestic Life*, 62–63.

16. Anburey, *Travels*, 2:316–18; McLaughlin, *Jefferson and Monticello*, 168; Burstein, *Inner Jefferson*, 11; Rhys Isaac, "The First Monticello," in Onuf, *Jeffersonian Legacies*, 77–103.

17. Rice, *Travels in North America*, 2:390–91; Peterson, *Visitors to Monticello*, 2, 9, 45–54; "A Bill for Proportioning Crimes and Punishments . . . ," 18 June 1779, *Papers*, 2:504.

18. "Reminiscences of Th. J. by MR, copied by Mary and Caryanne," [ca. 1826], Edgehill-Randolph Papers, ViU; Malone, *Jefferson the Virginian*, 160–65; Burstein, *Inner Jefferson*, 28–31, 56–57; Reinier, *From Virtue to Character*, 1–19; Smith, *Inside the Great House*, 31–33, 40–45. Some scholars have argued that Jefferson's relationship with his mother was strained and that her death therefore did not affect him significantly; see Brodie, *Thomas Jefferson*, 38–46; McLaughlin, *Jefferson and Monti-*

cello, 47–51; and Lockridge, *On the Sources of Patriarchal Rage*, 69–70. More recently, Virginia Scharff has argued persuasively otherwise; see *Women Jefferson Loved*, esp. chap. 4.

19. *Memorandum Books*, 1:403, 423, 426, 459.

20. Petition of Mary Webley, 11 Oct. 1776, Legislative Petitions, Norfolk City, LVa; Joan R. Gundersen, "'We Bear the Yoke with a Reluctant Impatience': The War for Independence and Virginia's Displaced Women," in Resch and Sargent, *War and Society in the America Revolution*, 270–74.

21. TJ to William Randolph, [ca. June 1776], *Papers*, 1:409.

22. TJ to Francis Eppes, 12 Nov. 1775, 16 July, 9 Aug. 1776, *Papers*, 1:86, 458, 508; TJ to John Page, 30 July 1776, *Papers*, 1:483; Edmund Pendleton to TJ, 26 Aug. 1776, *Papers*, 1:508.

23. Joan R. Gundersen, "Kith and Kin Women's Networks in Colonial Virginia," in Clinton and Gillespie, *Devil's Lane*, 90–102; Smith, *Inside the Great House*, 197–230; Scharff, *Women Jefferson Loved*, 106–9.

24. Edmund Pendleton to TJ, 10 Aug. 1776, *Papers*, 1:489; TJ to John Hancock, 11 Oct. 1776, *Papers*, 1:524; Burstin, *Inner Jefferson*, 63; Brady, *Martha Washington*, 97; Norton, *Liberty's Daughters*, 216–18, 222; Berkin, *Revolutionary Mothers*, 29–31.

25. "Itinerary and Chronology of Thomas Jefferson, 1771–1779," *Writings*, 2:xvii–xxiii; Malone, *Jefferson the Virginian*, 287; TJ to Skelton Jones, 28 July 1809, *Papers: Retirement Series*, 1:381–4.

26. Malone, *Jefferson the Virginian*, 287–90; Scharff, *Women Jefferson Loved*, 124–26; Smith, *Inside the Great House*, 26–31, 176–77; Censer, *North Carolina Planters and their Children*, 24–25.

27. Moore, *Albemarle*, 56–57; Selby, *Revolution in Virginia*, 177–83; Cresswell, *Journal of Nicholas Cresswell*, 192; Anburey, *Travels*, 2:246–47, 429; Shammas, "Black Women's Work," 24; Kierner, *Southern Women in Revolution*, 9–10; Frances Bland Randolph to St. George Tucker, [July 1777], Tucker-Coleman Papers, ViWM; *Memorandum Books*, 1:391n.

28. TJ to MJ, 28 Nov. 1783, *Papers*, 6:360; "1783 Catalog of Books," [ca. 1775–1812], 81, at http://www.thomasjeffersonpapers.org/catalog1783/ (9 Mar. 2010); "List of Books for a Lady's Library," n.d., Jefferson Papers, LC; Kierner, *Beyond the Household*, 28, 40–41, 51, 60–61.

29. Norton, *Separated by Their Sex*, 112–20; Reinier, *From Virtue to Character*, 5–19; *Virginia Gazette* (Purdie and Dixon), 4 Mar. 1773. Norton argues persuasively that Addison and Steele's contention that women, regardless of rank, had no appropriate political role or voice was a relatively new idea in the early eighteenth-century Anglo-American world. The notion of a feminine private sphere (and its masculine public counterpart), however, was widely accepted in both Britain and its colonies by the 1770s.

30. "Reminiscences of Th. J. by MR, copied by Mary and Caryanne," [ca. 1826], Edgehill-Randolph Papers, ViU; TJ to Henry Skipwith, 3 Aug. 1771, *Papers*, 1:76–78; TJ to Peter Carr, 19 Aug. 1785, *Papers*, 8:405–8; TJ to MJ, 28 Nov., 11 Dec. 1783, 15 Jan., 19 Mar. 1784, 28 Mar. 1787, 2 Feb. 1791, *Papers*, 6:359–61, 380–81, 465–66, 7:43–44, 11:250–52, 19:239; Smith, *Inside the Great House*, 63–64.

31. Randolph, *Domestic Life*, 343–44; EWRC to Henry S. Randall, 31 Mar. 1856, Coolidge Correspondence, ViU.

32. Birle and Francavilla, *Thomas Jefferson's Granddaughter*, 160; EWRC to Henry S. Randall, 31 Mar. 1856, Coolidge Correspondence, ViU.

33. Riedesel to TJ, 4 Dec. 1779, *Papers*, 3:212; Jacob Rubsamen to TJ, 1 Dec. 1780, *Papers*, 4:174; Mazzei to Giovanni Fabbroni, 30 Jan. 1775, in Marchione et al., *Philip Mazzei*, 2:391.

34. Dabney, "Jefferson's Albemarle," 47–56; Moore, *Albemarle*, 57–64; Randolph, *Domestic Life*, 50–51; TJ to Patrick Henry, 27 Mar. 1779, *Papers*, 2:242.

35. Brown, *Baroness von Riedesel and the American Revolution*, xxvii, xxix, xxxiii–xxxiv; Cripe, *Thomas Jefferson and Music*, 17; William Phillips to TJ, 11 Apr. 1779, *Papers*, 2:252; TJ to Riedesel, 4 July 1779, *Papers*, 3:24.

36. Elizabeth Ambler to Mildred Smith, [1780], and to Ann Ambler Fisher, 1809, Ambler Papers, Colonial Williamsburg.

37. Malone, *Jefferson the Virginian*, 75, 301–2; Wenger, "Thomas Jefferson's Design for Remodeling the Governor's Palace."

38. "Itinerary and Chronology of Thomas Jefferson, 1771–1779," *Writings*, 2:xxiii; Malone, *Jefferson the Virginian*, 301–2; *Virginia Gazette* (Dixon and Hunter), 20 Nov. 1779.

39. Selby, *Revolution in Virginia*, 235–36; Isaac, *Transformation of Virginia*, 80–87; Isaac Jefferson, "Memoirs of a Monticello Slave," in Bear, *Jefferson at Monticello*, 4–5; *Memorandum Books*, 1:487, 490, 495; Tyler-McGraw, *At the Falls*, 64–65.

40. Malone, *Jefferson the Virginian*, 302, 327–28, 393; Martha Wayles Skelton Jefferson to Eleanor Conway Madison, 8 Aug. 1780, *Papers*, 3:532–33; Norton, *Liberty's Daughters*, 177–88.

41. Selby, *Revolution in Virginia*, chaps. 13–14; "The Affair of Westover," *Papers*, 5:671–705.

42. Selby, *Revolution in Virginia*, 223–24; Malone, *Jefferson the Virginian*, 336–41; Isaac Jefferson, "Memoirs of a Monticello Slave," in Bear, *Jefferson at Monticello*, 7–8; "Diary of Arnold's Invasion . . . ," [1796?], *Papers*, 4:259.

43. Isaac Jefferson, "Memoirs of a Monticello Slave," in Bear, *Jefferson at Monticello*, 10–11; Stanton, *Free Some Day*, 33; Frey, *Water from the Rock*, 155–68; Frey, "Between Slavery and Freedom," 381–86; Thomas Jefferson, *Notes on the State of Virginia*, in *Writings*, 3:244.

44. Malone, *Jefferson the Virginian*, 349–50; Selby, *Revolution in Virginia*, 273–77.

45. Malone, *Jefferson the Virginian*, 358; Elizabeth Ambler to Mildred Smith, 1781, Ambler Papers, Colonial Williamsburg.

46. Malone, *Jefferson the Virginian*, 350, 355–58; Selby, *Revolution in Virginia*, 281–83; Kranish, *Flight from Monticello*, 267–82; Moore, *Albemarle*, 64–65; Townsend, *Country Life in America*, 100.

47. TJ to George Nicholas, 28 July 1781, *Papers*, 6:14–15; TJ to James Monroe, 20 May 1782, *Papers*, 6:185; TJ to William Gordon, 16 July 1788, *Papers*, 13:363–64; Stanton, *Free Some Day*, 53–55. On Elk Hill, see Scharff, *Women Jefferson Loved*, 92–93, 106–8.

48. TJ to Lafayette, 4 Aug. 1781, *Papers*, 6:112; TJ to Horatio Gates, 14 Dec. 1781, *Papers*, 6:139; TJ to George Rogers Clark, 19 Dec. 1781, *Papers*, 6:139.

49. Rice, *Travels in North America*, 2:391.

50. Hamilton Wilcox Pierson, "Jefferson at Monticello: The Private Life of Thomas Jefferson," in Bear, *Jefferson at Monticello*, 99–100.

51. "Reminiscences of Th. J. by MR, copied by Mary and Caryanne," [ca. 1826], Edgehill-Randolph Papers, ViU; Edmund Randolph to James Madison, 20 Sept. 1782, *Papers*, 6:199n; Malone, *Jefferson the Virginian*, 393–96; Burstein, *Inner Jefferson*, 60–64.

52. "Reminiscences of Th. J. by MR, copied by Mary and Caryanne," [ca. 1826], Edgehill-Randolph Papers, ViU; TJ to Elizabeth Wayles Eppes, [3 Oct. 1782], *Papers*, 6:198–99.

53. Fenn, *Pox Americana*, esp. 38–40, 127–34; Malone, *Jefferson the Virginian*, 100, 399; TJ to Chastellux, 26 Nov. 1782, *Papers*, 6:203–4; TJ to William Gordon, 16 July 1788, *Papers*, 13:363–64.

54. TJ to Robert R. Livingston, 26 Nov. 1782, *Papers*, 6:206; TJ to Chastellux, 26 Nov., 1782, *Papers*, 6:203–4; TJ to James Madison, 26 Nov. 1782, *Papers*, 6:206–7; *Virginia Gazette* (Hayes), 28 Dec. 1782.

55. TJ to John Jay, 3 Jan. 1783, *Papers*, 6:218; TJ to James Madison, 31 Aug. 1783, *Papers*, 6:336.

Chapter 2

1. *Memorandum Books*, 1:524–25, 526n; Dumbauld, *Thomas Jefferson, American Tourist*, 9, 13; Gordon-Reed, *Hemingses of Monticello*, 124–25, 154–55.

2. *Memorandum Books*, 1:525–26, 527n; Dumbauld, *Thomas Jefferson, American Tourist*, 15; Thompson, *Rum, Punch, and Revolution*, 59; Malone, *Jefferson the Virginian*, 399–400; Smith, *Life in Early Philadelphia*, 3.

3. Rice, *Travels in North America*, 1:130, 136, 145, 164, 174–77, 179–80, 182; Martha Bland to Frances Bland Tucker, 30 Mar. 1781, in "Randolph and Tucker Letters," 41; Haulman, "Fashion and the Culture Wars of Revolutionary Philadelphia."

4. *Memorandum Books*, 1:524–26.

5. Annette L. Kolodny, ed., "The Travel Diary of Elizabeth House Trist: Philadelphia to Natchez, 1783–84," in Andrews, *Journeys in New Worlds*, 183–84.

6. Ibid., 186–87; TJ to MJ, 28 Nov. 1783, *Papers*, 6:361; Elizabeth House Trist to TJ, 25 Dec. 1784, 12 Mar. 1785, *Papers*, 7:584, 8:25; MJ to Elizabeth House Trist, [after 24 Aug. 1785], *Papers*, 8:436–38.

7. Malone, *Jefferson the Virginian*, 400; TJ to James Madison, 7 Feb. 1783, *Papers*, 6:230–32; TJ to Francis Eppes, 4 Mar. 1783, *Papers*, 6:252–53; *Memorandum Books*, 1:528–30.

8. *Memorandum Books*, 1:531–37; Gordon-Reed, *Hemingses of Monticello*, 155; TJ to James Madison, 31 Aug. 1783, *Papers*, 6:335–36; Judith Randolph to MJ, 5 June 1784, 12 Feb. 1785, Trist Papers, NcU.

9. TJ to James Madison, 31 Aug. 1783, *Papers*, 6:335–36; *Memorandum Books*, 1:539–40.

10. Bell, *Patriot-Improvers*, 1:11, 14, 2:24–25, 30–31; Hastings, *Life and Works of Francis Hopkinson*, 31–32, 36, 342; Kerrison, *Claiming the Pen*, 164, 167; Fatherly, *Gentlewomen and Learned Ladies*, 158.

11. *Memorandum Books*, 1:539; Bell, *Patriot-Improvers*, 1:504–12; Sifton, "Disordered Life"; Cripe, *Thomas Jefferson and Music*, 32, 49–51; "Bentley, John," in *The Encyclopedia of Music in Canada*, at http://www.thecanadianencyclopedia.com/index.cfm?PgNm=TCE&Params=U1ARTU0000280 (20 Apr. 2009); TJ to Marbois, 5 Dec. 1783, *Papers*, 6:374. See also Sellers, *Mr. Peale's Museum*, chap. 1.

12. TJ to MJ, 11, 22 Dec. 1783, *Papers*, 6:360, 417; Elizabeth House Trist to TJ, 13 Dec. 1783, *Papers*, 27:734. See also Gregory, *Father's Legacy*, 55–56, and Lockridge, *On the Sources of Patriarchal Rage*, 71.

13. TJ to MJ, 28 Nov., 22 Dec. 1783, 15 Jan., 18 Feb., 19 Mar., 4 Apr. 1784, *Papers*, 6:360, 417, 465–66, 544, 7:44; MJ to Elizabeth House Trist, [after 24 Aug. 1785], *Papers*, 8:438.

14. TJ to MJ, 28 Nov. 1783, *Papers*, 6:359–60.

15. Francis Hopkinson to TJ, 4 Jan. 1784, *Papers*, 6:444–45; TJ to MJ, 28 Mar. 1787, *Papers*, 251; Kerrison, *Claiming the Pen*, 36–46.

16. TJ to Marbois, 5 Dec. 1783, *Papers*, 6:374. On Jefferson's belief in the need for improvement in the education of boys and men in Virginia, even at a much later date, see his Report to the Commissioners for the University of Virginia, [4 Aug. 1818], in Peterson, *Portable Thomas Jefferson*, 333–37.

17. Benjamin Rush, *Thoughts Upon Female Education*, in Rudolph, *Essays on Education*, 25–40; Benjamin Rush, *Of the Mode of Education Proper in a Republic*, in Runes, *Selected Writings of Benjamin Rush*, 95–96; Noah Webster, "On the Education of Youth in America," in *Collection of Essays and Fugitiv Writings*, 27–29; Kerber, *Women of the Republic*, 204–13; Jefferson to Nathaniel Burwell, 14 Mar. 1818, *Writings*, 10:104–6.

18. Francis Hopkinson to TJ, 4 Jan., 18 Feb. 1784, *Papers*, 6:444–45, 542; TJ to MJ, 15 Jan., 18 Feb., 19 Mar. 1784, *Papers*, 6:466, 543, 7:43–44; Gregory, *Father's Legacy*, 57–58.

19. TJ to MJ, 18 Feb., 19 Mar. 1784, *Papers*, 6:543–44, 7:43–44; TJ to Nathaniel Burwell, 14 Mar. 1818, *Writings*, 10:105.

20. References to letters from Patsy received by Jefferson are in *Papers*, 6:381n, 466n, 544n, 7:56n, 93n, 95n. For Jefferson's letters to Patsy, see *Papers*, 6:359–61, 380–81, 416–17, 465–66, 543–44, 7:43–44, 62, 110. See also the discussion in Wayson, "Martha Jefferson Randolph," 95–99. On letter-writing generally, see Goodman, *Becoming a Woman*, esp. 1–9, 76–79.

21. TJ to MJ, 28 Nov. 1783, *Papers*, 6:359; Elizabeth House Trist to TJ, 13 Dec. 1783, *Papers*, 27:734; Francis Hopkinson to TJ, 4 Jan. 1784, *Papers*, 6:444–45; Mary Jefferson to TJ, 1 Apr. 1784, *Papers*, 7:58. On Jefferson, denial, and the ideal of familial happiness, see Jan Ellen Lewis, "The White Jeffersons," in Lewis and Onuf, *Sally Hemings and Thomas Jefferson*, 129–33.

22. Malone, *Jefferson the Virginian*, 419; Gordon-Reed, *Hemingses of Monticello*, 156; *Memorandum Books*, 1:548–53. On New York, see Van Buskirk, *Generous Enemies*, chap. 6.

23. TJ to John Adams, 19 June 1784, *Papers*, 7:309; TJ to David Humphreys, 21, 27 June 1784, *Papers*, 7:311, 321; TJ to Elbridge Gerry, 2 July 1784, *Papers*, 7:357-58; *Memorandum Books*, 1:553.

24. *Memorandum Books*, 1:553n; Abigail Adams to John Lowell, 29 Nov. 1779, in Butterfield et al., *Adams Family Correspondence*, 3:240; Hutchinson et al., *Papers of James Madison*, 4:255n, 331n, 352, 380; Edward W. Hanson, "Lowell, John," *ANB*.

25. See, for instance, Margaret Bayard Smith to Susan Bayard Smith, 26 Dec. 1802, in Smith, *First Forty Years*, 33; Tinkcom, "Caviar along the Potomac," 73; Smith, "Carysbrook Memoir," 74-75, ViU; and Hamilton Wilcox Pierson, "Jefferson at Monticello: The Private Life of Thomas Jefferson," in Bear, *Jefferson at Monticello*, 83-84.

26. *Memorandum Books*, 1:553n, 554n; TJ to James Monroe, 11 Nov. 1784, *Papers*, 7:508; MJ to Elizabeth House Trist, [after 24 Aug. 1785], *Papers*, 8:436; Abigail Adams to Mary Smith Cranch, 6 July 1784, in Butterfield et al., *Adams Family Correspondence*, 5:358-59.

27. Flavell, *When London Was Capital of America*; Kilbride, "Travel, Ritual, and National Identity." On Franklin, see Schiff, *Great Improvisation*, 38-42.

28. *Memorandum Books*, 1:555-56, 557n; TJ to James Monroe, 11 Nov. 1784, *Papers*, 7:508; MJ to Elizabeth House Trist, [after 24 Aug. 1785], *Papers*, 8:436-37.

29. *Memorandum Books*, 1:557-58; Rice, *Thomas Jefferson's Paris*, 13-15; Goodman, *Becoming a Woman*, 166-68; Adams, *Paris Years*, 46-47, 56-58; Papayanis, *Planning Paris*, 40; [Smith], *Journal and Correspondence of Miss Adams*, 14, 45; MJ to Elizabeth House Trist, [after 24 Aug. 1785], *Papers*, 8:437.

30. Goodman, *Becoming a Woman*, 74-75, 84-85; Rogers, *From the Salon to the Schoolroom*, 46; Abigail Adams to Lucy Cranch, 5 Sept. 1784, in Butterfield et al., *Adams Family Correspondence*, 5:438; Chastellux to TJ, 24 Aug. 1784, *Papers*, 7:410-11; *Memorandum Books*, 1:560.

31. MJ to Elizabeth House Trist, [after 24 Aug. 1785], *Papers*, 8:437; Sarah N. Randolph, "Mrs. Thomas Mann Randolph," in Wister and Scott, *Worthy Women*, 12-13; Kimball, *Jefferson*, 251; Rice, *Thomas Jefferson's Paris*, 65-67; [Smith], *Journal and Correspondence of Miss Adams*, 27; Choudhury, *Convents and Nuns*, 20; Rousseau, "Histoire de l'Abbaye de Pentemont," 207-8; Zujovic, *Short History of Pentemont*, 4-5; Birle and Francavilla, *Thomas Jefferson's Granddaughter*, 149, 159, 161-62.

32. TJ to John Bannister, 15 Oct. 1785, *Papers*, 8:635-37; Peter Carr to TJ, 18 Apr. 1787, *Papers*, 11:299.

33. Choudhury, *Convents and Nuns*, 129-40.

34. TJ to Mary Jefferson Bolling, 23 July 1787, *Papers*, 11:612; Abigail Adams to TJ, 10 Sept. 1787, *Papers*, 12:122. On American anti-Catholicism and its British origins, see McConville, *King's Three Faces*.

35. "Reminiscences of Th. J. by MR, copied by Mary and Caryanne," [ca. 1826], Edgehill-Randolph Papers, ViU; Sarah N. Randolph, "Mrs. Thomas Mann Randolph," in Wister and Scott, *Worthy Women*, 13; MJ to Elizabeth House Trist, [after 24 Aug. 1785], *Papers*, 8:437; TJ to Francis Eppes, [30 Aug. 1785], *Papers*, 8:451; Judith Randolph to MJ, 12 Feb. 1785, Trist Papers, NcU. Patsy's letters, which Judith mentioned in her own, unfortunately have not survived.

36. MJ to Elizabeth House Trist, [after 24 Aug. 1785], *Papers*, 8:438; J. Annesley to MJ, 20 Apr. 1786, and B[ettie] Carson to MJ, [1789], Edgehill-Randolph Papers, ViU; Jurgrau, *Story of My Life*, 638–39, 677–78.

37. Randolph, *Domestic Life*, 202–3; Pocock, *Memorials of the Family of Tufton*, 147; Caroline Tufton to MJ, 2 May [1789 or 1790]; Elizabeth Tufton to MJ, [Aug. 1789], 2, 18, 24 Sept. 1789; [J. Annesley] to MJ, 27 Apr. 1786; B[ettie] Hawkins to MJ, [1788]; and B[ettie] Carson to MJ, [1789], all in Edgehill-Randolph Papers, ViU; Marie de Botidoux to MJ, 4 Nov. 1789, 12 Mar. 1790, 31 Oct. 1798, 4 Oct. 1809, Botidoux Letters, ViU; Rousseau, "Histoire de l'Abbaye de Pentemont," 208–11; Birle and Francavilla, *Thomas Jefferson's Granddaughter*, 149, 159, 161–62.

38. J. Annesley to MJ, 20 Apr. 1786; B[ettie] Hawkins to MJ, 6 May [1786 or 1787], [1788]; and B[ettie] Carson to MJ, [1789], all in Edgehill-Randolph Papers, ViU; Marie de Botidoux to MJ, 4 Nov. 1789, 4 Oct. 1809, Botidoux Letters, ViU; Richard Garnett and J. Gilliland, "Lee [*née* Dashwood], Rachel Fanny Antonina," and Patrick Woodland, "Dashwood, Francis," *DNB*.

39. Marie de Botidoux to MJ, 31 Oct. 1798, Botidoux Letters, ViU; MJ to Elizabeth House Trist, [after 24 Aug. 1785], *Papers*, 8:438; Birle and Francavilla, *Thomas Jefferson's Granddaughter*, 160; TJ to MJ, 28 Mar. 1787, *Papers*, 11:250.

40. Adams, *Paris Years*, 46–52; Kimball, *Jefferson*, 263; Rice, *Thomas Jefferson's Paris*, 51–53; "Reminiscences of Th. J. by MR, copied by Mary and Caryanne," [ca. 1826], Edgehill-Randolph Papers, ViU.

41. [Smith], *Journal and Correspondence of Miss Adams*, 44–47, 73; Elizabeth Wayles Eppes to TJ, 13 Oct. 1784, *Papers*, 7:441, Francis Eppes to TJ [14 Oct. 1784], *Papers*, 7:441–42; TJ to Francis Eppes, 5 Feb, 11 May, 30 Aug. 1785, 24 Jan., 22 Apr. 1786, *Papers*, 7:602, 636, 8:141, 451, 9:211, 396; MJ to TJ, 9 Apr. 1787, *Papers*, 11:281–82.

42. Malone, *Thomas Jefferson and the Rights of Man*, chaps. 4–5; *Memorandum Books*, 1:625–27. On the Cosway episode, see, for instance, Adams, *Paris Years*, 222–27, 238–50, and Kukla, *Mr. Jefferson's Women*, chap. 5.

43. TJ to MJ, 6 Mar. 1786, *Papers*, 9:318; William Short to TJ, 2 Apr. 1786, 26 Mar. 1787, *Papers*, 9:367–68, 11:240; TJ to Francis Hopkinson, 9 May 1786, *Papers*, 9:482–83. On Short, see Malone, *Thomas Jefferson and the Rights of Man*, 8–9.

44. *Memorandum Books*, 1:560–649, passim; [Smith], *Journal and Correspondence of Miss Adams*, 44–47, 73.

45. TJ to John Adams, 25 Aug. 1785, *Papers*, 8:164; TJ to James Madison, 20 June 1787, *Papers*, 11:482; MJ to Elizabeth House Trist, [after 24 Aug. 1785], *Papers*, 8:436; *Memorandum Books*, 1:604, 610.

46. TJ to MJ, [Oct. 1786], 4 Nov. [1786], 28 Mar., 14 June 1787, *Papers*, 10:499, 507, 11:251, 472; TJ to Elizabeth House Trist, 18 Aug. 1785, *Papers*, 8:404; TJ to Elizabeth Wayles Eppes, 12 July 1788, *Papers*, 13:347 (emphasis in original). See also, Kukla, *Mr. Jefferson's Women*, 154–59.

47. MJ to TJ, 9 Apr. 1787, *Papers*, 11:282; Thomas Jefferson, *Notes on the State of Virginia*, in *Writings*, 3:250.

48. MJ to TJ, 3 May 1787, *Papers*, 11:334.

49. MJ to TJ, 8 [Mar.] 1787, 25 Mar., 9 Apr. 1787, *Papers*, 11:203–4, 238, 281–82.

50. TJ to MJ, 28 Mar., 7 Apr., 5, 21 May, 1 June 1787, *Papers*, 11:250–52, 277–78, 348–49, 369–70, 394–95.

51. TJ to MJ, 7 Apr. 1787, *Papers*, 11:278.

52. Abigail Adams to TJ, 26 June, 6, 10 July 1787, *Papers*, 11:501–2, 551, 573; John Adams to TJ, 10 July 1787, *Papers*, 11:575; TJ to Elizabeth Wayles Eppes, 28 July 1787, *Papers*, 11:634; TJ to George Gilmer, 12 Aug. 1787, *Papers*, 12:26. See also Isaac Jefferson, "Memoirs of a Monticello Slave," 5, and Hamilton Wilcox Pierson, "Jefferson at Monticello: The Private Life of Thomas Jefferson," 83, both in Bear, *Jefferson at Monticello*.

53. Mary Jefferson to TJ, [ca. 13 Sept. 1785], [ca. 22 May 1786?], [ca. 31 Mar. 1787], *Papers*, 8:517, 9:561, 11:260; TJ to Mary Jefferson, 20 Sept. 1785, *Papers*, 8:532–33; TJ to Elizabeth Wayles Eppes, 14 Dec. 1786, *Papers*, 10:594; Martha Jefferson Carr to TJ, 2 Jan. 1787, *Papers*, 11:632–33; Elizabeth Wayles Eppes to TJ, [ca. 31 Mar. 1787], *Papers*, 11:260.

54. Abigail Adams to TJ, 27 June, 6 July 1787, *Papers*, 11:501–2, 551.

55. TJ to Francis Eppes, [30 Aug. 1785], *Papers*, 8:451; William Short to TJ, 12 Mar. 1787, *Papers*, 11:209; John Blair to TJ, 28 Mar. 1787, *Papers*, 11:248–49; Francis Eppes to TJ, 30 Mar. 1787, *Papers*, 11:256; William Fleming to TJ, 2 May 1787, *Papers*, 11:330–31; Abigail Adams to TJ, 27 June, 6 July 1787, *Papers*, 11:501–2, 551; Gordon-Reed, *Hemingses of Monticello*, 191–92.

56. Gordon-Reed, *Hemingses of Monticello*, 143–44, 193, 210; Stanton, *Free Some Day*, 103.

57. Isaac Jefferson, "Memoirs of a Monticello Slave," in Bear, *Jefferson at Monticello*, 4. See also the discussion in Gordon-Reed, *Hemingses of Monticello*, 195–201.

58. Gordon-Reed, *Hemingses of Monticello*, 209, 211, 226–27, 236–38; TJ to Mary Jefferson Bolling, 23 July 1787, *Papers*, 11:612; Elizabeth Eppes, 28 July 1787, *Papers*, 11:634.

59. MJ to TJ, 27 May 1787, *Papers*, 11:380–81; Abigail Adams to TJ, 16 July 1787, *Papers*, 11:592; TJ to Mary Jefferson Bolling, 23 July 1787, *Papers*, 11:612; TJ to Elizabeth Wayles Eppes, 28, 12 July 1788, *Papers*, 11:634, 13:347.

60. *Memorandum Books*, 1:690–704, 712n, 724; Rice, *Thomas Jefferson's Paris*, 103–4; TJ to Dabney Carr, 24 Sept. 1794, *Papers*, 28:166; Smith, "Carysbrook Memoir," 24–25, ViU.

61. B[ettie] Hawkins to MJ, [1788], Edgehill-Randolph Papers, ViU; MJR to Benjamin Franklin Randolph, [1836?], Smith Papers, ViU.

62. Randolph, *Domestic Life*, 146; Sarah N. Randolph, "Mrs. Thomas Mann Randolph," in Wister and Scott, *Worthy Women*, 20–21; Melville, *John Carroll of Baltimore*, 102; MJR to Septimia Randolph, 2 Dec. 1832, Meikleham Papers, ViU; *Memorandum Books*, 1:692, 708, 709, 712, 718, 723, 724, 729; Gordon-Reed, *Hemingses of Monticello*, 260; TJ to John Jay, 19 Nov. 1788, *Papers*, 14:215–16.

63. TJ to MJ, 28 Mar., 14, 28 June 1787, *Papers*, 11:252, 472, 503; B[ettie] Hawkins to MJ, [1788], Edgehill-Randolph Papers, ViU; Zujovic, *Short History of Pentemont*, 2.

64. TJ to Elizabeth Wayles Eppes, 15 Dec. 1788, *Papers*, 14:355; TJ to John Trumbull, 12 Jan. 1789, *Papers*, 14:441; Jefferson to William Short, 22 Jan., 6 Feb. 1789, *Papers*,

14:483, 531; TJ to James Madison, 13 Jan. 1821, *Writings*, 10:181–82; MJR to Ann Cary Randolph Morris, 16 May 1827, Smith-Houston-Morris-Ogden Family Papers, APS; Kimball, *Jefferson*, 277.

65. Rice, *L'Hôtel de Langeac*, 8–14; *Memorandum Books*, 1:722.

66. Gordon-Reed, *Hemingses of Monticello*, 172–76, 182–84, 264; "The Memoirs of Madison Hemings," in Gordon-Reed, *Thomas Jefferson and Sally Hemings*, 246. Jon Kukla posits that the sexual relationship between Jefferson and Hemings began not in Paris but, rather, after their return to Monticello. Even so, it was in Paris that Jefferson first lived in close quarters with a mature Sally Hemings, whom he came to see, at some point, as a prospective sexual partner. See Kukla, *Mr. Jefferson's Women*, 125–27.

67. Gordon-Reed, *Hemingses of Monticello*, 242–43; Burstein, *Jefferson's Secrets*, 154, 157–58, 164–66. For Patsy's comments on French marriage and morality, see MJ to TJ, 9 Apr. 1787, *Papers*, 11:282.

68. Morris, *Diary*, 1:8, 10, 29, 49, 159n, 163, 166, 218, 220–21.

69. Gordon-Reed, *Hemingses of Monticello*, esp. chap. 13; Kukla, *Mr. Jefferson's Women*, 91–108, 125–27; *Memorandum Books*, 1:712n.

70. *Memorandum Books*, 1:732–43; Kimball, *Jefferson*, chap. 6; [Virginia Randolph Trist], "Description of Martha Randolph," Edgehill-Randolph Papers, ViU.

71. Sarah N. Randolph, "Mrs. Thomas Mann Randolph," in Wister and Scott, *Worthy Women*, 20–21; Adams, *Paris Years*, 213, 233–35; TJ to Anne Willing Bingham, 7 Feb. 1787, *Papers*, 11:122–24; TJ to Angelica Schuyler Church, 21 Sept. 1788, *Papers*, 13:521. On the salons generally, see Goodman, *Republic of Letters*, chaps. 2–3.

72. *Memorandum Books*, 1:734n; Gordon-Reed, *Hemingses of Monticello*, 260–62; Thomas Jefferson, *Notes on the State of Virginia*, in *Writings*, 3:246; "Black Europeans: George Polgreen Bridgetower," at http://www.bl.uk/onlinegallery/features/blackeuro/bridgetowerbackground.html (29 June 2009).

73. Sarah N. Randolph, "Mrs. Thomas Mann Randolph," in Wister and Scott, *Worthy Women*, 21; TJ to MJ, 15 Oct., 4 Nov. 1786, *Papers*, 10:499, 507; TJ to Dorcas Montgomery, 19 Nov. 1786, *Papers*, 10:543–44. On the Duchess of Devonshire in the 1780s, see Foreman, *Georgiana, Duchess of Devonshire*, 224–28.

74. Malone, *Thomas Jefferson and the Rights of Man*, 8–9; Sarah N. Randolph, "Mrs. Thomas Mann Randolph," in Wister and Scott, *Worthy Women*, 24; Bizardel and Rice, "'Poor in Love Mr. Short,'" 516–18; [Smith], *Journal and Correspondence of Miss Adams*, 45; TJ to MJ, 22 Dec. 1783, *Papers*, 6:417; MJ to TJ, 9 Apr. 1787, *Papers*, 11:281–82.

75. Bizardel and Rice, "'Poor in Love Mr. Short,'" 518–19, 521–27, 530–33; Gordon-Reed, *Hemingses of Monticello*, 254–55, 274.

76. Bizardel and Rice, "'Poor in Love Mr. Short,'" 527–30.

77. TJ to William Short, 24 Mar. 1789, *Papers*, 14:694–97. On Patsy's supposed "impatience to return to her own country," see TJ to Elizabeth Wayles Eppes, 15 Dec. 1788, *Papers*, 14:355.

78. Marie de Botidoux to MJ, [Jan. 1790], 1 May 1790, Botidoux Letters, ViU; George Green Shackelford, "Short, William," *ANB*.

79. Morris, *Diary*, 1:146–50; Adams, *Paris Years*, 278–88; TJ to Thomas Paine, 17 July 1789, *Papers*, 15:279.

80. Sarah N. Randolph, "Mrs. Thomas Mann Randolph," in Wister and Scott, *Worthy Women*, 22; Adams, *Paris Years*, 289–91.

81. Marie de Botidoux to MJ, [Jan. 1790], 31 Oct. 1798, Botidoux Letters, ViU; Bax, *Jean-Paul Marat*, 20–22; Bizardel and Rice, "'Poor in Love Mr. Short,'" 531. On Lafayette, see generally, Gottschalk and Maddox, *Lafayette and the French Revolution*.

82. "The Memoirs of Madison Hemings," in Gordon-Reed, *Thomas Jefferson and Sally Hemings*, 246; Gordon-Reed, *Hemingses of Monticello*, chaps. 16–18, 452–53, 504–5.

83. "Extract of the Diary of Nathaniel Cutting at Le Havre and Cowes," [28 Sept.–12 Oct. 1789], *Papers*, 15:490–98; Randolph, *Domestic Life*, 150–51; *Memorandum Books*, 1:743–45; Isaac Jefferson, "Memoirs of a Monticello Slave," in Bear, *Jefferson at Monticello*, 21.

84. *Memorandum Books*, 1:747; Randolph, *Domestic Life*, 151–52; John Trumbull to TJ, 22 Sept. 1789, *Papers*, 15:468.

85. Judith Randolph to MJ, 5 June 1784, 12 Feb. 1785, Trist Papers, NcU; Anne Willing Bingham to TJ, 1 June 1787, *Papers*, 11:394. On Bingham, see also Branson, *These Fiery, Frenchified Dames*, 135–40.

86. *Memorandum Books*, 1:748n.

Chapter 3

1. "Reminiscences of Th. J. by MR, copied by Mary and Caryanne," [ca. 1826], and [Virginia Randolph Trist], "Description of Martha Jefferson Randolph," undated, Edgehill-Randolph Papers, ViU. See also Randolph, *Domestic Life*, 152.

2. Malone, *Thomas Jefferson and the Rights of Man*, 234–35, 245–49; TJ to Elizabeth Wayles Eppes, 31 Oct. 1790, *Papers*, 17:658.

3. Gaines, *Thomas Mann Randolph*, 4–7, 22.

4. Malone, *Jefferson the Virginian*, 339; *Memorandum Books*, 1:531, 748n, 749; TMR to TJ, 16 Aug. 1786, *Papers*, 10:261; TJ to James Madison, 14 Feb. 1790, *Papers*, 16:182; TJ to Madame de Corny, 2 Apr. 1790, *Papers*, 16:290; Randolph, *Domestic Life*, 138–39; TMR to Septimia Randolph, 6 Aug. 1827, Meikleham Papers, ViU.

5. For disparaging views of Patsy's future husband, see Brodie, *Thomas Jefferson*, 28, and Gordon-Reed, *Hemingses of Monticello*, 418–19. For the view that Jefferson sabotaged his daughter's marriage, which Gordon-Reed argues persuasively was not the case, see especially Wayson, "Martha Jefferson Randolph," chap. 5 (quote on 200). On the young Thomas Mann Randolph and his father, see Gaines, *Thomas Mann Randolph*, 8–24.

6. TMR to Ann Cary Randolph, 1 May 1788, Trist Papers, NcU; Gaines, *Thomas Mann Randolph*, 26; Hamilton Wilcox Pierson, "Jefferson at Monticello: The Private Life of Thomas Jefferson," in Bear, *Jefferson at Monticello*, 83–84, 89–91.

7. TMR to TJ, 16 Aug. 1786, *Papers*, 9:260; TJ to Thomas Mann Randolph Sr., 11 Apr. 1787, *Papers*, 11:21–22; TMR to TJ, 14 Apr. 1787, *Papers*, 11:291–93; TJ to Thomas Mann

Randolph Sr., 4 Feb. 1790, *Papers*, 16:154; TJ to Madame de Corny, 2 Apr. 1790, *Papers*, 16:290; TJ to Dr. Richard Gem, 4 Apr. 1790, *Papers*, 16:297. See also, Gaines, *Thomas Mann Randolph*, 13–23.

8. Smith, *Inside the Great House*, 128; Clinton, *Plantation Mistress*, 60; Carson, *Colonial Virginians at Play*, 5–9; Montague, "Cornelia Lee's Wedding," 457–60. The Virginia legislature granted no divorce petitions until 1802; divorce remained rare thereafter. See Kierner, *Southern Women in Revolution*, 195–98, and Buckley, *Great Catastrophe of My Life*, 22–23.

9. Ann Cary Randolph to St. George Tucker, 23 Sept. 1788, Tucker-Coleman Papers, ViWM.

10. Kierner, *Scandal at Bizarre*, 23–24; Thomas Mann Randolph Sr. to TJ, 30 Jan. 1790, *Papers*, 16:135; TJ to MJR, 4 Apr. 1790, *Papers*, 16:300.

11. On Hemings's pregnancy as a factor in the timing of Patsy's wedding, see Brodie, *Thomas Jefferson*, 250, and Gordon-Reed, *Hemingses of Monticello*, 420–22.

12. TJ to Thomas Mann Randolph Sr., 4 Feb. 1790, *Papers*, 16:154–55, 155n; Thomas Mann Randolph Sr. to TJ, 15 Feb. 1790, *Papers*, 27:776–77.

13. Marriage Settlement for Martha Jefferson, 21 Feb. 1790, *Papers*, 16:189–91; Main, "The One Hundred," 377, 380; Gaines, *Thomas Mann Randolph*, 29.

14. *Memorandum Books*, 1:750.

15. TJ to MJR, 4 Apr. 1790, *Papers*, 16:300–301; MJR to TJ, 25 Apr. 1790, *Papers*, 16:384–85; Gaines, *Thomas Mann Randolph*, 31–32.

16. Kierner, *Beyond the Household*, 164–67; Jabour, *Scarlett's Sisters*, 186, 191–94; Gaines, *Thomas Mann Randolph*, 23–24.

17. TJ to Thomas Mann Randolph Sr., 11 Aug. 1787, *Papers*, 12:21; TMR to TJ, 23 Apr. 1790, *Papers*, 16:370; TJ to TMR, 30 May 1790, *Papers*, 16:449.

18. MJR to TJ, 25 Apr. 1790, *Papers*, 16:384–85.

19. TJ to MJR, 26 Apr. 1790, *Papers*, 16:386–87.

20. Weld, *Travels through the States of North America*, 1:205–6; Burstein, *Jefferson's Secrets*, 79.

21. TMR to TJ, 25 May 1790, *Papers*, 16:441; TJ to TMR, 20 June 1790, *Papers*, 16:540; TJ to Thomas Mann Randolph Sr., 25 July 1790, *Papers*, 17:274–75.

22. TJ to MJR, 17 July 1790, *Papers*, 7:215; TMR to Thomas Mann Randolph Sr., Oct. 1790, Edgehill-Randolph Papers, ViU; Gaines, *Thomas Mann Randolph*, 32–33.

23. TJ to MJR, 17 July 1790, *Papers*, 7:215.

24. TJ to TMR, 11 July 1790, *Papers*, 7:26; Memorandum to Nicholas Lewis, [ca. 7 Nov. 1790], *Papers*, 18:29; "Nicholas Lewis," in *Thomas Jefferson Encyclopedia* at http://wiki.monticello.org/mediawiki/index.php/Nicholas_Lewis (12 Aug. 2009).

25. TMR to TJ, 5 Mar. 1791, *Papers*, 19:420; MJR to TJ, 3 May 1787, 20 Feb. 1792, *Papers*, 11:334, 23:126.

26. TJ to TMR, 4 Mar. 1792, *Papers*, 23:193; Wolf, *Race and Liberty in the New Nation*, 28–38; Egerton, *Gabriel's Rebellion*, 6–13. Virginians' antislavery commitment should not be exaggerated. See Schmidt and Wilhelm, "Early Proslavery Petitions in Virginia."

27. Albemarle County Personal Property Tax Lists, 1790–99, LVa. Census data ob-

tained from http://fisher.lib.virginia.edu/collections/stats/histcensus/php/county
.php (25 Aug. 2009).

28. TJ to TMR, 18 Apr. 1790, 1 Jan., 6, 12 Apr., 15 June, 19 Oct. 1792, 9 Jan. 1797, *Papers*, 16:351–52, 23:7–8, 160, 411, 24:83, 501, 29:260; TMR to TJ, 4 June, 7 Oct. 1792, *Papers*, 24:33, 449; Taylor, "Edgehill," 62–63; Moore, *Albemarle*, 88–89; MJR to EWRC, [1826?], Martha Jefferson Randolph Letter, VHi.

29. Randolph, *Virginia House-Wife*, x. In general, see Clinton, *Plantation Mistress*, 16–35.

30. TJ to Elizabeth Wayles Eppes, 7 Mar. 1790, *Papers*, 16:208; TJ to MJR, 4 Dec. 1791, *Papers*, 22:376–77; MJR to TJ, 7 May 1792, *Papers*, 23:486; Birle and Francavilla, *Thomas Jefferson's Granddaughter*, 160; EWRC to Henry S. Randall, 31 Mar. 1856, Coolidge Correspondence, ViU.

31. MJR to TJ, 16 Jan. 1791, *Papers*, 18:499–500; Mary Walker Lewis to TJ, 23 Jan. 1791, *Papers*, 18:594; TMR to TJ, 2 Feb. 1791, *Papers*, 19:239–40.

32. TMR to TJ, 14 Nov. 1793, *Papers*, 27:378; Kierner, *Scandal at Bizarre*, 17, 32–33, 103, 109.

33. MJR to TJ, 16 Jan. 1791, *Papers*, 18:499–500; TMR to TJ, 2 Feb. 1791, *Papers*, 19:239–40; Mary Walker Lewis to TJ, 23 Jan. 1791, *Papers*, 18:594; Malone, *Jefferson the Virginian*, 428; "Col. Nicholas Lewis (1728–1808) and Mary Walker Lewis (1742–1824)," at http://www.monticello.org/library/exhibits/lucymarks/lucymarks/bios/colnandmwlewis.html (12 Aug. 2009).

34. TMR to TJ, 2, 21 Feb., 14 Mar. 1791, *Papers*, 19:239, 323, 556; Mary Jefferson to TJ, 13 Feb., 6 Mar. 1791, *Papers*, 19:271, 423; MJR to TJ, 22 Mar. 1791, *Papers*, 19:599.

35. TMR to TJ, 8 Feb. 1791, *Papers*, 19:259; Mary Jefferson to TJ, 13 Feb., 6 Mar. 1791, *Papers*, 19:271, 423; TJ to TMR, 17 Mar. 1791, *Papers*, 19:582; Mary Jefferson to TJ, 12 June 1797, *Papers*, 29:428; Hamilton Wilcox Pierson, "Jefferson at Monticello: The Private Life of Thomas Jefferson," in Bear, *Jefferson at Monticello*, 85.

36. Randolph, *Domestic Life*, 192–94; MJ to TJ, 16 Jan., 22 Mar. 1791, *Papers*, 18:499–500, 19:598–99; TJ to Elizabeth Wayles Eppes, 15 May 1791, *Papers*, 19:413; Smith, "Carysbrook Memoir," 23, ViU; Kierner, *Scandal at Bizarre*, 29–30.

37. TMR to TJ, 16 Apr., 4 May, 12 Oct. 1792, *Papers*, 23:429, 481, 24:473–74; MJR to TJ, 7 May, 2 July 1792, *Papers*, 23:487, 24:147–48.

38. Kierner, *Scandal at Bizarre*, 29–30.

39. Ibid., 1–7.

40. Ibid., 8–39.

41. Ibid., 31–32; TMR to TJ, 1 Feb. 1792, *Papers*, 23:95; MJR to TJ, 20 Feb., 18 Nov. 1792, *Papers*, 23:125–26, 24:634.

42. MJR to TJ, 18 Nov. 1792, *Papers*, 24:634; "Notes of Evidence," Apr. 1793, in Cullen and Johnson, *Papers of John Marshall*, 2:171.

43. Kierner, *Scandal at Bizarre*, 42, 51.

44. Ibid., 42.

45. Klepp, *Revolutionary Conceptions*, 179–95; "Notes of Evidence," Apr. 1793, in Cullen and Johnson, *Papers of John Marshall*, 2:168–75.

46. "Notes of Evidence," Apr. 1793, in Cullen and Johnson, *Papers of John Mar-*

shall, 2:168–69; Munger, "Guaiacum," 218; Moss, *Southern Folk Medicine*, 82, 84, 186; Smith, *Professor Cullen's Treatise*, 2:139–42; Cook, *Physiomedical Dispensary*, at http://medherb.com/cook/html/GUAIACUM_OFFICINALE.htm#VPID_175 (15 Aug. 2009); *PDR for Herbal Medicines*, 884.

47. Smith, *Professor Cullen's Treatise*, 2:142; Riddle, *Eve's Herbs*, 193–96, 202; Cook, *Physiomedical Dispensary*. Modern authorities do not classify gum guaiacum as an abortifacient. See, for instance, *PDR for Herbal Medicines*, 884.

48. Kierner, *Scandal at Bizarre*, 59–60; John Wayles Eppes to TJ, 1 May 1793, *Papers*, 25:632–33; MJR to TJ, 16 May 1793, *Papers*, 26:53.

49. TJ to MJR, 28 Apr. 1793, *Papers*, 25:621–22; MJR to TJ, 16 May 1793, *Papers*, 26:53; Kierner, *Scandal at Bizarre*, 86–92; Ely, *Israel on the Appomattox*, chap. 2.

50. MJR to TJ, 16 May 1793, *Papers*, 26:53.

51. Kierner, *Scandal at Bizarre*, 94, 104; Gaines, *Thomas Mann Randolph*, 37–38; TMR to TJ, 30 Nov. 1793, *Papers*, 27:465.

52. Malone, *Jefferson and the Ordeal of Liberty*, chaps. 8–9; Jan Lewis, "'The Blessings of Domestic Society': Thomas Jefferson's Family and the Transformation of American Politics," in Onuf, *Jeffersonian Legacies*, 111–18; TJ to Elizabeth House Trist, 17 Sept. 1794, *Papers*, 28:155.

53. TJ to Elizabeth House Trist, 17 Sept. 1794, *Papers*, 28:155; TJ to Dabney Carr, 24 Sept. 1794, *Papers*, 28:166; TJ to TMR, 27 Oct. 1794, *Papers*, 28:182; Peterson, *Visitors to Monticello*, 29.

54. Gaines, *Thomas Mann Randolph*, 40–41; MJR to TJ, 31 Mar. 1797, *Papers*, 29:334; TJ to TMR, 9 Apr. 1797, *Papers*, 29:349. On gentry and the courts, see Isaac, *Transformation of Virginia*, 88–94, and Roeber, *Faithful Magistrates and Republican Lawyers*, esp. chap. 2.

55. Gaines, *Thomas Mann Randolph*, 42; TJ to MJR, 8 June 1797, *Papers*, 29:424; TJ to TMR, 3 May 1798, *Papers*, 30:325; TJ to Mary Jefferson, [14 June 1797], *Papers*, 29:429–30; Mary Jefferson to TJ, 27 Feb. [1797], *Papers*, 29:308; TJ to Francis Eppes, 24 Sept. 1797, *Papers*, 29:532–33; TJ to Catherine Church, 11 Jan. 1798, *Papers*, 30:24–25; MJR to TJ, [23 June 1798], *Papers*, 30:424; Malone, *Jefferson and the Ordeal of Liberty*, 238–41; Albemarle County Personal Property Tax Lists, 1797–98, and Henrico County Personal Property Tax Lists, 1797, 1799, LVa; McLaughlin, *Jefferson and Monticello*, 262–64; Taylor, "Edgehill," 62–63; National Register of Historic Places Nomination Form for Edgehill, at http://165.176.125.227/registers/Counties/Albemarle/002-0026_Edgehill_1982_Final_Nomination.pdf (2 Mar. 2010).

56. MJR to TJ, 16 May 1793, 31 Mar. 1797, [23 June 1798], *Papers*, 26:53, 29:334, 30:424; TJ to Mary Jefferson, 11 Mar. 1797, *Papers*, 29:314. On migration out of Virginia during this period, see, for instance, Davis, "Jeffersonian Expatriate," and Terry, "Sustaining the Bonds of Kinship."

57. McMillen, *Motherhood in the Old South*, 31–33, 107; Censer, *North Carolina Planters and Their Children*, 24–25.

58. TJ to MJR, 12 Nov. 1792, 17 June 1793, *Papers*, 24:610, 26:307.

59. Thomas Elder to TJ, Oct. 1785, *Papers*, 8:687; TMR to TJ, 25 May 1790, 19 July 1793, *Papers*, 26:541, 16:441; Judith Randolph to Mary Randolph Harrison, 18 June 1801, Harrison Family Papers, VHi; Gaines, *Thomas Mann Randolph*, 39.

60. TJ to TMR, 14 July 1794, [8 Jan. 1795], 29 Jan. 1795, *Papers*, 28:104, 242, 251; TJ to MJR, 22 Jan., 5 Feb. 1795, *Papers*, 28:249, 260; Gaines, *Thomas Mann Randolph*, 39.

61. TJ to James Madison, 13 July 1795, *Papers*, 28:408; TJ to MJR, 28 Mar. 1787, *Papers*, 11:250–52; Lewis, *Ladies and Gentlemen on Display*, 18, 49, 58, 61, 66, 80; Thomas Jefferson, *Notes on the State of Virginia*, in *Writings*, 3:121.

62. TJ to TMR, 26 July, 11, 20 Aug. 1795, *Papers*, 28:419, 434–35, 439; TJ to MJR, 31 July 1795, *Papers*, 28:429; TJ to Elizabeth House Trist, 23 Sept. 1795, *Papers*, 28:478; George Green Shackelford, "Unmarried Children of Martha Jefferson Randolph and Thomas Mann Randolph, Jr.," in Shackelford, *Collected Papers*, 124.

63. MJR to TJ, 31 Mar. 1797, *Papers*, 29:334; Lewis, *Pursuit of Happiness*, 98–103; Lewis, *Ladies and Gentlemen on Display*, 18, 120.

64. TJ to TMR, 18 Jan., 12, 19 Aug. 1796, *Papers*, 28:592–93, 29:168–69, 170–71; TMR to TJ, 6 Nov. 1797, 3 Feb. 1798, *Papers*, 29:568–69, 30:79; TJ to MJR, 8 Feb. 1798, *Papers*, 30:92.

65. TJ to TMR, 24 Feb. 1791, *Papers*, 19:328; TMR to TJ, 14 Mar. 1791, *Papers*, 19:556.

66. Gregory, *Comparative View*, 23, 29–34, 37, 82, 125–26; Doyle, "'Highest Pleasure'"; Paul Lawrence, "Gregory, John," *DNB*.

67. Gregory, *Comparative View*, 36, 40; Lewis and Lockridge, "'Sally Has Been Sick,'" 9–10; Klepp, *Revolutionary Conceptions*, 97–98, 265, 268; Kierner, *Beyond the Household*, 174–75.

68. TMR to TJ, 10 Jan. 1801, *Papers*, 32:440; MJR to TJ, 31 Jan. 1801, *Papers*, 32:526; Gordon-Reed, *Hemingses of Monticello*, 519.

69. MJR to TJ, 30 Jan. 1800, *Papers*, 31:347; TJ to MJR, 11 Feb. 1800, *Papers*, 31:368; John Wayles Eppes to TJ, 20 Feb., 16 Mar., 22 Apr. 1800, *Papers*, 31:386–87, 440, 533; TMR to TJ, 22 Feb. 1800, *Papers*, 31:389; Gregory, *Comparative View*, 59–60; Isaac Jefferson, "Memoirs of a Monticello Slave," in Bear, *Jefferson at Monticello*, 5.

70. Gregory, *Comparative View*, 44, 61, 66; TJ to MJR, 22 Jan. 1795, *Papers*, 28:249; TJ to TMR, 18 Jan. 1796, [25 Apr. 1796], *Papers*, 28:592–93, 28:90. On the painting, see Stein, *Worlds of Thomas Jefferson*, 148–49.

71. Gregory, *Comparative View*, 117–18; Kerber, *Women of the Republic*, chap. 9; TJ to Marbois, 5 Dec. 1783, *Papers*, 6:374.

72. MJR to TJ, 16 Jan. 1793, 12 May 1798, *Papers*, 25:64, 30:346; Gregory, *Comparative View*, 72; Thomas Jefferson Randolph memoirs, 1874, Edgehill-Randolph Papers, ViU, 3–4, 6–7; Moore, *Albemarle*, 102–3; Woods, *Albemarle County*, 86–87.

73. MJR to TJ, 31 Jan. 1801, *Papers*, 32:527.

74. Shammas, "Black Women's Work," 18–19, 25; Betts, *Thomas Jefferson's Farm Book*, 7; Stanton, *Free Some Day*, 102–6.

75. Gordon-Reed, *Hemingses of Monticello*, 423–24; Stanton, *Free Some Day*, 33, 103–4.

76. Isaac Jefferson, "Memoirs of a Monticello Slave," in Bear, *Jefferson at Monticello*, 16.

77. MJR to TJ, 15 Jan. 1795, 22 Jan. 1798, *Papers*, 28:247, 30:43; TMR to TJ, 13 Jan. 1798, *Papers*, 28:28. See also Weiner, *Mistresses and Slaves*, 2, 72–80.

78. Gordon-Reed, *Thomas Jefferson and Sally Hemings*, 195–201; Gordon-Reed, *Hemingses of Monticello*, 431, 530–35.

79. Wyatt-Brown, *Southern Honor*, 295–97, 305–24; Clinton, *Plantation Mistress*, chap. 11; Rothman, *Notorious in the Neighborhood*, 4–5, 40–51; Kierner, *Scandal at Bizarre*, 74–76; Gordon-Reed, *Hemingses of Monticello*, 429–36.

80. MJR to TJ, 31 Jan. 1801, *Papers*, 32:527; McLaughlin, *Jefferson and Monticello*, 255–56.

81. TJ to Mary Jefferson Eppes, 4 July 1800, *Papers*, 32:39; TJ to MJR, 5 Feb. 1801, *Papers*, 32:556–57; Malone, *Jefferson and the Ordeal of Liberty*, 459–63, 477–79.

Chapter 4

1. TJ to TMR, 19 Feb. 1801, *Papers*, 33:20–21.

2. MJR to TJ, 8 Feb. 1799, *Papers*, 31:20.

3. Allgor, *Parlor Politics*, 9. Allgor's pathbreaking work was the essential first step in discerning the central role of social life—balls, receptions, dinners, and other official and quasi-official social gatherings—in the conduct of political business in the early American republic. Finding women in these social venues and taking seriously the significance of their activities, she argues perceptively, "produces not politically correct history but correct political history" (ibid., 246).

4. Eleanor Parke Custis to Elizabeth Bordley, 14 May 1798, in Brady, *George Washington's Beautiful Nelly*, 52; Ann Cary Randolph to St. George Tucker, 29 Oct. 1797, and Judith Randolph to St. George Tucker, 5 Nov. 1797, Tucker-Coleman Papers, ViWM; Kierner, *Scandal at Bizarre*, 141–43; Zagarri, *Revolutionary Backlash*, esp. chap. 2.

5. On Jefferson and Abigail Adams, see Kukla, *Mr. Jefferson's Women*, 143–53.

6. TJ to Anne Willing Bingham, 11 May 1788, *Papers*, 13:151–52; Thomas Jefferson, "Autobiography," in *Writings*, 1:140. See also Steele, "Thomas Jefferson's Gender Frontier," 17–42.

7. Branson, *These Fiery, Frenchified Dames*, chap. 4; Kukla, *Mr. Jefferson's Women*, 160–62; TJ to MJR, 17 May 1798, 11 Feb. 1800, *Papers*, 30:355, 31:366.

8. TJ to MJR, 5 Feb. 1801, *Papers*, 32:556–57; Malone, *Jefferson and the Ordeal of Liberty*, 478–82. See also Lewis, *Pursuit of Happiness*, 171–72, 187–88, 209–10, and Allgor, *Parlor Politics*, 27–29.

9. Elizabeth House Trist to TJ, 1 Mar. [1801], *Papers*, 33:115–16. A thoughtful overview of Jefferson's attitudes toward politically minded women appears in Kukla, *Mr. Jefferson's Women*, chap. 7. Kukla's view differs somewhat from mine in part because he does not consider Jefferson's friendship with Trist or with other women—such as Dolley Madison or Margaret Bayard Smith—who admired him and supported him politically.

10. Allgor, *Parlor Politics*, 20–21; TJ to MJR, 17 May 1798, 11 Feb. 1800, *Papers*, 30:355, 31:366.

11. TJ to MJR, 28 May 1801, *Papers*, 34:200; Scofield, "Fatigues of His Table," 460, 463–64; Cullen, "Jefferson's White House Dinner Guests"; Allgor, *Parlor Politics*, 19–23, 38–40.

12. Kann, *Republic of Men*, chap. 4; Gundersen, "Independence, Citizenship, and the American Revolution." For Jefferson's invitations, see TJ to Maria Jefferson Eppes, 28 May 1801, 3, 29 Mar. 1802, *Family Letters*, 203, 219–20; TJ to MJR, 28 May,

19 Oct. 1801, 24 Apr., 18 June, 18 Oct. 1802, *Family Letters*, 202, 209, 224–25, 228–29, 237; MJR to TJ, 10 July 1802, *Family Letters*, 233; TJ to TMR, 28 Mar., 22 Oct. 1802, Jefferson Papers, LC.

13. Allgor, *Parlor Politics*, 24–26, 29–30; Zagarri, *Revolutionary Backlash*, 158–60; Young, *Washington Community*, 168–69; Margaret Bayard Smith to Maria Bayard, 28 May 1801, in Smith, *First Forty Years*, 29.

14. TJ to Maria Jefferson Eppes, 3, 29 Mar. 1802, *Family Letters*, 219–20; TJ to MJR, 24 Apr., 18 June, 18 Oct. 1802, *Family Letters*, 224–25, 228–29, 237; MJR to TJ, 10 July 1802, *Family Letters*, 233; TJ to TMR, 28 Mar., 22 Oct. 1802, Jefferson Papers, LC.

15. MJR to TJ, 29 Oct., 9 Nov. 1802, *Family Letters*, 238, 239; TJ to MJR, 2 Nov. 1802, *Family Letters*; 238; Mary Jefferson Eppes to TJ, 5 Nov. 1802, 11 Jan. 1803, *Family Letters*, 239, 240; Smith, *First Forty Years*, 33. For Jefferson's rate of travel, see Bear, "Chronologies of the Whereabouts of Martha Jefferson," Monticello Research Files, ICJS.

16. Busey, *Pictures of the City of Washington*, 57, 73–74; Young, *Washington Community*, 19–24, 41–44; Mason, *Extracts from a Diary*, 16–17; Mordecai, *Richmond in By-Gone Days*, 214–18; Abigail DeHart Mayo to Dolley Madison, 23 Feb. 1804, *DMDE*.

17. Abigail Adams to Abigail Adams Smith, 21 Nov. 1800, in Adams, *Letters of Mrs. Adams*, 2:240–42.

18. Malone, *Jefferson the President: First Term*, 40–46; Young, *Washington Community*, 45–47; Jeffrey L. Pasley, "The Cheese and the Words: Popular Political Culture and Participatory Democracy in the Early American Republic," in Pasley, Robertson, and Waldstreicher, *Beyond the Founders*, 31–38; Cutler and Perkins, *Life Journals and Correspondence of Manasseh P. Cutler*, 2:116; "Presentation of the 'Mammoth Cheese,'" *Papers*, 36:248.

19. TJ to Maria Jefferson Eppes, 18 Jan. 1803, *Family Letters*, 241; TJ to MJR, 27 Jan. 1803, *Family Letters*, 242; Virginia J. Trist cookbook, Papers of the Trist, Burke, and Randolph Families, ViU; Septimia Randolph Meikleham cookbook, Monticello Research Files, ICJS; Stanton, "Well-Ordered Household." See also Kimball, *Thomas Jefferson's Cookbook*, 12–13, 26.

20. Benjamin Henry Latrobe to Mary Elizabeth Latrobe, 24 Nov. 1802, in Van Horne and Formwalt, *Correspondence and Miscellaneous Papers of Benjamin Henry Latrobe*, 1:232; Cutler and Perkins, *Life Journals and Correspondence of Manasseh P. Cutler*, 2:113; "Dr. Mitchill's Letters from Washington, 1801–1813," *Harper's New Monthly Magazine* 58 (Dec. 1878–May 1879): 741; VJRT to Laura Carter Holloway, [ca. 1870], in Holloway, *Ladies of the White House*, 150; Septimia Anne Randolph Meikleham, "Montpelier: Quiet Homelife of Mr and Mrs Madison," [after 1836], Meikleham Papers, ViU.

21. Margaret Bayard Smith to Susan Bayard Smith, 26 Dec. 1802, in Smith, *First Forty Years*, 33.

22. For Jefferson's attendance at religious services, see Cutler and Perkins, *Life Journals and Correspondence of Manasseh P. Cutler*, 2:72, 113, 172. Allgor has explored the political significance of women's visiting in early Washington; see *Parlor Politics*, 120–25, and *Perfect Union*, chap. 4.

23. Gaines, *Thomas Mann Randolph*, 41–49; MJR to TJ, 18 Nov. 1801, *Papers*, 35:690; TMR to TJ, 29 Oct. 1802, Coolidge Collection.

24. *Richmond Recorder*, 1 Sept. 1802; TMR to Peter Carr, 24 Dec. 1802, Carr-Cary Papers, ViU. See also Rothman, *Notorious in the Neighborhood*, 26–38, and Gordon-Reed, *Hemingses of Monticello*, 554–58.

25. On the family's defense of Jefferson's reputation and the careful construction of his public image after his death in 1826, see, for instance, Jan Ellen Lewis, "The White Jeffersons," in Lewis and Onuf, *Sally Hemings and Thomas Jefferson*, 144–54; Burstein, *Jefferson's Secrets*, 69, 172–82, and chap. 8; Scharff, *Women Jefferson Loved*, 379–82.

26. Gaines, *Thomas Mann Randolph*, 50–51; John Barnes to William Short, 28 Dec. 1802, Short Papers, LC; TMR to John Milledge, 5 Jan. 1803, Milledge Family Papers, NcD; Maria Jefferson Eppes to TJ, 11 Jan. 1803, *Family Letters*, 240; TJ to MJR, 7 Nov. 1803, *Family Letters*, 248; Mary Trist to Catharine Bache, 8 Apr. 1803, and to William Bache, 27 Aug. 1803, *FLDA*.

27. For an assessment of Thomas Mann Randolph's career in Congress, see Gaines, *Thomas Mann Randolph*, 66–67.

28. TJ to MJR, 23 Nov. 1807, *Family Letters*, 315; Zagarri, *Revolutionary Backlash*, 62–63; Allgor, *Parlor Politics*, 110–11, and *Perfect Union*, 41–42.

29. MJR to TJ, 2 Jan. 1808, *Family Letters*, 318; TJ to TMR, 8 Oct. 1801, 5 July 1803, Jefferson Papers, LC.

30. Gaines, *Thomas Mann Randolph*, 41–47; TJ to TMR, 28 Mar., 15 Dec. 1802, Jefferson Papers, LC; TJ to Mary Jefferson Eppes, 29 Mar. 1802, *Family Letters*, 220; MJR to TJ, 2 Jan. 1808, *Family Letters*, 318.

31. TMR to TJ, 6 Mar. 1802, Coolidge Collection; Wallenstein, *Cradle of America*, 122–23, 155; Schwarz, *Migrants against Slavery*, esp. 1–17; Terry, "Sustaining the Bonds of Kinship," 455–76. For two views of southern women's attitudes toward westward migration, see Cashin, *Family Venture*, chap. 2, and Censer, "Southwestern Migration among North Carolina Planter Families," 409–13.

32. TMR to TJ, 6 Mar. 1802, Coolidge Collection; Lee, "Problem of Slave Community"; Morgan, *Slave Counterpoint*, chap. 9; Allan Kulikoff, "Uprooted Peoples: Black Migrants in the Age of the American Revolution," in Berlin and Hoffman, *Slavery and Freedom in the Age of the American Revolution*, 143–71; Sidbury, *Ploughshares into Swords*, 27–39. For a telling first-person account of a Maryland slave who was moved to the cotton states around 1800, see Ball, *Fifty Years in Chains*, esp. 112–28.

33. Lebsock, *Free Women of Petersburg*, 137–43; Weiner, *Mistresses and Slaves*, 72–88.

34. Thomas Jefferson, *Notes on the State of Virginia*, in *Writings*, 3:267; Cary, *Letters on Female Character*, 134–35, 173.

35. MJR to TJ, 14 Jan. 1804, *Family Letters*, 253.

36. MJR to TJ, 14 Jan., 30 Nov. 1804, 19 Apr. 1805, 14 Oct. 1806, *Family Letters*, 252, 264, 269, 288; TJ to MJR, 3 Dec. 1804, 24 June 1805, *Family Letters*, 265, 273.

37. TJ to MJR, 26 Apr. 1790, *Family Letters*, 54; TJ to Anne Cary, Thomas Jefferson, and Ellen Wayles Randolph, 2 Mar. 1802, *Family Letters*, 218.

38. Anne Cary Randolph to TJ, 21 Jan., 14 Feb. 1804, 4 July, 12 Dec. 1806, 9 Nov. 1807, *Family Letters*, 254, 257, 287, 292, 314; TJ to Anne Cary Randolph, 9 Jan. 1804, 8 Dec. 1806, *Family Letters*, 251, 291–92; EWR to TJ, 22 Feb., 10 Nov. 1805, 14 Nov.,

27 Dec. 1806, 30 Jan., 17 Feb., 11 Nov. 1807, 8 Jan. 1808, *Family Letters*, 267–68, 281–82, 289–91, 294, 295–96, 296, 314; TJ to EWR, 30 Nov. 1806, 8 Feb. 1807, *Family Letters*, 291, 295; Cornelia Randolph to TJ, 1 Feb. 1808, *Family Letters*, 325; MJR to TJ, 11 July 1805, *Family Letters*, 278.

39. MJR to TJ, 18 Nov. 1801, *Papers*, 35:690; MJR to TJ, 14 Jan. 1804, *Family Letters*, 252–53.

40. TJ to Maria Jefferson Eppes, 26 Dec. 1803, *Family Letters*, 250; Randolph, *Domestic Life*, 299; Malone, *Jefferson the President: First Term*, 411–13.

41. Randolph, *Domestic Life*, 300; Malone, *Jefferson the President: First Term*, 413; *Memorandum Books*, 2:1125.

42. MJR to TJ, 31 May 1804, *Family Letters*, 260–61.

43. TJ to MJR, 3 Dec. 1804, 21 Jan. 1805, *Family Letters*, 266–67; MJR to TJ, 28 Feb. 1805, *Family Letters*, 268; TMR to TJ, 26 Jan. 1805, Edgehill-Randolph Papers, ViU.

44. TMR to TJ, 27 Apr. 1805, Edgehill-Randolph Papers, ViU; Dolley Madison to Anna Payne Cutts, 26 Apr. 1804, 8 Sept. [1804], *DMDE*; Kierner, *Scandal at Bizarre*, 108–11; Kierner, "'Dark and Dense Cloud Perpetually Lowering over Us,'" 210.

45. Kierner, *Scandal at Bizarre*, 94, 111–14, 121; TMR to TJ, 6 Mar. 1802, 22 June 1805, Edgehill-Randolph Papers, ViU; MJR to TJ, 11 July 1805, 2 Jan., 24 Nov. 1808, *Family Letters*, 278–79, 318, 361; Smith, "Carysbrook Memoir," 23–25, 32, ViU. For other job-seekers, see TJ to TMR, 2 Jan. 1808, Jefferson Papers, LC; MJR to Dolley Madison, 15 Jan. 1808, *DMDE*; MJR to TJ, 16 Jan. 1808, 1 Jan. 1809, *Family Letters*, 323, 375; TJ to MJR, 25 Apr., 18 Oct. 1808, *Family Letters*, 343–44.

46. TJ to MJR, 7 Jan., 6 May, 7, 25 Nov. 1805, *Family Letters*, 265, 270, 281, 283; MJR to TJ, 26 Oct. 1805, *Family Letters*, 280.

47. MJR to TJ, 23 Nov., 1805, *Family Letters*, 282; TJ to MJR, 25, 29 Nov. 1805, *Family Letters*, 283–84; Dolley Madison to Anna Payne Cutts, 3 May [1806], *DMDE*.

48. TJ to MJR, 6 May 1805, *Family Letters*, 270; Melish, *Travels through the United States*, 145, 153–54; Jeffrey L. Pasley, "The Cheese and the Words: Popular Political Culture and Participatory Democracy in the Early American Republic," in Pasley, Robertson, and Waldstreicher, *Beyond the Founders*, 36.

49. MJR to Ann Cary Randolph Morris, 1 May 1832, Smith-Houston-Morris-Ogden Family Papers, APS. See also Quimby, "Political Art of James Akin."

50. Werner Sollors, "Presidents, Race, and Sex," 199–200, and Jan Ellen Lewis, "The White Jeffersons," 138, both in Lewis and Onuf, *Sally Hemings and Thomas Jefferson*.

51. Margaret Bayard Smith to Mrs. Kirkpatrick, 4 May 1806, in Smith, *First Forty Years*, 49–50; Malone, *Jefferson the President: Second Term*, 108–13.

52. MJR to TJ, 2 Mar. 1809, *Family Letters*, 386–87; Margaret Bayard Smith's Account of a Visit to Monticello, [29 July–2 Aug.] 1809, *Papers: Retirement Series*, 1:393.

53. List of Diners at the President's House, 1804–1808, Coolidge Collection; Busey, *Pictures of the City of Washington*, 333; "The Memoirs of Madison Hemings," in Gordon-Reed, *Thomas Jefferson and Sally Hemings*, 247; Sarah N. Randolph, "Mrs. Thomas Mann Randolph," in Wister and Scott, *Worthy Women*, 41.

54. List of Diners at the President's House, 1804–1808, Coolidge Collection; Scofield, "Fatigues of His Table," 456–60, 460n; Nevins, *Diary of John Quincy Adams*, 38.

55. Smith, *First Forty Years*, 404–5; Tinkcom, "Caviar along the Potomac," 73; All-gor, *Parlor Politics*, 35, 44–45.

56. Allgor, *Perfect Union*, 50–59; TJ to MJR, 16 June 1806, and to EWR, 24 June 1806, *Family Letters*, 284–85.

57. EWR to TJ, 26 Feb., 18 Mar. 1808, *Family Letters*, 330, 335; Anne Cary Randolph to TJ, 18 Mar. 1808, *Family Letters*, 334; Zagarri, *Revolutionary Backlash*, 95–97; Kier-ner, *Beyond the Household*, 135.

58. MJR to TJ, 14 Oct. 1806, *Family Letters*, 288; Gaines, *Thomas Mann Randolph*, 59–61; Kierner, *Scandal at Bizarre*, 109–10, 115–16, 137.

59. MJR to TJ, 18 Nov. 1808, *Family Letters*, 360; Dawidoff, *Education of John Randolph of Roanoke*, 25, 99; Bouldin, *Home Reminiscences of John Randolph of Roanoke*, 10–13, 28, 35–36; Gaines, *Thomas Mann Randolph*, 57; Randolph Memo-randum Book, ca. 1790, copy, ICJS; TMR to Peachy R. Gilmer, 11 May 1804, Randolph-Gilmer Letters, LVa. See also Hamilton Wilcox Pierson, "Jefferson at Monticello: The Private Life of Thomas Jefferson," in Bear, *Jefferson at Monticello*, 90; Freeman, *Affairs of Honor*, 167–80.

60. *Annals of Congress*, House of Representatives, 9th Congress, 1st Session, 1102–6; Gaines, *Thomas Mann Randolph*, 61–62.

61. TJ to TMR, 23 June 1806, Edgehill-Randolph Papers, ViU; Freeman, *Affairs of Honor*, 177–80. On the fifty-year widowhood of Elizabeth Schuyler Hamilton, see Chernow, *Alexander Hamilton*, 724–27.

62. TJ to TMR, 18, 19, 28 Feb. 1807, Jefferson Papers, LC; TJ to MJR, 2 Feb., 6, 9, 12 Mar. 1807, *Family Letters*, 297–301; Gaines, *Thomas Mann Randolph*, 65–67; EWRC to Henry S. Randall, 13 Mar. 1856, Coolidge Correspondence, ViU.

63. MJR to TJ, 2 Jan. 1808, *Family Letters*, 318.

64. MJR to TJ, 16 Apr. 1802, *Family Letters*, 222–23.

65. TJ to Nathaniel Burwell, 14 Mar. 1818, *Writings*, 10:104.

On schools generally, see Turnbull, "Private Schools in Norfolk"; Meagher, *History of Education in Richmond*, 36–78; Knight, *Academy Movement in the South*, 23–24; Kierner, *Beyond the Household*, 155–61. On Jefferson's library, see Hayes, *Road to Monticello*, chaps. 37–38.

66. TJ to Nathaniel Burwell, 14 Mar. 1818, *Writings*, 10:104–5; EWR to TJ, 11 Mar., 14 Apr. 1808, *Family Letters*, 332–33, 341; MJR to Septimia Randolph, 30 July 1832, 5 Dec. 1835, Meikleham Papers, ViU; VJRT to Laura Carter Holloway, [ca. 1870], in Holloway, *Ladies of the White House*, 150–51; Cripe, *Thomas Jefferson and Music*, 36–40; Burstein, *Jefferson's Secrets*, 92–101; "Children's Reading," in *Thomas Jefferson Encyclopedia*, at http://wiki.monticello.org/mediawiki/index.php/Children's_Reading (21 Sept. 2009).

On Edgeworth's popularity in postrevolutionary America, see Kelley, *Learning to Stand and Speak*, 39, 163, 172, 179. See also "Children's Reading," in *Thomas Jefferson Encyclopedia*, at http://wiki.monticello.org/mediawiki/index.php/Children's_Reading (21 Sept. 2009).

67. Davidson, *Revolution and the Word*; Kerrison, "Novel as Teacher."

68. MJR to TJ, 24 Nov. 1808, Coolidge Collection; TJ to Ann C. Bankhead, 26 May

1811, *Papers: Retirement Series*, 3:633; Edgeworth, *Modern Griselda*; Gillooly, *Smiles of Discontent*, 5–7.

69. Birle and Francavilla, *Thomas Jefferson's Granddaughter*, 162–63.

70. Ibid., 2:47, 64; Smith, "Carysbrook Memoir," 43–44, ViU.

71. Birle and Francavilla, *Thomas Jefferson's Granddaughter*, 160; TJ to Anne Cary Randolph, 6 July 1805, 7 June 1807, *Family Letters*, 275, 307–8; TJ to EWR, 29 June 1807, *Family Letters*, 309–10; TJ to MJR, 5 Jan. 1808, *Family Letters*, 319–20; MJR to TJ, 16 Jan. 1808, *Family Letters*, 322; Anne Cary Randolph to TJ, 9 Nov. 1807, 22 Jan. 1808, *Family Letters*, 314, 323–24; EWR to TJ, 11 Nov. 1807, 11 Mar. 1808, *Family Letters*, 314, 332.

72. TMR to TJ, 6 Mar. 1802, Coolidge Collection; TJ to MJR, 11 July 1808, *Family Letters*, 347–48; MJR to TJ, 15 July 1808, *Family Letters*, 348–49.

73. MJR to TJ, 15 July 1808, *Family Letters*, 348–49.

74. MJR to TJ, 16 Jan. 1808, *Family Letters*, 322; TJ to MJR, 18 Oct. 1808, *Family Letters*, 351; TJ to TJR, 3 Jan. 1809, *Family Letters*, 376.

75. Gordon-Reed, *Hemingses of Monticello*, 601–3; Gordon-Reed, *Thomas Jefferson and Sally Hemings*, 14–15, 18–19, 196, 199; Dolley Madison to Anna Payne Cutts, 28 Aug. [1808], *DMDE*.

Chapter 5

1. MJR to TJ, 24 Feb. 1809, *Family Letters*, 384; TJ to Charles Bankhead, 27 Feb. 1809, Coolidge Collection; To the Inhabitants of Albemarle County, 3 Apr. 1809, *Papers: Retirement Series*, 1:102–3; Malone, *Sage of Monticello*, 3–17.

2. MJR to Margaret Bayard Smith, 10 Nov. 1828, Henley Smith Papers, LC; Busey, *Pictures of the City of Washington*, 311; EWRC to Nicholas Trist, 27 Sept. 1826, Coolidge Correspondence, ViU; MJR to EWRC, [1826], Martha Jefferson Randolph Letter, VHi.

3. Gaines, *Thomas Mann Randolph*, 58–59, 77; TMR to TJ, 6 Mar. 1802, Edgehill-Randolph Papers, ViU; Brooke Hunter, "Creative Destruction: The Forgotten Legacy of the Hessian Fly," in Matson, *Economy of Early America*, 242–44.

4. Randolph Memorandum Book, ca. 1790 (copy), ICJS; Gaines, *Thomas Mann Randolph*, 71–74, 110–11.

5. TMR to TJ, 6 Jan. 1809, Edgehill-Randolph Papers, ViU; TJ to TMR, 17 Jan. 1809, Jefferson Papers, LC.

6. Gaines, *Thomas Mann Randolph*, 77; TMR and MJR's Conveyance of Bedford County Land to Anne Moseley, 19 Feb. 1810, *FLDA*; *Papers: Retirement Series*, 2:239n.

7. Gaines, *Thomas Mann Randolph*, 73–75; Elizabeth Trist to Catharine Wistar Bache, 28 Dec. 1810, *FLDA*; TMR to Joseph C. Cabell, 23 Mar. 1810, Coolidge Correspondence, ViU.

8. Elizabeth Trist to Catharine Wistar Bache, 18 Oct. [1811], *FLDA*; Peter Minor to TMR, 11 July 1812, *Papers: Retirement Series*, 5:227–28. For industries and changing land use at Monticello, see "Monticello Explorer: Buildings & Features," at http://explorer.monticello.org/text/index.php?sect=plantation&sub=buildings (28 Sept. 2009); "Monticello Explorer: Farms & Fields," at http://explorer.monticello.org/text/index.php?sect=plantation&sub=farms (28 Sept. 2009); and Tyler-McGraw, *At the Falls*, 70–71, 86–90.

9. TJ to William McClure, 10 Sept 1811, *Papers: Retirement Series*, 4:143, 143n; TJ to James Ronaldson, 11 Oct. 1812, *Papers: Retirement Series*, 5:384; TJ to Philip Mazzei, 29 Dec. 1813, *Papers: Retirement Series*, 7:87–89. See also, "The Monticello Textile Factory," at http://www.monticello.org/plantation/work/textile.html (28 Sept. 2009).

10. Stanton, *Free Some Day*, 92–93; "The Memoirs of Madison Hemings," in Gordon-Reed, *Thomas Jefferson and Sally Hemings*, 248; Extract from TJ to James Maury, 16 June 1815, *FLDA*; EWR to MJR, 27 Sept. [1816], Coolidge Collection; TJ to Richard Fitzhugh, 27 May 1813, *Papers: Retirement Series*, 6:140; Sarah N. Randolph, "Mrs. Thomas Mann Randolph," in Wister and Irwin, *Worthy Women*, 44; "Textile Factory," in *Thomas Jefferson Encyclopedia*, at http://wiki.monticello.org/mediawiki/index.php/Textile_Factory (29 Sept. 2009).

11. Census of Inhabitants and Supplies at Monticello, 8 Nov. 1810, *Papers: Retirement Series*, 3:202; Elizabeth Trist to Catharine Wistar Bache, 24 Oct. 1810, *FLDA*; VJRT to Laura Carter Holloway, [ca. 1870], in Holloway, *Ladies of the White House*, 150.

12. Anna Maria Brodeau Thornton diary, 18–22 Sept. 1802, Thornton Papers, LC.

13. Ibid., 21, 25 Sept. 1806; EWR to TJ, 14 Apr. 1808, *Family Letters*, 341; McLaughlin, *Jefferson and Monticello*, 329–33.

14. "The House," at http://www.monticello.org/house/house_faq.html#style (30 Sept. 2009); Stevenson, *Life in Black and White*, 21–22; TJ to TMR, 31 Jan. 1809, Jefferson Papers, LC.

15. MJR to TJ, 2 Mar. 1809, *Family Letters*, 386–87.

16. Margaret Bayard Smith's Account of a Visit to Monticello, [29 July-2 Aug.] 1809, *Papers: Retirement Series*, 1:387–95; Allgor, "Margaret Bayard Smith's 1809 Journey to Monticello and Montpelier."

17. Gilmer, *Sketches of Some of the First Settlers of Upper Georgia*, 242; Ticknor, *Life, Letters, and Journals of George Ticknor*, 1:34–35; Stein, *Worlds of Thomas Jefferson*, 28, 61–62, 67–68, 71; McLaughlin, *Jefferson and Monticello*, 356–63.

18. Margaret Bayard Smith's Account of a Visit to Monticello, [29 July-2 Aug.] 1809, *Papers: Retirement Series*, 1:386–401; David Baillie Warden to TJ, 11 Dec. 1810, 5, 28 Mar. 1811, *Papers: Retirement Series*, 3:251, 427, 512; David Baillie Warden to MJR, [ca. 15 Jan., 14 Apr. 1811], *FLDA*; Harriet Randolph Hackley to Dolley Madison, 27 Apr. 1810, *DMDE*; Davis, *Abbe Correa in America*, 36–37, 40–41; Randolph, *Domestic Life*, 401.

19. Margaret Bayard Smith's Account of a Visit to Monticello, [29 July-2 Aug.] 1809, *Papers: Retirement Series*, 1:387–90, 393, 395; TJ to Edmund Bacon, 5 Dec. 1811, *Papers: Retirement Series*, 4:306; Anna Maria Brodeau Thornton diary, 18–22 Sept. 1802, 24 Sept, 1806, Thornton Papers, LC; Tinkcom, "Caviar along the Potomac," 101–2; Caldwell, *Tour through Part of Virginia*, 36–37; Ticknor, *Life, Letters, and Journals of George Ticknor*, 1:36.

20. Hamilton Wilcox Pierson, "Jefferson at Monticello: The Private Life of Thomas Jefferson," in Bear, *Jefferson at Monticello*, 83–84.

21. Margaret Bayard Smith's Account of a Visit to Monticello, [29 July-2 Aug.]

1809, *Papers: Retirement Series*, 1:387, 389, 391–92; Elizabeth Trist to Catharine Wistar Bache, 10 July 1809, *FLDA*.

22. Brodie, *Thomas Jefferson*, 429; Gordon-Reed, *Hemingses of Monticello*, 603–4.

23. Gaines, *Thomas Mann Randolph*, 68.

24. Morgan, *Slave Counterpoint*, 284–96; Census of Inhabitants and Supplies at Monticello, 8 Nov. 1810, *Papers: Retirement Series*, 3:202; Hamilton Wilcox Pierson, "Jefferson at Monticello: The Private Life of Thomas Jefferson," in Bear, *Jefferson at Monticello*, 83–85, 97–103; Stanton, "Other End of the Telescope," 139–52.

25. Kann, *Republic of Men*, chaps. 3–4.

26. TJ to TMR, 14 May 1809, *Papers: Retirement Series*, 2:393; TJ to John Wayles Eppes, 6 Sept. 1811, *Papers: Retirement Series*, 4:132–33; Elizabeth Trist to Catharine Wistar Bache, 18 Oct. [1811], *FLDA*; Gaines, *Thomas Mann Randolph*, 76. On the harvest feast, which was rooted in both English and African tradition, see Sobel, *World They Made Together*, 52–53.

27. "Reminiscences of Th. J. by MR, copied by Mary and Caryanne," [ca. 1826], Edgehill-Randolph Papers, ViU; Lovell, *Art in a Season of Revolution*, 54, 79, 81–82, 146–47; Stein, *Worlds of Thomas Jefferson*, 142.

28. MJR to Elizabeth Trist, 12 Nov. 1811, *FLDA*.

29. Malone, *Sage of Monticello*, 154; MJR to Elizabeth Trist, 12 Nov. 1811, Edgehill-Randolph Papers, ViU.

30. John Wayles Eppes to TJ, 10 July 1809, 10 Jan. 1810, *Papers: Retirement Series*, 1:336–37, 2:130; Francis Eppes to TJ, 2 Sept. 1811, *Papers: Retirement Series*, 4:115; EWRC to Henry S. Randall, 13 Mar. 1856, Coolidge Correspondence, ViU; Malone, *Sage of Monticello*, 285–86.

31. Margaret Bayard Smith's Account of a Visit to Monticello, [29 July-2 Aug.] 1809, *Papers: Retirement Series*, 1:387; Elizabeth Trist to Catharine Wistar Bache, 1 Feb. 1813, *FLDA*.

32. TJ to Elizabeth Trist, 10 May 1812, *Papers: Retirement Series*, 5:26; TJ to Tadeusz Kosciuszko, 28 June 1812, *Papers: Retirement Series*, 5:187; Elizabeth Trist to TJ, 7 June 1812, *Papers: Retirement Series*, 5:112; Elizabeth Trist to Catharine Wistar Bache, 3 May 1812, *FLDA*; TMR to Peachy R. Gilmer, 30 May 1812, Randolph Papers, LVa.

33. Gaines, *Thomas Mann Randolph*, 68–69, 83; James Madison to TJ, 10 Mar. 1813, *Papers: Retirement Series*, 5:684–85.

34. James Madison to TJ, 10 Mar. 1813, *Papers: Retirement Series*, 5:684; Gaines, *Thomas Mann Randolph*, 84–85; Laver, *Citizens More Than Soldiers*, 98–101.

35. For evidence of Martha's awareness of these attacks on her father's reputation, see MJR to Ann Cary Randolph Morris, 1 May 1832, Smith-Houston-Morris-Ogden Family Papers, APS.

36. Skelton, "High Army Leadership," 256–62.

37. Will of Thomas Mann Randolph, 16 Mar. 1813, Jefferson Papers, LC; Hickey, *War of 1812*, 302–3. On widows, see Lebsock, *Free Women of Petersburg*, 26–27, and Wood, *Masterful Women*, 9.

38. Gaines, *Thomas Mann Randolph*, 83–85; TJ to Elizabeth Trist, 10 May 1813,

Papers: Retirement Series, 6:110–11; TMR to Harry Heth, 12 June 1813, Heth Papers, ViU.

39. Olivia Taylor, "Charles Lewis and Anne Cary Randolph Bankhead," in Shackelford, *Collected Papers*, 71–73; Hamilton Wilcox Pierson, "Jefferson at Monticello: The Private Life of Thomas Jefferson," in Bear, *Jefferson at Monticello*, 94–96; Anne Cary Randolph Bankhead to MJR, 2 Feb. 1810, Trist Papers, NcU; Archibald Robertson to TJ, 16 May 1812, *Papers: Retirement Series*, 5:51; Elizabeth Trist to Catharine Wistar Bache, 28 Dec. 1810, 7 May 1811, 22 Aug. 1814, *FLDA*; Household Accounts Maintained by Anne Cary Randolph, 1805–1808, at http://memory.loc.gov/ammem/collections/ jefferson_papers/ser7v011.html (6 Oct. 2009).

40. Dolley Madison to Hannah Nicholson Gallatin, 30 Aug. 1813, *DMDE*; TMR to James Madison, 11 Dec. 1813, Madison Papers, LC; TMR to Joseph C. Cabell, 20 July 1820, Randolph Papers, NcD.

41. Gaines, *Thomas Mann Randolph*, 88–91; Hickey, *War of 1812*, 145–46; TMR to James Madison, 11 Dec. 1813, Madison Papers, LC.

42. Gaines, *Thomas Mann Randolph*, 91–93; TJ to TMR, 14 Nov. 1813, and to Elizabeth Trist, 1 Feb. 1814, Coolidge Collection; TJ to EWR, 26 Nov. 1813, *Family Letters*, 404; Elizabeth Trist to Catharine Wistar Bache, 13 Dec. 1813, *FLDA*.

43. Dolley Madison to Hannah Nicholson Gallatin, 30 Aug. 1813, *DMDE*; Allgor, *Perfect Union*, 220–26.

44. TMR to James Madison, 11 Dec. 1813, Madison Papers, LC; TMR to Joseph C. Cabell, 29 Dec. 1813, Randolph Papers, NcD; Hickey, *War of 1812*, 122–23, 247–49.

45. TMR to James Madison, 11 Dec. 1813, Madison Papers, LC; Laver, *Citizens More Than Soldiers*, 128–43; Purcell, *Sealed with Blood*; Wyatt-Brown, *Southern Honor*, 70, 78, 191–92. For a telling confrontation between tax men and militia, see Slaughter, *Whiskey Rebellion*, 176–89.

46. TMR to Joseph C. Cabell, 29 Dec. 1813, Randolph Papers, NcD; TJ to Elizabeth Trist, 1 Feb. 1814, Coolidge Collection.

47. TMR to Joseph C. Cabell, 29 Dec. 1813, 8 Jan. 1814, Randolph Papers, NcD.

48. Gaines, *Thomas Mann Randolph*, 95; TJ to Elizabeth Trist, 1 Feb., 10 June 1814, Coolidge Collection; TMR to Harry Heth, 17 Apr. 1814, Heth Papers, ViU.

49. J. Macrae to TMR, 8 Mar. 1814, *FLDA*; Skelton, "High Army Leadership," 265, 270–71.

50. Gaines, *Thomas Mann Randolph*, 96–100; Hickey, *War of 1812*, chaps. 8–11.

51. Gaines, *Thomas Mann Randolph*, 87, 99–100; David Campbell to TMR, 22 Nov. 1813, and Peter Carr to TMR, [31 Aug. 1814], Coolidge Collection; Samuel Mordecai to Rachel Mordecai, 11 Sept. 1814, Mordecai Letter, VHi.

52. Elizabeth Trist to Catharine Wistar Bache, 22 Aug. 1814, *FLDA*; MJR to Benjamin Franklin Randolph, 27 Jan. [1836?], Smith Papers, ViU; Lewis, *Pursuit of Happiness*, chap. 2.

53. MJR to Elizabeth Trist, 31 May 1815, Elizabeth House Trist Papers, VHi; Kierner, "'Dark and Dense Cloud Perpetually Lowering over Us,'" 198–99.

54. McCoy, *Elusive Republic*, 227–33; Zagarri, *Revolutionary Backlash*, 98–102.

55. MJR to Elizabeth Trist, 31 May 1815, Elizabeth House Trist Papers, VHi; Kierner, *Scandal at Bizarre*, 136–43.

56. Gaines, *Thomas Mann Randolph*, 101–4; TMR to Thomas Taylor, 2 Jan., 30 Dec. 1815, 23 Jan., 22 Nov. 1816, Thomas Mann Randolph Letters, VHi; [TMR] to [Ann Cary Randolph Morris], 10 Apr. 1817, Smith-Houston-Morris-Ogden Family Papers, APS; TMR's Bill of Sale, 9 Oct. 1818, *FLDA*.

57. TJ to George Jefferson, 31 Oct. 1809, *Papers: Retirement Series*, 1:634; John Wood to TJ, 21 Jan. 1810, *Papers: Retirement Series*, 2:171; TJ to TJR, 14 Mar. 1810, *Papers: Retirement Series*, 2:295; TJ to Caspar Wistar, 11 Oct. 1811, *Papers: Retirement Series*, 4:191; TJ to TMR, 14 Nov. 1813, Coolidge Collection; Gaines, *Thomas Mann Randolph*, 102–3.

58. TJ to Elizabeth Trist, 1 Feb. 1814, Coolidge Collection; Description of Conversations about Jane H. Nicholas, [1813 or 1814?], *FLDA*; George Green Shackelford, "Jane Hollins Nicholas and Thomas Jefferson Randolph," in Shackelford, *Collected Papers*, 77.

59. TJR to Wilson C. Nicholas, 4 Feb. 1815, Edgehill-Randolph Papers, ViU; TJ to TJR, 31 Mar. 1815, *Family Letters*, 409.

60. Vance, "Thomas Jefferson Randolph," 41–46; George Green Shackelford, "Jane Hollins Nicholas and Thomas Jefferson Randolph," in Shackelford, *Collected Papers*, 77, 86; MJR to Elizabeth Trist, 31 May 1815, Elizabeth House Trist Papers, VHi; Margaret Nicholas to Jane Randolph, 19 Mar. 1818, Edgehill-Randolph Papers, ViU; Lease from TJ to TJR, [Jan. 1818], Coolidge Collection.

61. MJR to VJR, 24 Sept. 1817, Trist Papers, NcU. For a pioneering assessment of the economic value of women's domestic and non-waged work, see Boydston, *Home and Work*.

62. Malone, *Sage of Monticello*, 14–15, 290–93; Gordon-Reed, *Hemingses of Monticello*, 618–19; EWR to MJR, 27 Sept. [1816], [10 Nov. 1816], Coolidge Collection; EWR to MJR, 14 Apr. 1818, Coolidge Correspondence, ViU; TJ to MJR, 31 Aug. 1817, *Family Letters*, 419; [EWRC,] "Closing Scenes," Bulfinch Papers, Boston Athenaeum; George Green Shackelford, "Unmarried Children of Martha Jefferson Randolph and Thomas Mann Randolph, Jr.," in Shackelford, *Collected Papers*, 152.

63. MJR to Elizabeth Trist, 31 May 1815, Elizabeth House Trist Papers, VHi; TJ to John Bankhead, 28 Oct. 1815, Edgehill-Randolph Papers, ViU; MJR to TJ, 20 Nov. 1816, *Family Letters*, 416–17.

64. Malone, *Sage of Monticello*, 157–60; Gaines, *Thomas Mann Randolph*, 106–7; Bardaglio, *Reconstructing the Household*, chaps. 1–2; Wyatt-Brown, *Southern Honor*; Bloch, "American Revolution, Wife Beating, and the Emergent Value of Privacy," 225–27, 238, 245–49.

65. MJR to Elizabeth Trist, 31 May 1815, Elizabeth House Trist Papers, VHi.

66. Dolley Madison to MJR, 9 Jan. 1814, *DMDE*; Daniels, *Randolphs of Virginia*, 196–202, 221–24; George Jefferson to TJ, 13 Nov. 1809, *Papers: Retirement Series*, 1:669–70.

67. EWR to MJR, [2 Mar. 1814], 30 Mar. [1814], 24 Apr. 1814, Coolidge Correspondence, ViU.

68. Ibid., 22 Jan., 7 Feb. 1816, 7–17 Feb. 1816, 28 Feb. [1816].

69. Ibid., 14–26 Mar. 1816, [ca. 26 Mar. 1816], [Apr. 1816], 1 May 1816; EWR to TJ, 19 Mar. 1816, *Family Letters*, 413.

70. EWR to MJR, 17 Feb. [1816], Coolidge Correspondence, ViU.

71. Ibid.; Jabour, *Scarlett's Sisters*, 116–25.

72. VJR to MJR, 6 Sept. 1817; VJR to [Jane Randolph], 16 Sept. 1817; Cornelia Randolph to Virginia Randolph and Mary Elizabeth Randolph, 24 Sept. 1817; and MJR to VJR, 24 Sept. 1817, all in Trist Papers, NcU; Sarah E. Nicholas to Jane Randolph, 28 Nov. 1817, Edgehill-Randolph Papers, ViU; Lewis, *Ladies and Gentlemen on Display*, 175–86.

73. Sarah E. Nicholas to Jane Randolph, 26 Dec. 1817, and Margaret Nicholas to Jane Randolph, 8 Jan. 1818, Edgehill-Randolph Papers, ViU; EWR to MJR, 28 Jan. 1818, Coolidge Correspondence, ViU; Cornelia Randolph to VJR, 14, 19 Dec. 1817, 28 Jan. 1818, Trist Papers, NcU. Although there is no evidence of anti-Semitism in the Jefferson-Randolph family circle, a later attempt by a Jewish man to court one of Martha's daughters was coolly received; see VJRT to NPT, 3 Feb. 1835, and NPT to VJRT, 14 Mar. 1835, Trist Papers, NcU. On the Mordecai family in Richmond, see Bingham, *Mordecai*, esp. chaps. 5–6.

74. NPT to MJR, 18, 20 Sept. 1818, and MJR to NPT, [19 Sept. 1818], Trist Papers, NcU; Willard Carl Klunder, "Trist, Nicholas Philip," *ANB*.

Chapter 6

1. Elizabeth Trist to NPT, 3 Feb. 1819, Trist Papers, LC; Elizabeth Trist to NPT, 24 Feb., 9 Mar. 1819, Trist Papers, NcU; Hetty Carr to Dabney S. Carr, 5 Feb. 1819, Carr-Cary Papers, ViU. See also Vance, "Thomas Jefferson Randolph," 61–75. Bankhead's letter to Jane Randolph is not extant.

2. Elizabeth Trist to NPT, 3 Feb. 1819, and Cornelia Randolph to VJR, 11 Aug. 1819, Trist Papers, LC; Hetty Carr to Dabney S. Carr, 5 Feb. 1819; John A. Carr to Dabney S. Carr, 22 Feb. 1819; and M. Gilmer to Virginia Randolph Cary, 11 Mar. 1819, Carr-Cary Papers, ViU; Peggy Nicholas to Jane Randolph, 18 Mar. 1819, Edgehill-Randolph Papers, ViU. On the Bankheads' marriage generally, see Cockerham, Keeling, and Parker, "Seeking Refuge at Monticello," 34–42, and Ann Cary Randolph Bankhead diary, 26 Nov. 1820–27 Nov. 1825, *FLDA*.

3. TMR to Edmund Bacon, 9 May 1819, *FLDA*; EWR to MJR, 28 July 1819, Coolidge Correspondence, ViU; Elizabeth Trist to NPT, 15 Sept. 1819, Trist Papers, LC; EWR to Dolley Madison, 24 Apr. [1820], *DMDE*; Elizabeth Trist to NPT, 31 July 1820, Trist Papers, NcU.

4. MJR to Ann Cary Randolph Morris, 28 Dec. 1821, Smith-Houston-Morris-Ogden Family Papers, APS; VJR to NPT, 21 Nov. 1821, 31 Oct., 12 Nov. 1822, 7 Mar. 1824, Trist Papers, LC; Elizabeth Trist to NPT, 19 Aug. 1822, Papers of the Trist, Burke, and Randolph Families, ViU. On Jefferson's headaches, see Burstein, *Jefferson's Secrets*, 31; Schneeberg, "Medical History of Thomas Jefferson," 119–20.

5. MJR to VJR, 10 Jan. 1822, and to Virginia Randolph Cary, 29 Dec. 1822, Trist Papers, NcU. See also Chew, "Inhabiting the Great Man's House," 241; email from Elizabeth Chew, curator at Monticello, 31 Aug. 2010, in author's possession.

6. TMR, "Song dreamed at day break," 1 Apr. 1818, *FLDA*; Chew, "Inhabiting the Great Man's House," 231–32.

7. Cornelia Randolph to VJR, 1 Dec. 1820, Trist Papers, NcU; EWR to MJR, 18 July

1819; Cornelia Randolph to EWR, 24 Nov. 1825; and VJRT to EWRC, 3 Sept. 1825, Coolidge Correspondence, ViU; VJR to NPT, 4 Feb. 1823, Trist Papers, LC; Chew, "Inhabiting the Great Man's House," 229–33.

8. Viard, *Le Cuisinier Royal*; DeBures Frères to TJ, 11 Sept. 1819, Coolidge Collection.

9. VJR to NPT, 12 Nov. 1822, 4 Feb. 1823, Trist Papers, LC; MJR to Virginia Randolph Cary, 29 July 1822, Trist Papers, NcU.

10. TJ to TMR, 8 Oct. 1820, 30 July 1821, Jefferson Papers, LC; VJRT to EWRC, 3 Sept. 1825, and Cornelia Randolph to EWRC, 23 Feb. 1826, Coolidge Correspondence, ViU; MJR to Ann Cary Randolph Morris, 22 Mar. 1827, Smith-Houston-Morris-Ogden Family Papers, APS.

11. Benjamin Vaughan to MJR, 23 June 1819, Coolidge Collection; MJR to Ann Cary Randolph Morris, 8 Aug. 1825, Smith-Houston-Morris-Ogden Family Papers, APS; James W. Wallace to MJR, 14 Oct. 1825, Jefferson Papers, LC.

12. Margaret Bayard Smith's Account of a Visit to Monticello, [29 July-2 Aug.] 1809, *Papers: Retirement Series*, 1:387–90, 393, 395; Anonymous Description of a Visit to Monticello, [post-1819], Randolph-Meikleham Family Papers, ViU.

13. Sloan, *Principle and Interest*, 11, 218–20; MJR to TJ, 7 Aug. 1819, *Family Letters*, 430; EWR to MJR, 11, 24 Aug. 1819, Coolidge Correspondence, ViU.

14. Elizabeth Trist to NPT, 25 Aug., 15 Sept. 1819, 15 June 1820, Trist Papers, LC. See also Daniel S. Dupre, "The Panic of 1819 and the Political Economy of Sectionalism," in Matson, *Economy of Early America*, 263–93.

15. Peggy Nicholas to Jane Randolph, 20 May 1819, Edgehill-Randolph Papers, ViU; Elizabeth Trist to NPT, 15 June 1820, 21 Jan. 1823, Trist Papers, LC; MJR to Nicholas Trist, 7 Mar. 1822, Trist Papers, NcU; MJR to Ann Cary Randolph Morris, 27 May 1822, Smith-Houston-Morris-Ogden Family Papers, APS; TMR to Edmund Bacon, 9 May 1819, and TMR's receipt to Edmund Bacon, 10 May 1819, *FLDA*; Henry Remsen to TJ, 25 Nov. 1823, Coolidge Collection.

16. Gaines, *Thomas Mann Randolph*, 112–55.

17. EWR to Dolley Madison, 17 Jan. 1820, *DMDE*; TMR to Joseph C. Cabell, 20 July 1820, Randolph Papers, NcD; Hamilton Wilcox Pierson, "Jefferson at Monticello: The Private Life of Thomas Jefferson," in Bear, *Jefferson at Monticello*, 91; Gaines, *Thomas Mann Randolph*, 116–17, 122; Searle, *Virginia's Executive Mansion*, 13–26.

18. Elizabeth Trist to NPT, 2 Jan. 1820, Trist Papers, NcU; *Richmond Enquirer*, 19 Dec. 1820; Gaines, *Thomas Mann Randolph*, 124–26.

19. Elizabeth Trist to NPT, 2 Jan. 1820, Trist Papers, NcU; Searle, *Virginia's Executive Mansion*, 26; Gaines, *Thomas Mann Randolph*, 127–32.

20. MJR to Ann Cary Randolph Morris, 4 Dec. 1820, Smith-Houston-Morris-Ogden Family Papers, APS; MJR to VJR, 13 Dec. 1820, Trist Papers, NcU; *Richmond Enquirer*, 7, 14, 30 Dec. 1820.

21. David Campbell to John Campbell, 22 Jan. 1821, Campbell Family Papers, NcD.

22. MJR to Ann Cary Randolph Morris, 28 Dec. 1821, Smith-Houston-Morris-Ogden Family Papers, APS; MJR to NPT, 8 Jan., 7 Mar. 1822, Trist Papers, NcU.

23. Elizabeth Trist to NPT, 9 Mar. 1819, and MJR to VJR, 14 Feb. 1822, Trist Papers, NcU; MJR to Ann Cary Randolph Morris, 28 Dec. 1821, Smith-Houston-Morris-Ogden Family Papers, APS; VJR to NPT, 28 Jan., 18 Feb. 1822, 7 Mar. 1823, Trist Papers,

LC; Peggy Nicholas to Jane Randolph, 14 Mar. 1822, Edgehill-Randolph Papers, ViU; EWR to MJR, 29 Mar., 9 Apr. 1819, 25 Apr. [1819], 31 May 1820, 14–15 Dec. 1821, 30 Dec. [1821], 9 Mar. [1822], 3 Apr. 1822, Coolidge Correspondence, ViU; Wilson J. Cary to Virginia Randolph Cary, 16 Jan. 1822, Carr-Cary Papers, ViU; Gaines, *Thomas Mann Randolph*, 132; Fitzpatrick, *Autobiography of Martin Van Buren*, 2:182–83.

24. VJR to NPT, 13 May 1823, Trist Papers, LC; NPT to [MJR], [July 1821]; MJR to NPT, 1 Sept. 1822; and NPT to VJR, 20 Sept. 1822, 18 Mar. 1823, Trist Papers, NcU; Wilson Miles Cary to Virginia Randolph Cary, Jan. 1825, Carr-Cary Papers, ViU; VJRT to EWRC, 27 June 1825, and MJR to ERWC, 13 Oct. 1825, Coolidge Correspondence, ViU; MJR to Ann Cary Randolph Morris, 8 Aug. 1825, Smith-Houston-Morris-Ogden Family Papers, APS; Ohrt, *Defiant Peacemaker*, 43–45; Walter Muir Whitehead, "Eleanora Wayles Randolph and Joseph Coolidge, Jr.," in Shackelford, *Collected Papers*, 89–91.

25. MJR to EWRC, 13 Oct. 1825, Coolidge Correspondence, ViU.

26. Gordon-Reed, *Hemingses of Monticello*, 115, 285, 597–98, 601, 648–49, 657.

27. Elizabeth Trist to NPT, 23 Dec. 1822, Trist Papers, LC.

28. TMR to NPT, 27 July 1821, Trist Papers, LC; TMR to NPT, 5 June 1820, 6 May 1821; NPT to TMR, 14 May 1821; and MJR to NPT, 7 Mar., 1 Sept. 1822, Trist Papers, NcU; Edmund Bacon to TJ, 7 Feb. 1826, Coolidge Collection.

29. MJR to Elizabeth Trist, 31 May 1815, Elizabeth House Trist Papers, VHi; Hamilton Wilcox Pierson, "Jefferson at Monticello: The Private Life of Thomas Jefferson," in Bear, *Jefferson at Monticello*, 90, 94.

I do not believe that either Martha or Tom purposefully destroyed the letters they exchanged. The fact that Martha's life is so well documented even without these letters is mostly attributable to her connection to Jefferson, who self-consciously preserved all his papers for posterity. Because it was common for people not to preserve family letters—and women's letters especially—writing biographies of early American women who lacked connections to famous men who were also prolific correspondents is difficult (and rarely done).

30. VJR to NPT, 9 Jan. 1824, and MJR to VJR, 27 Jan. 1822, Trist Papers, NcU; Mary Jefferson Randolph to EWRC, 11–13 Sept. 1825, Coolidge Correspondence, ViU. Jefferson erroneously predicted that Unitarianism, or the rationalist belief in the "pure and simple unity of the creator of the universe," would soon become "the general religion of the United States" (TJ to James Smith, 8 Dec. 1822, Jefferson Papers, LC). On interest in mummies and Egypt generally, which peaked in later decades, see Trafton, *Egypt Land*.

31. Gaines, *Thomas Mann Randolph*, 146–49, 155; TMR to Henry Remsen, 10 Jan. 1824, Thomas Mann Randolph Letters, VHi; MJR to NPT, [4 Apr. 1824], Trist Papers, NcU; Deed of trust between TMR and TJR, 1 Apr. 1824, *FLDA*.

32. Burstein, *Jefferson's Secrets*, 70–72. For a larger intergenerational context, see Appleby, *Inheriting the Revolution*, 3–11, 88–89.

33. Gaines, *Thomas Mann Randolph*, 97, 99; Kennedy, *Memoirs of the Life of William Wirt*, 1:337; TJR memoirs, 1874, Edgehill-Randolph Papers, ViU, 304.

34. TJR to Dabney S. Carr, 11 July 1826, Carr-Cary Papers, ViU; Hamilton Wilcox Pierson, "Jefferson at Monticello: The Private Life of Thomas Jefferson," in Bear,

Jefferson at Monticello, 94, 135. On caning, see Greenberg, *Honor and Slavery*, 123. Although some historians cite this statement about Tom's violent temper as evidence of his abusiveness toward his son (and possibly toward Martha), Jeff was actually describing his father's supposed hostility toward Jefferson during the last year of the latter's life.

35. TJR to Jane Randolph, 14 Feb. 1825, Edgehill-Randolph Papers, ViU; MJR to EWRC, 1 Sept. 1825, and VJRT to EWRC, 3 Sept. 1825, Coolidge Correspondence, ViU; VJRT to NPT, 4 Sept. 1825, Trist Papers, NcU; MJR to Ann Cary Randolph Morris, 8 Aug. 1825, 5 Apr. 1826, Smith-Houston-Morris-Ogden Family Papers, APS; Shade, *Democratizing the Old Dominion*, 50–59.

36. TMR to Septimia Randolph, 6 Aug. 1827, Meikleham Papers, ViU.

37. Gaines, *Thomas Mann Randolph*, 149; Horace Holley to his brother, 6 Sept. 1824, *University of Virginia Alumni Bulletin*, 3rd ser., no. 2, 415–17 (photocopy in ICJS Special Collections); Smith, "Carysbrook Memoir," 69–75, ViU; *Richmond Enquirer*, 16 Nov. 1824. See also Purcell, *Sealed with Blood*, chap. 5. Tom's membership in the state legislature in 1824 does not explain his absence. That body was in recess when Lafayette arrived and would not reconvene until more than three weeks after he visited Monticello.

38. Smith, "Carysbrook Memoir," 70–71, ViU; TJR memoirs, 1874, Edgehill-Randolph Papers, ViU; Peter Fossett's account of Lafayette's visit, 1898, in *Thomas Jefferson Encyclopedia*, at http://wiki.monticello.org/mediawiki/index.php/Lafayette%27s_Visit_to_Monticello_%281824%29#Peter_Fossett_.07UNIQ48c9289f2e2f2616-nowiki-00000013-QINU5.07UNIQ48c9289f2e2f2616-nowiki-00000014-QINU (10 Nov. 2009).

39. Smith, "Carysbrook Memoir," 74–75, ViU; James Madison to Dolley Madison, 5 Nov. 1824, *DMDE*; Levasseur, *Lafayette in America*, 237.

40. TJ to Lafayette, 4 Nov. 1823, *Writings*, 10:282; Smith, "Carysbrook Memoir," 72–74, ViU; Morris, *Fanny Wright*, 1–3, 80–85; Burstein, *Jefferson's Secrets*, 140–45.

41. Frances Wright to MJR, 4 Dec. 1824, Jefferson Papers, LC; EWRC to MJR, 21 July 1829, 6 June 1830, Coolidge Correspondence, ViU; Morris, *Fanny Wright*, 171–75.

42. Gaines, *Thomas Mann Randolph*, 155–60; TJR to Jane Randolph, 14 Feb. 1825, Edgehill-Randolph Papers, ViU; TMR to Francis Walker Gilmer, 21 June, 12 July 1825, Gilmer Correspondence, ViU; MJR to Ann Cary Randolph Morris, 8 Aug. 1825, Smith-Houston-Morris-Ogden Family Papers, APS; Cornelia Randolph to EWRC, Coolidge Correspondence, ViU.

43. MJR to Ann Cary Randolph Morris, 8 Aug. 1825, Smith-Houston-Morris-Ogden Family Papers, APS; MJR to EWRC, 1 Sept. 1825, Coolidge Correspondence, ViU; Gaines, *Thomas Mann Randolph*, 162.

44. EWRC to Henry S. Randall, 13, 27 Mar. 1856, and MJR to EWRC, [30 June 1828], Coolidge Correspondence, ViU; TMR to Septimia Randolph, 6 Aug. 1827, Meikleham Papers, ViU.

45. EWRC to Henry S. Randall, 27 Mar. 1856, Coolidge Correspondence, ViU; TJR memoirs, 1874, Edgehill-Randolph Papers, ViU; George Green Shackelford, "Septimia Anne Randolph and David Scott Meikleham," 133, and Olivia Taylor, "Charles Lewis and Anne Cary Randolph Bankhead," 75, in Shackelford, *Collected Papers*.

46. TJ to TMR, 5 June 1825, 8 Jan. 1826, Jefferson Papers, LC.

47. *Richmond Enquirer*, 22 Dec. 1822.

48. MJR to EWRC, 2 Aug. 1825, Coolidge Correspondence, ViU.

49. Ibid.; MJR to Ann Cary Randolph Morris, 22 Jan. 1826, Smith-Houston-Morris-Ogden Family Papers, APS; Gordon-Reed, *Hemingses of Monticello*, 519, 621–23; Gaines, *Thomas Mann Randolph*, 161–62.

50. MJR to Ann Cary Randolph Morris, 22 Jan. 1826, Smith-Houston-Morris-Ogden Family Papers, APS; Gordon-Reed, *Hemingses of Monticello*, 611, 657.

51. MJR to Ann Cary Randolph Morris, 22 Jan. 1826, Smith-Houston-Morris-Ogden Family Papers, APS.

52. MJR to EWRC, 5 Apr. 1826, Coolidge Correspondence, ViU; Gaines, *Thomas Mann Randolph*, 161–62.

53. MJR to Ann Cary Randolph Morris, 22 Jan. 1826, Smith-Houston-Morris-Ogden Family Papers, APS.

54. Malone, *Sage of Monticello*, 473–77; MJR to EWRC, 5 Apr. 1826, Coolidge Correspondence, ViU.

55. Vance, "Thomas Jefferson Randolph," 94–98.

56. Cornelia Randolph to EWRC, 23 Feb. 1826; MJR to Joseph Coolidge, 1 Mar. 1826; and MJR to EWRC, 5 Apr. 1826, Coolidge Correspondence, ViU; Hetty Carr to Dabney S. Carr, 13 Mar. 1826, Carr-Cary Papers, ViU; Malone, *Sage of Monticello*, 478–81.

57. Jane Randolph to Cary Anne Smith, 27 June 1826, Edgehill-Randolph Papers, ViU.

58. Ann Cary Randolph Bankhead diary, 26 Nov. 1820–27 Nov. 1825, *FLDA*. The diary includes only one mildly critical reference to Charles Bankhead. Anne described her husband as having been "far from prudent" on Christmas 1823, which probably meant that he was drunk.

59. Ibid.; "Ann Cary Randolph Bankhead," in *Thomas Jefferson Encyclopedia* at http://wiki.monticello.org/mediawiki/index.php/Ann_Cary_Randolph_Bankhead (12 Nov. 2009); MJR to Ann Cary Randolph Morris, 22 Jan. 1826, Smith-Houston-Morris-Ogden Family Papers, APS; [Cornelia Randolph] to Mary Randolph, 11 Feb. 1826, Edgehill-Randolph Papers, ViU; TJ to TJR, 11 Feb. 1826, *Family Letters*, 470; Cornelia Randolph to EWRC, 23 Feb. 1826, Coolidge Correspondence, ViU; Radbill, *Autobiographical Ana of Robley Dunglison*, 34.

60. Cornelia Randolph to EWRC, 23 Feb. 1826, and MJR to Joseph Coolidge, 1 Mar. 1826, Coolidge Correspondence, ViU; Jane Margaret Carr to Dabney S. Carr, 27 Feb. 1826, Edgehill-Randolph Papers, ViU.

61. Cornelia Randolph to EWRC, 23 Feb. 1826, and MJR to Joseph Coolidge, 1 Mar. 1826, Coolidge Correspondence, ViU; TJ to Anne Cary Randolph, 16 Feb., 22 Mar. 1808, *Family Letters*, 328, 337; Lewis, *Genealogy of the Lewis Family*, 35; Gordon-Reed, *Hemingses of Monticello*, 638; Stanton, *Free Some Day*, 133–35, 143–44, and Hughes family tree on back endpaper.

62. Joseph Coolidge to MJR, 8 Feb. 1826; Cornelia Randolph to EWRC, 23 Feb. 1826; EWRC to MJR, 23 Mar. 1826; TJR to Jane Randolph, 14 Apr. 1826; and EWRC to VJRT, 9–10 May 1826, all in Coolidge Correspondence, ViU; Malone, *Sage of Monticello*, 480–82.

63. EWRC to VJRT, 9–10, 29 May 1826, and Mary Randolph to EWRC, 15 May 1826, Coolidge Correspondence, ViU.

64. Jefferson's last will and testament, 16 Mar. 1826, *FLDA*; Gaines, *Thomas Mann Randolph*, 164; TJR to Henry S. Randall, [ca.1856], and Dr. Dunglison's memoranda, in Randall, *Life of Thomas Jefferson*, 3:543, 547.

65. Codicil to Jefferson's last will and testament, 17 Mar. 1826, *FLDA*.

66. TJR to Henry S. Randall, [ca.1856]; Dr. Dunglison's memoranda; and Henry Lee to NPT, 20 July 1826, in Randall, *Life of Thomas Jefferson*, 3:543, 547, 663; Peterson, *Visitors to Monticello*, 108–10; Burstein, *Jefferson's Secrets*, 271–74; TJ to Roger C. Weightman, 24 June 1826, *Writings*, 10:390–92; TJ to George Stevenson, 25 June 1826 (transcription), Page Papers, VHi.

67. TJR to Henry S. Randall, [ca.1856], in Randall, *Life of Thomas Jefferson*, 3:543; Peterson, *Visitors to Monticello*, 109–10; Gordon-Reed, *Hemingses of Monticello*, 650–52; Jane Randolph to Cary Anne Smith, 27 June 1826, Edgehill-Randolph Papers, ViU; VJRT to Cornelia Randolph, 30 June 1826, Coolidge Correspondence, ViU.

68. VJRT to Cornelia Randolph, 30 June 1826; NPT to Joseph Coolidge, 4 July 1826; and Joseph Coolidge to NPT, [5 July 1826], Coolidge Correspondence, ViU.

69. Gordon-Reed, *Hemingses of Monticello*, 657–60; will of MJR, 18 Apr. [1834], *FLDA*.

70. Randall, *Life of Thomas Jefferson*, 3:545; "Deathbed Adieu," in Burstein and Onuf, *Letters from the Head and Heart*, 87; Lewis, *Pursuit of Happiness*, 69–70, 81.

71. Malone, *Sage of Monticello*, 464–68, 498; TJR to Henry S. Randall, [ca.1856], in Randall, *Life of Thomas Jefferson*, 3:543; Louise McIntyre to Jane Margaret Carr, 26 July 1826, Carr-Cary Papers, ViU; Henry H. Worthington to Reuben B. Hicks, 5 July 1826, and Andrew K. Smith's Account of Thomas Jefferson's Funeral, 1875, *FLDA*.

72. TMR to NPT, 6 July 1826, Trist Papers, LC; TJR to Dabney S. Carr, 11 July 1826, Carr-Cary Papers, ViU; Gaines, *Thomas Mann Randolph*, 166.

73. Peterson, *Jefferson Image in the American Mind*, 3–5; Madison to TJR, 14 July 1826, Madison Papers, LC; Edward Everett to MJR, and Citizens of Germantown to MJR, 20 July 1826, Edgehill-Randolph Papers, ViU; James Monroe to MJR, 16 July 1826; Lydia Sigourney to MJR, Aug. 1826; "Ode: Sur La Mort De Thomas Jefferson," [1826]; and A. H. Hubbard to MJR, 17 July 1826, Jefferson Papers, LC. On Hubbard, see Caulkins, *History of Norwich*, 613.

74. MJR to EWRC, [Sept. 1826?], Martha Jefferson Randolph Letter, VHi; Vance, "Thomas Jefferson Randolph," 103–6; Malone, *Sage of Monticello*, 511–12.

75. MJR to EWRC, [Sept. 1826?], Martha Jefferson Randolph Letter, VHi; MJR to Ann Cary Randolph Morris, 4 Dec. 1826, Smith-Houston-Morris-Ogden Family Papers, APS.

76. MJR to Ann Cary Randolph Morris, 4 Dec. 1826, Smith-Houston-Morris-Ogden Family Papers, APS; Sarah Elizabeth Nicholas to Jane Randolph, 26 Sept. 1826, Edgehill-Randolph Papers, ViU; MJR to VJRT, 30 Oct. 1826, Trist Papers, NcU; Cornelia Randolph to EWRC, 11 Sept. 1826; Mary Randolph to EWRC, 1 Oct. 1826; and MJR to EWRC, 2 May 1828, Coolidge Correspondence, ViU.

77. Cornelia Randolph to EWRC, 11 Sept. 1826, and Mary Randolph to EWRC,

1, 30 Oct. 1826, Coolidge Correspondence, ViU; MJR to TJR, 2 Mar. 1827, Edgehill-Randolph Papers, ViU.

Chapter 7

1. MJR to Ann Cary Randolph Morris, 16 May 1827, Smith-Houston-Morris-Ogden Family Papers, APS.

2. For Jefferson's objections to inherited or unmerited privilege, see, for instance, his famous letter to John Adams, 28 Oct. 1813, *Writings*, 9:425–29. On use of patronage in his administration, see Cunningham, *Jeffersonian Republicans in Power*, 33–36, 69–70.

3. Mary Randolph to EWRC, 25 Jan., 11 June, 29 July 1827, and Cornelia Randolph to EWRC, 18 May 1827, Coolidge Correspondence, ViU; Gaines, *Thomas Mann Randolph*, 166–67; Ohrt, *Defiant Peacemaker*, 52–53; George Green Shackelford, "Unmarried Children of Martha Jefferson Randolph and Thomas Mann Randolph, Jr.," in Shackelford, *Collected Papers*, 148.

4. EWRC to MJR, 20 Nov. 1825, Coolidge Correspondence, ViU; Cornelia Randolph to VJRT, 30 Mar. 1828, Trist Papers, NcU; MJR to Ann Cary Randolph Morris, 24 Jan. 1828, Smith-Houston-Morris-Ogden Family Papers, APS.

5. EWRC to Nicholas Trist, 26 Sept. 1826, Coolidge Correspondence, ViU; MJR to EWRC, [1826], Martha Jefferson Randolph Letter, VHi.

6. MJR to Margaret Bayard Smith, 10 Nov. 1828, Henley Smith Papers, LC. Scholars have noted that Martha and her children carefully constructed what one historian has called the "Jefferson Family Story," which emphasized the happiness of his domestic circle and denied his relationship with Sally Hemings. A lesser-known aspect of that narrative involved his descendants' efforts to absolve him of blame for his family's financial problems. See Rhys Isaac, "Monticello Stories Old and New," 114–25, and Jan Ellen Lewis, "The White Jeffersons," 127–57, both in Lewis and Onuf, *Sally Hemings and Thomas Jefferson*; Burstein, *Jefferson's Secrets*, 69, 172–82, and chap. 8; Scharff, *Women Jefferson Loved*, 379–82; and Gordon-Reed, *Thomas Jefferson and Sally Hemings*, chap. 3.

7. Kierner, "'Dark and Dense Cloud Perpetually Lowering over Us,'" 207, 210–12; ERW to MJR, 28 Jan. 1818, 29 Mar. [1819], and Mary Randolph to EWRC, 26 Nov. 1826, Coolidge Correspondence, ViU; MJR to Ann Cary Randolph Morris, 24 Jan. 1826, Smith-Houston-Morris-Ogden Family Papers, APS.

8. Mary Randolph to EWRC, 25 Jan., 18 Mar. 1827; Cornelia Randolph to EWRC, 4 Feb. 1827; and VJRT to EWRC, 11 Feb. 1827, Coolidge Correspondence, ViU; MJR to Jane Randolph, 5 Feb. 1827, Meikleham Papers, ViU; MJR to TJR, 2 Mar. 1827, Edgehill-Randolph Papers, ViU; MJR to Ann Cary Randolph Morris, 4 Dec. 1826, 22 Mar. 1827, Smith-Houston-Morris-Ogden Family Papers, APS.

9. Cornelia Randolph to EWRC, 24 Nov. 1825, Coolidge Correspondence, ViU.

10. Joseph Coolidge to NPT, [5 Jan. 1827], 15 May 1828, Trist Papers, LC; Lewis Randolph to Septimia Randolph, 28 July 1830, Randolph-Meikleham Family Papers, ViU; Mary Randolph to EWRC, 25 Jan. 1827, Coolidge Correspondence, ViU; Peggy Nicholas to Jane Randolph, 17 Jan. 1829, Edgehill-Randolph Papers, ViU; Gordon-

Reed, *Hemingses of Monticello*, 655–61. See also Casper, *Constructing American Lives*, 1–10.

11. James Barbour to MJR, 9 Nov. 1826, *FLDA*; Gaines, *Thomas Mann Randolph*, 166; John Ramsay to MJR, 29 Sept. 1827, and John Vaughn to MJR, 17 Dec. 1827, Jefferson Papers, LC; TMR to Septimia Randolph, 6 Aug. 1827, Meikleham Papers, ViU; Francis Eppes to NPT, 7 Nov. 1826, Trist Papers, NcU; Cornelia Randolph to EWRC, 10 Apr. 1827, Coolidge Correspondence, ViU; MJR to Margaret Bayard Smith, 10 Nov. 1828, Henley Smith Papers, LC.

12. Wayson, "Martha Jefferson Randolph," 480; Resch, "Politics and Public Culture."

13. MJR to TJR, 2 Mar. 1827, Edgehill-Randolph Papers, ViU; MJR to Ann Cary Randolph Morris, 22 Mar. 1827, Smith-Houston-Morris-Ogden Family Papers, APS.

14. MJR to TJR, 2 Mar. 1827, and TJR to MJR, 9 Apr. 1827, Edgehill-Randolph Papers, ViU; VJRT to EWRC, 1 May 1827, Coolidge Correspondence, ViU; Eliza S. Quincy to Margaret Bayard Smith, 15 Jan. 1828, Margaret Bayard Smith Papers, LC.

15. Kennedy, *Planning the City upon a Hill*, 261; "Population of the 90 Urban Places: 1830," at http://www.census.gov/population/www/documentation/twps0027/tab06.txt (15 Dec. 2009).

16. O'Connor, *Athens of America*, 3–4, 28–33; Kennedy, *Planning the City upon a Hill*, 24, 43–50; Burrill, *State House*, 6; Wenger, "Thomas Jefferson and the Virginia State Capitol"; email from James E. Wootton, Executive Director at Capitol Square Preservation Council, Richmond, 23 Dec. 2009, in author's possession.

17. Royall, *Sketches of History*, 307–26.

18. EWRC to MJR, 27 Sept. 1818, 20 Nov. 1825, 27 Feb., 14 Sept. 1826, and EWRC to VJRT, 20 Mar. 1827, Coolidge Correspondence, ViU.

19. Kennedy, *Planning the City upon a Hill*, 32–33; O'Connor, *Athens of America*, 36–37; Blackmar, *Manhattan for Rent*, esp. chap. 4; "Population of the 100 Largest Urban Places: 1840," at http://www.census.gov/population/www/documentation/twps0027/tab07.txt (15 Dec. 2009); Isaac, "Stories and Constructions of Identity," 209–12; Sarah N. Randolph, "Mrs. Thomas Mann Randolph," in Wister and Irwin, *Worthy Women*, 44.

20. MJR to EWRC, 2 Aug. 1825; EWRC to MJR, 2 Jan. 1826, 28 May 1828, 25 Sept. 1831; EWRC to VJRT, 20 Mar. 1827, 15 Oct. 1830, Coolidge Correspondence, ViU; MJR to Ann Cary Randolph Morris, 8 Aug. 1825, Smith-Houston-Morris-Ogden Family Papers, APS; Kierner, *Scandal at Bizarre*, 152, 158.

21. Bushman, *Refinement of America*, 256–62, 353–65; Chew, "Inhabiting the Great Man's House," 234–36, 239; Joseph Coolidge to NPT, 18 Apr. 1827, Trist Papers, LC; *Boston Directory*.

22. TJR to Jane Randolph, 14, 25 Apr. 3 May 1826, Edgehill-Randolph Papers, ViU.

23. EWRC to VJRT, 7 Jan. 1827, Coolidge Correspondence, ViU; Joseph Coolidge to NPT, 15 Mar., 18 Apr. 1827, Trist Papers, LC; MJR to Jane Randolph, 5 Feb. 1827, Meikleham Papers, ViU; O'Connor, *Athens of America*, chap. 5; Nissenbaum, *Battle for Christmas*, esp. chaps. 3 and 7. See also *Family Letters*, 70n.

24. Royall, *Sketches of History*, 307; Nelson, *Blessed Company*, 24; Woods, *Albe-*

marle County, 127, 132–34; Rawlings, *Early Charlottesville*, 50–51, 68–69; Meade, *Old Churches*, 2:52; TJ to Thomas Cooper, 2 Nov. 1822, *Writings*, 242–43; Mary Randolph to EWRC, 6 June 1826, Coolidge Correspondence, ViU; Joseph Coolidge to NPT, 5 Jan. 1827, Trist Papers, LC.

25. Joseph Coolidge to MJR, 11 Nov. 1825; EWRC to MJR, 20 Nov. 1825, 2 Jan. 1826; and EWRC to VJRT, 24 June 1828, Coolidge Correspondence, ViU; O'Connor, *Athens of America*, 10–11.

26. Joseph Coolidge to NPT, 5 Jan. 1827, Trist Papers, LC; Kierner, "'Dark and Dense Cloud Perpetually Lowering over Us,'" 196–98; Daniel Walker Howe, "Channing, William Ellery," *ANB*.

27. MJR to NPT, 4 Apr. 1827, Trist Papers, NcU.

28. Joseph Coolidge to NPT, 8, 15 Mar., 18 Apr., 16 Oct. 1827, Trist Papers, NcU; EWRC to VJRT, 20 Mar. 1827, and VJRT to EWRC, 1 May 1827, Coolidge Correspondence, ViU; MJR to NPT, 14 Sept. 1827, Trist Papers, NcU; MJR to Ann Cary Randolph Morris, 16 May 1827, Smith-Houston-Morris-Ogden Family Papers, APS.

29. Royall, *Sketches of History*, 307; MJR to Ann Cary Randolph Morris, 16 May 1827, 24 Jan. 1828, Smith-Houston-Morris-Ogden Family Papers, APS; Joseph Coolidge to VJRT, 23 July 1827, Coolidge Correspondence, ViU; Joseph Coolidge to NPT, 24 Mar. 1828, Trist Papers, LC; Cornelia Randolph to VJRT, 30 Mar. 1828, Trist Papers, NcU; MJR to TJR, 29 Feb. 1828, and EWRC to Jane Randolph, 10 May 1828, Edgehill-Randolph Papers, ViU; Capper, *Margaret Fuller*, 95–96.

30. VJRT to EWRC, 1 May 1827, Coolidge Correspondence, ViU; Gaines, *Thomas Mann Randolph*, 177.

31. TMR to Mary Randolph, 25 Feb. 1827, Trist Papers, NcU; EWRC to VJRT, 20 Mar. 1827, Coolidge Correspondence, ViU; Gaines, *Thomas Mann Randolph*, 170; "Thomas Spaulding (1774–1851)," in *New Georgia Encyclopedia*, at http://www.georgia encyclopedia.org/nge/Article.jsp?id=h-901 (17 Dec. 2009).

32. MJR to Ann Cary Randolph Morris, 22 Mar., 16 May 1827, Smith-Houston-Morris-Ogden Family Papers, APS.

33. Joseph Coolidge to NPT, 18 Apr. 1827, 14 May 1828, Trist Papers, LC.

34. Joseph Coolidge to NPT, 17 Aug. 1828, Trist Papers, LC; Joseph Coolidge to TJR, 13 Aug. 1827, Edgehill-Randolph Papers, ViU; Joseph Coolidge to VJRT, 23 July 1827, Coolidge Correspondence, ViU.

35. Joseph Coolidge to TJR, 13 Aug. 1827, Edgehill-Randolph Papers, ViU; Cott, "Divorce and the Changing Status of Women," 597, 606–8; Riley, *Divorce*, 36–38, 44–45; Buckley, *Great Catastrophe of My Life*, esp. 4–9, 32–33.

36. Joseph Coolidge to NPT, 17 Aug. 1828, Trist Papers, LC; Joseph Coolidge to TJR, 13 Aug. 1827, Edgehill-Randolph Papers, ViU.

37. MJR to NPT, 2 Aug. 1828, Trist Papers, NcU.

38. Ibid.; Grossberg, "Who Gets the Child?," 236–44; Bardaglio, *Reconstructing the Household*, chap. 3; Buckley, *Great Catastrophe of My Life*, 38, 39, 144, 183–84.

39. TMR to Septimia Randolph, 6 Aug. 1827, Meikleham Papers, ViU.

40. Ibid., and MJR to Septimia Randolph, 27 Mar. 1833, Meikleham Papers, ViU.

41. TMR to Mary Randolph, 24, 25 Sept., 6 Oct. 1827, and to NPT, 3 Nov. 1827, Trist Papers, NcU; Gaines, *Thomas Mann Randolph*, 176–77, 184.

42. Joseph Coolidge to NPT, 4 Dec. 1827, Trist Papers, LC; MJR to TJR, 29 Feb. 1828, Edgehill-Randolph Papers, ViU; MJR to EWRC, [30?] June 1828, Coolidge Correspondence, ViU.

43. TMR to NPT, 10, 11 Mar. 1828; NPT to TMR, 10 Mar. 1828; and VJRT to EWRC, 19 Mar. 1828, Coolidge Correspondence, ViU; NPT to TMR, 11 Mar. 1828, Trist Papers, LC.

44. VJRT to EWRC, 19 Mar. 1828, Coolidge Correspondence, ViU; Joseph Coolidge to NPT, 24 Mar., 14 May 1828, Trist Papers, LC.

45. Joseph Coolidge to NPT, 14 May 1828, Trist Papers, LC; TJR to Jane Randolph, 27 Apr. 1828, Edgehill-Randolph Papers, ViU; MJR to EWRC, 2 May 1828, and Cornelia Randolph to EWRC, 24 May 1828, Coolidge Correspondence, ViU; NPT to James Madison, 30 May 1828, Nicholas Trist Papers, VHi; VJRT to Laura Carter Holloway, [ca.1870], in Holloway, *Ladies of the White House*, 169.

46. Cornelia Randolph to EWRC, 24 May 1828, and MJR to EWRC, [30] June 1828, Coolidge Correspondence, ViU; Appraisal of the Books of Thomas Mann Randolph, 3 Feb. 1834, Albemarle County Will Books, 11:346–49, LVa; Tay and Dibbell, "George Wythe's 'legacie' to President Thomas Jefferson."

47. MJR to EWRC, [30] June 1828; to George Wythe Randolph, 30 June 1828; and Cornelia Randolph to EWRC, 6 July 1828, Coolidge Correspondence, ViU; Aries, *The Hour of Our Death*.

48. MJR to EWRC, [30] June 1828, and Cornelia Randolph to EWRC, 6 July 1828, Coolidge Correspondence, ViU. See also Lewis, *Pursuit of Happiness*, 89–98.

49. MJR to EWRC, 21 July 1828, Coolidge Correspondence, ViU.

50. Margaret Bayard Smith to Mrs. Boyd, 12 Aug. 1828, in Smith, *First Forty Years*, 230–32; NPT to William Wirt, 1 July 1828, Trist Papers, NcU.

51. Mary Randolph to EWRC, 18 Mar. 1827, 20 July 1828; VJRT to EWRC, 28 Mar. 1827; and Joseph Coolidge to MJR, 7 Aug. 1828, Coolidge Correspondence, ViU; NPT to James Madison, 30 May 1828, Nicholas Trist Papers, VHi; NPT to William Wirt, 1 July, 13 Aug. 1828, Trist Papers, NcU; NPT to Dolley Madison, 23 Sept. 1828, *DMDE*.

52. Ohrt, *Defiant Peacemaker*, 57; Allgor, *Parlor Politics*, 117, 132–37; Margaret Bayard Smith to Mrs. Kirkpatrick, 21 Nov. 1828, in Smith, *First Forty Years*, 242; MJR to Margaret Bayard Smith, 7 Oct., 10 Nov. 1828, Henley Smith Papers, LC; Henry Clay to Nicholas Trist, 10 Oct. 1828, in Hopkins et al., *Papers of Henry Clay*, 7:489.

53. MJR to Margaret Bayard Smith, 7 Oct. 1828, Henley Smith Papers, LC; VJRT to NPT, 22 Nov. 1828, Trist Papers, NcU; Joseph Coolidge to TJR, 7 Aug. 1829; TJR to Joseph Coolidge, 22 Nov. 1828; and Jane Randolph to Sarah Elizabeth Nicholas, 25 Nov. 1828, Edgehill-Randolph Papers, ViU; Joseph Coolidge to MJR, 8 Aug. 1828, Coolidge Correspondence, ViU; Joseph Coolidge to NPT, [Dec. 1828], Trist Papers, LC.

54. VJRT to NPT, 23 Dec. 1828, 20 Jan., 8, 14 Feb. 1829, Trist Papers, NcU; MJR to Joseph Coolidge, 25 Jan. 1829, Coolidge Correspondence, ViU; Kierner, "'Dark and Dense Cloud Perpetually Lowering over Us,'" 216–17.

55. MJR to Joseph Coolidge, 25 Jan. 1829, Coolidge Correspondence, ViU; VJRT to NPT, 31 Jan., 8, 14 Feb. 1829, Trist Papers, NcU.

56. Joseph Coolidge to Nicholas Trist, [22 Mar. 1829], Trist Papers, LC; MJR to

Joseph Coolidge, 12 May 1829, and MJR to EWRC, [28 May 1829], Coolidge Correspondence, ViU; Lewis Randolph to Septimia Randolph, 12 Jan. 1830, Meikleham Papers, ViU; Willard Carl Klunder, "Trist, Nicholas Philip," *ANB*; Randolph, *Writings of Thomas Jefferson*. For a modern appraisal of this first edition of Jefferson's writings, see Cogliano, *Thomas Jefferson*, chap. 3.

57. MJR to Joseph Coolidge, 12 May 1829; MJR to EWRC, [28 May 1829]; and Cornelia Randolph to EWRC, 12 Aug. 1829, Coolidge Correspondence, ViU; MJR to NPT, 24 Feb. 1829; NPT to VJRT, 8, 25 May 1829; and VJRT to NPT, 12 May, 13 Aug. 1829, Trist Papers, NcU.

58. Francis Eppes to NPT, 2 Mar., 9 June 1828, and VJRT to NPT, 10 Dec. 1828, 4 Mar. 1829, Trist Papers, NcU; MJR to Ann Cary Randolph Morris, 6 Sept. 1829, Smith-Houston-Morris-Ogden Family Papers, APS; MJR to Septimia Randolph, 29 Jan. 1829, Trist Papers, NcU; Will of Anna Scott Jefferson Marks, 11 Aug. 1825, Albemarle County Will Books, 9:281, LVa; "Anna Scott Jefferson Marks," in *Thomas Jefferson Encyclopedia* at http://wiki.monticello.org/mediawiki/index.php/Anna_Scott_Jefferson_Marks (6 Jan. 2010).

59. Mary Randolph to EWRC, 23 Aug., 25 Nov. 1829, Coolidge Correspondence, ViU; VJRT to NPT, 30 Sept. 1829, and MJR to EWRC, [Dec. 1829], Trist Papers, NcU.

60. NPT to VJRT, Oct. 1829, 18 Sept. 1831; VJRT to NPT, 16 Oct. 1829, 12 Sept. 1831; VJRT to Jane Randolph, 17 Oct. 1829; MJR to NPT, 26 Oct. 1829; VJRT to Mrs. Rives, 18 Jan. 1834, Trist Papers, NcU; MJR to TJR, 7 Feb. 1830, Edgehill-Randolph Papers, ViU; MJR to Septimia Randolph, 11 July, 2 Sept. 1830, Meikleham Papers, ViU; MJR to Joseph Coolidge, 15 Dec. 1830, *FLDA*; Stein, *Worlds of Thomas Jefferson*, 124, 141, 198, 256, 288, 320–23, 328; Young, *Washington Community*, 71, 74.

61. "Population of the 90 Urban Places, 1830," at http://www.census.gov/population/www/documentation/twps0027/tab06.txt (10 Jan. 2010); *Washington Directory*, 21; Vedder, *Reminiscences of the District of Columbia*, 69–71; Smith, *What Is Gentility?*, esp. 83–84; Allgor, *Parlor Politics*, esp. 120–23, 156–57, 163–70, 211.

62. Margaret Bayard Smith to Mrs. Kirkpatrick, Jan. 1829, 11 Mar., 27 Nov. 1829, in Smith, *First Forty Years*, 253, 294–96, 307–8; MJR to EWRC, [Dec. 1829], Coolidge Correspondence, ViU; VJRT to Jane Randolph, 27 Dec. 1829, Trist Papers, NcU.

63. On the Jacksonian Democrats' hostility to women's political activism, see Allgor, *Parlor Politics*, chap. 5; Zagarri, *Revolutionary Backlash*, 149–52, 155–60; and Varon, *We Mean to Be Counted*, chap. 3. On Jefferson and Jackson as symbols, see, respectively, Peterson, *Jefferson Image in the American Mind*, and Ward, *Andrew Jackson*.

64. Margaret Bayard Smith to Mrs. Kirkpatrick, 27 Nov., 27 Dec. 1829, in Smith, *First Forty Years*, 307–9.

65. Ibid.; Ohrt, *Defiant Peacemaker*, 60–61; Cole, *Martin Van Buren*, 192; Fitzpatrick, *Autobiography of Martin Van Buren*, 2:349.

66. MJR to EWRC, [Dec. 1829], Coolidge Correspondence, ViU; VJRT to Jane Randolph, 27 Dec. 1829, Trist Papers, NcU; Fitzpatrick, *Autobiography of Martin Van Buren*, 2:349.

67. Allgor, *Parlor Politics*, 198–204; Wood, "'One Woman So Dangerous to Pub-

lic Morals,'" 237–39, 244–52; Margaret Bayard Smith to Mrs. Kirkpatrick, [Jan. 1829], 25 Feb. 1829, in Smith, *First Forty Years*, 252, 281–82; Cole, *Martin Van Buren*, 204–6.

68. Marszalek, *Petticoat Affair*, 108–9.

69. Ibid.; Fitzpatrick, *Autobiography of Martin Van Buren*, 2:347–48.

70. Fitzpatrick, *Autobiography of Martin Van Buren*, 2:348–49.

71. Ibid., 2:349–50; Marszalek, *Petticoat Affair*, 109–10.

72. Randall, *Life of Thomas Jefferson*, 2:224.

73. MJR to TJR, 7 Feb. 1830, Edgehill-Randolph Papers, ViU; Cornelia Randolph to EWRC, 18 May 1831, and MJR to EWRC, 15 July 1833, Coolidge Correspondence, ViU; NPT to VJRT, 25 May 1829, and VJRT to Mrs. Rives, 18 Jan. 1834, Trist Papers, NcU; VJR to NPT, 15 Mar. 1822, Trist Papers, LC; Ohrt, *Defiant Peacemaker*, 62–63, 66, 69–70.

74. Andrew Jackson to MJR, 31 Dec. 1829, Jefferson Papers, LC; MJR to TJR, 7 Feb. 1830, Edgehill-Randolph Papers, ViU.

75. MJR to EWRC, 22 Feb., 1 Apr., 21 June 1831, and Cornelia Randolph to EWRC, 10 May 1931, Coolidge Correspondence, ViU; Fitzpatrick, *Autobiography of Martin Van Buren*, 2:345.

76. MJR to EWRC, 8 Mar. 1831, Coolidge Correspondence, ViU; *Senate Journal*, 27 June 1832, 370; Freehling, *Prelude to Civil War*, 207–10. On Poindexter, see Fitzpatrick, *Autobiography of Martin Van Buren*, 2:754–62; Miles, "Andrew Jackson and Senator George Poindexter," 51–58; Remini, *Andrew Jackson and the Course of American Freedom*, 327, 347–50.

77. MJR to EWRC, 22 Feb., 8 Mar., 21 June 1831, Coolidge Correspondence, ViU; *Senate Journal*, 10 Feb. 1831, 140.

78. MJR to TJR, 6 Feb. 1831, and Joseph Coolidge to TJR, 29 Aug. 1830, 7 Sept. 1831, Edgehill-Randolph Papers, ViU; [Cornelia Randolph] to VJRT, 20, 26 June 1831, and MJR to VJRT, 5 July 1831, Trist Papers, NcU; MJR to EWRC, 6 June 1831, 15 Aug. 1831, Coolidge Correspondence, ViU.

Chapter 8

1. VJRT to NPT, 12 July 1832, Trist Papers, NcU.

2. MJR to EWRC, 15 Sept. 1833, Coolidge Correspondence, ViU. See also Dunn, *Dominion of Memories*.

3. Cornelia Randolph to VJRT, 26 June, 6 Aug. 1831, Trist Papers, NcU; Cornelia Randolph to EWRC, 29 June 1831, and MJR to EWRC, 15 Aug. 1831, Coolidge Correspondence, ViU; Leepson, *Saving Monticello*, 25–26.

4. Cornelia Randolph to EWRC, 29 June, 28 Aug. 1831, Coolidge Correspondence, ViU; Lewis Randolph to Septimia Randolph, 31 July 1832, Randolph-Meikleham Papers, ViU; VJRT to NPT, 3 Feb. 1835, Trist Papers, NcU; Leepson, *Saving Monticello*, 26–27, 30–32, 38–45.

5. MJR to Ann Cary Randolph Morris, 1 Aug. 1831, Smith-Houston-Morris-Ogden Family Papers, APS; MJR to EWRC, 27 Oct. 1833, and EWRC to VJRT, 15 Apr. 1834, Coolidge Correspondence, ViU.

6. For a concise account of the insurrection and its aftermath, see Ford, *Deliver Us from Evil*, 338–57.

7. Jane Randolph to Sarah E. Nicholas, [Aug. 1831], and TJR to Jane Randolph, 29 Jan. 1832, Edgehill-Randolph Papers, ViU; VJRT to NPT, 19, 25 Sept. 1831, Trist Papers, NcU; Mary Randolph to EWRC, 25 Sept. 1831, Coolidge Correspondence, ViU; Albemarle County Personal Property Tax Lists, 1831, LVa.

8. Jane Randolph to Sarah E. Nicholas, [Aug. 1831], Edgehill-Randolph Papers, ViU; Cornelia Randolph to EWRC, 28 Aug. 1831, and Mary Randolph to EWRC, 25 Sept. 1831, Coolidge Correspondence, ViU.

9. Tyler-McGraw, *African Republic*, chaps. 1-4; Ford, *Deliver Us from Evil*, chap. 2.

10. MJR to Joseph Coolidge, 27 Oct. 1831, Coolidge Correspondence, ViU; Tyler-McGraw, *African Republic*, 28-29, 83-101; Varon, *We Mean to Be Counted*, 42-45; Ford, *Deliver Us from Evil*, 330-38.

11. Freehling, *Drift toward Dissolution*, 129-30, 135; Ford, *Deliver Us from Evil*, 367-69, 373; TJR to NPT, 4 Apr. 1832, Trist Papers, LC.

12. Freehling, *Drift toward Dissolution*, 124-25, 165-67, 194-95; Ford, *Deliver Us from Evil*, 367, 373-75; Freehling, *Road to Disunion*, 183, 188-89; TJR to Jane Randolph, 29 Jan. 1832, Edgehill-Randolph Papers, ViU; MJR to Ann Cary Randolph Morris, 6 Sept. 1832, Smith-Houston-Morris-Ogden Family Papers, APS.

13. Freehling, *Drift toward Dissolution*, 216-30, 247; Tyler-McGraw, *African Republic*, 72-73.

14. Peggy Nicholas to Jane Randolph, 4 Apr. 1832, and VJRT to Jane Randolph, 6 Apr. 1833, Edgehill-Randolph Papers, ViU; MJR to Septimia Randolph, 18 Apr. 1833, Meikleham Papers, ViU; MJR to EWRC, 15 Sept. 1833, Coolidge Correspondence, ViU. See also Schwarz, *Migrants against Slavery*.

15. MJR to Septimia Randolph, 18 Apr. 1833, Meikleham Papers, ViU; MJR to EWRC, 15 Sept. 1833, Coolidge Correspondence, ViU.

16. Morgan, *Slave Counterpoint*, 503-11; Stevenson, *Life in Black and White*, 208-21.

17. MJR to Joseph Coolidge, 27 Oct. 1831, Coolidge Correspondence, ViU; MJR to NPT, 17 Apr. 1833, Trist Papers, NcU; MJR to Benjamin Randolph, 27 Jan. [1836?], Smith Papers, ViU.

18. MJR to Benjamin Randolph, 27 Jan. [1836?], Smith Papers, ViU. The Colbert sisters—Susan, Emily, Martha Ann, and Thenia—narrowly escaped separation when their mother, Critta Hemings Colbert, died in 1819. At the time, Martha apparently promised Ellen "any one of them who was not disposed of," though Ellen said that she would relinquish her "claim" if she married and left Monticello. See Gordon-Reed, *Hemingses of Monticello*, 622-24.

19. Thomas Jefferson, *Notes on the State of Virginia*, in *Writings*, 3:266-67; Cornelia Randolph to VJRT, 11 Aug. 1833, Trist Papers, NcU. See also Cole, "Changes for Mrs. Thornton's Arthur."

20. Cornelia Randolph to VJRT, 11 Aug. 1833, Trist Papers, NcU; Stanton, *Free Some Day*, 185; Stanton, "Well-Ordered Household," 11-12, 19.

21. Gordon-Reed, *Hemingses of Monticello*, 602; Ohrt, *Defiant Peacemaker*, 77.

22. Cary, *Letters on Female Character*, 134-35, 172-74; Breen, "Female Antislavery Petition Campaign of 1831-32," 378-79; Wood, *Masterful Women*, 48-53; Weiner, *Mistresses and Slaves*, 85-87.

23. MJR to EWRC, 21 June 1831, Coolidge Correspondence, ViU; MJR to VJRT, 5 July 1831; Nicholas Trist to VJRT, 2 Oct. 1831; VJRT to Jane Randolph, 5 Nov. 1831; and MJR to Jane Randolph, 20 Nov. 1831, Trist Papers, NcU.

24. MJR and VJRT to EWRC, [1832], Trist Papers, NcU; MJR to Septimia Randolph, 27 Feb. 1833, Meikleham Papers, ViU.

25. Lewis Randolph to NPT, 28 Sept. 1831, Trist Papers, LC; MJR to EWRC, 15 July 1833, Coolidge Correspondence, ViU; Lewis Randolph to Septimia Randolph, 24 Mar. 1834, Randolph-Meikleham Family Papers, ViU; VJRT to NPT, 3 Mar. 1835, and Lewis Randolph to VJRT, 13 Apr. 1836, Trist Papers, NcU; MJR to Ann Cary Randolph Morris, 22 Mar. 1835, Smith-Houston-Morris-Ogden Family Papers, APS; Ohrt, *Defiant Peacemaker*, 75–79; Burke, *Emily Donelson of Tennessee*, 260, 274, 285–86.

26. Peggy Nicholas to Jane Randolph, 29 Mar., 4 Apr. 1832, and MJR to TJR, 8 Feb. 1833, Edgehill-Randolph Papers, ViU; Shade, *Democratizing the Old Dominion*, 238–44.

27. MJR to Septimia Randolph, 22 Feb. 1836, Meikleham Papers, ViU; Shade, *Democratizing the Old Dominion*, 238; Remini, *Andrew Jackson and the Course of American Democracy*, esp. chaps. 11 and 20.

28. Margaret Bayard Smith to Mrs. Kirkpatrick, 4 Feb. 1835, in Smith, *First Forty Years*, 362–64; VJRT to NPT, 3 Feb. 1835, Trist Papers, NcU.

29. MJR to Joseph Coolidge, 2 Nov. 1832, Coolidge Correspondence, ViU; MJR to Septimia Randolph, 31 Jan. 1833, Meikleham Papers, ViU; Rhodes, *John James Audubon*, 369–71.

30. VJRT to NPT, 9 Sept. 1832, Trist Papers, NcU; MJR to Septimia Randolph, 25 Sept. 1832, Meikleham Papers, ViU; Rosenberg, *Cholera Years*, chaps. 1–2; Mayer, *All on Fire*, 62–68.

31. NPT to MJR, 22 Mar. 1833, and MJR to NPT, 27 Mar. 1833, Trist Papers, NcU; MJR to Ann Cary Randolph Morris, 30 June 1833, Smith-Houston-Morris-Ogden Family Papers, APS; VJRT to Laura Carter Holloway, [ca. 1870], in Holloway, *Ladies of the White House*, 174–75.

32. MJR to EWRC, 24 June 1833, 7 Jan., 20 June 1834, Coolidge Correspondence, ViU; MJR to Ann Cary Randolph Morris, 3 Nov. 1833, Smith-Houston-Morris-Ogden Family Papers, APS; Lewis Randolph to VJRT, 24 Jan., 6, 16 Mar. 1834, Trist Papers, NcU.

33. MJR to Septimia Randolph, 2 Dec. 1832, 1 Jan. 1833, Meikleham Papers, ViU; Margaret Bayard Smith to Anna Maria H. Smith, 15 Dec. 1832, in Smith, *First Forty Years*, 340.

34. MJR to Septimia Randolph, 2 Dec. 1832, 31 Jan. 1833, Meikleham Papers, ViU; MJR to EWRC, 10 June 1833, Coolidge Correspondence, ViU; Ohrt, *Defiant Peacemaker*, 42, 64–66.

35. MJR to Septimia Randolph, 30 July 1832, 1 Jan., 27 Feb. 1833, Meikleham Papers, ViU.

36. VJRT to NPT, 4, 10, 29 Jan. 1834, Trist Papers, NcU; MJR to Ann Cary Randolph Morris, 16 Feb. 1834, Smith-Houston-Morris-Ogden Family Papers, APS.

37. VJRT to NPT, 22 Mar., 3 Apr. 1834, Trist Papers, NcU.

38. MJR to EWRC, 20 June 1834, Coolidge Correspondence, ViU; MJR to Ann Cary Randolph Morris, 17 Sept. 1834, Smith-Houston-Morris-Ogden Family Papers, APS.

39. MJR to Ann Cary Randolph Morris, 17 Sept. 1834, Smith-Houston-Morris-Ogden Family Papers, APS.

40. MJR to Ann Cary Randolph Morris, 22 Mar. 1835, Smith-Houston-Morris-Ogden Family Papers, APS; VJRT to NPT, 18 Feb., 3 Mar. 1835, Trist Papers, NcU; Margaret Bayard Smith to Mrs. Kirkpatrick, 16 Apr. 1835, in Smith, *First Forty Years*, 373–74.

41. Will of MJR, 18 Apr. [1835], Edgehill-Randolph Papers, ViU.

42. Gordon-Reed, *Thomas Jefferson and Sally Hemings*, 78–98; Henry S. Randall to James Parton, 1 June 1868, in ibid., 254–55; Nathaniel Francis Cabell to Henry S. Randall, 17 Dec. 1838, Nathaniel Francis Cabell Letters, VHi; Jan Ellen Lewis, "The White Jeffersons," in Lewis and Onuf, *Sally Hemings and Thomas Jefferson*, 136–48.

43. Jan Ellen Lewis, "The White Jeffersons," in Lewis and Onuf, *Sally Hemings and Thomas Jefferson*, 146; Henry S. Randall to James Parton, 1 June 1868, and EWRC to Joseph Coolidge, 24 Oct. 1858, in Gordon-Reed, *Sally Hemings and Thomas Jefferson*, 255, 258–60. Madison Hemings publicly challenged the authorized Jefferson family story in 1873; Fawn Brodie was the first of Jefferson's biographers to do so. Brodie's book was published in 1974. See "The Memoirs of Madison Hemings," in Gordon-Reed, *Thomas Jefferson and Sally Hemings*, 245–48, and Brodie, *Thomas Jefferson*, esp. chaps. 20–21.

44. TJR to Jane Randolph, 24, 26 Apr. 1835, Edgehill-Randolph Papers, ViU; VJRT to NPT, 10–19 Apr., 4, 8, 21 June 1835, Trist Papers, NcU; Cornelia Randolph to Ann Cary Randolph Morris, 10 May 1835, Smith-Houston-Morris-Ogden Family Papers, APS.

45. VJRT to NPT, 7 Apr., 21 June 1835, and Mary Randolph to VJRT, 8, 20 July 1835, Trist Papers, NcU; MJR to Ann Cary Randolph Morris, 22 Mar. 1835, Smith-Houston-Morris-Ogden Family Papers, APS.

46. MJR to NPT, 24 Aug. 1835, Trist Papers, NcU; Wyatt-Brown, "Abolitionists' Postal Campaign of 1835," 227–31.

47. MJR to VJRT, 17 July 1835, and Mary Randolph to VJRT, 5 Dec. 1835, Trist Papers, NcU; MJR to Septimia Randolph, 8, 22 Feb. 1836, Meikleham Papers, ViU; MJR to Ann Cary Randolph Morris, 22 Mar. 1835, 5 Apr. 1836, Smith-Houston-Morris-Ogden Family Papers, APS.

48. MJR to VJRT, 17 July 1835, and Mary Randolph to VJRT, 5 Dec. 1835, Trist Papers, NcU; MJR to Septimia Randolph, 5 Dec. 1835, Meikleham Papers, ViU; MJR to Ann Cary Randolph Morris, 22 Mar., 4 Dec. 1835, 5 Apr. 1836, Smith-Houston-Morris-Ogden Family Papers, APS; Gaines, *Thomas Mann Randolph*, 4.

49. [Mary Randolph] to VJRT, 20 July, 6 Sept. 1835, and Mary Randolph to Martha Jefferson Trist, 24 Sept. [1835], Trist Papers, NcU; EWRC to VJRT, 27 Sept. 1835, Coolidge Correspondence, ViU; Mary Randolph to Septimia Randolph, 5 Feb. 1836, Meikleham Papers, ViU; Will of MJR, 24 Jan. 1836, *FLDA*; MJR to Benjamin Randolph, 27 Jan. [1836?], Smith Papers, ViU.

50. MJR to Ann Cary Randolph Morris, 5 Apr. 1836, Smith-Houston-Morris-Ogden Family Papers, APS; Mary Randolph to VJRT, 17 Apr. 1836, Trist Papers, NcU; Mary Randolph to Susan Coolidge, 25 July 1836, Randolph-Meikleham Family Papers, ViU.

51. MJR to Septimia Randolph, 3 Mar. 1836, Meikleham Papers, ViU; NPT to VJRT,

5 May 1834, 14 Mar., 18 May 1835, 23 Mar. 1836, and VJRT to NPT, 29 Mar., 7 Apr. 1835, 31 Jan. 1836, Trist Papers, NcU; MJR to Ann Cary Randolph Morris, 8 Feb. 1833, Smith-Houston-Morris-Ogden Family Papers, APS; EWRC to Henry S. Randall, 2 Mar. 1856, Coolidge Correspondence, ViU.

52. VJRT to NPT, 27 May 1836, Trist Papers, NcU; Biddle and Fielding, *Life and Works of Thomas Sully*, 191, 256; Rhodes, *John James Audubon*, 219–20.

53. Stein, *Worlds of Thomas Jefferson*, 142; VJRT to Laura Carter Holloway, [ca. 1870], in Holloway, *Ladies of the White House*, 178; VJRT to NPT, 5 June 1836, Trist Papers, NcU; Biddle and Fielding, *Life and Works of Thomas Sully*, 256.

54. VJRT to NPT, 18 June 1836, and MJR to VJRT, 20 June 1836, Trist Papers, NcU; MJR to Ann Cary Randolph Morris, 17 Aug. 1836, Smith-Houston-Morris-Ogden Family Papers, APS; Mary Randolph to Susan Coolidge, 25 July 1836, and Septimia Anne Randolph Meikleham, "Montpelier: Quiet Homelife of Mr and Mrs Madison," [after 1836], Randolph-Meikleham Family Papers, ViU; Allgor, *Perfect Union*, chap. 17.

55. MJR to EWRC, 22 Aug. 1836, Coolidge Correspondence, ViU; MJR to Ann Cary Randolph Morris, 17 Aug. 1836, Smith-Houston-Morris-Ogden Family Papers, APS; VJRT to NPT, 5 Oct. 1836, Trist Papers, NcU.

56. MJR to EWRC, 22 Aug. 1836, Coolidge Correspondence, ViU; MJR to Ann Cary Randolph Morris, 17 Aug. 1836, Smith-Houston-Morris-Ogden Family Papers, APS; Cornelia Randolph to NPT, 31 Aug. 1836, Trist Papers, NcU; Kierner, *Scandal at Bizarre*, 163, 167.

57. MJR to EWRC, 22 Aug. 1836, Coolidge Correspondence, ViU; MJR to Ann Cary Randolph Morris, 17 Aug. 1836, Smith-Houston-Morris-Ogden Family Papers, APS; Cornelia Randolph to NPT, 31 Aug. 1836, Trist Papers, NcU; Kierner, *Scandal at Bizarre*, 167.

58. VJRT to NPT, 16 Oct. 1836, Trist Papers, LC; EWRC to Henry S. Randall, 2 Mar. 1856, Coolidge Correspondence, ViU; Sarah N. Randolph, "Mrs. Thomas Mann Randolph," in Wister and Irwin, *Worthy Women*, 69–70.

59. VJRT to NPT, 16 Oct. 1836, Trist Papers, LC; EWRC to Henry S. Randall, 2 Mar. 1856, Coolidge Correspondence, ViU; Randall, *Life of Thomas Jefferson*, 3:564; VJRT to Laura Carter Holloway, [ca. 1870], in Holloway, *Ladies of the White House*, 179–80.

60. NPT to VJRT, 13 Oct. 1836, Trist Papers, NcU; VJRT to NPT, 16 Oct. 1836, Trist Papers, LC; George Wythe Randolph to TJR, 17 Oct. 1836, Edgehill-Randolph Papers, ViU; EWRC to Henry S. Randall, 2 Mar. 1856, Coolidge Correspondence, ViU.

61. Epitaph of Martha Jefferson Randolph, [1836], Edgehill-Randolph Papers, ViU; Sarah N. Randolph, "Mrs. Thomas Mann Randolph," in Wister and Scott, *Worthy Women*, 70.

62. Birle and Francavilla, *Thomas Jefferson's Granddaughter*, 160.

63. *Richmond Enquirer*, 18 Oct. 1836. The issue of the *Charlottesville Jeffersonian Republican* in which the obituary originated is not extant.

Epilogue

1. Birle and Francavilla, *Thomas Jefferson's Granddaughter*, 160; Smith "Carysbrook Memoir," ViU.

2. Randolph, *Domestic Life*, viii.

3. Sarah N. Randolph, "Mrs. Thomas Mann Randolph," in Wister and Scott, *Worthy Women*, 4.

4. Ibid., esp. 24–25, 43–44, 51, 61.

5. Davis, *Francis Walker Gilmer*, 373; Smith, "Carysbrook Memoir," 47–48, ViU.

6. Survey of Virginia newspapers based on Brigham, *History and Bibliography of American Newspapers*, 2:1104–75, and "Virginia in Newspapers Bibliography," at http://www.lva.virginia.gov/public/vnp/results.asp?rl=Richmond&rt=City (23 Feb. 2010). Generalizations in this epilogue are based on material published in the *Richmond Enquirer*, 7–18 Oct. 1836.

7. Gordon-Reed, *Thomas Jefferson and Sally Hemings*, 23–24, 78–79.

8. *Richmond Enquirer*, 11 Oct. 1836.

9. Majewski, *House Dividing*, 60–65.

10. *Richmond Enquirer*, 18 Oct. 1836.

11. Ibid., 7 Oct. 1836.

12. Information on the lives of the Randolph siblings after 1836 is taken primarily from the pertinent essays in Shackelford, *Collected Papers*.

13. Robinson, *Jefferson's Granddaughter*, 1, 10.

14. Albemarle County Personal Property Tax Lists, 1840, LVa; National Register of Historic Places Nomination Form for Edgehill, at http://165.176.125.227/registers/Counties/Albemarle/002-0026_Edgehill_1982_Final_Nomination.pdf (2 Mar. 2010). On Thomas Jefferson Randolph and secession, see Vance, "Thomas Jefferson Randolph," 225.

bibliography

PRIMARY SOURCES

Manuscripts

American Philosophical Society, Philadelphia, Pa.
  Catharine Wistar Bache Papers
  Smith-Houston-Morris-Ogden Family Papers
Boston Athenaeum, Boston, Mass.
  Charles Bulfinch Papers
College of William and Mary, Swem Library, Williamsburg, Va.
  Tucker-Coleman Papers
Colonial Williamsburg, Inc., Williamsburg, Va.
  Elizabeth Ambler Papers
Duke University, Perkins Library, Durham, N.C.
  Campbell Family Papers
  Milledge Family Papers
  Thomas Mann Randolph Papers
Florida State Archives, Tallahassee
  Randolph Family Papers
International Center for Jefferson Studies, Monticello, Charlottesville, Va.
  Carter-Smith Papers (transcripts)
  Horace Holley Letter (copy)
  Monticello Research Files
      James A. Bear Jr., "Chronologies of the Whereabouts of Martha Jefferson
          (1784–1809), Mary Jefferson (1784–1809), Thomas Jefferson (1767–1826)"
      Septimia Randolph Meikleham cookbook
  Thomas Mann Randolph Memorandum Book
Library of Congress, Washington, D.C.
  Thomas Jefferson Papers
  James Madison Papers
  William Short Papers
  Henley Smith Papers
  Margaret Bayard Smith Papers
  Anna Maria Brodeau Thornton Papers
  Nicholas P. Trist Papers
Library of Virginia, Richmond
  Albemarle County Personal Property Tax Lists
  Albemarle County Will Books
  Henrico County Personal Property Tax Lists
  Legislative Petitions
  Thomas Mann Randolph Papers
  Randolph-Gilmer Letters

Massachusetts Historical Society, Boston
    Coolidge Collection of Thomas Jefferson Manuscripts
    Ellen Wayles Randolph Coolidge Diaries
University of North Carolina, Southern Historical Collection, Chapel Hill
    Nicholas Philip Trist Papers
University of Virginia, Small Special Collections Library, Charlottesville
    Marie Jacinthe de Botidoux Letters
    Carr-Cary Papers
    Ellen Wayles Randolph Coolidge Correspondence
    Edgehill-Randolph Papers
    Francis Walker Gilmer Correspondence
    Henry Heth Papers
    Septimia Anne Cary Randolph Meikleham Papers
    Martha Jefferson Randolph Letters
    Martha Jefferson Randolph Papers
    Randolph-Meikleham Family Papers
    Rives Family Papers
    Jane Blair Cary Smith, "The Carysbrook Memoir" (typescript)
    Samuel Smith Papers
    Papers of the Trist, Burke, and Randolph Families
Virginia Historical Society, Richmond
    Nathaniel Francis Cabell Letters
    Joseph Coolidge Memoranda
    Harrison Family Papers
    Samuel Mordecai Letter
    Gabriella Page Papers
    Martha Jefferson Randolph Letter
    Mary Jefferson Randolph Commonplace Book
    Thomas Mann Randolph Letters
    Elizabeth House Trist Papers
    Nicholas Trist Papers

Newspapers
    Richmond Enquirer
    Richmond Recorder
    Virginia Gazette

Books and Articles
Adams, Charles Francis, ed. *Letters of Mrs. Adams.* 2 vols. Boston, 1840.
Anburey, Thomas. *Travels Through the Interior Parts of America.* 2 vols. London, 1789.
Andrews, William L., ed. *Journeys in New Worlds: Early American Women's Narratives.* Madison, Wisc., 1990.
Ball, Charles. *Fifty Years in Chains; or, The Life of an American Slave.* Indianapolis, 1859.
Bear, James A., Jr., ed. *Jefferson at Monticello.* Charlottesville, 1967.

Bear, James A., Jr., and Lucia Stanton, eds. *Jefferson's Memorandum Books: Accounts, with Legal Records and Miscellany.* 2 vols. Princeton, 1997.

Betts, Edwin Morris, ed. *Thomas Jefferson's Farm Book.* Chapel Hill, 2002.

Betts, Edwin Morris, and James Adam Bear Jr., eds. *The Family Letters of Thomas Jefferson.* Columbia, Mo., 1966.

Birle, Ann Lucas, and Lisa A. Francavilla, eds. *Thomas Jefferson's Granddaughter in Queen Victoria's England: The Travel Diary of Ellen Wayles Coolidge, 1838–1839.* Boston, 2011.

The Boston Directory. Boston, 1828.

Bouldin, Powhatan. *Home Reminiscences of John Randolph of Roanoke.* Danville and Richmond, 1887.

Boyd, Julian P., et al., eds. *The Papers of Thomas Jefferson.* Princeton, 1954– .

Brady, Patricia, ed. *George Washington's Beautiful Nelly: The Letters of Eleanor Parke Custis Lewis to Elizabeth Bordley Gibson, 1794–1851.* Columbia, S.C., 1991.

Brown, Everett Somerville, ed. *William Plumer's Memorandum of Proceedings in the United States Senate, 1803–1807.* New York, 1923.

Brown, Marvin L., ed. *Baroness von Riedesel and the American Revolution: Journal and Correspondence of a Tour of Duty, 1776–1783.* Chapel Hill, 1965.

Burstein, Andrew, and Peter S. Onuf, eds. *Letters from the Head and Heart: Writings of Thomas Jefferson.* Charlottesville, 2002.

Butterfield, L. H., et al., eds. *Adams Family Correspondence.* Cambridge, Mass., 1963– .

Caldwell, John Edwards. *A Tour through Part of Virginia in the Summer of 1808.* Edited by William M. E. Rachal. Richmond, 1951.

Cary, Virginia Randolph. *Letters on Female Character, Addressed to a Young Lady on the Death of Her Mother.* Richmond, 1828.

Cook, William, M.D. *The Physiomedical Dispensary.* Cincinnati, 1869.

Cresswell, Nicholas. *The Journal of Nicholas Cresswell.* Port Washington, N.Y., 1968.

Cullen, Charles T., and Herbert A. Johnson, eds. *The Papers of John Marshall.* Chapel Hill, 1974– .

Cutler, William P., and Julia Perkins, eds. *Life Journals and Correspondence of Manasseh P. Cutler.* 2 vols. Cincinnati, 1888.

Davis, Richard Beale, ed. *The Abbe Correa in America, 1812–1820: The Contributions of the Diplomat and Natural Philosopher to the Foundations of our Nation.* Philadelphia, 1955.

Dumbauld, Edward. *Thomas Jefferson, American Tourist.* Norman, Okla., 1946.

Edgeworth, Maria. *The Modern Griselda; A Tale.* London, 1805.

Fitzpatrick, John C., ed. *The Autobiography of Martin Van Buren.* 2 vols. Washington, D.C., 1920.

Ford, Paul Leicester, ed. *The Writings of Thomas Jefferson.* 10 vols. New York: G. P. Putnam's Sons, 1892–99.

Gilmer, George R. *Sketches of Some of the First Settlers of Upper Georgia, of the Cherokees, and of the Author.* New York, 1855.

Gregory, John. *A Comparative View of the State and Faculties of Man with those of the Animal World.* 1765; London, 1798.

———. *A Father's Legacy to His Daughters*. London, 1774.

Holloway, Laura Carter. *The Ladies of the White House*. New York, 1870.

Hopkins, James F., et al., eds. *The Papers of Henry Clay*. Lexington, Ky., 1959–92.

Hutchinson, William T., et al., eds. *The Papers of James Madison*. Chicago and Charlottesville, 1962– .

Jurgrau, Thelma, ed. *Story of My Life: The Autobiography of George Sand*. Albany, N.Y., 1991.

Kennedy, John Pendleton. *Memoirs of the Life of William Wirt*. 2 vols. Philadelphia, 1854–56.

Levasseur, Auguste. *Lafayette in America in 1824 and 1825: Journal of a Voyage to the United States*. Translated by Alan R. Hoffman. Manchester, N.H., 2006.

Looney, J. Jefferson, et al., eds. *The Papers of Thomas Jefferson: Retirement Series*. Princeton, 2004– .

Marchione, Margherita, et al., eds. *Philip Mazzei: Selected Writings and Correspondence*. 2 vols. Prato, 1983.

Mason, Jonathan. *Extracts from a Diary kept by the Hon. Jonathan Mason of a Journey from Boston to Savannah in the Year 1804*. Cambridge, Mass., 1885.

Meade, Bishop [William]. *Old Churches, Ministers and Families of Virginia*. 2 vols. Philadelphia, 1857.

Melish, John. *Travels through the United States of America, in the years 1806 & 1807, and 1809, 1810, & 1811*. London, 1818.

Montague, Lee Ludwell, ed. "Cornelia Lee's Wedding, As Reported in a Letter from Ann Calvert Stuart to Mrs. Elizabeth Lee, October 19, 1806." *Virginia Magazine of History and Biography* 80 (1972): 453–60.

Mordecai, Samuel. *Richmond in By-Gone Days*. 1856; Richmond, 1946.

Morris, Gouverneur. *A Diary of the French Revolution*. 2 vols. Edited by Beatrix Cary Davenport. Boston, 1939.

Nevins, Allan, ed. *Diary of John Quincy Adams: American Political, Social, and Intellectual Life from Washington to Polk*. New York, 1929.

Peterson, Merrill D., ed. *The Portable Thomas Jefferson*. New York, 1975.

———. *Visitors to Monticello*. Charlottesville, 1989.

Pocock, Robert. *Memorials of the Family of Tufton, Earls of Thanet*. Gravesend, 1800.

Radbill, Samuel X., ed. *The Autobiographical Ana of Robley Dunglison, M.D.* Philadelphia, 1963.

Randall, Henry S. *The Life of Thomas Jefferson*. 3 vols. New York, 1858.

Randolph, Mary. *The Virginia House-Wife*. Edited by Karen Hess. Columbia, S.C., 1984.

Randolph, Sarah N. *The Domestic Life of Thomas Jefferson*. New York, 1871.

Randolph, Thomas Jefferson, ed. *The Writings of Thomas Jefferson*. 4 vols. Charlottesville, 1829.

"Randolph and Tucker Letters." *Virginia Magazine of History and Biography* 43 (1935): 41–46.

Rawlings, Mary, ed. *Early Charlottesville: Recollections of James Alexander, 1828–1874*. Charlottesville, 1963.

Rice, Howard C., ed. *Travels in North America in the Years 1780, 1781 and 1782 by the Marquis de Chastelleux*. 2 vols. Chapel Hill, 1963.

Robinson, William E. *Jefferson's Granddaughter: Speech of Hon. William E. Robinson, of New York, in the House of Representatives, Friday, March 14, 1884*. Washington, D.C., 1884.

Royall, Anne Newport. *Sketches of History, Life and Manners in the United States, by a Traveller*. New Haven, 1826.

Rudolph, Frederick, ed. *Essays on Education in the Early Republic*. Cambridge, Mass., 1965.

Runes, Dagobert G., ed. *The Selected Writings of Benjamin Rush*. New York, 2007.

[Smith, Abigail Adams]. *Journal and Correspondence of Miss Adams, Daughter of John Adams, Second President of the United States, Written in France and England, in 1785*. New York, 1841.

Smith, Benjamin Barton. *Professor Cullen's Treatise of the Materia Medica*. Philadelphia, 1812.

Smith, Margaret Bayard. *The First Forty Years of Washington Society*. Edited by Galliard Hunt. New York, 1906.

———. *What Is Gentility?: A Moral Tale*. Washington, D.C., 1828.

———. *A Winter in Washington; or, Memoirs of the Seymour Family*. New York, 1824.

Ticknor, George. *Life, Letters, and Journals of George Ticknor*. 2 vols. Boston, 1876.

Tinkcom, Margaret Bailey, ed. "Caviar along the Potomac: Sir Augustus John Foster's 'Notes on the United States,' 1804-1812." *William and Mary Quarterly*, 3rd ser., 8 (1951): 68-107.

Van Horne, John C., and Lee W. Formwalt, eds. *The Correspondence and Miscellaneous Papers of Benjamin Henry Latrobe*. 3 vols. New Haven, 1984-88.

Vedder, Sarah E. *Reminiscences of the District of Columbia, or Washington City, Seventy-nine years Ago, 1830-1909*. St. Louis, 1909.

Viard, A. *Le Cuisinier Royal*. Paris, 1817.

The Washington Directory. Washington, D.C., 1830.

Webster, Noah. *A Collection of Essays and Fugitiv Writings: On Moral, Historical, Political and Literary Subjects*. Boston, 1790.

Weld, Isaac, Jr. *Travels through the States of North America and the Provinces of Upper and Lower Canada, during the years 1795, 1796, and 1797*. 3rd ed. 2 vols. London, 1800.

Electronic Sources

Annals of Congress. http://rs6.10c.gov/ammem/amlaw/lwac.html.

"Household Accounts Maintained by Anne Cary Randolph, 1805-1808." http://memory.loc.gov/ammem/collections/jefferson_papers/ser7v011.html.

"Population of the 90 Urban Places: 1830." http://www.census.gov/population/www/documentation/twps0027/tab06.txt.

"Population of the 100 Largest Urban Places: 1840." http://www.census.gov/population/www/documentation/twps0027/tab07.txt.

Senate Journal. http://memory.loc.gov/ammem/amlaw/lwsj.html.

Shulman, Holly C., ed. *The Dolley Madison Digital Edition*. Charlottesville, 2004. http://p8080-rotunda.upress.virginia.edu.mutex.gmu.edu/dmde/default.xqy.

Thomas Jefferson Foundation, Inc. *Family Letters Digital Archive*. http://retirementseries.dataformat.com.

University of Virginia Geospatial and Statistical Data Center. *Historical Census Data Browser*. http://mapserver.lib.virginia.edu/.

SECONDARY SOURCES

Books, Articles, and Dissertations

Adams, William Howard. *The Paris Years of Thomas Jefferson*. New Haven, 1997.

Allgor, Catherine. "Margaret Bayard Smith's 1809 Journey to Monticello and Montpelier: The Politics of Performance in the Early Republic." *Early American Studies*, forthcoming.

———. *Parlor Politics: In Which the Ladies of Washington Help Build a City and a Government*. Charlottesville, 2000.

———. *A Perfect Union: Dolley Madison and the Creation of the American Nation*. New York, 2006.

Appleby, Joyce. "Commercial Farming and 'the Agrarian Myth' in the Early Republic." *Journal of American History* 68 (1982): 833–49.

———. *Inheriting the Revolution: The First Generation of Americans*. Cambridge, Mass., 2000.

Aries, Philippe. *The Hour of Our Death*. Translated by Helen Weaver. New York, 1981.

Bailyn, Bernard, and John B. Hench, eds. *The Press and the American Revolution*. Boston, 1981.

Bardaglio, Peter W. *Reconstructing the Household: Families, Sex, and the Law in the Nineteenth-Century South*. Chapel Hill, 1995.

Bax, Ernest Belford. *Jean-Paul Marat, The People's Friend: A Biographical Sketch*. London, 1879.

Bearss, Sara B., et al., eds. *Dictionary of Virginia Biography*. Richmond, 1988– .

Bell, Whitfield J., Jr. *Patriot-Improvers: Biographical Sketches of Members of the American Philosophical Society*. 2 vols. Philadelphia, 1997–99.

Berkin, Carol. *Revolutionary Mothers: Women in the Struggle for America's Independence*. New York, 2005.

Berlin, Ira, and Ronald Hoffman, eds. *Slavery and Freedom in the Age of the American Revolution*. Urbana, Ill., 1983.

Biddle, Edward, and Mantle Fielding. *The Life and Works of Thomas Sully, 1783–1872*. Lancaster, Pa., 1921.

Bingham, Emily. *Mordecai: An Early American Family*. New York, 2003.

Bizardel, Yvon, and Howard C. Rice, Jr. "'Poor in Love Mr. Short.'" *William and Mary Quarterly*, 3rd ser., 21 (1964): 516–33.

Blackmar, Elizabeth. *Manhattan for Rent, 1785–1850*. Ithaca, N.Y., 1989.

Bloch, Ruth H. "American Feminine Ideals in Transition: The Rise of the Moral Mother." *Feminist Studies* 4 (1978): 100–126.

———. "The American Revolution, Wife Beating, and the Emergent Value of Privacy." *Early American Studies* 5 (2007): 223–51.

Boydston, Jeanne. *Home and Work: Housework, Wages, and the Ideology of Labor in the Early Republic.* New York, 1990.

Brady, Patricia. *Martha Washington: An American Life.* New York, 2005.

Branson, Susan. *These Fiery, Frenchified Dames: Women and Political Culture in Early National Philadelphia.* Philadelphia, 2001.

Breen, Patrick. "The Female Antislavery Petition Campaign of 1831–32." *Virginia Magazine of History and Biography* 110 (2002): 377–98.

Breen, T. H. *Tobacco Culture: The Mentality of the Great Tidewater Planters on the Eve of Revolution.* Princeton, 1985.

Brigham, Clarence S. *History and Bibliography of American Newspapers, 1690–1820.* 2 vols. 1947; Westport, Conn., 1975.

Brodie, Fawn M. *Thomas Jefferson: An Intimate History.* New York, 1974.

Buckley, Thomas E., S.J. *The Great Catastrophe of My Life: Divorce in the Old Dominion.* Chapel Hill, 2002.

Burke, Pauline Wilcox. *Emily Donelson of Tennessee.* Edited by Jonathan M. Atkins. Knoxville, Tenn., 2001.

Burrill, Ellen Mudge. *The State House, Boston, Massachusetts.* Boston, 1907.

Burstein, Andrew. *The Inner Jefferson: Portrait of a Grieving Optimist.* Charlottesville, 1995.

———. *Jefferson's Secrets: Death and Desire at Monticello.* New York, 2005.

Busey, Samuel C. *Pictures of the City of Washington in the Past.* Washington, D.C., 1898.

Bushman, Richard L. *The Refinement of America: Persons, Houses, Cities.* New York, 1992.

Capper, Charles. *Margaret Fuller: An American Romantic Life.* New York, 1992.

Carson, Jane. *Colonial Virginians at Play.* Williamsburg, 1989.

Cashin, Joan E. *A Family Venture: Men and Women on the Southern Frontier.* New York, 1991.

Casper, Scott E. *Constructing American Lives: Biography and Culture in Nineteenth-Century America.* Chapel Hill, 1999.

Caulkins, Frances Manwaring. *History of Norwich, Connecticut.* Hartford, Conn., 1866.

Censer, Jane Turner. *North Carolina Planters and Their Children, 1800–1860.* Baton Rouge, La., 1984.

———. "Southwestern Migration among North Carolina Planter Families: 'The Disposition to Emigrate.'" *Journal of Southern History* 57 (1991): 407–26.

Chernow, Ron. *Alexander Hamilton.* New York, 2004.

Chew, Elizabeth V. "Inhabiting the Great Man's House: Women and Space at Monticello." In *Structures and Subjectivities: Attending to Early Modern Women,* edited by Joan E. Hartman and Adele Seeff, 223–52. Newark, Del., 2007.

Choudhury, Mita. *Convents and Nuns in Eighteenth-Century French Politics and Culture.* Ithaca, N.Y., 2004.

Clinton, Catherine. *The Plantation Mistress: Woman's World in the Old South.* New York, 1982.

Clinton, Catherine, and Michele Gillespie, eds. *The Devil's Lane: Sex and Race in the Early South.* New York, 1997.

Cockerham, Anne Z., Arlene W. Keeling, and Barbara Parker. "Seeking Refuge at Monticello: Domestic Violence in Thomas Jefferson's Family." *Magazine of Albemarle County History* 64 (2006): 34–42.

Cogliano, Francis D. *Thomas Jefferson: Reputation and Legacy.* Charlottesville, 2006.

Cohen, William. "Thomas Jefferson and the Problem of Slavery." *Journal of American History* 56 (1969): 503–26.

Cole, Donald B. *Martin Van Buren and the American Political System.* Princeton, 1984.

Cole, Stephanie. "Changes for Mrs. Thornton's Arthur: Patterns of Domestic Service in Washington, D.C., 1800–1835." *Social Science History* 15 (1991): 367–79.

Cott, Nancy. "Divorce and the Changing Status of Women in Eighteenth-Century Massachusetts." *William and Mary Quarterly*, 3rd ser., 33 (1976): 586–614.

Cripe, Helen. *Thomas Jefferson and Music.* Charlottesville, 1974.

Cullen, Charles T. "Jefferson's White House Dinner Guests." *White House History* 17 (2006): 25–43.

Cunningham, Noble E., Jr. *The Jeffersonian Republicans in Power: Party Operations, 1801–1809.* Chapel Hill, 1963.

Dabney, William M. "Jefferson's Albemarle: History of Albemarle County, Virginia, 1727–1829." Ph.D. diss., University of Virginia, 1951.

Daniels, Jonathan. *The Randolphs of Virginia.* Garden City, N.Y., 1972.

Davidson, Cathy N. *Revolution and the Word: The Rise of the Novel in America.* New York, 1988.

Davis, R. B. *Francis Walker Gilmer.* Richmond, 1939.

Davis, Richard Beale. "The Jeffersonian Expatriate in the Building of a Nation." *Virginia Magazine of History and Biography* 70 (1960): 49–61.

Dawidoff, Robert. *The Education of John Randolph of Roanoke.* New York, 1979.

Doyle, Nora. "'The Highest Pleasure of Which Woman's Nature Is Capable': Breast-Feeding and the Sentimental Maternal Ideal in America, 1750–1860." *Journal of American History* 97 (2011): 958–73.

Dunn, Susan. *Dominion of Memories: Jefferson, Madison, and the Decline of Virginia.* New York, 2007.

Egerton, Douglas R. *Gabriel's Rebellion: The Virginia Slave Conspiracies of 1801 and 1802.* Chapel Hill, 1993.

Ely, Melvin Patrick. *Israel on the Appomattox: A Southern Experiment in Black Freedom from the 1790s through the Civil War.* New York, 2004.

Fatherly, Sarah. *Gentlewomen and Learned Ladies: Women and Elite Formation in Eighteenth-Century Philadelphia.* Bethlehem, Pa., 2008.

Fenn, Elizabeth A. *Pox Americana: The Great Small Pox Epidemic of 1775–1783.* New York, 2001.

Finkelman, Paul. "Thomas Jefferson and Antislavery: The Myth Goes On." *Virginia Magazine of History and Biography* 102 (1994): 193–228.

Flavell, Julie. *When London Was Capital of America*. New Haven, 2010.

Ford, Lacy K. *Deliver Us from Evil: The Slavery Question in the Old South*. New York, 2009.

Foreman, Amanda. *Georgiana, Duchess of Devonshire*. New York, 1998.

Fox-Genovese, Elizabeth. *Within the Plantation Household: Black and White Women of the Old South*. Chapel Hill, 1988.

Freehling, Alison Goodyear. *Drift toward Dissolution: The Virginia Slavery Debate of 1831–1832*. Baton Rouge, La., 1982.

Freehling, William W. *Prelude to Civil War: The Nullification Controversy in South Carolina, 1816–1836*. New York, 1966.

———. *The Road to Disunion: Secessionists at Bay, 1776–1854*. New York, 1990.

Freeman, Joanne B. *Affairs of Honor: National Politics in the New Republic*. New Haven, 2001.

Frey, Sylvia R. "Between Slavery and Freedom: Virginia Blacks in the American Revolution." *Journal of Southern History* 49 (1983): 375–98.

———. *Water from the Rock: Black Resistance in a Revolutionary Age*. Princeton, 1991.

Gaines, William H., Jr. *Thomas Mann Randolph: Thomas Jefferson's Son-in-Law*. Baton Rouge, La., 1966.

Gillooly, Eileen. *Smiles of Discontent: Humor, Gender, and Nineteenth-Century British Fiction*. Chicago, 1999.

Glassie, Henry. *Folk Housing in Middle Virginia: A Structural Analysis of Historic Artifacts*. Knoxville, Tenn., 1975.

Goodman, Dena. *Becoming a Woman in the Age of Letters*. Ithaca, N.Y., 2009.

———. *The Republic of Letters: A Cultural History of the French Enlightenment*. Ithaca, N.Y., 1994.

Gordon-Reed, Annette. *The Hemingses of Monticello*. New York, 2008.

———. *Thomas Jefferson and Sally Hemings: An American Controversy*. Charlottesville, 1997.

Gottschalk, Louis, and Margaret Maddox. *Lafayette and the French Revolution*. 2 vols. Chicago, 1969–73.

Greenberg, Kenneth S. *Honor and Slavery*. Princeton, 1996.

Grossberg, Michael. "Who Gets the Child?: Custody, Guardianship, and the Rise of Judicial Patriarchy in Nineteenth-Century America." *Feminist Studies* 9 (1983): 235–60.

Gundersen, Joan R. "Independence, Citizenship, and the American Revolution." *Signs* 13 (1987): 59–77.

Hastings, George Everett. *The Life and Works of Francis Hopkinson*. Chicago, 1926.

Haulman, Kate. "Fashion and the Culture Wars of Revolutionary Philadelphia." *William and Mary Quarterly*, 3rd ser., 62 (2005): 625–62.

Hayes, Kevin J. *The Road to Monticello: The Life and Mind of Thomas Jefferson*. New York, 2008.

Hemphill, John M., ed. "John Wayles Rates His Neighbors." *Virginia Magazine of History and Biography* 66 (July 1958): 302–6.

Hickey, Donald R. *The War of 1812: A Forgotten Conflict*. Urbana, Ill., 1989.

Holton, Woody. *Abigail Adams*. New York, 2009.

———. *Forced Founders: Indians, Debtors, Slaves, and the Making of the American Revolution in Virginia*. Chapel Hill, 1999.

Isaac, Rhys. "Stories and Constructions of Identity: Folk Tellings and Diary Inscriptions in Revolutionary Virginia." In *Through a Glass Darkly: Reflections on Personal Identity in Early America*, edited by Ronald Hoffman, Mechal Sobel, and Fredrika J. Teute, 206–37. Chapel Hill, 1997.

———. *The Transformation of Virginia, 1740–1790*. Chapel Hill, 1982.

Jabour, Anya. *Scarlett's Sisters: Young Women in the Old South*. Chapel Hill, 2007.

Kann, Mark. *A Republic of Men: The American Founders, Gendered Language, and Patriarchal Politics*. New York 1998.

Kelley, Mary. *Learning to Stand and Speak: Women, Education, and Public Life in America's Republic*. Chapel Hill, 2006.

Kennedy, Lawrence W. *Planning the City upon a Hill: Boston since 1630*. Amherst, Mass., 1992.

Kerber, Linda K. "Separate Spheres, Female Worlds, Woman's Place: The Rhetoric of Women's History." *Journal of American History* 75 (1988): 9–39.

———. *Women of the Republic: Intellect and Ideology in Revolutionary America*. Chapel Hill, 1980.

Kern, Susan. "The Material World of the Jeffersons at Shadwell." *William and Mary Quarterly*, 3rd ser., 62 (2005): 213–42.

Kerrison, Catherine. *Claiming the Pen: Women and Intellectual Life in the Early America South*. Ithaca, N.Y., 2006.

———. "The Novel as Teacher: Learning to be Female in the Early American South." *Journal of Southern History* 69 (2003): 513–48.

Kierner, Cynthia A. *Beyond the Household: Women's Place in the Early South, 1700–1835*. Ithaca, N.Y., 1998.

———. "'The Dark and Dense Cloud Perpetually Lowering over Us': Gender and the Decline of the Gentry in Postrevolutionary Virginia." *Journal of the Early Republic* 20 (2000): 185–217.

———. *Scandal at Bizarre: Rumor and Reputation in Jefferson's America*. New York, 2004.

———. *Southern Women in Revolution: Personal and Political Narratives, 1776–1800*. Columbia, S.C., 1998.

Kilbride, Daniel. "Travel, Ritual, and National Identity: Planters on the European Tour, 1820–1860." *Journal of Southern History* 69 (2003): 549–84.

Kimball, Marie. *Jefferson: The Scene of Europe, 1784 to 1789*. New York, 1950.

———. *Thomas Jefferson's Cookbook*. Charlottesville, 1979.

Klepp, Susan E. *Revolutionary Conceptions: Women, Fertility, and Family Limitation in America, 1760–1820*. Chapel Hill, 2009.

Knight, Edgar W. *The Academy Movement in the South*. Chapel Hill, 1919.

Kranish, Michael. *Flight from Monticello: Thomas Jefferson at War*. New York, 2010.

Kukla, Jon. *Mr. Jefferson's Women*. New York, 2007.

Laver, Harry S. *Citizens More Than Soldiers: The Kentucky Militia and Society in the Early Republic*. Lincoln, Neb., 2007.

Lebsock, Suzanne D. *The Free Women of Petersburg: Status and Culture in a Southern Town, 1784–1860*. New York, 1985.

Lee, Jean Butenhoff. "The Problem of Slave Community in the Eighteenth-Century Chesapeake." *William and Mary Quarterly*, 3rd ser., 43 (1986): 333–61.

Leepson, Marc. *Saving Monticello: The Levy Family's Epic Quest to Restore the House That Jefferson Built*. New York, 2001.

Lerner, Gerda. "New Approaches to the Study of Women in American History." *Journal of Social History* 3 (1969): 53–62.

Lewis, Charlene M. Boyer. *Ladies and Gentlemen on Display: Planter Society at the Virginia Springs, 1790–1860*. Charlottesville, 2001.

Lewis, Jan. *The Pursuit of Happiness: Family and Values in Jefferson's Virginia*. Cambridge, Eng., 1983.

———. "The Republican Wife: Virtue and Seduction in the Early Republic." *William and Mary Quarterly*, 3rd ser., 44 (1987): 689–721.

Lewis, Jan, and Kenneth A. Lockridge. "'Sally Has Been Sick': Pregnancy and Family Limitation among Virginia Gentry Women, 1780–1830." *Journal of Social History* 22 (1988): 5–20.

Lewis, Jan, and Peter S. Onuf., eds. *Sally Hemings and Thomas Jefferson: History, Memory, and Civic Culture*. Charlottesville, 1999.

Lewis, Jan, et al. "Forum: Thomas Jefferson and Sally Hemings Redux." *William and Mary Quarterly*, 3rd ser., 57 (2000): 121–210.

Lewis, William Terrell. *Genealogy of the Lewis Family in America*. Louisville, Ky., 1893.

Lockridge, Kenneth A. *On the Sources of Patriarchal Rage: The Commonplace Books of William Byrd and Thomas Jefferson and the Gendering of Power in the Eighteenth Century*. New York, 1992.

Lovell, Margaretta M. *Art in a Season of Revolution: Painters, Artists, and Patrons in Early America*. Philadelphia, 2005.

Maier, Pauline. *From Resistance to Revolution: Colonial Radicals and the Development of American Opposition to Britain, 1765–1776*. New York, 1972.

Main, Jackson Turner. "The One Hundred." *William and Mary Quarterly*, 3rd ser., 11 (1954): 354–84.

Majewski, John. *A House Dividing: Economic Development in Pennsylvania and Virginia before the Civil War*. Cambridge, Eng., 2000.

Malone, Dumas. *Jefferson and His Time*. 6 vols. Boston, 1951–82.

———. *Jefferson and the Ordeal of Liberty*. Boston, 1962.

———. *Jefferson the President: First Term, 1801–1805*. Boston, 1970.

———. *Jefferson the President: The Second Term, 1805–1809*. Boston, 1974.

———. *Jefferson the Virginian*. Boston, 1948.

———. *The Sage of Monticello*. Boston, 1982.

———. *Thomas Jefferson and the Rights of Man*. Boston, 1951.

Marszalek, John F. *The Petticoat Affair: Manners, Mutiny, and Sex in Andrew Jackson's White House.* New York, 1997.

Matson, Cathy D., ed. *The Economy of Early America: Historical Perspectives and New Directions.* Philadelphia, 2006.

Mayer, Henry. *All on Fire: William Lloyd Garrison and the Abolition of Slavery.* New York, 2008.

Mayer, Holly A. *Belonging to the Army: Camp Followers and Community during the American Revolution.* Columbia, S.C., 1996.

McConville, Brendan. *The King's Three Faces: The Rise and Fall of Royal America, 1688-1776.* Chapel Hill, 2006.

McCoy, Drew R. *The Elusive Republic: Political Economy in Jeffersonian America.* Chapel Hill, 1980.

McLaughlin, Jack. *Jefferson and Monticello: The Biography of a Builder.* New York, 1988.

McMillen, Sally G. *Motherhood in the Old South: Pregnancy, Childbirth, and Infant Rearing.* Baton Rouge, La., 1990.

Meagher, Margaret. *History of Education in Richmond.* Richmond, 1939.

Melville, Annabelle M. *John Carroll of Baltimore: Founder of the Catholic Hierarchy.* New York, 1955.

Meyers, Robert Manson. "The Old Dominion Looks to London: A Study of English Literary Influences on the *Virginia Gazette* (1736-1766)." *Virginia Magazine of History and Biography* 54 (1946): 195-217.

Miles, Edwin A. "Andrew Jackson and Senator George Poindexter." *Journal of Southern History* 24 (1958): 51-66.

Moore, John Hammond. *Albemarle: Jefferson's County, 1727-1976.* Charlottesville, 1976.

Morgan, Philip D. *Slave Counterpoint: Black Culture in the Eighteenth-Century Chesapeake and Lowcountry.* Chapel Hill, 1998.

Morris, Celia. *Fanny Wright: Rebel in America.* Cambridge, Mass., 1984.

Moss, Kay K. *Southern Folk Medicine, 1750-1820.* Columbia, S.C., 1999.

Munger, Robert S. "Guaiacum: The Holy Wood from the New World." *Journal of the History of Medicine and Allied Sciences* 4 (1949): 196-229.

Nelson, John K. *A Blessed Company: Parishes, Parsons, and Parishioners in Anglican Virginia, 1690-1776.* Chapel Hill, 2002.

Nissenbaum, Stephen. *The Battle for Christmas: A Cultural History of America's Most Cherished Holiday.* New York, 1996.

Norton, Mary Beth. *Liberty's Daughters: The Revolutionary Experience of American Women, 1750-1800.* Boston, 1980.

———. *Separated by Their Sex: Women in Public and Private in the Colonial Atlantic World.* Ithaca, N.Y., 2011.

O'Connor, Thomas H. *The Athens of America: Boston, 1825-1845.* Amherst, Mass., 2006.

Ohrt, Wallace. *Defiant Peacemaker: Nicholas Trist in the Mexican War.* College Station, Tex., 1997.

Onuf, Peter S., ed. *Jeffersonian Legacies.* Charlottesville, 1993.

Papayanis, Nicholas. *Planning Paris before Haussmann*. Baltimore, 2004.

Pasley, Jeffrey L., Andrew W. Robertson, and David Waldstreicher, eds. *Beyond the Founders: New Approaches to the Political History of the Early American Republic*. Chapel Hill, 2004.

PDR for Herbal Medicines. 1st ed. Montvale, N.J., 1998.

Peckham, Howard H. *The Toll of Independence: Engagements and Battle Casualties of the American Revolution*. Chicago, 1974.

Peterson, Merrill D. *The Jefferson Image in the American Mind*. New York, 1970.

Purcell, Sarah J. *Sealed with Blood: War, Sacrifice, and Memory in Revolutionary America*. Philadelphia, 2002.

Quimby, Maureen O'Brien. "The Political Art of James Akin." *Winterthur Portfolio* 7 (1972): 59–112.

Ragsdale, Bruce A. *A Planter's Republic: The Search for Economic Independence in Revolutionary Virginia*. Madison, Wisc., 1996.

Reinier, Jacqueline S. *From Virtue to Character: American Childhood, 1775–1850*. New York, 1996.

Remini, Robert V. *Andrew Jackson and the Course of American Democracy, 1833–1845*. New York, 1984.

———. *Andrew Jackson and the Course of American Freedom, 1822–32*. New York, 1981.

Resch, John R. "Politics and Public Culture: The Revolutionary War Pension Act of 1818." *Journal of the Early Republic* 8 (1988): 139–58.

Resch, John, and Walter Sargent, eds. *War and Society in the America Revolution: Mobilization and Home Fronts*. DeKalb, Ill., 2006.

Rhodes, Richard. *John James Audubon: The Making of an American*. New York, 2004.

Rice, Howard C., Jr. *L'Hôtel de Langeac: Jefferson's Paris Residence, 1785–1789*. Paris, 1947.

———. *Thomas Jefferson's Paris*. Princeton, 1976.

Riddle, John M. *Eve's Herbs: A History of Abortion and Contraception in the West*. Cambridge, Mass., 1997.

Riley, Glenda. *Divorce: An American Tradition*. New York, 1991.

Risjord, Norman K. *The Old Republicans: Southern Conservatism in the Age of Jefferson*. New York, 1983.

Roeber, A. G. *Faithful Magistrates and Republican Lawyers: Creators of Virginia Legal Culture, 1680–1810*. Chapel Hill, 1981.

Rogers, Rebecca. *From the Salon to the Schoolroom: Educating Bourgeois Girls in Nineteenth-Century France*. University Park, Pa., 2005.

Rosenberg, Charles E. *The Cholera Years: The United States in 1832, 1849, and 1866*. 2nd ed. Chicago, 1987.

Rothman, Joshua D. *Notorious in the Neighborhood: Sex and Families across the Color Line in Virginia, 1787–1861*. Chapel Hill, 2003.

Rousseau, François. "Histoire de l'Abbaye de Pentemont depuis sa Translation à Paris jusqu'a la Révolution." *Société de l'Histoire de Paris et de l'Ile-de-France* 45 (1918): 171–227.

Rutman, Darrett B., and Anita H. Rutman. *A Place in Time: Explicatus.* New York, 1984.

Scharff, Virginia. *The Women Jefferson Loved.* New York, 2010.

Schiff, Stacy. *A Great Improvisation: Franklin, France, and the Birth of America.* New York, 2005.

Schmidt, Fredrika Teute, and Barbara Ripel Wilhelm. "Early Proslavery Petitions in Virginia." *William and Mary Quarterly,* 3rd ser., 30 (1973): 133–46.

Schneeberg, Norman G. "The Medical History of Thomas Jefferson (1743–1826)." *Journal of Medical Biography* 16 (2008): 118–25.

Schwarz, Philip J. *Migrants against Slavery: Virginians and the Nation.* Charlottesville, 2001.

Scofield, Merry Ellen. "The Fatigues of His Table: The Politics of Presidential Dining during the Jefferson Administration." *Journal of the Early Republic* 26 (2006): 449–69.

Scott, Joan W. "Gender: A Useful Category of Historical Analysis." *American Historical Review* 5 (1986): 1053–75.

Searle, William. *Virginia's Executive Mansion: A History of the Governor's House.* Richmond, 1988.

Selby, John E. *The Revolution in Virginia, 1775–1783.* Charlottesville, 1988.

Sellers, Charles Coleman. *Mr. Peale's Museum: Charles Willson Peale and the First Popular Museum of Natural Science and Art.* New York, 1980.

Shackelford, George Green, ed. *Collected Papers to Commemorate Fifty Years of the Monticello Association of Descendants of Thomas Jefferson.* Princeton, 1965.

Shade, William G. *Democratizing the Old Dominion: Virginia and the Second Party System, 1824–1861.* Charlottesville, 1996.

Shammas, Carole. "Black Women's Work and the Evolution of Plantation Society in Virginia." *Labor History* 26 (1985): 5–28.

Sidbury, James. *Ploughshares into Swords: Race, Rebellion, and Identity in Gabriel's Virginia.* Cambridge, Eng., 1997.

Sifton, Paul G. "A Disordered Life: The American Career of Pierre Eugène du Simitière." *Manuscripts* 25 (1953): 235–53.

Skelton, William B. "High Army Leadership in the Era of the War of 1812: The Making and Remaking of the Officer Corps." *William and Mary Quarterly,* 3rd ser., 51 (1994): 253–74.

Slaughter, Thomas P. *The Whiskey Rebellion: Frontier Epilogue to the American Revolution.* New York, 1986.

Sloan, Herbert E. *Principle and Interest: Thomas Jefferson and the Problem of Debt.* New York, 1995.

Smith, Billy G., ed. *Life in Early Philadelphia: Documents from the Revolutionary and Early National Periods.* University Park, Pa., 1995.

Smith, Daniel Blake. *Inside the Great House: Planter Family Life in Eighteenth-Century Chesapeake Society.* Ithaca, N.Y., 1980.

Sobel, Mechal. *The World They Made Together: Black and White Values in Eighteenth-Century Virginia.* Princeton, 1988.

Stanton, Lucia. *Free Some Day: The African American Families of Monticello.* Charlottesville, 2000.

———. "The Other End of the Telescope: Jefferson through the Eyes of His Slaves." *William and Mary Quarterly*, 3rd ser., 57 (2000): 139–52.

———. "A Well-Ordered Household: Domestic Servants in Jefferson's White House." *White House History* 17 (2006): 4–23.

Steele, Brian. "Thomas Jefferson's Gender Frontier." *Journal of American History* 95 (2008): 17–42.

Stein, Susan M. *The Worlds of Thomas Jefferson at Monticello.* New York, 1993.

Stevenson, Brenda E. *Life in Black and White: Family and Community in the Slave South.* New York, 1996.

Sydnor, Charles S. *Gentlemen Freeholders: Political Practices in Washington's Virginia.* Chapel Hill, 1952.

Taylor, Olivia. "Edgehill, 1735–1902." *Magazine of Albemarle County History* 30 (1972): 61–67.

Terry, Gail S. "Sustaining the Bonds of Kinship in a Trans-Appalachian Migration, 1790–1811: The Cabell-Breckinridge Slaves Move West." *Virginia Magazine of History and Biography* 102 (1994): 455–76.

Thompson, Peter. *Rum, Punch, and Revolution: Taverngoing and Public Life in Eighteenth-Century Philadelphia.* Philadelphia, 1998.

Townsend, Edward Booth. *Country Life in America as Lived by Ten Presidents of the United States.* New York, 1947.

Trafton, Scott. *Egypt Land: Race and Nineteenth-Century American Egyptomania.* Durham, N.C., 2004.

Turnbull, L. Minerva. "Private Schools in Norfolk, 1800–1860." *William and Mary Quarterly*, 2nd ser., 11 (1931): 277–301.

Tyler-McGraw, Marie. *An African Republic: Black and White Virginians in the Making of Liberia.* Chapel Hill, 2007.

———. *At the Falls: Richmond, Virginia, and Its People.* Chapel Hill, 1994.

Van Buskirk, Judith. *Generous Enemies: Patriots and Loyalists in Revolutionary New York.* Philadelphia, 2002.

Vance, Joseph Carroll. "Thomas Jefferson Randolph." Ph.D. diss., University of Virginia, 1957.

Varon, Elizabeth R. *We Mean to Be Counted: White Women and Politics in Antebellum Virginia.* Chapel Hill, 1998.

Wallenstein, Peter. *Cradle of America: Four Centuries of Virginia History.* Lawrence, Kans., 2007.

Ward, John William. *Andrew Jackson: Symbol for an Age.* New York, 1962.

Wayson, Billy Lee. "Martha Jefferson Randolph: The Education of a Republican Daughter and Plantation Mistress, 1782–1809." Ph.D. diss., University of Virginia, 2008.

Weiner, Marli F. *Mistresses and Slaves: Plantation Women in South Carolina.* Urbana, Ill., 1998.

Wenger, Mark R. "Thomas Jefferson and the Virginia State Capitol." *Virginia Magazine of History and Biography* 101 (1993): 77–102.

———. "Thomas Jefferson's Design for Remodeling the Governor's Palace." *Winterthur Portfolio* 32 (1997): 223–42.

Wister [Sarah Butler], and Agnes Scott, eds. *Worthy Women of Our First Century*. Philadelphia, 1877.

Wolf, Eva Sheppard. *Race and Liberty in the New Nation: Emancipation in Virginia from the Revolution to Nat Turner's Rebellion*. Baton Rouge, La., 2006.

Wood, Kirsten E., *Masterful Women: Slaveholding Widows from the American Revolution through the Civil War*. Chapel Hill, 2004.

———. "'One Woman So Dangerous to Public Morals': Gender and Power in the Eaton Affair." *Journal of the Early Republic* 17 (1997): 237–75.

Woods, Edgar. *Albemarle County in Virginia*. Charlottesville, 1901.

Wyatt-Brown, Bertram. "The Abolitionists' Postal Campaign of 1835." *Journal of Negro History* 50 (1965): 227–38.

———. *Southern Honor: Ethics and Behavior in the Old South*. New York, 1982.

Young, James Sterling. *The Washington Community, 1800–1828*. New York, 1966.

Zagarri, Rosemarie. *Revolutionary Backlash: Women and Politics in the Early American Republic*. Philadelphia, 2007.

Zujovic, Danica. *A Short History of Pentemont*. N.p., n.d.

Electronic Sources

American National Biography Online. http://www.anb.org/articles/03/03-00500.html.

British Library Online Gallery: Black Europeans. http://www.bl.uk/onlinegallery/features/blackeuro/homepage.html.

The Encyclopedia of Music in Canada. http://www.thecanadianencyclopedia.com/index.cfm?PgNm=EMCSubjects&Params=U2.

Monticello. http://monticello.org/.

Monticello Explorer. http://explorer.monticello.org/text/index.php.

National Register of Historic Places. Edgehill Nomination. http://165.176.125.227/registers/Counties/Albemarle/002-0026_Edgehill_1982_Final_Nomination.pdf.

The New Georgia Encyclopedia. http://www.georgiaencyclopedia.org/nge/Home.jsp.

Oxford Dictionary of National Biography. http://www.oxforddnb.com.mutex.gmu.edu/index.jsp.

Tay, Edrina, and Jeremy Dibbell. "George Wythe's 'legacie' to President Thomas Jefferson." *Common-Place* 10 (Jan. 2010). http://www.common-place.org/vol-10/no-02/tales/.

The Thomas Jefferson Encyclopedia. http://wiki.monticello.org/mediawiki/index.php/Thomas_Jefferson_Encyclopedia.

Virginia Newspapers Project. http://www.lva.virginia.gov/public/vnp/.

Acknowledgments

Martha Jefferson Randolph, her husband, and her father spent most of their adult lives lamenting their debts. I happily acknowledge mine.

As someone who is not a Jefferson scholar, I have benefited enormously from the work of historians, editors, and curators whose research has revolutionized our understanding of Jefferson, his family, and the wider Monticello community. My endnotes show the profound influence of scholars such as Annette Gordon-Reed, Jan Ellen Lewis, and Lucia Stanton, whose research on Jefferson, gender, family life, and slavery has informed my understanding of Martha Jefferson Randolph and her world. At Monticello, curator Elizabeth Chew provided insights on the use of domestic space and gave me a special upstairs tour, which included Martha's room. Editors at the *Papers of Thomas Jefferson*, both at Monticello and at Princeton, shared sources and their own vast knowledge of Jefferson and his times. I am especially grateful to Martha J. King, who sent me letters and citations pertaining to Martha's visits to Washington during her father's presidency, and to Lisa A. Francavilla, who shared her research on Ellen Coolidge and various family documents and also alerted me to the location of one of Martha's French cookbooks and Anne Cary Randolph Bankhead's diary. The *Family Letters Digital Archive*—overseen by Lisa Francavilla, *Retirement Series* editor J. Jefferson Looney, and others at the International Center for Jefferson Studies—is a boon to scholars, students, and anyone else who is interested in Martha Jefferson Randolph and her extended circle of family and friends.

Others answered my questions or generously offered leads on sources that I otherwise might have missed. Brent Tarter shared his knowledge of petitioning in postrevolutionary Virginia. Jim Wootton provided architectural information on Virginia's Capitol in Richmond, which Jefferson designed. A discussion with Scott Casper helped clarify the complicated origins of the seemingly un-republican notion of an American "first family." Francis Pollard located information in a rare Boston city directory that oddly turned up in the collections of the Virginia Historical Society. At the University of Virginia, Regina Rush promptly responded to requests for copies of documents from the Small Special Collections Library, saving me several trips to Charlottesville. Jurretta Heckscher sent me excerpts from an obscure nineteenth-century book, which included a valuable letter in which Virginia Trist reminisced about her mother. Jon Kukla kindly provided some digital images he had used for his own book on Jefferson and women. (The credit line for the Panthemont image should really be "Author's *friend's* collection.") Sandra Gioia Treadway told me about Russell Smith's previously unpublished sketch of Monticello and its environs, which became my book's final illustration.

Friends and colleagues read all or part of my work-in-progress, and their suggestions and comments invariably improved the finished product. Jane Turner Censer read the entire manuscript and offered good advice from her perspective as a historian of southern women. Lisa Francavilla, Martha King, and Jon Kukla corrected some errors pertaining to Jefferson and his world. Michele Gillespie, Lorri Glover, and Rosie Zagarri raised important questions or issues, which I previously overlooked, concerning Martha's public life and its significance. Catherine Allgor, an accomplished biographer and historian of women whose work engages both scholarly and general audiences, was an especially generous and insightful critic. My ideal informed general reader, Sandy Treadway, reassured me that this book would be accessible to nonspecialists—so long as I did not overuse the word "quotidian"—and offered spa-like accommodations when I did research in Richmond.

My editor at the University of North Carolina Press, Chuck Grench, wisely recognized that illustrations—and lots of them—would be essential to this book. I thank the press for funding the illustrations and the many librarians, archivists, and others for helping me to obtain the images and the rights to publish them. At the Library of Congress, Paul Hogroian efficiently processed my complicated request for multiple images in various formats. At the Library of Virginia, Audrey Johnson got me a superb reproduction of an early nineteenth-century newspaper advertisement. Meghan Budinger of the James Monroe Museum & Memorial Library, Hillary Crehan of the White House Historical Association, and Virginia Hart at the U.S. State Department each provided me with a digital image of a relatively obscure object. Tad and Sue Thompson, the current residents of Tuckahoe, the boyhood home of Thomas Mann Randolph, allowed me to publish a photograph of their beautiful house (for a second time). Finally, I thank Leah Stearns, the Digital Images Coordinator at Monticello, for her assistance in securing so many indispensable illustrations for this book, including the two portraits of Martha Jefferson Randolph that hang in Jefferson's iconic home.

This project has received generous institutional support at virtually every stage. Fellowships from the Virginia Historical Society and the International Center for Jefferson Studies supported some early research, as did a one-semester leave from the College of Arts and Sciences (and the late Dean Schley R. Lyons) at the University of North Carolina at Charlotte. A fellowship from the National Endowment for the Humanities funded a year's leave during which I wrote and revised most of my chapters. I thank my new dean, Jack R. Censer, and department chair, Brian Platt, for letting me take that time away from teaching and other departmental work, after I spent less than a year as their colleague at George Mason University.

My agent, Lisa Adams, believed that this book could be both interesting and important and convinced Chuck Grench and his colleagues at UNC Press that she was right. Lisa's advice significantly improved my book proposal, and her subsequent reading of my chapters helped me to clarify Martha's story and its significance. Chuck Grench has been an ideal editor for this project—knowledgeable, supportive, and full of good counsel.

Martha Jefferson Randolph's life was all about family, but I think it's fair to say that I have been more fortunate than her in mine. My parents, Bob and Bea Kierner, don't live on a mountain—they live at the shore, which I like better anyway—and they have always encouraged my brothers and me to do our own things. I can honestly say that they never expected me to run their plantation or help them evade troublesome visitors. My husband, Tom Bright, shares Tom Randolph's love of science but thankfully not much else. Middle age has definitely been kinder to us than to Tom and Martha. As for children, Martha had twelve and I have only two, but they are awfully good guys. When I began this project roughly eight years ago, Zack and Anders were first-graders who played Little League baseball in Charlotte. This year, they made their high school baseball team in northern Virginia. Between now and the next book, I hope that they live their dreams, get their mom a beach house, and maybe even rescue the New York Mets.

Fairfax Station, Virginia
June 2011

Index

Hughes, Ursula, 117
Hughes, Wormley, 200, 203–4, 262

Indiana, 251
Indian removal, 256
Indians. *See* Native Americans
Ingham, Deborah, 240
Inoculations, 36–37, 98, 100
Iris (slave), 166
Izard, Mrs., 37

Jackson, Andrew, 233, 236, 251, 277; MJR
    and, 238–39, 241–42; as president,
    237, 238, 239, 241, 242, 255–56, 259
Jackson, Rachel Donelson Robards, 239
James City County, Va., 19
Jay, John, 37
Jefferson, Isaac, 31, 63, 106
Jefferson, Elizabeth, 22
Jefferson, Jane (1774–75), 22
Jefferson, Jane Randolph, 15, 22, 76
Jefferson, Lucy Elizabeth (1780–81), 30,
    32
Jefferson, Lucy Elizabeth (1782–84), 35,
    36, 39, 42, 57–58, 63
Jefferson, Martha (Patsy). *See* Ran-
    dolph, Martha Jefferson
Jefferson, Martha Wayles Skelton, 17,
    23–24, 30, 80, 203, 236; childbirth
    and, 15, 22, 30, 35; death of, 7, 11,
    35–36, 63; described, 16, 27; marriage
    of to TJ, 16; as mistress of Monticello,
    25, 110; as mother, 26; pregnancies of,
    24, 30, 34
Jefferson, Mary (Polly). *See* Eppes,
    Mary (Maria) Jefferson
Jefferson, Peter, 16, 76
Jefferson, Thomas (TJ)
—attitudes of toward women, 6, 12, 13,
    44, 46, 95, 110–12, 241
—biographies of, 6, 120, 274
—death and funeral of, 202–4
—debts of, 6, 7, 121, 140, 143, 180–81,
    197–98, 205
—early political career of, 16, 20, 22, 24

—education and, 6, 16, 26, 53, 140, 181
—estate of, 107, 205, 209, 211, 233, 243,
    246
—as father, 13, 14, 23, 26, 44–47, 50,
    58–61, 80–81, 84, 98, 125, 126
—as governor, 28–34, 157, 163
—as grandfather, 150, 153, 168, 171, 172
—health of, 198, 199, 200
—Hemings family and, 17, 63, 73
—marriage of, 16
—papers of, 213, 231, 232, 243
—in Paris, 50–51, 53, 56–57, 66–67
—in Philadelphia, 20, 22, 23, 36, 39–41,
    86, 97
—as president, 12, 109, 113–14, 117–18,
    127, 128, 131–32, 133, 208, 237
—race and, 68–69, 191, 249, 256
—reliance of on TJR, 6, 87–88, 97, 166–
    67, 189, 198
—religion and, 44, 45, 64, 117, 118, 164,
    203, 204, 229
—reputation of, 9, 13, 14, 34, 118, 119–20,
    130, 147–48, 202, 211, 262–64, 274–75,
    280
—in retirement, 9, 142, 152, 267
—Sally Hemings and, 6, 12, 66–67, 73,
    106–7, 119, 128, 130, 203, 250, 262–64,
    294 (n. 66)
—as secretary of state, 75, 76, 82, 86, 97
—slavery and, 60, 122, 249, 253, 284
    (n. 11)
—slaves manumitted by, 106, 186, 201,
    233
—TMR and, 6, 77, 79, 80, 85–86, 87–88,
    100, 118, 119, 135, 166, 189, 201, 205
—as vice president, 75, 97, 108, 111
—will of, 200–201, 224
Jews, 173, 310 (n. 73)
John (slave), 123
Julien, Honoré, 117
Jupiter (slave), 31

Kentucky, 190, 252, 257
Kit (slave), 123
Kukla, Jon, 294 (n. 66), 300 (n. 9)

cumstances of, 98, 121, 135–36, 166, 185–86, 196

Reading, 15, 20, 26, 43, 45, 136, 168, 176, 177; as leisure, 16, 60

Religion, 30, 199; evangelical, 164, 187, 217, 221, 276; MJR and, 13, 64–65, 164, 187, 220–21, 259–60; TJ and, 44, 45, 64, 117, 118, 164, 203, 204, 229; TMR and, 164, 182, 188, 229

Remsen, Henry, 181, 188

Republican party (Jeffersonians), 109, 110, 113, 156

Revolution, American, 24–25, 40, 42, 50, 89, 110, 214, 216; coming of, 18, 20–21; slaves in, 22, 34, 35; in Virginia, 21, 22, 26, 30–34, 76, 163

Richard (slave), 236

Richmond, 30, 74, 82, 87, 106, 133, 173, 187, 188, 191, 212, 215, 228; British attacks on, 30–31, 32, 76, 163; growth of, 145; MJR in, 106, 181, 182–83, 215; social life in, 30, 115, 166, 169–70, 182–83, 184, 185, 215

Richmond Enquirer, 134, 277

Richmond Recorder, 119

Riedesel, Baron von, and family, 28

Ritchie, Thomas, 134

Rittenhouse, David, 44

Rittenhouse family, 45, 48

Rivanna River, 84, 145

Rives, William Cabell, 258–59

Rochefoucauld, Rosalie, 69

Rochefoucauld-Liancourt, Duc de la, 69, 72, 97

Rouen, 50

Royall, Anne Newport, 216–17, 222

Royer, Lilite, 69–70

Rush, Benjamin, 46

Sackets Harbor, N.Y., 159

Saint-Germain-en-Laye, 69, 70

Sally (slave), 253–54

Salons, 113; in Paris, 67, 68, 111; in Philadelphia, 9, 74, 111

Saratoga, battle of, 27, 34

Savannah, Ga., 28

Scharff, Virginia, 284 (n. 3)

Schools, 20, 42, 51, 206, 209, 215, 220, 225; convent, 53–54; at Edgehill, 207, 212–13, 231, 232, 243, 261, 280; in Virginia, 104, 136, 166, 212, 277–78. *See also* Education; Panthemont, Abbaye Royale de

Science, 46, 77, 79, 88, 111, 140, 179, 226

Serra, Abbé Correa de, 149

Servants, free, 19, 40, 66, 218–19

Sewing, 25, 45, 60, 63, 88, 177, 203, 233

Shadwell, 15, 21, 205; gristmill at, 145, 162, 166

Shopping, 110, 170–71, 216, 236, 278; in Philadelphia, 22, 41, 42, 115, 127; in Paris, 50–51, 57, 65, 67–68

Short, William, 58, 66, 69–71

Sigourney, Lydia, 204

Simitière, Pierre Eugène, 43, 44, 46

Skipwith, Robert, 26

Slave auctions, 11, 194, 196, 213–14

Slave insurrections, 247; white fears of, 20, 31–32, 123, 181, 248, 251

Slavery: abolished in Massachusetts, 49, 218; defense of, 9; ill effects of on whites, 122–23, 253, 254; MJR and, 11, 60, 121–22, 194, 196, 209, 211, 213, 218, 221, 243, 252–53, 254, 262, 265, 270, 276, 277, 280; plantation mistresses and, 11, 105, 106; TJ and, 60, 122, 249, 253, 284 (n. 11); TJR and, 250–51, 252, 270; TMR and, 87, 121–22, 181, 186; in Virginia, 87, 96, 181, 201, 203, 211, 247–51

Slaves, 15, 16, 40, 89, 92, 93, 209, 220, 248; as artisans, 18, 105, 145, 168, 196; as domestic servants, 15, 30, 102, 105–6, 121, 122, 196, 253, 260; at Edgehill, 86, 87, 98, 145, 153, 252, 280; escaped, 19, 31–32, 34, 35, 123, 186, 279; forced migration of, 121–22, 181, 266; manumission of, 96, 106, 186, 201, 203, 233, 262; at Monticello, 25, 34, 35, 75, 86, 123, 145, 191, 218, 277; Revolution and,

22, 31–32, 87; sale of, 166, 181, 193–94, 218, 258; whipping of, 174, 253–54

Smallpox, 36, 98, 100

Smith, Jane Blair Cary, 5

Smith, Margaret Bayard, 118, 130, 156, 236, 238; MJR and, 211, 231, 257, 262; visits Monticello, 147–48, 150–51, 179, 230; in Washington society, 132, 236

Smith, Samuel Harrison, 118, 131, 134, 148, 257

Social life, 27–28, 37, 39, 45, 76, 100, 185, 267; in Boston, 219–20, 222, 257; in Paris, 50, 59, 60, 64, 65, 67–69; in Philadelphia, 40, 115, 171; politics and, 9, 110, 111–14, 117–18, 131–32; in Richmond, 30, 115, 166, 169–70, 181, 182–83, 184, 185; in Washington, 117–18, 131–32, 184–85, 236–37, 238–40, 255, 257

Southampton County, Va., 247

South Carolina, 30, 121; gift from to MJR, 214, 215; nullification in, 256

Sparks, Jared, 213

Spaulding, Thomas, 223

Spectator, The, 25

Spinning, 25, 145

Spotsylvania County, Va., 209

Staunton, Va., 34, 100

Stearns, Hannah, 232

Steele, Richard, 25

Steuart, Jenny, 23

Stowe, Harriet Beecher, 252

Sukey (slave), 31

Sully, Thomas, 267–69

Susan (slave), 194

Sweet Springs, Va., 100

Tarleton, Banastre, 32, 34

Tatler, The, 25

Taverns, 40, 227

Taxes, 133, 134, 161; collection of, 160

Textiles, 216; homespun, 25, 110, 133; made at Monticello, 25, 110, 133, 145

Theater, 56, 59, 222, 228

Thornton, Anna Maria Brodeau, 146

Tobacco, 17, 88, 122, 159; prices of, 18, 87

Tom (slave), 106

Tracy, Nathaniel, 49

Trade, 18, 48, 133, 216; blockade of, 25, 157, 158

Transylvania College, 190

Travel, 50, 160; by carriage, 39–40, 48, 75, 115, 120, 127, 168, 228; by ferry, 40, 48, 74; by horse, 74, 182, 187; by rail, 264–65; by ship, 49, 73–74, 228, 257, 269

Tripoli, 131

Trist, Elizabeth House, 49, 50, 59, 124, 158, 159, 165, 168, 180–81, 182; MJR and, 44, 48, 53, 208, 236; at Monticello, 144, 148, 175, 208, 233; in Philadelphia, 40, 41, 43; political opinions of, 112, 148, 156

Trist, Hore Browse, 41

Trist, Martha Jefferson, 200, 208, 279

Trist, Nicholas, 41

Trist, Nicholas P., 191, 202, 208, 221, 222, 224, 257, 259, 265, 271, 272; career of, 230, 232, 238, 242, 255–56, 259, 267, 279; courtship and marriage of, 173, 177, 185, 245; education of, 173, 230; MJR and, 173, 186–87, 232–33; TMR and, 185, 186–87; Washington residences of, 232–33, 254, 258, 261

Trist, Thomas Jefferson, 231, 279

Trist, Virginia Jefferson Randolph, 102, 155, 168, 172, 176, 179, 183, 188, 200, 202, 206, 207, 208, 212, 224, 227, 228, 231, 232, 233, 247, 257, 259, 267, 270, 271, 272; children of, 200, 279; courtship and marriage of, 173, 177, 185, 245; in Washington, 236, 238, 258, 262–63

Tristram Shandy (Sterne), 16

Tuckahoe, 16, 82, 91, 96, 107, 266; MJR visits, 31, 32, 42

Tucker, St. George, 79

Tufton, 55, 167, 194, 199, 205, 209

Tufton, Caroline, 54, 69

Tufton, Elizabeth, 54, 69